Constructivism Reconsidered

The constructivist challenge to the rational-structural approaches that dominate the study of international relations in the United States lies in the argument that structure is in fact constructed by and through social ideas and practice. The complicated web of international relations is not the result of basic human nature or some other unchangeable aspect, but has been built up over time and through shared ideas, experience, and assumptions. *Constructivism Reconsidered* is a twenty-first-century primer on the approach, synthesizing the nature of and debates on constructivism in international relations. It examines the (dis)agreement with regard to the meaning of constructivism and to what extent constructivism is regarded as a successful alternative approach to rationalism to explaining and understanding international affairs. The volume explores constructivism's theoretical, empirical, and methodological strengths and weaknesses, and it debates what these say about constructivism's past, present, and future. In that spirit, *Contructivism Reconsidered* makes a significant contribution by establishing a path for moving forward the constructivist research program in international relations, so as to reach a better understanding of international affairs in general and where constructivism fits in relation to the discipline of international relations in particular.

Mariano E. Bertucci is a Visiting Assistant Professor of International Relations at the Department of Political Science at Loyola Marymount University.

Jarrod Hayes is a Visiting Associate Professor of International Relations in the MIT Department of Political Science and Associate Professor of International Security at the University of Massachusetts, Lowell.

Patrick James is Dornsife Dean's Professor of International Relations at the University of Southern California, and president of the International Studies Association, 2018–19.

CONSTRUCTIVISM RECONSIDERED

Past, Present, and Future

Mariano E. Bertucci, Jarrod Hayes, Patrick James, Editors

University of Michigan Press
Ann Arbor

Copyright © 2018 by Mariano E. Bertucci, Jarrod Hayes, Patrick James
All rights reserved

This book may not be reproduced, in whole or in part, including illustrations, in any form
(beyond that copying permitted by Sections 107 and 108 of the U.S. Copyright Law and
except by reviewers for the public press), without written permission from the publisher.

Published in the United States of America by the
University of Michigan Press
Manufactured in the United States of America
Printed on acid-free paper
First published November 2018

A CIP catalog record for this book is available from the British Library.

Library of Congress Cataloging-in-Publication data has been applied for.

ISBN: 978-0-472-13110-5 (Hardcover : alk paper)
ISBN: 978-0-472-03715-5 (Paper : alk paper)
ISBN: 978-0-472-12376-6 (ebook)

Contents

Figures

List of Tables

Acknowledgments

This edited volume is the result of efforts from many people. We greatly appreciate those who prepared chapters for this volume as well as all the other participants in the workshop at the University of Southern California (USC) in January 2015. Those who attended the workshop and provided valuable insights that have impacted upon the contents, but are not represented in this book, include Ted Hopf, Brian Rathbun, and Wayne Sandholtz.

Mariano Bertucci would like to especially thank Patrick James and Jarrod Hayes for co-organizing and convening an outstanding group of scholars to discuss these issues and for working closely with him in preparing this volume. Mariano also would like to express his gratitude to Ludovico Feoli, executive director of the Center for Inter-American Policy and Research (CIPR) at Tulane University, for making available valuable resources to help build the dataset upon which chapter 2 is based. Mariano, Jarrod, and Pat also thank Cecily Montgomery, Parker Bradley, Tom Jamieson, and Mayagüez Salinas for their outstanding work as research assistants on that chapter.

Jarrod Hayes thanks Patrick James for motivating this whole project. He has enjoyed working with both Mariano and Pat. Jarrod also is grateful to his friends and colleagues for their participation in the conference at USC and their resulting contributions, and to his wife and daughters Janelle, Isabelle, and Mackenzie for their support and inspiration.

Patrick James appreciates the support USC provided through its Center for International Studies (CIS), which enabled the workshop to take place in January 2015. Exchanges back and forth at that event produced a host of improvements throughout the chapters of this volume. Pat is grateful to Indira Persad at CIS for her valuable work in organizing the above-noted workshop. He also appreciates very much the abilities of Mariano and Jarrod, who have been outstanding in their work throughout this project.

Finally, the editors are very grateful to the University of Michigan Press for their splendid work on this volume.

Preface

The Dinosaur Speaks!

Nicholas Onuf

When it comes to constructivism in International Relations (IR), I am one of the dinosaurs. We dinosaurs are still in a reasonably good state of preservation, and still talking. When a dinosaur speaks, we generally expect the old fossil to talk, well, like a dinosaur. And so I shall.

There are not very many of us; Alexander Wendt, Friedrich Kratochwil, and I are usually put together in a museum display called "IR in the 80s" (Wendt 1987, 1992; Kratochwil 1989; Onuf 1989). John Ruggie should be added to this group, thanks chiefly to an early essay he wrote with Kratochwil (1986), as should Raymond (Bud) Duvall, mentor to Wendt and a number of other constructivists (and see Wendt and Duvall 1989). Nearby are feminists and a variety of self-styled "posties"—postmodernists, post-structuralists, and postcolonial thinkers—who are occasionally grouped with us as constructivists, despite reservations on both sides. No doubt the familiar dynamic of "us" versus a stigmatized "them" or "other" helps to account for this inappropriate simplification. So does the sociocultural context of the 1980s.

I will talk as if nothing much has happened since the dinosaurs came on the scene, although I am happy to say that this symposium volume is evidence to the contrary. I will talk about meta-theory—the philosophical rationale behind constructivism—although the dinosaurs have been pushed aside by a bunch of furry little creatures with close-at-hand concerns. I will talk as if the issues animating philosophy (and especially the philosophy of science in the 1970s and 1980s) have changed very little. And I could talk as if IR theory lost its way once the dinosaurs had their say. But I will not, at least not here.

Instead let me say this about the time of the dinosaurs. The end of the Cold War had nothing to do with constructivism's arrival on the scene, despite what I hear younger museum visitors saying to each other. I suspect Wendt is at least partly responsible for this vagrant belief. All those young visitors, not to mention their parents, read the following passage from his great book, *Social Theory of International Politics* (1999, 4): "constructivist thinking about international politics was accelerated by the end of the Cold War, which caught scholars on all sides off guard but left orthodoxies particularly exposed."

Wendt already had muddied the waters by claiming that "a constructivist worldview underlies the classical international theories of Grotius, Kant and Hegel" and that many post–World War II writers advanced "important constructivist approaches to international politics" (1998, 3). If constructivist thinking had always been around, then it does make sense to say that it accelerated *after* 1989. Yet by exposing old orthodoxies, Wendt himself gave constructivism much of its initial momentum in 1987, *before* the Cold War ended (for an example of Wendt's misguidance, see Kurki 2008, 277). This said, I have not the slightest doubt that the end of the Cold War and the rise of identity politics gave constructivism an unexpected relevance to scholars in the field, prompted the emergence of a second generation of constructivists, and accounts for the empirical thrust (typically manifested in case studies) of so much scholarship undertaken in name of constructivism.

Constructivism, in my view as a participant-observer, arose in the context of a "culture war" conducted chiefly in research universities in the United States. This is how I would describe the uprising of scholars in the humanities chafing under the dramatic shift in resources from the liberal arts to the sciences, including the applied social sciences. Drawing inspiration from continental social theory, humanists declared that the philosophical assumptions underlying modern science are untenable. Self-styled "posties"—postmodernists, postpositivists, poststructuralists, and postcolonial thinkers—repudiated the "Enlightenment project" of universal reason in favor of local, practical knowledge and multiple rationalities. We in the field are familiar with this development as the "Third Debate." As described by Lapid (1989), the Third Debate reinforced the tendency, already evident in Keohane's edited volume *Neorealism and Its Critics* (1986), to segregate positivists and postpositivists into hostile camps. What Lapid, who had been Kratochwil's student, failed to make clear is how this ostensible debate relates to constructivism's early days.

There are, of course, many factors giving rise to constructivism. I have addressed them elsewhere as they affected me: feminist theory and the linguistic turn top the list (Onuf 2002). Here I want to emphasize a factor that I think motivated the three of us who are generally taken to represent constructivism's founding generation: Wendt, Kratochwil, and myself. This factor is the philosophy of science, which surged into prominence with the humanist campaign against science. Most conspicuously, Wendt plumbed the literature on the philosophy of science even as a student. Kratochwil did so least conspicuously in the early days, though some of his later work constitutes a trenchant critique of misappropriated philosophy of science (see especially 2007a, b, c). In my own case, I ransacked the literature to support a constructivism that went "all the way down." When I got there, even "below" philosophy devoted specifically to science, I found myself with Wittgenstein's *Philosophical Investigations* and Goodman's *Ways of Worldmaking* (1978) for company.

The question of foundations animated the post-movement. In my view, then and now, this question must be addressed by anyone who could plausibly claim to be a constructivist. I do not mean to suggest that we must all become philosophers or even that we should preface anything we say as scholars with pseudo-philosophical boilerplate. I do think *you* should be prepared to say, "this is what I think about the so-called Third Debate," and then actually have something to say if, against the odds, anyone—student or colleague—actually asks your opinion.

In all likelihood you will say, with ample precedent, that constructivism is the middle way, Adler's "middle ground" (1997), Wendt's "*via media*" (1999). I myself suggested that constructivism functions as a four-way bridge between phenomenology, poststructuralism, rational choice, and functionalism/structuralism (1989, 57–60), cleverly worked out perhaps, but ignored. So the question remains: Between what and what is it the middle way? Between positivism and postpositivism? Philosophical realism and philosophical idealism? Science and art? None of these formulations sounds right, I think because they ignore the metaphorical power of the term *foundation*. Foundations or their repudiation must come first, and not somewhere in the middle.

My own preference is for a Kantian frame of reference, that is to say, a philosophical idealism that takes Immanuel Kant's First Critique (1965) as a point of departure. In that context, I have recently urged my colleagues in the field to consider constructivism as having a specific focus applicable to social relations in general. In short, we are best equipped to study the human disposition to fill the world with "moderate-sized dry goods." I have borrowed this expression from Austin (1962, 8; see also Onuf 2016) and attempted to locate it in a Kantian framework. Almost needless to say, my colleagues have paid me no mind whatsoever, something I attribute to their sense that philosophical idealism is no answer to the question of foundations.

Fair enough. If I nagged you all about foundations long enough, most of you would admit to being philosophical realists of one sort or another, and you probably would prefer to have the dinosaur stand silent in its 1980s diorama. But the question remains: What is it about constructivism that makes it seem like the middle way?

Constructivism is much discussed and well-practiced in several disciplines. My question is specific to IR and its history as a field of study. Are constructivist scholars in IR temperamentally inclined to go for the "middle" in most situations they find themselves in? Do zealous "rat choice" theorists and scorched-earth "posties" make us nervous? For that matter, do fundamentalists of any sort give us the willies? Are we disproportionately centrist on matters of politics? Are we drawn to middle range theory as a practical goal? Do most of us think that talk about world-making is actually pretty pretentious?

I think the answer to these questions is *yes*. So let me return to the claim I made a moment ago: that we humans are disposed to fill the world with the moderate-sized dry goods type of objects to which we assign value (and this is what makes them goods). And let me do so without the encumbrance of a Kantian framework. Instead I will rely on science for inspiration, the science of perception and its relation to cognition.

First, an observation about "the world." Here I am talking about one's world, one's perceptual field, which each of us construe as an integrated whole, with one's perceiving self at its center. (This is Kant's faculty of apperception, but never mind.) We see this world in three dimensions; as it changes we add time as a fourth dimension. *What* we see is a world, a perceptual field, full of things, things-in-themselves (oops, more Kant), things with discernible boundaries and determinate properties, things that change in strict relation to other things. I do not need to tell you that there is an enormous amount of science dedicated to understanding how we "resolve" the world out there into the things we know we see (and I acknowledge the visual bias in my remarks and indeed most of the relevant science).

The things we see most clearly are in the *middle* of our visual field. Things at the edges are relatively fuzzy; the retinal image is hyperbolic (Heelan 1983), if we bother to notice. Most of the time we automatically rescale things so that they have the same ascertainable properties wherever they are in the visual field. (Psychologists call this "size constancy scaling"; see Gregory 1997, chaps. 9–10.) As a cognitive operation, rescaling constitutes a world of moderate-sized objects. Midway between the granular foreground and the gauzy backdrop, these objects are available for metrical comparison. Thanks to the instruments of modern science, we have been able to extend the range of rescaled objects from the infinitesimal to the astronomic.

Furthermore, we moderns *may* perform these operations more "naturally" than other people because we have replaced the hyperbolic visual field with a Euclidian field. In a "carpentered world," as some psychologists have hypothesized, space and time have become metricized constants, such that we see objects in illusory geometric patterns. Whether the human mind always operates in what we often refer to as Kantian space-time, or this is a peculiar, deeply internalized feature of modern experience, is an open question. Field researchers testing the hypothesis on non-Western subjects disagree on interpretation of their tests.

What the relevant science does not say, but I will, is that rescaling in Kantian space-time also applies to "social facts." We make these fuzzy, formless, fluid things into moderate-sized dry goods when we talk about them. I give you some obvious examples.

- Ideas are effectively formless until they are linguistically or symbolically represented. Even then they are too elusive to serve as social facts until they are endowed with additional properties.
- Norms are merely nebulous ideas until we give them the properties of rules.
- People are turned into moderate-sized objects by assigning them identities that they need not know themselves to possess.
- Agents have powers that they may take for granted but that observers associate with the causal powers of some class of moderate-sized objects.
- Structures are arrangements of agents who have powers that observers see as having an effect on those agents and their jointly constructed world.
- States are social constructions *only* because we can visualize them as dry goods having more or less comparable properties.

- Scholars resort to moderate-sized goods they call frameworks, approaches, or theories to study complex phenomena such as international relations; they say they work within fields, such as International Relations, to locate themselves, as a familiar class of goods, in metaphorically contained, manageably scaled space.

The point should be clear. The way we make useful, moderate-sized social objects with material properties, the way we infuse them with value, the way we do it together through a myriad of cognitive and linguistic operations: this is exactly what seems to entrance constructivists. And only constructivists. Everyone else starts with goods already in place.

REFERENCES

Adler, Emanuel. 1997. "Seizing the Middle Ground: Constructivism in World Politics." *European Journal of International Relations* 3, no. 3: 319–63.

Austin, J. L. 1962. *Sense and Sensibilia.* Oxford: Clarendon Press.

Goodman, Nelson 1978. *Ways of Worldmaking.* Indianapolis, IN: Hackett.

Gregory, Richard L. 1997. *Eye and Brain: The Psychology of Seeing*, 5th ed. Princeton, NJ: Princeton University Press.

Heelan, Patrick A. 1983. *Sense Perception and the Philosophy of Science.* Berkeley: University of California Press.

Kant, Immanuel. 1965. *Critique of Pure Reason.* Translated by Norman Kemp Smith (New York: St. Martin's).

Keohane, Robert O., ed. 1986. *Neorealism and Its Critics.* New York: Columbia University Press.

Kratochwil, Friedrich V. 1989. *Rules, Norms, and Decisions: On the Conditions of Practical and Legal Reasoning in International Relations and Domestic Affairs.* Cambridge: Cambridge University Press.

Kratochwil, Friedrich. 2007a. "Of False Promises and Good Bets: A Plea for a Pragmatic Approach to Theory Building (The Tartu Lecture)." *Journal of International Relations and Development* 10, no. 1: 1–15.

Kratochwil, Friedrich. 2007b. "Of Communities, Gangs, Historicity and the Problem of Santa Claus: Replies to My Critics." *Journal of International Relations and Development* 10, no. 1: 57–78.

Kratochwil, Friedrich. 2007c. "Evidence, Inference, and Truth as Problems of Theory Building in the Social Sciences." In *Theory and Evidence in Comparative Politics and International Relations*, edited by Richard Ned Lebow and Mark Irving Lichbach, 25–54. New York: Palgrave Macmillan.

Kratochwil, Friedrich, and John Gerard Ruggie. 1986. "International Organization: A State of the Art on an Art of the State." *International Organization* 40, no. 4: 753–75.

Kurki, Milja. 2008. *Causation in International Relations: Reclaiming Causal Analysis.* Cambridge: Cambridge University Press.

Lapid, Yosef. 1989. "The Third Debate: On the Prospects of International Theory in a Post-Positivist Era." *International Studies Quarterly* 33, no. 3: 235–54.

Onuf, Nicholas. 2002. "Worlds of Our Making: The Strange Career of Constructivism in International Relations," in *Visions of International Relations: Assessing an Academic Field*, edited by Donald J. Puchala, 119–41. Columbia: University of South Carolina Press.

Onuf, Nicholas. 2016. "Constructivism at the Crossroads; or, the Problem of Moderate-Sized Dry Goods." *International Political Sociology* 10, no. 2: 115–32.

Onuf, Nicholas Greenwood. 1989. *World of Our Making: Rules and Rule in Social Theory and International Relations*. Columbia: University of South Carolina Press.

Wendt, Alexander. 1992. "Anarchy Is What States Make of It: The Social Construction of Power Politics." *International Organization* 46, no. 2: 391–425.

Wendt, Alexander. 1999. *Social Theory of International Politics*. Cambridge: Cambridge University Press.

Wendt, Alexander E. 1987. "The Agent-Structure Problem in International Relations Theory." *International Organization* 41, no. 3 (1987): 335–70.

Wendt, Alexander, and Raymond Duvall. 1989. "Institutions and International Order." In *Global Changes and Theoretical Challenges: Approaches to World Politics for the 1990s*, edited by Ernst-Otto Czempiel and James N. Rosenau, 51–73. Lexington, MA: Lexington Books.

Wittgenstein, Ludwig. 1968. *Philosophical Investigations*, 3rd ed. Translated by G. E. M. Anscombe. Oxford: Basil Blackwell.

ONE

A New Look at Constructivism

Mariano E. Bertucci
Jarrod Hayes
Patrick James

Three decades ago, a small group of scholars, responding to the intellectual poverty of neorealism, sought to develop an alternative approach to international relations (IR). Termed "constructivism" by one of its progenitors (Onuf 1989), the new approach would be more sociologically aware, with different ontological—and to a far lesser degree epistemological—foundations than the prevailing structural forms of realism and liberalism. In contradistinction to so-called postmodern approaches to IR, constructivism would come to draw more on sociologist Peter Berger than on continental philosophers like Michel Foucault. But it might be argued that at its heart constructivism represented an "embourgeoisement" of postmodernist theoretical perspectives, importing aspects of the latter's core insights about the social construction of reality but wrapping them in less radical, more politically safe theoretical trappings.[1] Constructivism's repurposing and repackaging has not been without cost, as suggested by tensions between "mainstream" and "critical" constructivists.[2] This gentrification, combined with the unexpected end of the Cold War, catalyzed the rise to prominence of constructivism as *the* alternative to rationalist and materialist approaches to the study of international relations (Barder and Levine 2012; Onuf in this volume).

The world since has upheld the significance of constructivism's central focus on interpretation, the practices of meaning making, and social structures like norms and identity. Studies of terrorism increasingly have turned toward constructivist analysis (Onuf 1989; Stump and Dixit 2012). The same can be said for other major issues in the international system, from climate change to Russia's invasion and annexation of Crimea (Hayes and Knox-Hayes 2014; Faizullaev and Cornut 2016). Despite initial expectations of a more stable world (e.g., the "peace dividend") after the Cold War, international relations has refused to return to the superficial simplicity of the Cold War. As a result, constructivism's embrace of complexity, contingency, and the interplay between actors and their societal contexts make it a theoretical approach for the twenty-first century.

It is not surprising, then, that in the study of international relations in the United States it is now trite to say that constructivism comprises, alongside variants of realism and liberalism, one third of a "mainstream" theoretical trinity. There are good reasons to ask, however, where constructivism is, where it has been, and where it is going. One reason is that there is a need for a certain amount of ground clearing. The groundbreaking texts of constructivism emerged almost thirty years ago in the late 1980s (Kratochwil 1989; Onuf 1989; Wendt 1992), with a second wave ten years later in the late 1990s (Katzenstein 1996; Acharya 2000, 2001). Efforts to come to terms with these waves date from roughly the same period (Finnemore and Sikkink 2001) or, as in the case of Guzzini and Leanders's *Constructivism and International Relations*, are more recent (2006) but focus on scholarship from these periods. The apparent success of constructivism (Guzzini 2000), however, has generated a wide-ranging research program that expanded theoretical and conceptual depth and breadth, necessitating periodic assessments of trajectories within constructivist scholarship. This volume undertakes one such assessment.

Another reason for the present type of review is that constructivism resists assessment through the Lakatosian science framework that seems to be the favorite of IR scholars, making it difficult to clearly define the core and auxiliary elements of the constructivist "research program." In part this resistance lies in the nature of constructivism as a social theory rather than a substantive theory. Thus, like rationalist approaches, it is difficult to say whether constructivism is progressive or degenerative in Lakatosian terms because it does not generate novel predictions of unobserved phenomena or core and auxiliary sets of testable hypotheses that can be tested, altered, or abandoned. But in part the resistance is because constructivists disagree on whether constructivism should be subject to assessments like Lakatos's research program designed for the natural—not social—sciences. For an example of such a disagreement, see Kessler and Steele's critique in this volume of Finnemore and Sikkink's (2001) moderate effort to fit constructivism to a Lakatosian appraisal.

Perhaps arising from the resistance of constructivism to Lakatosian-style appraisals, there seems to be a persistent question of what is this thing we call constructivism. In the neat packaging of theory for students, and indeed in the convenient linguistic shorthand of academics, constructivism is represented as a theory. But many constructivists chafe at this characterization, preferring to conceive of it as a general analytical perspective. Others, usually critics, term it a methodology and thus—intentionally or not—attempt to displace constructivism from its place in IR theory's trinity. Often these debates focus on trying to clearly delineate constructivism as, in Onuf's terminology, a medium-sized dry good. We ourselves undertake such an exercise in chapter 2 when we define constructivism as an "approach to social analysis that: (a) emphasizes ideational factors, and not just material ones, in explaining social action and interactions, (b) asserts that the most relevant ideational factors are shared, "intersubjective" beliefs not reducible to particular individuals, and (c) contends that such ideational factors construct the interests and identities of actors." We did not, however, impose this definition on the contributors to this volume. Further, we suggest that these debates miss part of the point of constructivism by applying an objectivist lens to an approach that emphasizes inter-subjectivity and social construction. Thus, rather than seek to establish a definitive conception of constructivism by definitional fiat or otherwise, this volume seeks to understand constructivism as an intersubjectively constructed intellectual field given shape both by those who conceive of themselves as constructivists and by those who do not.

Third, as David McCourt argues in this volume, there is reason to be pessimistic about the future of constructivism. While constructivism may be considered part of the theoretical mainstream, in teaching (Maliniak et al. 2014) and in professional practice constructivists are relatively marginalized vis-à-vis their more rationalist and neopositivist colleagues (Subotic 2017; Zarakol 2017). Given the victory lap taken by many constructivists in the early years of the twenty-first century (Guzzini 2000), the situation confronting practicing constructivists in the second decade of the century is sobering. Yet in practical terms, constructivism is increasingly working its way into everyday policy analysis. Take terrorism, thus far the leading threat of the twenty-first century. Analysis has migrated from largely rationalist assessments of economic costs and benefits to focusing on the social foundations of terrorist violence and questions of identity and belonging (Arena and Arrigo 2005). A similar dynamic is happening in scholarship on climate change (Hayes and Knox-Hayes 2014), and the list goes on. Thus, while constructivism's status in the IR scholarly community is in some doubt, its policy and practical applicability continues to expand. Thus, this volume seeks to renew scholarly engagement with constructivism within the study of international relations to match its growing practical importance.

In line with these goals, and unlike the typical edited volume, the editors did not set out a framework and ask contributors to engage with it in some way. Rather, we asked contributors to engage with a series of questions: What is constructivism? What is its place in IR intellectually and professionally? Where has constructivism been? Where is it going? In part, our desire to learn how constructivism is understood in the discipline required that we refrain from harnessing the contributors into a framework straightjacket. That would have put them in the position of reacting to the editors' conceptions of constructivism, which would have both essentialized constructivism and produced a far less interesting collection of essays. Our interest in where constructivism has been as well as where it is going also shaped the roster of our contributors. While the volume has well-established scholars—Samuel Barkin, Charles Glaser, Stacie Goddard, Oliver Kessler, Audie Klotz, Ron Krebs, Nick Onuf, Laura Sjoberg, and Brent Steele—it also has emerging scholars such as David Blagden, Jordan Branch, Jérémie Cornut, Thomas Jamieson, David McCourt, and Jennifer Ramos, who will continue to shape IR and constructivism for many years to come.

To our delight, the contributions to the volume developed organically in a way that addresses the continued promise and challenge of constructivism in the study of international relations. The essays cluster around four themes. The first considers the nature of constructivism and its place in the American study of international relations. The second considers constructivism from the inside, with contributors elaborating ideas and concepts that hold the potential to extend and enrich constructivist scholarship. Third, a group of scholars consider the ways that constructivism interfaces with, and can benefit from, theories outside the traditional purview of international relations. Fourth and finally, scholars outside of constructivism offer critiques and observations both sympathetic and distinctly unsympathetic. The volume clusters the contributions around these themes and, in the epilogue, offers reflections by Amitav Acharya, a renowned scholar linked to constructivism but critical of its preoccupation with the Euro-Atlantic. In what follows, we provide a brief overview of the contributions to orient the reader and provide a sense of the ideas and arguments to come.

In the preface, Nick Onuf starts the conversation, returning to the meta-theoretical foundations of constructivism. Onuf argues that constructivism emerged out an effort of scholars in the humanities to push back against the increasing emphasis in the liberal arts on the natural sciences and epistemologies attributed to them. The Cold War, while useful in terms of making space in the study of international relations, was incidental to the theoretical currents that created constructivism. To understand what constructivism is requires a return to foundations, a shift in perspective that marginalizes the oft-repeated claim that constructivism can be defined as some kind of middle ground in the debates that periodically roil IR. For Onuf, those foundations are rooted in the work of Kant and Austin and they lead constructivists—uniquely—to explore how social objects are infused with value and meaning.

In counterpoint to Onuf's contribution, chapter 2 takes a decidedly empirical approach. Here the editors of the volume present not a framework paper, but rather an unparalleled dataset addressing how constructivism has manifested in major IR journals since Onuf coined the term in 1989. Based on the systematic analysis of constructivist articles published from 1989 to 2014, the editors of the volume present the first quantitative assessment of the constructivist research program. By analyzing more than six hundred articles along more than twenty dimensions, the chapter sheds light on three questions about the contributions of constructivism to knowledge: (a) knowledge about what? (b) knowledge for what? and (c) how has knowledge been generated? The chapter places constructivism's patterns of publication within trends exhibited by the field of IR as a whole and leads into more in-depth explorations of the approach's value in subsequent chapters.

David McCourt in chapter 3 takes a more sociological and practice-oriented approach in an effort to assess the future of constructivism. To do so requires an effort to understand how constructivism is typically understood in IR. This, however, raises questions about how best to understand the significance of constructivism in IR when there are multiple studies of IR, each imparting a different meaning and significance onto constructivism. These contending conceptions of constructivism, combined with constructivism's disposition toward examining how social things are socially constituted, lead McCourt to assess how constructivism as a specific socially constituted practice fares in the field of American IR. His conclusions—

that there is precious little and decreasing space for constructivism—make for sobering reading. But McCourt remains optimistic that there has been and will be space in IR for theorizing the social, even if that theorizing is not carried out under the banner of constructivism.

Chapters 4, 5, and 6 address issues and concepts within constructivism, demonstrating the rich promise of constructivism to continue to illuminate international relations. In chapter 4, Oliver Kessler and Brent Steele take on the relationship between constructivism and realism. To do so, they draw attention to the importance of contingency, a concept implicit but underspecified in not only constructivist scholarship but IR in general. Kessler and Steele intend their contribution in part to be a stock-taking exercise, and to this end they provide a valuable assessment of the shifting relationship between constructivism and its purported theoretical rivals, liberalism and realism. Here they mount a critique on what they call moderate constructivism as captured by a desire to oppose rationalism in neorealism and neoliberalism while at the same time seeking to rationalize and scientificize constructivism. The evolution of constructivism, they argue, and its relationship with other approaches in international relations, can be traced through the changing role of contingency.

For example, Kessler and Steele point to similarities between the conception of agency and contingency of that agency shared between classical realism and early constructivism. In the former, the search for security is predicated on double contingency: the way meanings are—through language—received, interpreted, and expressed between actors. Likewise, early constructivists pointed to the importance of language for communicating rules and norms that cannot be reduced to a single actor and that perform social action. The contingency in this early constructivist work lies in the interrelationship between intention and effect in a social setting. Kessler and Steele go on to argue that a defining feature of moderate constructivism—which they claim has "left the constructivist building"—is the replacement of double contingency with single contingency "in the name of science." Kessler and Steele conclude with a proposition of a triple contingency, a concept that might serve as a basis for moving constructivism forward into a new generation of scholarship.

Stacie Goddard and Ron Krebs, in chapter 5, highlight legitimation as crucial to the practice of international relations. While legitimacy has long been a point of investigation in constructivism, it has gained traction in more rationalist-oriented approaches like realism and liberalism. Yet Goddard and Krebs argue that within constructivism the politics and process of legitimation remains underexamined. In their approach, Goddard and Krebs open up a rich avenue for constructivist inquiry and position constructivism as central to any effort to come to terms with legitimation. This is because, while legitimation is increasingly important to most, if not all, theories of international relations, taking the concept seriously requires a social constructivist ontology. Legitimation requires a social constructivist approach because, in the final analysis, it is a process by which actors attempt to imbue their action with a specific set of meanings. Those meanings are not created whole cloth by the legitimating actor, but rather are tied to the specific social context in which legitimation takes place. This process, of "providing reasons for our own actions, and making sense of others' actions," is, according to Goddard and Krebs, "central to our existence."

The centrality of meaning making in social life places legitimation at the center of global politics. Goddard and Krebs' approach is predicated on four "analytical wagers": that actors are both strategic and social, that legitimation imparts meaning, that contestation is interwoven into legitimation, and contentious dialogue gives rise to the power of language. Building on these wagers, Goddard and Krebs discuss when legitimation might be expected to be most important. They conclude by arguing that the significance of legitimation in political and social life offers substantial scholarly promise that constructivism is well, and perhaps best, placed to explore.

In chapter 6, Audie Klotz underlines the importance of race for constructivist scholarship and the critical failure of constructivists to adequately address the phenomenon of racism. Pointing to gaps identified by scholars in constructivist treatments of gender, Klotz argues a parallel problem holds for race in constructivist analyses. Despite a smattering of superb publications that have straddled the divide between scholarship on race and that of constructivism, including Klotz's own seminal work, the gap remains. Klotz's chapter explores this race gap and suggests future directions for research in two core areas of constructivism: norm diffusion and state identity.

For Klotz, the key to incorporating race into constructivism lies in a recognition of the prevalence of hierarchies. In the case of norm diffusion, including race in analysis highlights the ways in which norms that often are held up as having significant impact in the international system—democracy for example—often operated only within and across societies of European extraction, and often to the detriment of racial "others." For tools to pick apart the scholarly silence on race, Klotz points to another prominent aspect of the constructivist research program: state identity. Here the corporate aspect of identity (who is part of the self) provides a

means by which constructivism can begin to assess the ongoing significance of race in international relations. Klotz argues that in the final analysis race has substantial promise to re-energize the conceptual workhorses
of constructivism—norms and identity—as well as the research program
as a whole.

In chapters 7 through 9, the contributors explore the interconnections
between constructivism and other theoretical perspectives. In chapter 7,
Jordan Branch takes on the tension between ideas and materiality that is
central to constructivism and increasingly important for all of international
relations in the context of the rapid technologicalization that characterizes the twenty-first century. While constructivism initially distinguished
itself from other approaches by privileging the ideational, more recently
constructivist scholars have presented a variety of theorizing about the
material-ideational intersection. Branch considers that intersection by
focusing on one empirical domain: technology and technological change.
Technologies, being themselves simultaneously material and ideational (or
social), provide a useful lens for thinking about what constructivism has
contributed and can continue to contribute. Branch reviews how existing
constructivist theories address technology; considers the broader array of
arguments and theoretical tools offered by other fields, particularly science
and technology studies (STS); and highlights theoretical issues and empirical topics where constructivist approaches could be fruitfully applied.

Jennifer Ramos examines in chapter 8 the significant possibilities that
emerge when scholars link constructivism with social psychology, with a
specific focus on the phenomenon of cognitive dissonance. Ramos starts
with an old question for constructivists: how do international norms
evolve? Her focus in the chapter narrows to considering the role of military intervention on international norms, centering on the question of
how the outcome of military intervention influences the evolution of the
norm of state sovereignty. Social psychology enters the picture through the
concept of cognitive dissonance. Social psychology, Ramos argues, gives
constructivists a vector through which they can link microfoundations of
agential action to social context.

Echoing Goddard and Krebs' discussion of legitimation, Ramos argues
that the use of legitimating language by a policy elite in the context of
military interventions drives sovereignty norm evolution. She goes on to
examine the role of cognitive dissonance through two case studies: the US
interventions in Afghanistan and Iraq. At the heart of these cases, Ramos
points to the ways action can allow for unarticulated ideas to be expressed,
which in turn may become sources of explicit general principles to guide

state behavior as states try to minimize the dissonance between the norms they espouse and the actions they undertake.

Jérémie Cornut turns in chapter 9 to practice theory, arguing that it has the potential to expand constructivism in important ways from ontology—allowing constructivism to account for the materialization of ideas, identity, and culture—to epistemology, strengthening constructivism's meta-theoretical foundations. Helpfully, both constructivism and practice theory focus on the social construction of reality. The differences between the two, however, are what allow practice theory to make its contribution.

Specifically, Cornut argues that practice theory's broad ontology is structural *and* agential, as well as ideational *and* material. It puts power relationships at the center of its understanding of politics and complements the text-based methods that predominate in constructivism with interviews and participant observation. Finally, practice theory is based on a reflexive and pragmatic epistemology. Cornut explores these differences and the contribution they can make to constructivism and concludes that these characteristics show that practice theory answers important objections raised against constructivism. By bringing new wine into the (not so) old constructivist bottle, practice theory offers a promising path for the next generation of constructivists.

In chapters 10 through 12, scholars outside constructivism offer thoughts on constructivism's place in IR. In chapter 10's very personal essay, Thomas Jamieson argues that Constructivism needs a greater embrace of positivist epistemology if it is to keep and expand the foothold it has developed in the United States. While Jamieson appreciates the pluralist space that constructivism has opened up in American IR, he argues that constructivist methodology, linked to its general rejection of positivism, makes replication difficult. This in turn limits the appeal of constructivism in the social context of American IR, where a particular conception of methodological rigor is dominant.

Jamieson focuses specifically on securitization theory as both exemplar of constructivism's failings and avatar of the promise it holds if positivist approaches gain greater appeal. Regarding the failings, Jamieson argues that applications of securitization theory lack a cohesive methodology, one that would allow for rigorous testing of propositions and avoid pitfalls such as confirmation bias. Moreover, he argues that the failure to ground securitization theory in positivist epistemology has allowed scholars to focus on speech without taking account of material manifestations of that speech. These failings lay not in the original securitization framework, which Jamieson argues placed equal emphasis on action taken in response to securitization, but rather with the indeterminate epistemological foundations. To this end, Jamieson proposes a four-sided framework for securitization that positions it as an exemplar of positivist, constructivist IR.

Chapter 11 sees Charles Glaser offering a rationalist realist perspective on constructivism. Although the two are often characterized as competing, Glaser argues that that key strands of the two theoretical families are better understood as complementary research projects that have much to offer each other. Rationalist realist theory takes much as given, including states' preferences and norms that influence their identities. Conversely, constructivist theories, especially the Wendtian version that focuses on states—exploring the formation of their interests and of their beliefs about the international system—address those realist assumptions. Thus for Glaser the combination of constructivism and rationalist realism holds the potential to provide a much fuller explanation of international politics than either alone.

All is not complementary, however. Glaser does see rational realist theory and those constructivist theories that focus on the impact of the international system—which he terms structural constructivism—as in direct competition as they seek to explain many of the same phenomena from different theoretical perspectives. Here Glaser asserts realism's advantages for explaining states' strategic interaction and the possibilities for international cooperation under anarchy, holding that rational theory relies on more analytically demanding assumptions about states' preferences and provides arguments that are more parsimonious and direct than are the key structural constructivist alternative.

In chapter 12, David Blagden offers a more forceful take on constructivism. He accepts a range of constructivist premises: Identity matters in international politics; the pursuit of status and the desire to play a particular international-social role can condition states' foreign and defense policy choices; culture impacts the way states interpret security threats, formulate strategy, and—ultimately—fight; and that nationalism causes political communities to be constituted as nation-states. Despite these concessions, Blagden rejects what he argues is the central pillar of constructivism: the promise of a fundamental transformation of international relations—particularly great power relations—away from the competition and periodic conflict predicted by realism. While social role may be *an* interest of states, for Blagden it is necessarily subordinate to—rather than constitutive of—survival, security, and prosperity, all of which have a material base. Drawing on classic realist logics, Blagden argues that since states cannot be sure of other states' intentions—particularly their future intentions—securing these materially underpinned interests requires guarding against the threat potentially posed by others, and thus threatening them back. In the end, then, Blagden holds that constructivism can only ever matter at the margins of an international system primarily driven by material considerations.

Laura Sjoberg and Samuel Barkin in chapter 13 are altogether more sympathetic to the constructivist agenda than is Blagden. Both argue that there is much to interest IR scholars—intellectually and normatively—in many of the intents and promises of constructivism. Despite these merits, however, Sjoberg and Barkin nonetheless find themselves steering clear of both the label "constructivist" and research programs that self-identify as a part of "constructivist IR." This is because, they argue, there are a number of "constructivisms" in IR, the various parts of which feel muddled, underspecified, and underdeveloped, even thirty years into constructivist IR. Their chapter focuses on three: the tendency to associate constructivisms with progressive politics, the tendency to apply overbroad notions of the social and of norms to global politics, and problematic (mis)understandings of the notion of "social construction." In engaging all three of these problems, they make the argument that the disciplinary politics of *having a constructivism in IR* is a positive one, but that in practice IR constructivisms often destroy their potential contributions by overstretch and underspecification.

In the final chapter, we the editors return to the questions that animated the conference we hosted at the University of Southern California, at which contributors presented initial drafts of what ultimately became chapters in this volume. With respect to the question of what is constructivism, the volume reflects both convergence and divergence. Many of the contributors agree with Nicholas Onuf's positioning of the approach as one centrally concerned with the social construction of reality through linguistic and cognitive processes. Often these processes of social construction take the form of normative structures. While the consensus regarding constructivism's general orientation and research program is strong, it is weaker when it comes to questions of epistemology. This perhaps reflects the tension between some of the original formulations, those of Onuf and Kratochwil, and the empirical research that constructivist scholars have undertaken in the American context where the pressures to adhere to positivist notions of scholarly inquiry are strong.

These tensions aside, the programs of research within constructivism are strong, as even critics like Charles Glaser seem willing to acknowledge. Indeed, looking at constructivism through the perspective of Bunge's

(1996) systemism—which seeks to link macro-level phenomena with micro-level mechanisms—reveals an evolving research program. In the past, constructivism primarily focused on macro- or systemic-level linkages, typified by Wendt's cultures or anarchy. The constructivist scholarship described in this volume has shifted focus to mechanisms within states that drive forward the systemic-level behavior as well as how the macro- and micro-levels link together.

While the agenda of constructivism exhibits many strengths, critics in this volume point to weaknesses as well. While some, notably Blagden, see these weaknesses as positioning constructivism as moderately interesting but ultimately not relevant, many of the critics position their critiques as opportunities for growth. A common complaint lies in the lack of specificity as to what, precisely, constructivism represents in the scholarly practice of IR. To this end, Sjoberg and Barkin argue for an opportunity to reform constructivism around a coherent conversation focused on the processes of social construction. Many of the contributors also pushed for greater separation from the implicit idealism that seems to have pervaded much of constructivist scholarship. This has been a theme in recent scholarship by Hopf, who has challenged the possibility of change through his work on habit and common sense (Hopf 2010, 2013).

A final theme we note is the willingness of many of the authors to countenance analytical eclecticism (Sil and Katzenstein 2010) when it comes to thinking about constructivism. Even the most distant critic in the volume (Blagden) notes that constructivism and more materialist/rationalist approaches can make shared contributions to our understanding of important international practices and outcomes. Likewise, the willingness of Goddard and Krebs to countenance social actors as strategic actors points to the possibility of shared insights. It is of course possible to take the analytical eclectic point too far; at their starting points, Blagden and Goddard and Krebs are materialist and constructivists, respectively. Indeed, the same can be said for all the authors in this volume. Analytical eclecticism does not extend down to the theoretical foundations. But the willingness of all the authors here to embrace intellectual and theoretical flexibility speaks highly of an evolving IR discipline and its ability to engage with real-world problems that do not cleave along ontological, theoretical, epistemological, or methodological lines.

Throughout the process of putting this volume together, the editors have sought to provide not the first or last word on constructivism but rather a platform for discussion. Thus, just as Onuf has the first word through his preface, Amatav Acharya has the last word in his epilogue.

There he interrogates constructivism's ability to engage with IR theory and practice outside the narrow confines of the West. Acharya argues that while constructivism initially had promise to become a "vanguard theory of Global IR," scholars within the tradition did not seek to realize that potential. That promise, however, has not been lost. Acharya details the aspects of constructivism that enable it—rather than its theoretical competitors—to reach beyond the sociocultural milieu of the West. Acharya concludes with a robust program for realizing constructivism's promise as a vanguard theory of Global IR, one powerful answer to one of the motiving questions of this volume: where is constructivism going?

NOTES

1. We are grateful to an anonymous reviewer for raising this point.
2. For example, consider the tension between Jamieson's (chapter 10) and Kessler and Steele's (chapter 4) conception of positivism.

REFERENCES

Acharya, Amitav. 2000. *The Quest for Identity: International Relations of Southeast Asia.* Singapore: Oxford University Press.

Acharya, Amitav. 2001. *Constructing a Security Community in Southeast Asia: ASEAN and the Problem of Regional Order.* Politics in Asia series. London: Routledge.

Arena, Michael P., and Bruce A. Arrigo. 2005. "Social Psychology, Terrorism, and Identity: A Preliminary Re-examination of Theory, Culture, Self, and Society." *Behavioral Sciences & the Law* 23, no. 4: 485–506.

Barder, Alexander D., and Daniel J. Levine. 2012. "'The World Is Too Much with Us': Reification and the Depoliticising of Via Media Constructivist IR." *Millennium—Journal of International Studies* 40, no. 3: 585–604.

Bunge, Mario. 1996. *Finding Philosophy in Social Science.* New Haven, CT: Yale University Press.

Faizullaev, Alisher, and Jérémie Cornut. 2016. "Narrative Practice in International Politics and Diplomacy: The Case of the Crimean Crisis." *Journal of Int Relations and Development* 20, no. 3: 578–604.

Finnemore, Martha, and Katheryn Sikkink. 2001. "Taking Stock: The Constructivist Research Program in International Relations and Comparative Politics." *Annual Review of Political Science* 4: 391–416.

Guzzini, Stefano. 2000. "A Reconstruction of Constructivism in International Relations." *European Journal of International Relations* 6, no. 2: 147–82.

Hayes, Jarrod, and Janelle Knox-Hayes. 2014. "Security in Climate Change Discourse: Analyzing the Divergence between US and EU Approaches to Policy." *Global Environmental Politics* 14, no. 2: 82–101.

Hopf, Ted. 2010. "The Logic of Habit in International Relations." *European Journal of International Relations* 16, no. 4: 539–61.

Hopf, Ted. 2013. "Common-sense Constructivism and Hegemony in World Politics." *International Organization* 67, no. 2: 317–54.

Katzenstein, Peter J. 1996. *The Culture of National Security: Norms and Identity in World Politics.* New York: Columbia University Press.

Kratochwil, Friedrich V. 1989. *Rules, Norms, and Decisions on the Conditions of Practical and Legal Reasoning in International Relations and Domestic Affairs.* Cambridge: Cambridge University Press.

Maliniak, Daniel, Susan Peterson, Ryan Powers, and Michael J. Tierney. 2014. TRIP 2014 Faculty Survey Report. https://trip.wm.edu/reports/2014/rp_2014/index.php. Accessed January 18, 2016.

Onuf, Nicholas Greenwood. 1989. *World of Our Making: Rules and Rule in Social Theory and International Relations.* Columbia: University of South Carolina Press.

Sil, Rudra, and Peter J. Katzenstein. 2010. *Beyond Paradigms: Analytical Eclecticism in the Study of World Politics.* Basingstoke: Palgrave Macmillan.

Stump, Jacob L., and Priya Dixit. 2012. "Toward a Completely Constructivist Critical Terrorism Studies." *International Relations* 26, no. 2: 199–217.

Subotic, Jelena. 2017. "Constructivism as Professional Practice in the US Academy." *PS: Political Science & Politics* 50, no. 1: 84–88.

Wendt, A. 1992. "Anarchy Is What States Make of It: The Social Construction of Power Politics." *International Organization* 46, no. 2: 391–425.

Zarakol, Ayşe. 2017. "TRIPping Constructivism." *PS: Political Science & Politics* 50, no. 1: 75–78.

TWO

Constructivism in International Relations

The Story So Far

Mariano E. Bertucci
Jarrod Hayes
Patrick James

Constructivism and International Relations

International relations (IR) continues to struggle with constructivism. Is it a method? Is it a space for social inquiry? Is it a paradigm in competition with rationalist-based approaches? Add to these questions further concerns about the place of constructivism in the discipline in professional terms. The Teaching, Research, and International Policy (TRIP) survey shows constructivism as the single largest "paradigm" globally and in the United States, second in self-identified scholars only to "non-paradigmatic." Scholars have argued, however, that these results are deceptive.[1] Others note that constructivists are exceedingly rare in the United States, accounting for slightly more than 6 percent of the IR faculty in the top fifty political science departments, and completely absent at the most prestigious levels.[2]

This chapter presents an alternative assessment of the constructivist research program in International Relations.[3] Specifically, our focus lies on how constructivism is manifested in one of the most important professional practices scholars undertake: journal publishing. The analysis, based on works published during the period from 1989 to 2014, seeks to shed light on the empirical content, purpose, and methodology of IR constructivism. It is concerned with three key questions about the contributions of this approach to knowledge: Knowledge about what? Knowledge for what? And how has knowledge been generated?

The assessment is based on an analysis of journal articles published in seventeen leading International Relations journals: *International Organization, International Security, World Politics, European Journal of International Relations, International Studies Quarterly, Review of International Studies, International Studies Review, International Studies Perspectives, Review of International Political Economy, Millennium, International Theory, Foreign Policy Analysis, International Political Sociology, Conflict and Cooperation, Security Studies, Security Dialogue,* and *Journal of International Relations and Development.* In all, 676 works have been selected and coded along the lines of twenty-five variables such as the question or topics being addressed; the country or region being covered in the study; whether the generation of theory or empirical analyses is the research goal; whether the goal is also to offer descriptions, causal accounts, constitutive accounts, or prescriptions; and what methods are used to generate theory, among other variables.[4] The goal is to try to paint a picture of the intellectual agenda of constructivism.

By necessity, this picture is only partial. Constructivist research analyzing international relations issues appears in a myriad of journals in history, economics, comparative politics, and other political science outlets, as well as in books catalogued under a variety of names and topics. While it would be ideal to know the universe of works on the matter and to have included items from those sources, such an undertaking may very well be impossible. At present, we know of no way to locate all the relevant articles and books produced by scholars interested in constructivism. Thus we present here a sample, albeit one we believe to be an inclusive and fair representation of the practice of constructivism. There is always a danger that constructivist research published in other outlets and formats could diverge systematically from the sources we review, but by including what are widely regarded as the leading sources that set the collective standards for IR research in general and IR constructivist research in particular, we believe the danger is minimized. Thus our choice of journals is suited to the goal of providing a characterization and assessment of the current state of the constructivist research program in IR.

The chapter is organized as follows. First, an overview of the scope of constructivist research is presented. To this end, the literature is characterized in terms of the subject matter or issues it covers. Where relevant, information about the empirical scope or cases studied is provided, and to place this literature in context, trends in world politics and the field of IR are considered. Subsequently, the objectives, methods, and research designs of constructivist work are considered. The analysis of research objectives distinguishes between theory generation and empirical analysis and, furthermore, distinguishes among (a) descriptive research, which advances propositions about *what* the state of the world is, (b) causal research, which articulates propositions about *why* the world is as it is, (c) constitutive research, which seeks to establish the properties of things by reference to the structures in virtue of which they exist, and (d) prescriptive research, which argues how the world should be. In turn, the analysis of research design and methods focuses on the distinction between qualitative and quantitative methods of empirical analysis and on whether constructivist research addresses variation across variables in its accounts of international relations. Finally, we summarize the findings and flesh out the reasons why the challenges facing constructivism are not insuperable.

This new data enables a more robust and systematic analysis of constructivism as an approach to the study of international relations that previously had not been available. Specifically, it is possible to compare constructivist research against available data on the IR field in general. In doing so, it is also possible to assess prevailing perceptions about constructivism's allegiance to so-called poststructuralism and its perceived distance from what might pass for IR's orthodoxy or its mainstream positivist epistemology. In taking such a data-driven approach to describing the world of constructivism and its place in IR, we aim to ground and complement the valuable and more thematic contributions to this volume and those published elsewhere.[5] But by centering on questions of substance, research goals, and methodology in particular, we reveal where disconnects between constructivism and IR mainstream approaches may continue to exist as well as partially dispel some myths about the perceived quantitative, paradigmatic, and positivist turn in IR research. Constructivism has helped shaped the IR field as we know it today. But, at the same time, it has helped carve out an alternative theoretical, epistemological, and methodological space to understanding international affairs that three decades ago was simply not available and is now—and will continue to be—one of the leading approaches to making sense of world politics.

A Brief Note on Concepts and Methods

Defining any research program is an exercise fraught with danger; almost any definition is likely to do violence to how practitioners (within and without) the program understand it. As one of us has noted, definitions also provide the basis for disciplining efforts and identity dynamics of inclusion and exclusion.[6] Nonetheless, any effort to come to terms with constructivism as a research program and scholarly practice must start with some working conception of it. Drawing on Guzzini (2000), we define constructivism as an approach to social analysis that (a) emphasizes ideational factors, and not just material ones, in explaining social action and interactions, (b) asserts that the most relevant ideational factors are shared, "intersubjective" beliefs not reducible to particular individuals, and, (c) contends that such ideational factors construct the interests and identities of actors.[7] Social reality, including scientific knowledge, is thus constructed socially and cannot be explained as the product of human calculation and bargaining alone. We believe this conceptualization is broad enough to capture a substantial amount of constructivist scholarship of both the conventional and critical varieties without making constructivism so shapeless as to mean anything. Central to our conception of constructivism is the role of shared ideational factors in shaping international relations.

This starting point is crucial in the sampling process. First, the authors read the abstract (and, when necessary, the introductions) of every article published in the target journals in the time frame. Candidate articles—those fitting within our conceptualization—were logged for coding. Where ambiguity existed, the authors read the articles until satisfied they either did or did not fit the definitional criteria. This did not require that the term "constructivist" be used at all in a given article. Since those who built the sample did not necessarily do the actual coding, we used the coding process as a second check against poor sampling decisions; that is, coders could flag articles that did not belong to the dataset.

To ensure intercoder reliability, we conducted three test rounds of coding. In the first test, all coders—a coauthor of this chapter plus two graduate students in international relations at the University of Southern California—followed the code book with no further instructions and coded a sample of articles chosen at random. The coders agreed on 81 percent of coding decisions prior to debriefing. We compared results and discussed our discrepancies, which allowed us to refine our code book and coding rules. We conducted a second initial test over a different subsample of articles chosen at random. In this instance, coders agreed on 93 percent of coding decisions; after this second test, all coders began to code independently different subsamples of articles. If a coder could not be sure about the value of a particular variable, he met with the co-author of this chapter—also a coder—to agree on a final coding decision. The third coding test was performed by the coder who is the coauthor of this chapter, on a subsample of articles chosen at random. In this third instance, coders agreed on 92 percent of coding decisions.[8]

The Substance and Empirical Scope of Constructivist Research

General Patterns

Some interesting trends immediately emerge in the literature. Consider the contents of table 2.1, which focuses on the substantive scope of constructivist research. Despite the initial strength of norms-based constructivist research, identity-oriented scholarship enjoys substantially greater attention in constructivist scholarship overall. Not surprisingly, more recent advances in constructivism—such as the practice turn—are so far less prevalent in the literature. Surprisingly, established issues, such as processes of socialization or dynamics of legitimacy, which would seem to be obvious areas of interest for constructivist scholarship, are relatively neglected. The attention paid to security in the constructivist literature follows from the early example set by Katzenstein's agenda-setting volume *The Culture of National Security* (1996). Interestingly, however, no single issue within the broader security umbrella seems to have garnered significant attention; the field appears to be extremely fragmented. In other areas, observations match expectations. Scholars, including Klotz in chapter 6, have noted that IR has overlooked race to a substantial degree. Constructivism appears to be no different in this regard.[9] Along similar lines, calls for a global IR, with emphasis on material and ideational elements that transcend Westernized frameworks that have dominated the field for a long time, are gaining prominence (Acharya 2014). Constructivism also appears to have been generally reticent to take on aspects from disciplines such as social psychology that could bolster constructivist microfoundations.

But beyond its expected emphasis on ideas and security—the former by definition and the latter as a natural extension of traditional IR emphasis on security matters—constructivism also has covered, in a relatively even fashion, a myriad of issues ranging from human rights and international law to trade, economic regionalism, and development. The effects of the structure of the international system and—considerably less prominently—that of domestic systems on international affairs, also has been an important area of study for constructivists. Indeed, as per table 2.2, this subject matter makes up more than 50 percent of all constructivist work and more than

70 percent of the total if foreign policy analyses and studies pertaining to nonstate actors are considered.

The new data allows us to highlight gaps in the constructivist research agenda, and there are many. Pressing issues such as terrorism, the environment, drugs, economic sanctions, refugee crises, and the roles of race and technology in world politics are virtually absent from constructivism. While such issues are relatively new to IR in general, the time seems ripe for constructivism in particular to stress the nonmaterial factors shaping such new issues and developments (see Klotz in chapter 6 and Branch in chapter 7, for example).

TABLE 2.1. *Knowledge about What? I:* The Substantive Scope of Constructivist International Relations Research

Subject Matter	Articles (%)
Ideas	**105.1**
Identity	26.1
Norms	19.2
Speech, argument, discourse, rhetoric, narratives, and persuasion	14.7
Culture	11.6
International governance (i.e., intl. organizations, institutions, multilateralism)	9.1
Institutionalization/socialization (e.g. learning, emulation, diffusion, etc.)	7.9
Practices	6.9
Sovereignty	4.8
Legitimacy	2.6
Religion	2.2
Security	**43.5**
National interest, military culture/strategy/doctrine	8.7
Securitization	6
Security dilemma	5.1
Security communities	3.9
Power	3.5
Conflict resolution	3.2
International society	3.1
Cold War/post–Cold War order	2.9
Humanitarianism	1.6
Nuclear proliferation	1.4
Assassination	1.4
R2P	0.8
Hegemony	0.8
Regime change/maintenance	0.7
Neutrality	0.4
Subtotal	148.6

Note: N = 676. The subtotal percentage exceeds 100 percent because individual articles frequently address multiple subject matters.

Source: Author's calculations on data on the variable *Question* from the Bertucci, Hayes, and James constructivist IR research dataset.

As part of a not-so-international field of inquiry (Tickner and Waever 2010), constructivist scholars also focus most of their attention on Europe and the United States; almost 45 percent of all sampled research covers cases and issues in the North Atlantic region. Within this general pattern, however, there is a notable difference in application between Europe and North America that may reflect the divergent acceptance of constructivism in the two zones. About 13 percent of articles have focused on Asia,

TABLE 2.2. *Knowledge about What? I (Cont.)*: The Substantive Scope of Constructivist International Relations Research

Subject Matter	Articles (%)
Other Issues	**17.4**
Human rights	4.7
Democratization/democracy	2.9
International law	2.3
Gender	2.3
Environment	1.9
Psychology/social psychology	1.4
Public health	1.1
Race	0.8
Public opinion	–
Drugs	–
Energy	–
System-Domestic Structures	**15.1**
Structure of the international system	11.6
Structure of the domestic system	3.5
IPE	**13.4**
Trade	4.4
Economic integration/regionalism	4.2
Economic development	4.2
Foreign aid	0.5
Economic sanctions	0.1
FPA	**9.7**
Foreign policy analysis	9.7
Non-State Actors	**7.5**
NGOs/transnational advocacy networks	3.1
International organizations	2.8
Epistemic communities	1.4
Moral communities	0.2
Refugees	–
Subtotal	63.1
Grand Total (Tables 1 and 2)	211.7

Note: N = 676. The Grand Total percentage exceeds 100 percent because individual articles frequently address multiple subject matters. The "–" symbol denotes that the given issue area is not represented in the literature in any significant number (or at all).

Source: Author's calculations on data on the variable *Question* from the Bertucci, Hayes, and James constructivist IR research dataset.

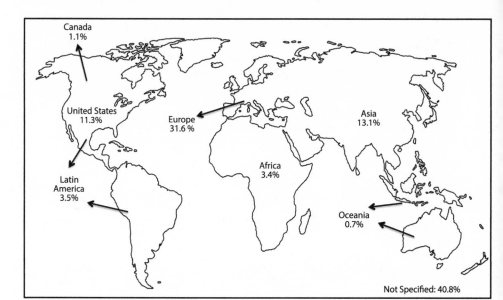

Figure 2.1. Knowledge about what? III: The geographic scope of constructivist IR research

but regions such as Latin America, Africa, and, most notably, the Middle East have received only scant attention. Tellingly, figure 2.1 reveals that 40 percent of all published constructivist research does not specify the cases or regions upon which its analyses is based, which signals the strong preference on the part of constructivists to engage with strictly theoretical, conceptual, and epistemological debates and analyses rather than with carefully crafted empirical works on the different processes and phenomena shaping outcomes of interest (more on this below).[10]

Emphasis on the North Atlantic region could be due to sampling—leading IR journals are mostly based in the United States and western Europe—and, more specifically, to IR's characteristic parochialism. As table 2.3 below shows, at the time of publication, more than 80 percent of all authors were based either in Europe or the United States. And, save for the relatively marginal exceptions of scholars working in Canada, Oceania, and Asia, constructivist work by African, Latin American, and Middle Eastern scholars is almost nonexistent in leading IR journals. To be sure, IR scholars outside the United States and western Europe tend to face different professional structures of incentives compared to those in the North Atlantic region; peer-reviewed publications in leading journals are not as important as policy-oriented research, for example (Tickner and Waever 2009). Still, and even though correlation is not causation, the fact that most constructivists are (a) based in Europe and the United States and (b) study Europe and the United States seems to confirm the adage that "what you see depends on where you stand."

TABLE 2.3. *Knowledge by Whom?* Geographic Location of Author at the Time of Publication

Country/Region	Articles (%)
Europe	41.8
United States	39.9
Canada	7.1
Oceania	4.7
Asia	4.1
Independent Scholar	0.8
Africa	0.4
Latin America	0.4
Middle East	0.2
Total	99.4

Note: N = 676.

Source: Author's calculations on data on the variable *Space* from the Bertucci, Hayes, and James constructivist IR research dataset.

Thus, despite constructivism's place as the leading theoretical alternative to rationalist approaches to the study of international relations,[11] in terms of its substantive and empirical scope, constructivism does not look much different than rationalist alternatives like realism and liberalism. In all cases, scholarship primarily focuses on security processes and outcomes taking place in the North Atlantic region and Europe—broadly defined—whereas as subfields such as foreign policy analysis have been of secondary importance to constructivist research.[12]

Research Objectives and Methods

What researchers study is, obviously, a keen concern in any assessment of a given field. Equally important, however, are questions regarding the ends to which scholarship is directed and the methods by which knowledge is generated. These two issues get at the objectives of research (i.e., the distinction between theory generation and empirical analysis and between descriptive, causal, constitutive, and prescriptive goals and methods of research), at how research is generated (i.e., the distinction between qualitative and quantitative methods of empirical analysis), and whether research seeks to explain variation across variables. Thus, moving beyond a concern with matters of substantive and empirical scope is essential to an overall characterization and assessment of IR constructivist research.

Starting with the distinction between theory generation and empirical analysis, Table 2.4 shows that almost all constructivist research seeks to contribute mainly theoretical accounts of international affairs. Only one-tenth of all constructivist work advances inquiries based on observable manifestations of a concept or concepts about what the state of the world is without explicitly pursuing the further development of available theories or concepts to broaden current understandings of international politics. But more telling is the 60 percent of articles that, in addition to providing an empirical analysis of some sort, seek to contribute to the generation of theory. Even more interesting is that almost one-third of works seek to develop theoretical concepts and constructs specifically crafted to better understand international relations processes and outcomes. That is, almost

TABLE 2.4. *Knowledge for What?* The Objectives of Constructivist International Relations Research

Objectives		Articles (%)	Aggregate Options	Total (%)
Theory and empirics	Theory generation	29.2	Mainly theoretical	89.8
	Both theory generation and empirical analysis	60.6		
	Empirical analysis	10.0	Empirical	10.0
	Total	100		
Description, causation, constitution, and prescription	Descriptive	20.4		
	Causal and descriptive	26.0	Mainly causal	30.4
	Causal	4.4		
	Constitutive and descriptive	19.5	Mainly constitutive	47.1
	Constitutive	13.7		
	Causal and constitutive	13.9		
	Prescriptions	1.9		
	Total	100		

Note: N = 676. A *theory* is understood here to consist of a proposition or set of propositions about how or why the world is as it is. An *empirical analysis* is understood here to consist of an inquiry based on observable manifestations of a concept or concepts about what the state of the world is. A study making use of a theory/ theories and/or concepts to help make better sense what the state of the world is, but that does not engage with broader theoretical debates/developments, is considered an empirical analysis. *Descriptions* answer the question what is the state of the world. *Causal* accounts answer the question what explains the outcomes we see in the world. The term "descriptive" is not used, as is common, in a critical fashion, as when a work is characterized as being merely descriptive. Here the term is used in a positive manner, as referring to accounts about *what* the state of the world is, that are differentiated from causal accounts that seek to explain *why* the state of the world is as it is. *Constitutive accounts* seek to establish the property of things by reference to the structures in virtue of which they exist, e.g., how structure X helps account for the properties of phenomenon Y. *Prescriptions* refer to whether policy recommendations are being offered or not.

Source: Author's calculations on data on the variables *Theory_Empirical* and *Descriptive_Causal_Constitutive_Prescription* from the Bertucci, Hayes, and James constructivism IR research dataset.

nine out of ten reviewed articles have the generation of theory as a main research goal, suggesting the prominent role the approach has played during the last three decades in helping turn the study of international affairs into a more theoretically-minded—rather than policy-oriented—research enterprise (Long et al. 2005).

Consider next the choice between descriptive, causal, constitutive, and prescriptive goals. The production of constitutive accounts—analyses seeking to establish the property of things by reference to the structures by virtue of which they exist—has been the dominant goal of constructivist research. Indeed, roughly half of all reviewed publications have explicitly focused on the description (19.5 percent) or causal and constitutive power of (13.9 percent and 13.7 percent, respectively) structures and how they help account for the properties of things under study. But the emphasis on constitution has not prevented constructivism from addressing causation. Indeed, just under one-third of all reviewed publications (30.4 percent) seek to explain outcomes by systematically identifying independent variables and spelling out arguments regarding how these independent variables affect certain dependent variables, a body of work worth highlighting given the perceived unusual marriage of constructivism and so-called positivist research considerations.

The prevalence of constitutive and causal accounts over descriptive research within constructivism follows trends in research goals in IR more generally. In IR research, there has been a steady decline in the number of descriptive work since the 1980s, even prior to the arrival of constructivism to the study of world politics. In 1980, "descriptive articles . . . accounted for 42% of all the articles published . . . but after 1986 [and until 2005, that figure] never moves above 30%" (Long et al. 2005, 25). Given the prominence of theory development as a goal in constructivist research, the approach has contributed significantly to IR becoming more of a theoretically rather than an empirically minded research field.

Finally, it must be noted that less than 2 percent of the publications under review offer prescriptions, that is, statements about how the world *should* be. This feature reflects the fact that "few articles in top journals offer explicit policy advice" (Maliniak et al. 2011, 437; see also Avey and Desch 2014) to begin with, and it shows a predisposition on the part of constructivists in particular not to engage with policy recommendations.[13] In this sense, it is important to stress that offering prescriptions is an important, albeit too frequently ignored, research goal and that in principle there is nothing inherent in constructivism that precludes many of its findings from being turned into knowledge useful to policymakers. But, at the same time, it is crucial to stress that whenever possible, policy prescriptions ought to be offered after arguments have been carefully developed and tested (a matter to which we turn next), the latter characteristic being one that has not been among the strengths of the constructivist literature because of issues of method and research design.

Turning to the methods of analysis, the review of constructivist literature reveals a clear pattern. In generating empirical analyses, almost 95 percent of all reviewed articles have used qualitative methods and only 5 percent have drawn on quantitative methodologies. Moreover, mixed-methods also are uncommon; they account for less than 9 percent of all publications. A similar pattern emerges regarding the methods used to generate theory. Table 2.5 shows that whether inductive or deductive, formal or informal, quantification is not favored by Constructivist researchers. This makes sense; constructivism, at its core, is about capturing meaning and meaning-making practices. Ideational factors shaping international affairs pose methodological challenges more amenable to interpretive and inductive qualitative methodologies than to quantitative methods.

These methodological preferences are not, in and of themselves, a problem. Although it has been argued that the rules of scientific inference in the social sciences "are sometimes more clearly stated in the style of quantitative research" (King, Keohane, and Verba 1994: 6), qualitative methods also can contribute to achieving valid inference. As Brady and Collier (2004, 12) remind us, "analytic leverage can derive from a close knowledge of cases and context, which can directly contribute to more valid descriptive and causal inference." Thus, beyond constructivism's inherent interest in ideas and meaning, within the approach there is no a priori reason to opt for qualitative or quantitative methods. After all, psychologists and social psychologists, for example, have been studying the influence of ideas on behavior for decades and a marriage between those fields of study and constructivism has offered novel ways of understanding international relations (Ramos, chap. 8 in this volume; see also Shannon and Kowert 2011; Hymans 2010).

Offering testable hypotheses has not been the name of the game, either, within constructivism. Although more than half of the peer-reviewed research analyzed does posit explicit associations among the variables under study, in more than 40 percent of the sampled publications the variables under study and the relationship among them are not clear. That is, basic questions of research design that would help make sense of what variables are shaping outcomes and processes of interests often are left unattended.[14]

When such methodological and research design preferences are seen in light of publication patterns in IR as a whole, a cautionary note is in order. Data show that since 1980 and until 2011, "more articles published in the top journals . . . employ quantitative tools than any other methodological approach [showcasing] the strong and growing commitment to positivism" on the part of IR scholars (Maliniak et al. 2011, 437, 454). This trend makes it particularly challenging for constructivists to publish in leading IR journals. And this is important because what has now become—along with real-

TABLE 2.5. *How Is Knowledge Generated?* The Methods and Research Design of Constructivist Research

Aim of Method/ Research Design	Options	Articles (%)	Aggregate Options	
Methods of empirical analysis	Qualitative	88.5	Mainly qualitative	94.7
	Mixed method, dominantly qualitative	6.2		
	Mixed method, dominantly quantitative	2.7	Mainly quantitative	5.2
	Quantitative	2.5		
	Total	100		
Methods to generate theory	Interpretive	20	Mainly qualitative	107.5
	Inductive, qualitative	87.5		
	Inductive, quantitative	1.8	Mainly quantitative	5.7
	Deductive, informal	3.6		
	Deductive, formal	0.3		
	Simulations	–		
	Total	113.2		
Testable hypothesis/es	Yes (explicit causal model; functional form)	3.7		
	Not exactly (only discussion of association among variables is posited)	55.9	No explicit causal model	97
	No (unclear what variables are)	41.1		
	Total	100		
Research Design	Variation in variables	26.3		
	No variation in variables	73.6		
	Total	100		

Note: The *N* for Methods of Empirical Analysis is 479 (i.e., all sampled articles minus those engaging with purely theoretical, conceptual, and/or epistemological debates). The *N* for Methods to Generate Theory and Testable Hypothesis/es is 608 (i.e., all sampled articles minus those empirical studies describing what the state of the world is that do not engage with broader theoretical debates/developments). The *N* for Research Design is 676. The percentage of articles using mainly qualitative methods exceeds 100 percent because individual articles frequently use multiple methods. *Quantitative* methods are those that rely on numbers and, more specifically, on statistical tools of analysis to determine causal significance amongst variables on any given subject matter. *Qualitative* methods are those that rely on words and, more specifically, on tools of analysis such as "process tracing," "historical narrative," etc.

Source: Author's calculations on data on the variables *Method_Empirical_Analysis*, *Method_Theory*, *Testable_Hypothesis*, and *Variation_Variable* from the Bertucci, Hayes, and James constructivism IR research dataset.

ism and liberalism—the third main pillar for making sense of international relations is not evenly represented in leading journals. This is also relevant because having a diminished chance to publish in top outlets is a fact that impacts on placement, hiring, and promotion decisions that eventually contribute to giving IR a very specific profile as a field of inquiry. If the data are accurate, IR would seem to be a field in which positivist epistemological commitments hold the upper hand on who publishes where, and it thus offers clear and specific incentives to future IR scholars regarding the type of work in which they ought to engage. By not trying to move some of constructivism's research practices closer to the mainstream—without, to be sure, giving up on its own theoretical, epistemological, and methodological preferences given the very nature of what constructivism is best at studying—the approach may be helping construct an ever-perpetuating self-fulfilling prophecy as "nonmainstream."

Conclusion

This study of journal articles yields the following conclusions. Constructivism is an approach to the study of international relations that (a) makes security issues in the North Atlantic region its salient substantive and empirical focus of analysis, (b) is heavily oriented toward theory development, (c) aims to mainly produce constitutive knowledge, (d) is far from having an active concern with policy debates and recommendations, (e) largely disregards empirical analyses, and (f) relies almost exclusively on qualitative methods of analysis. When juxtaposed with the salient trends in IR over the past twenty-five years, the contributions of constructivism to the field are apparent. In particular, constructivism has contributed to development of new theories that help highlight different dimensions of existing puzzles, offered a different logic of action than that of rationalist approaches, provided explanations of processes and outcomes that remain unexplained under mainstream approaches, and used interpretive methodologies. These features stand out and collectively tell the story of constructivism so far.

NOTES

1. Zarakol 2017.
2. Subotic 2017.
3. Finnemore and Sikkink 2001; Adler 2013; Keohane 1988.
4. The complete list of issue areas and categories considered in the code book

but not necessarily appearing in this paper's tables, since they are not represented in the literature in any significant number or at all, can be accessed by email request at marianobertucci@gmail.com. An intercoder reliability test was conducted on 5 percent of the total entries, selected at random. The coders agreed on 92 percent of coding decisions.

5. See, for example, Keohane 1988; Guzzini 2000; Finnemore and Sikkink 2001; and Adler 2013.

6. Hayes 2017.

7. See also Barnett 2005 and Reus-Smit 2005. To be sure, ideas, norms, and normative concerns have been central to the study of politics for more than two millennia. The meaning of justice and good society, as well as how such ideas influence human behavior, have been front and center in analyses of politics among thinkers ranging from Aristotle and Plato to E. H. Carr, Ernst Haas, and even realists such as Hans Morgenthau, who extensively referred to the limits that morality and international law impose on states' exercise of power (Finnemore and Sikkink 1998, 889). It was only after the late 1980s, however, that the more sweeping ideational turn in IR took place, helping constitute a distinct approach to the study of world politics as particularly interested in shared ideational factors that help construct and shape the identities, interests, and behavior of actors.

8. The code book can be accessed by email at marianobertucci@gmail.com.

9. Vucetic 2011.

10. This suggests that, as with the rest of IR, constructivists so far tend not to care much about regions of the world outside the North Atlantic. Of course, the data also could be because we have sampled only US and European journals. Without looking at journals published in other regions—although these are not the ones that conventionally set the standards of "quality" work in the field of IR—we cannot say more than that at present.

11. Maliniak et al. 2011.

12. To cite another example, in available surveys of IR, constructivism "shows up in less than 4 percent of IPE articles" (Sharman and Weaver 2013, 1088).

13. Some exceptions certainly exist; see, for example, Edelstein and Krebs 2015.

14. In general and compared to other approaches, in constructivism it is common to find works that ultimately do not pay much attention to research design. This could be due to the very nature of the subject matter, but it could also be traced to the fact that constructivists may not even consider it essential to work along such lines. This may represent a distinct epistemological commitment among constructivists.

REFERENCES

Acharya, Amitav. 2014. "Global International Relations (IR) and Regional Worlds: A New Agenda for International Studies," *International Studies Quarterly* 58, no. 4: 647–59.

Adler, Emanuel. 2013. "Constructivism in International Relations: Sources, Contributions and Debates." In *Handbook of International Relations*, edited by Walter Carlsnaes, Thomas Risse, and Beth A. Simmons. London: Sage.

Avey, Paul C., and Michael Desch. 2014. "What Do Policymakers Want from Us?

Result of a Survey of Current and Former Senior National Security Decision-makers." *International Studies Quarterly* 58, no. 2: 227–46.

Barnett, Michael. 2005. "Social Constructivism." In *The Globalization of World Politics: An Introduction to International Relations*, 3rd ed., edited by J. Baylis and S. Smith. Oxford: Oxford University Press.

Brady, Henry E., and David Collier, eds. 2004. *Rethinking Social Inquiry: Diverse Tools, Shared Standards*. New York: Rowman & Littlefield Publishers.

Edelstein, David M., and Ronald R. Krebs. 2015. "Delusions of Grand Strategy: The Problem with Washington's Planning Obsession." *Foreign Affairs* (November/December): 109–16.

Finnemore, Martha, and Kathryn Sikkink. 1998. "International Norm Dynamic and Political Change." *International Organization* 52, no. 4: 887–917.

Finnemore, Martha, and Kathryn Sikkink. 2001. "The Constructivism Research-Program in International Relations and Comparative Politics." *Annual Review of Political Science* 4: 391–416.

Guzzini, Stefano. 2000. "A Reconstruction of Constructivism in International Relations." *European Journal of International Relations* 6, no. 2: 147–82.

Hayes, Jarrod. 2017. "Reclaiming Constructivism: Identity and the Practice of the Study of International Relations." *PS: Political Science & Politics* 50, no. 1: 89–92.

Hymans, Jacques E. C. 2010. "The Arrival of Psychological Constructivism." *International Theory* 2, no. 3: 461–67.

Katzenstein, Peter J. 1996. *The Culture of National Security: Norms and Identity in World Politics*. New York: Columbia University Press.

Keohane, Robert. 1988. "International Institutions: Two Approaches." *International Studies Quarterly* 32, no. 4: 379–96.

King, Gary, Robert Keohane, and Sidney Verba. 1994. *Designing Social Inquiry. Scientific Inference in Qualitative Research*. Princeton, NJ: Princeton University Press.

Long, James D., Daniel Maliniak, Susan Peterson, and Michael J. Tierney. 2005. "Teaching and Research in International Politics: Surveying Trends in Faculty Opinion and Publishing." Prepared for the 46th Annual Convention of the International Studies Association, March 1–5, 2005, Honolulu, Hawaii. Available at trip.wm.edu/home/index.php/publications.

Maliniak, Daniel, Amy Oakes, Susan Peterson, and Michael J. Tierney. 2011. "International Relations in the U.S. Academy." *International Studies Quarterly* 55, no. 2: 437–64.

Reus-Smit, Christian. 2005. "Constructivism." In *Theories of International Relations*, 3rd ed., edited by S. Burchill et al. New York: Palgrave.

Shannon, Vaughn P., and Paul A. Kowert, eds. 2011. *Psychology and Constructivism in International Relations: An Ideational Alliance*. Ann Arbor: Michigan University Press.

Sharman, J. C., and Catherine Weaver. 2013. "RIPE, the American School and Diversity in Global IPE." *Review of International Political Economy* 20, no. 5: 1082–1100.

Subotic, Jelena. 2017. "Constructivism as Professional Practice in the US Academy." *PS: Political Science & Politics* 50, no. 1: 4–8.

Tickner, Arlene, and Ole Waever, eds. 2009. *International Relations Scholarship Around the World*. London: Routledge.

Vucetic, Srdjan. 2011. *The Anglosphere: A Genealogy of a Racialized Identity in International Relations*. Stanford, CA: Stanford University Press.

Zarakol, Ayşe. 2017. "TRIPping Constructivism." *PS: Political Science & Politics* 50, no. 1: 75–78.

THREE

The Future of Constructivism

A Constructivist Assessment

David M. McCourt

Assessing the future of constructivist theory in international relations (IR) requires an adequate understanding of what constructivism is, where it came from, and how it has traversed the disciplinary landscape since its emergence. But beyond broad agreement that constructivism first appeared in the late 1980s through the work of Friedrich Kratochwil, Nicholas Onuf, John Gerard Ruggie, and Alexander Wendt and that its focus is on the importance of norms, identities, and intersubjective meanings more broadly in world politics, there is little consensus on the essence of constructivism and its boundaries. For example, the emergence separately from constructivism of the "practice turn" (see Cornut, this volume) might be considered surprising given that the turn is inspired by the same impulse as constructivism: namely that the fundamental nature of international politics is not given, but constructed *in practice* (see McCourt 2016). Appearance of the practice turn separate from constructivism suggests that making predictions about constructivism's future requires first addressing the question of what "it" is.

In this chapter, consequently, I engage in a brush-clearing exercise along just those lines. I proceed in three parts. I first ask how constructivism is typically understood in IR. Constructivism is seen as an interpretive and ideational approach that stresses the role of intersubjective meaning in world politics, manifested through norms, identity, and culture (Steele 2017, 71). To what extent is this depiction accurate and useful?

In the second part, I ask how else we might view constructivism. I argue that viewing constructivism as a fixed set of intellectual ideas is a very *unconstructivist* way of thinking. Constructivism should be understood as less a coherent "thing" than a process within IR's distinct academic and national contexts. To illustrate, whereas in the United States constructivism represents one of a few nonpositivist or critical approaches deemed legitimate (see respectively Zarakol 2017 and Subotic 2017), my impression is that in Europe and Australia constructivism is not viewed as critical at all, perhaps even tainted with the associations with the positivist American-dominated mainstream. Substantiating perceptions like this is difficult given that the best available data—from the TRIPS survey—is heavily US-centric (see Maliniak et al. 2011). Nonetheless, assessing constructivism's future requires viewing it as a context-dependent process, not a single thing.

In a final part, I show that rethinking constructivism in this way allows for more nuanced assessments of where constructivism might be going. Put simply, the issue depends less on the innate value of constructivism as an approach and more on the actions of scholars in their ongoing struggles within IR's different contexts. I suggest that constructivism's future looks very different in the United States than it does, say, in Europe. I argue that in the United States, constructivism may either progressively disappear or persist as a minority position, acting as a useful historical and interpretive counterposition to the mainstream, but less powerful in the field as a result of its nonscientific associations. My contention is that in Europe, the term "constructivism" may become less useful as scholars with some affinities to constructivism identify themselves in different ways: international political sociologists, international political theorists, or scholars of critical security studies.

In conclusion, I note that although seemingly pessimistic, the argument presented in this chapter about constructivism's past and possible futures is indebted to the fundamental contributions of constructivism itself, proving the enduring value of constructivism, under whatever label.

IR Constructivism: The Standard View

The typical way of characterizing analytical approaches like constructivism in IR, like in any other discipline, is to grasp the core ideas they put forward, in this case about the basic features of world politics and how we should study it. From this perspective, although constructivism is acknowledged to be a broad approach rather than a theory (Adler 1997, 323), it has nevertheless been distilled to a set of core tenets.

The most basic tenet of constructivism is the primacy of social facts: how people act is conditioned by the meanings things have for them. As Finnemore and Sikkink put it, "Constructivism . . . asserts that human interaction is shaped primarily by ideational factors, not simply material ones; that the most important ideational factors are widely shared or 'intersubjective' beliefs, which are not reducible to individuals; and that these shared beliefs construct the interests of purposive actors" (2001, abstract). As a more recent contribution notes, "The central insight of constructivism is that collectively held ideas shape the social, economic, and political world in which we live" (Abdelal, Blyth, and Parson 2010, 2). Constructivism's emergence in IR is thus usually dated to the late 1980s–early 1990s, to the work of Kratochwil (1989), Onuf (who coined the term in 1989), and Ruggie (1993), who each stressed the intersubjective basis of social life, and to Wendt, who translated the insight into terms even the most ardent objectivist could understand: "anarchy is what states make of it." (Wendt 1992)

Constructivists' assertion of the primacy of intersubjective reality has important implications for what they think IR scholars should study. Indeed, arguably more important than the founding constructivist theories was a first wave of empirical contributions, which showed a field in the grips of a neorealist-neoliberal consensus (at least in the United States, Baldwin 1993) that norms and identities underpinned state interest formation (Klotz 1995; Finnemore 1996), that the practice of world politics had its basis in fundamental institutions (Reus-Smit 1997), that nonstate actors could be as important as states (Price 1998), and that security was rooted in different national cultures and self-conceptions (Katzenstein 1996a). These works launched constructivism as a *general theoretical orientation* (Katzenstein, Keohane, and Krasner 1998, 646), and *specific research programs* followed on the role of norms (Finnemore and Sikkink 1998), collective and state identity (Hall 1999), and political culture (Katzenstein 1996b) among others.

Viewed as a set of ideas, then, constructivism has been understood as a different approach to knowledge production than positivism, which remains predominant in US political science (Maliniak et al. 2011). Constructivism's methodological implications have been variously characterized, and there is far from a consensus (see Jackson 2011, 201–7). But given the stress constructivists place on intersubjective meaning, Max

Weber's notion of *verstehen* and its typical translation as "interpretation" have formed the bedrock of attempts to develop a specifically constructivist methodology (Klotz and Lynch 2007). Also prominent have been the notions of "constitutive" theory as opposed to purely "causal" analysis (Wendt 1998), the search for "understanding" over "explanation" (drawing on Hollis and Smith 1991).

Together, these core contributions have come to characterize constructivism as an approach to the study of international relations. Ideas, however, represent only one way of understanding what constructivism means. This is because research is only one of the processes by which approaches are produced and reproduced in academic disciplines. Approaches also diffuse through the writing and use of textbooks, the teaching of graduate students, and the placing of those graduate students in academic positions. Approaches and theories like constructivism thus enter academic fields at particular times and places, in the work of particular theorists, and are picked up and used by multiple actors for their own purposes. They are thus conditioned by forces beyond the control of any individual: they are, put simply, *socially constructed*.

To be clear: I am concerned with the predominant way of characterizing constructivism in IR; this is not a view to which I subscribe, nor is it the only way of characterizing constructivism. The predominant characterization outlined above is not wrong per se, so much as partial and problematic. It captures only the most prominent arguments made by the most prominent scholars and not all the claims that could be made in constructivism's name. One of the chief effects, then, is that constructivism has been essentialized—made into an essence, a thing—in two senses. First, constructivism has been made into a coherent approach. This is to some extent inevitable as the simple act of writing itself essentializes because language essentializes. If it did not, the human capacity to convey meaning would be impossible (see Emirbayer 1997). Second, constructivism is made into an essence that studies essences, be they norms, identities, or whatever. This serves in practice to close off constructivism to new objects of interest, like "emotions," the ignoring of which are invoked to criticize constructivism (e.g. Ross 2006).

What is needed, simply put, is a way of understanding what constructivism *is* in international relations that takes account of how it has been shaped by the field and therefore what it *may have been* and *could be in the future*. What is needed is an adequately constructivist assessment of the nature of constructivism.

Constructivism Revisited

Constructivism begins with social facts—practices, beliefs, and conventions—which Emile Durkheim, one of constructivism's main progenitors (Ruggie 1998; Kratochwil 1989), shows us constrain and enable individuals in their day-to-day interactions. Social facts are not, however, subjectively held ideas. Although they take the form of norms, institutions, and cultural patterns, which we often view as ideational, social facts are every bit as "thing-like" as natural facts (Durkheim 1982 [1895]). The upshot of this is that from a constructivist perspective the standard view of constructivism as a set of more or less coherent theoretical ideas is misguided. The important question is not what constructivism *is*, but what it *does*: how does constructivism constrain and enable scholars in their attempts to navigate the field? This leads to a concern with the concrete social context in which constructivism emerged and developed. Although a full account of the social construction of social constructivism is beyond the scope of this chapter, some key points can be made.

To begin, the significance of constructivism's emergence within the context of US international relations cannot be downplayed, as it draws attention to the nature of IR as a field and the specific social contexts in which constructivism exists. Traditionally traced back to the first chair at the University of Wales at Aberystwyth and especially to the United States, where it became bound up with postwar global hegemony, over the past few decades IR has gone global (see Tickner and Waever 2009). Yet strong national and regional characteristics remain. A straightforward distinction between IR as a subfield of political science—as in the United States—and as a stand-alone discipline—for much of the rest of the world—has important implications for what constructivism does in different contexts, and hence for the future of constructivism in these different locations.

In short, constructivism does something very different in the United States than outside of it. Constructivism emerged in the United States as a counterpoint to neorealism and neoliberal institutionalism and their specific arguments regarding the role of regimes in international organization (Kratochwil and Ruggie 1986), and more generally on the origins of state interests (Klotz 1995; Finnemore 1996). Over time, however, the center of gravity of US IR has shifted away from realism and toward rationalism (see Maliniak et al. 2011). In terms of what it *does*, consequently, constructivism in US IR is now the main counterpoint to rationalism (Fearon and Wendt 2002). Constructivism serves to remind rationalists that the initial actor type and background rules they model are not given by nature but by practice (Johnson 2002, 236).

In non-US IR, by contrast, neither the "neo-neos" nor more recently rationalism has ever been predominant. In Europe especially, more socio-logical approaches akin to constructivism—like the English School and the Copenhagen School, to name just two—were already there and remain strong (Friedrichs 2004). There was then no significant "other" for con-structivists to argue against, as the neo-neos provided in the United States.

Constructivism's insights thus look familiar beyond the United States and are problematically tied to older US-centric concerns and styles of theorizing (especially in its Wendtian variety.) Whereas US-based con-structivists drew on philosophical and social theoretic work from Europe to make arguments aimed at realists, neoliberal institutionalists, and rationalists—from Foucault and Habermas, to Giddens and Bourdieu (see e.g. Onuf 1989)—in European IR these thinkers have been drawn upon more organically and not as part of something that can only be brought into IR as "constructivism."

Emergence of the academic journal *International Political Sociology* in 2007 is significant in this regard. *IPS* is dominated by work that can be considered constructivist from the standard view above (Bertucci, Hayes, and James, this volume). But much of it does not label itself constructivist. This is because the research is largely European or at least non-US in ori-gin. This should come as no surprise. Beyond the United States, construc-tivism *is* international political sociology. As first-generation constructivist Christian Reus-Smit has noted, "Constructivists are political sociologists, nor more no less" (2008, 72).

Foregrounding the geographic context in which IR has developed also highlights the important fact that the discipline of IR sits within particular nationally and regionally rooted *professions*. These professions decide who counts as a member and who prospers, and these are achieved through cre-dentialing, publishing, the distribution of jobs, and thus the maintenance of an elaborate prestige hierarchy. As much a set of ideas, then, constructiv-ism is a stake within professional struggles. From this perspective the per-tinent issue is the professional standing constructivism has attained within IR's diverse professional contexts, especially the level of prestige accorded constructivist scholarship and scholars (for other takes along these lines, see Hayes 2017; Onuf 2017; Subotic 2017).

Constructivism's professional standing is difficult to measure. In the United States, surface assessments suggest a healthy standing. Alexander Wendt is often cited as among the most influential IR scholars (Maliniak et al. 2011, 10), and Kathryn Sikkink is now a professor at the Kennedy School at Harvard. But notwithstanding the fact that Wendt has openly recanted his constructivist beliefs (2006), the ability of the first generation of constructivists to position their students in the highest echelons of the political science profession has been limited (for a thorough analysis, see Subotic 2017). Beyond the United States, by contrast, constructivism's standing is very strong. If we define constructivism broadly, it can be seen to be in many ways predominant, with scholars such as Karin Fierke, Stefano Guzzini, Ole Waever, Lene Hansen, and Michael Williams at the top of the prestige hierarchy. Indeed, the two trends are not unrelated, as many of the first- and second-generation constructivists secured job and publication opportunities overseas, including Friedrich Kratochwil (European University Institute, Italy), Christian Reus-Smit (University of Queensland), Jutta Weldes (Bristol), Richard Price (University of British Columbia), Ted Hopf (National University of Singapore), and Janice Bially Mattern (also at the National University of Singapore).

These reflections are anecdotal. But they serve to highlight how an understanding of constructivism as a set of theoretical ideas and empirical arguments misrecognizes what constructivism is and does in IR when the latter is grasped as a set of overlapping professional contexts.

As a final point, then, thus far I have focused on dynamics internal to IR to explain constructivism's trajectory. As Barder and Levine (2012) note, however, the historical context of constructivism's emergence was and remains crucial. They show that at its birth constructivism held a radical promise: to fully historicize and contextualize the categories of thought IR scholars used to make sense of the world, including the primacy of the nation-state, raison d'etat, and sovereignty. For Ruggie, neorealism and neoliberal institutionalism—then constructivism's chief "others"—are "capable of explaining virtually nothing that is constitutive of the very possibility of international relations: not territorial states, not systems of states, not any concrete international order, nor the whole host of institutional forms that states use, ranging from concepts of contracts and treaties to multilateral organizing principles" (1998, 871). But over time so-called *Via Media* constructivism (Adler 1997) shook off its radical pretensions and adopted a more presentist and avowedly scientistic style.

The reason, for Barder and Levine, was that much *Via Media* constructivism imbibed the post–Cold War optimism in world politics and thus came to focus on the transformative and progressive potential of norms, human rights, taboos, culture, identity, and argument and persuasion in world politics. Constructivism, in other words—at least the *Via Media* variety popular in the United States—became quite idealist. Fast-forward a decade and this context has vanished. The terrorist attacks of September 11, the invasion of Iraq and the rise of the Islamic State, and the wars in Syria and the Ukraine cast doubt on the happy liberal norms the constructivist approach emerged trumpeting.

Constructivism's Future(s)

What does the foregoing mean for constructivism as it enters its second quarter century? Forecasting in the social sciences is notoriously controversial, especially for an approach such as constructivism that stresses the messiness and context-dependence of social life (Meyer 2011). Nonetheless, the reflections above suggest that constructivism's future cannot be grasped by reflecting only on the content of constructivism's ideas. Instead, extrapolations must be sought from current trends, sensitive to the contexts in which constructivism finds itself. Constructivism, in other words, has no single future, but a number of potential futures depending on how IR as a complex and partially internationalized discipline and set of interrelated professions evolves, which in turn depends on changes in international politics itself.

These are heady claims. To begin to make good on them, constructivism's US future looks especially uncertain. The question is whether political science departments will continue to produce enough scholars willing and able to stake their careers on making constructivist knowledge claims such that constructivism can remain a meaningful and powerful marker in the American academy. Neither the data collected by the editors of this volume, nor the Teaching, Research and International Policy (TRIP) survey—the most extensive data yet available on IR—speak directly to this issue. Two scenarios are possible.

The first possibility is that constructivism will remain a viable but marginal approach in US political science, akin to interpretivism in the broader discipline (see Monroe 2005). Sociologist Andrew Abbott (2001) goes further, noting that social constructivism in the broader social sciences has enjoyed cyclical popularity, re-emerging around every twenty years as a reminder on the part of more humanistic scholars to their more naturalistic colleagues to recognize the role of culture, beliefs, history, and practice in the study of the social world. From the perspective Abbott develops (2001, 88), constructivism in IR might be "doomed to be a perpetual succession of flare ups" in the same way constructionism is beyond IR. The reason, for Abbott, is that constructivism "is attractive for its cleansing, destructive powers until a particular end, for a particular group of people, is established. Then constructionism becomes an intellectual embarrassment to those very people" (Abbott 2001, 88). Because most sensible scholars do not want to spend their careers banging their heads against a brick wall, after making their names on the back of constructivism's theoretical claims, constructivists jettison the term in favor of empirical work more in line with the field's predominant norms.

If Abbott is correct, constructivism is due for a reappearance in IR, having first emerged in the late 1980s and early 1990s. The emergence of the practice turn, with its strong constructivist overtones, might be considered to be just this reappearance (Adler and Pouliot 2011; McCourt 2016; see Cornut, this volume). But if this is so, then a more pessimistic set of conclusions suggest themselves regarding constructivism's future in US IR.

First, the practice turn has been presented as nonparadigmatic, suggesting that constructivism as a label may have outlived its usefulness. Constructivism might thereby disappear, alongside the other "isms." For Jackson, for one, this is a desirable outcome, because in light of the dominance of neopositivism, "continuing to focus on 'constructivism' as a meaningful category for organizing the IR field is as philosophically nonsensical and practically counterproductive a move as any other attempt to break the grip of unselfconscious neopositivism has been over the past few decades" (Jackson 2011, 204).

Second, the prominent scholars advocating a practice turn are working outside the US academy (in Canada, Europe, and elsewhere). This suggests that US IR might already be closed to a re-emergence of constructivism given the hegemony of neopositivism and rationalism. To be sure, it is too early to accept this conclusion. How would we know? Might practice theory not be rejected for other reasons than a closure of the space of constructivism?

Tellingly, Abbott's optimistic conclusions regarding the cyclical nature of constructivism are tied to his experiences in the discipline of sociology in the United States and do not reflect the social context of political science. US sociology, put simply, has a long and distinguished tradition of grounded, contextual, and historical scholarship, focused on the identification and analysis of social problems. This tradition is centered, unsurprisingly, on the University of Chicago, where Abbott holds a chair (Abbott 1999). There are then limits on the extent to which sociology as a profession can ape the methods of the natural sciences without alienating large factions within its ranks.

The extent to which US political science can go in distancing itself from the messy world of practical US politics in order to become more adequately scientific, on the other hand, is an open question. Taken together— recent concerns about an ever-growing "gap" between the ivory tower and politics aside (Avey and Desch 2014)—the continued rise of rational choice theory in the guise of open economy politics (Oatley 2011), and the related success of economics in achieving political influence while mirroring the hard sciences, do not augur well for the future of constructivism in US political science as a space for work that is sensitive to historical and social context. They suggest that constructivism might at best achieve a permanently marginal position in the field, similar to that of political theory (Gunnell 1993), with periodic bursts of relative popularity.

Again, the pertinent question is not what constructivism itself will do as a set of ideas—which obviously cannot *do* anything—but what scholars working in the United States will do with and in the name of "constructivism." One strategy that presents itself is to push constructivism forward in more methodologically ambitious and rigorous ways, without—in Jackson's terms (2011)—simply engaging in "neopositivist research on norms." The reason for this is simple: the type of historical and qualitative analysis closely tied to constructivism is less highly regarded in the US academic marketplace—for both jobs and publications—than the display of mathematical competence, be it in the form of statistical modeling, formal game theoretic models, or any other technique.

Social network analysis (SNA) is a particularly promising avenue (Hafner-Burton, Kahler, and Montgomery 2009; Goddard 2012), one that is not only consistent with constructivist premises but is actually— like constructivism—a product of the humanist social sciences, particularly sociology (see White 2002). Social network analysis offers a way to objectify social processes and to explore their properties without falling into the trap of essentializing or reifying social structures. Nexon (2009), for example, draws on a network analysis to explain the degree of success rulers of dynastic empires had in suppressing rebellion during the European reformations. He shows that imperial political relationships can be viewed as networks, along two dimensions: how strongly they categorize the identities of those that populate them (English, King of France, etc.), a measure termed *catness*, and how dense the social ties that make up a network are, that is, how interdependent they are, or *netness* (Nexon 2009, 40–61). For Nexon (2009, 27), although the intersubjective meanings associated with the rebellions were crucial, as constructivists would already stress, the network structure produced by political relations between Madrid and the

Spanish Netherlands—which can be explored using network analysis—does a lot of explanatory work.

Of course, this presents a problem for constructivists, who invest time and energy in learning about the historical contexts they study, together with the social theory with which they can recognize the problems with the predominant positivist and behavioral approaches. Learning new methods represents another call on their limited time. Nonetheless, if constructivism is to thrive in US IR, the development of competency in SNA—together with other techniques, such as NVivo and Multiple Correspondence Analysis (MCA) (see Pouliot 2016)—is vital.

Outside of the United States, however, the story is different. The future(s) of constructivism globally thus depend on how US debates are translated into and engaged with by scholars rooted in diverse national contexts. Again, "constructivism" represents a category tied to the field of US IR. For now constructivism represents an approach many scholars around the world can identify with, since the United States is unique in its scientific pretensions, and elsewhere IR is a far more humanistic enterprise. Engaging with constructivism—to criticize it or deploy it empirically—thus serves as leverage which non-US scholars can use to participate in IR at the international level, that is, publish in the main English-language journals and presses and attend conferences such as the International Studies Association annual conventions. This in turn gains them capital within their own academic contexts. Should constructivism continue to lose momentum in the United States, it will also lose it ability to function in this way outside America.

In terms of the development of indigenous knowledges not tied to eurocentric concerns and US hegemony, it may be no bad thing if US political science becomes less of a model for other countries. But US hegemony and eurocentrism exist without constructivism in US IR. It remains imperative therefore that the space of constructivism remain open in American IR as a space for socially, culturally, and historically sensitive theorizing.

Conclusion

I have presented a strongly pessimistic view of the future(s) of constructivism in international relations. It is possible that the space of constructivism in US IR will diminish in size over time, as too few constructivists come through the ranks of top graduate programs. Internationally, the label "constructivism" may lose meaning. I want to end on a more optimistic note about what this means for constructivism and IR more generally: namely that *the argument I have presented is a constructivist argument.* I have foregrounded time, place, history, and culture. The norms of specific academic contexts have been central, as they shape how approaches such as constructivism emerge and develop. I also have highlighted the activities of actual people, particularly those with privileged positions on social systems. Whatever happens to the label "constructivism," so long as the way of thinking it represents continues—whether within specific disciplines like political or in others—all is not lost.

REFERENCES

Abbott, Andrew. 1999. *Discipline and Department: chicago sociology at One Hundred.* Chicago: Chicago University Press.

Abbott, Andrew. 2001. *The Chaos of Disciplines.* Chicago: Chicago University Press.

Abdelal, Rawi, Mark Blyth, and Craig Parsons. 2010. *Constructing the International Economy.* Ithaca, NY: Cornell University Press.

Adler, Emanuel. 1997. "Seizing the Middle Ground: Constructivism in World Politics." *European Journal of International Relations* 3, no. 3: 319–63.

Adler, Emanuel, and Vincent Pouliot. 2011. *International Practices.* Cambridge: Cambridge University Press.

Avey, Paul C., and Michael C. Desch. 2014. "What Do Policy-Makers Want from Us? Results of a Survey of Former and Current Senior National Security Decision-Makers." *International Studies Quarterly* 58, no. 4: 227–46.

Baldwin, David. 1993. *Neorealism and Neoliberalism: The Contemporary Debate.* New York: Columbia University Press.

Barder, Alexander, and Daniel J. Levine. 2012. "'The World Is Too Much with Us': Reification and the Depoliticising of *Via Media* Constructivist IR." *Millennium: Journal of International Studies* 40, no. 3: 585–604.

Durkheim, Emile. 1982 [1895]. *The Rules of Sociological Method.* New York: The Free Press.

Emirbayer, Mustafa. 1997. "Manifesto for a Relational Sociology." *American Journal of Sociology* 103, no. 2: 281–317.

Fearon, James, and Alexander Wendt. 2002. "Rationalism v. Constructivism: A Skeptical View." In *Sage Handbook of International Relations*, edited by Walter Carlsnaes, Thomas Risse, and Beth Simmons. London: Sage.

Finnemore, Martha. 1996. *National Interests in International Society.* Ithaca, NY: Cornell University Press.

Finnemore, Martha, and Kathryn Sikkink. 1998. "International Norm Dynamics and Political Change." *International Organization* 52, no. 4: 887–917.

Finnemore, Martha, and Kathryn Sikkink. 2001. "Taking Stock: The Constructivist Research Program in International Relations." *Annual Review of Political Science* 4: 391–416.

Friedrichs, Jörg. 2004. *European Approaches to International Relations Theory: A House with Many Mansions.* London: Routledge.

Goddard, Stacie. 2012. "Brokering Peace: Networks, Legitimacy, and the Northern Ireland Peace Process." *International Studies Quarterly* 56: 501–15.

Gunnell, John. 1993. *The Descent of Political Theory*. Chicago: Chicago University Press.

Hafner-Burton, Emilie M., Miles Kahler, and Alexander H. Montgomery. 2009. "Network Analysis for International Relations." *International Organization* 63: 559–92.

Hall, Rodney Bruce. 1999. *National Collective Identity: Social Constructs and International Systems*. New York: Columbia University Press.

Hayes, Jarrod. 2017. "Reclaiming Constructivism: Identity and the Practice of the Study of International Relations." *PS: Political Science and Politics* 50 (1): 89–92.

Hollis, Martin, and Steve Smith. 1991. *Explaining and Understanding in International Relations*. Oxford: Clarendon Press.

Jackson, Patrick Thaddeus. 2011. *The Conduct of Inquiry in International Relations: The Philosophy of Science and Its Implications for the Study of World Politics*. New York: Routledge.

Johnson, James. 2002. "How Conceptual Problems Migrate: Rational Choice, Interpretation, and the Hazards of Pluralism. *Annual Review of Political Science* 5: 223–48.

Katzenstein, Peter J., ed. 1996a. *The Culture of National Security: Norms and Identity in World Politics*. New York: Columbia University Press.

Katzenstein, Peter J. 1996b. *Cultural Norms and National Security: Police and Military in Postwar Japan*. Ithaca, NY: Cornell University Press.

Katzenstein, Peter J., Robert O. Keohane, and Stephen D. Krasner. 1998. "International Organization and the Study of World Politics." *International Organization* 52, no. 4: 645–85.

Klotz, Audie. 1995. "Norms Reconstituting Interests: Global Racial Equality and U.S. Sanctions Against South Africa." *International Organization* 49, no. 3: 451–78.

Klotz, Audie, and Cecilia Lynch. 2007. *Strategies for Research in Constructivist International Relations*. Armonk, NY: M. E. Sharpe.

Kratochwil, Friedrich V. 1989. *Rules, Norms, and Decisions: On the Conditions of Practical and Legal Reasoning in International Relations and Domestic Affairs*. Cambridge: Cambridge University Press.

Kratochwil, Friedrich V., and John Gerard Ruggie. 1986. "International Organization: A State of the Art on an Art of the State." *International Organization* 40, no. 4: 753–75.

Maliniak, Daniel, Amy Oakes, Susan Peterson, and Michael J. Tierney. 2011. "International Relations in the US Academy." *International Studies Quarterly* 55, no 1: 1–28.

McCourt, David M. 2016. "Practice Theory and Relationalism as the New Constructivism." *International Studies Quarterly* 60, no. 3: 475–85.

Meyer, Christoph O. 2011. "The Purpose and Pitfalls of Constructivist Forecasting: Insights from Strategic Culture Research for the European Union's Evolution as a Military Power." *International Studies Quarterly* 55, no. 3: 669–90.

Monroe, Kristen Renwick, ed. 2005. *Perestroika! The Raucous Rebellion in Political Science*. New Haven, CT: Yale University Press.

Nexon, Daniel H. 2009. *The Struggle for Power in Early Modern Europe: Religious Conflict, Dynastic Empires, and International Change*. Princeton, NJ: Princeton University Press.

Oatley, Thomas. 2011. "The Reductionist Gamble: Open Economy Politics in the Global Economy." *International Organization* 65, no. 2: 311–41.

Onuf, Nicholas. 1989. *World of Our Making: Rules and Rule in Social Theory and International Relations*. Columbia: South Carolina University Press.

Onuf, Nicholas. 2017. "The Bigger Story." *PS: Political Science and Politics* 50, no. 1: 93–95.

Pouliot, Vincent. 2016. *International Pecking Orders: The Politics and Practice of Multilateral Diplomacy*. Cambridge: Cambridge University Press.

Price, Richard. 1998. "Reversing the Gun Sights. Transnational Civil Society Targets Land Mines." *International Organization* 52, no. 3: 613–44.

Reus-Smit, Christian. 1997. "The Constitutional Structure of International Society and the Nature of Fundamental Institutions." *International Organization* 51, no. 4: 555–89.

Reus-Smit, Christian. 2008. "Constructivism and the Structure of Ethical Reasoning." In *Moral Limit and Possibility in World Politics*, edited by Richard Price, 53–82. Cambridge: Cambridge University Press.

Ross, Andrew A. G. 2006. "Coming In from the Cold: Constructivism and Emotions." *European Journal of International Relations* 12, no. 2: 197–222.

Ruggie, John Gerard. 1993. "Territoriality and Beyond: Problematizing Modernity in International Relations." *International Organization* 47, no. 1: 139–74.

Ruggie, John Gerard. 1998. "What Makes the World Hang Together? Neo-Utilitarianism and the Social Constructivist Challenge." *International Organization* 52, no. 4: 855–85.

Steele, Brent J. 2017. "Introduction: The Politics of Constructivist International Relations in the US Academy." *PS: Political Science and Politics* 50, no. 1: 71–73.

Subotic, Jelena. 2017. "Constructivism as Professional Practice in the US Academy." *PS: Political Science and Politics* 50, no. 1: 75–78.

Tickner, Arlene B., and Ole Waever. 2009. *International Relations Scholarship Around the World*. London: Routledge.

Wendt, Alexander. 1992. "Anarchy Is What States Make of It: The Social Construction of Power Politics." *International Organization* 46, no. 2: 391–425.

Wendt, Alexander. 1998. "On Constitution and Causation." *Review of International Studies* 24 (5): 101–18.

Wendt, Alexander. 2006. "*Social Theory* as Cartesian Science: An Auto-Critique from a Quantum Perspective." In *Constructivism and International Relations: Alexander Wendt and His Critics*, edited by Stefano Guzzini and Anna Leander. New York: Routledge.

White, Harrison C. 2002. *Markets from Networks: Socioeconomic Models of Production*. Princeton, NJ: Princeton University Press.

Zarakol, Ayse. 2017. "TRIPping Constructivism." *PS: Political Science and Politics* 50, no. 1: 75–78.

FOUR

On Constructivism, Realism, and Contingency

Oliver Kessler
Brent Steele

Disclosures and Caveats Regarding "Constructivism"

This chapter "takes stock" of the debate between constructivism and realism.[1] How these two "approaches" are linked, positioned, and separated has been contested since the turn of the century (see in particular Sterling-Folker 2000; Barkin 2003; Jackson and Nexon 2004; Steele 2010). As a "debate," it progressed much like previous ones within international relations (IR), that is to say, largely unidirectional. Constructivists turn to realism, but self-acclaimed realists are quite happy to treat most constructivists alike in order to deny any need for further engagement (see in particular Mearsheimer on "critical theory" 1994/95). The debate so far has been based largely on a narrative that unfolds from Morgenthau to Waltz, from Waltz to Wendt, and then closes with some critique on the liberal-moderate constructivists post-Wendt. That said, the realism-constructivism debate is driven by the conviction that during the "liberal moment" of the 1990s, constructivists flirted too heavily with liberal ideas.

Given that this story has been told several times already, we do not want to repeat it at this point. Yet in order to capture the complexity of the debate, it is important to see that the debates involving realism, liberalism, and constructivism encapsulate the question of science: what we mean by it, how it assumingly works best, and how it is to be practiced. That said, the debate between realism and constructivism is not merely different by empirics (like a reconfiguration of the global balance of power), but also by methodological considerations.

Before we move to this discussion, let us be open about what we mean by "taking stock." To take stock—as we understand it—means to take a deep breath, to stand still for a moment, and to observe with some distance. To take stock is a skeptical enterprise that raises doubts, identifies trends, and provides narratives about how constructivism developed within the field. It is a story of unfulfilled promises and detours added with suggestions of how to move on, and to move on requires a narrative about where we are coming from and who we are and want to be (see Kratochwil 2006 for an instructive discussion). This does not imply that one argues from a privileged position or can claim better knowledge than previous attempts. But it does mean that one has to provide an interpretation of the past and thereby make sense of what has happened.

In this chapter, we reconstruct the realism-constructivism conundrum in three steps. While previous contributions on realism-constructivism have focused predominantly on power (Barkin 2003; Jackson and Nexon 2004) and ethics (Steele 2013), we approach the discussion through a reconstruction of *contingency*. The first section shows how both classical realists and constructivists have acknowledged otherness, a plurality of perspectives, and politics as the mediation and interplay between them.[2] From this perspective, realism and constructivism do share some common ground. Yet we suggest what makes them different is the importance of language and meaning and hence a different understanding of power.

The second section then outlines how this focus on double contingency between ego and alter has been replaced by a single actor with crucial methodological consequences. While the focus on double contingency demands a reconstructive methodology that is open for historical specificity, normative theory, and most importantly translates "contingency" into constructivist methodology, the reinauguration of the single actor allows for "general" correlations, a subsumptionist logic (Herborth 2012), and in the end the production of necessary knowledge backed up by empirical tests.[3] The consequence is that constructivist concepts were relocated into a positivist methods-driven program (see Jackson 2011 on this point). This made it possible to talk about intersubjective ideas, norms, or agent-structure and to call for hypothesis testing at the same time (Klotz 2008).

Third, we propose a future route for engagement between realism and constructivists. We do not treat "double contingency" as a necessary and sufficient condition for "constructivism" to be enacted. Our task is not to re-examine "just" "honored ghosts" of realism's past (with intersubjective devices such as the balance of power). Instead, we want to broaden the debate to propose the concept of triple contingency. This third contingency addresses the question of how social arrangements are themselves formed and how they limit interactions, identities, and expectations. This allows both constructivists and realists to broaden the perspective beyond "realism is power" or "balance of power" only and to look more broadly at social arrangements that have not entered the debate thus far.

Setting the Stage: Realism and Constructivism

At the turn of the millennium, voices emerged that critically engaged constructivists for their hidden–and sometimes—open liberalism. Sterling-Folker (2000) set the tone when she accused constructivists of "adopt[ing] the same functional-institutional causal logic present in almost all variants of liberal IR theorizing. Constructivism has tended to replicate liberal arguments, conclusions and predictions about the future of international relations as such" (Sterling-Folker 2000, 98). By analyzing the work of Wendt, Ruggie, and Finnemore, she detected neofunctional arguments insofar as "some sort of collective interest is assumed as pre-given and hence exogenous to social interaction" (Ibid., 105). The consequence for Sterling-Folker was a theoretical choice between more moderate and more radical versions of liberal programs only (Ibid., 115). This critique on moderate constructivists can be considered the pivot point for the repositioning of constructivism vis-à-vis liberalism and realism. In particular, two "dimensions" were important in this debate: the question of power and the question of morality.

The issue of power was addressed in the context of Barkin's article on realist constructivism in the *International Studies Review* (Barkin 2003). In that early contribution, Barkin turned directly to the mutual misunderstandings between realists and constructivists rather than formulate another attack on moderate constructivism. As he notes, "Claims by constructivists that realist theory is incompatible with intersubjective epistemologies and methodologies are based on either caricatures or very narrow understandings of realism. And realist critics of constructivism are similarly guilty of inferring from the worldviews of some (perhaps many) practicing constructivists that the methodology is inherently biased toward liberalism" (Barkin 2003, 326). For Barkin, both realist and constructivist epistemologies are compatible. In line with Sterling-Folker, Barkin right-fully points out that nothing in constructivism demands a liberal world-view. When we take key realists concepts in their complexity seriously, such as power or human nature, then constructivists' arguments do show up at some point. As he concludes, "The path proposed by Barkin (2003) uses the realist's concept of power to redefine the constructivist's tenets of norms and change and then proposes to analyze them simultaneously.

This turn to power opened contentions about how that concept can be understood in realism-constructivism. Jackson and Nexon (2004) challenged Barkin on his take of power as he deliberately cuts more radical versions of constructivism from his discussion. Instead, they propose to exactly embrace poststructural and relational arguments where "power inheres in social practices, and that the (re)production of stable social relations is always a result of strategic (but not always rational) social action.[4] In short, power, by definition, is always present and implicated in any social formation" (Ibid., 340). Interestingly, they point out that the possibility of constructivism vis-à-vis its liberal and realist contenders thereby requires a further debate on the level of social theory in general, and Habermas vs. Foucault in particular. Thus we find a number of constructivist works in the 2000s critiquing Habermasian "argumentation" approaches from the 1990s precisely because the latter avoided grappling with power (Krebs and Jackson 2007; Steele 2010). Other constructivists would engage in a typology of power, as Barnett and Duvall (2005) did by bringing forth different kinds and expressions of power within social relations.

A second dimension to this debate, but a less focused one, was normative. Approaching the question of a possible realism-constructivism from the angle of normative theory looks like a classic nonstarter; ever since Carr's apparent devastating critique of "utopianism" (Wendt 1999, 33), the constructivists' interest in norms and ideas makes them subject to the common charge by realists. Yet the relationship is more complicated than that. First of all, "idealism" as in utopianism and the pursuit of a "normative ideal point" is quite different from "idealism" as in "acknowledging that ideas matter." Of course, we readily admit that maybe "ideas" is not a good term to start with in the first place (see Kessler 2007 for a discussion), yet it is problematic to fuse constructivism with the first understanding. Secondly, it is common knowledge that classical realists paid much attention to questions of morality, since morality plays an important part for successful politics (Niebuhr 1932; Carr 1964). Morgenthau devotes half of *Politics among Nations* to tracing the changing relationship of national and international politics due to a changed "international morality." He thereby turns against the "modern" radicalization of world politics through the formation of nation-states, nationalism, and nuclear weapons, all of which undermine the common and shared normative dimension of the balance of power and which today make a classic balance of power, as experienced in the eighteenth century, impossible. Classical realism's frank acknowledgment of "morality" was lost in the aftermath of Waltz's move to "scientifically" ground realism and thereby opened the gateway to treat the international system in purely formal terms (see Waltz 1979, chap. 5).

This dimension of the engagement of realism by constructivists thus allowed constructivists to challenge the alleged scientific basis of Waltz's structuralism and is still attractive for the younger generation of constructivists (see Kessler and Steele 2016). Further, Morgenthau's remarks on prudence could thus serve as a yardstick to develop a concept of order that is more prone to acknowledge otherness and difference and hence is more open for constructivist insights (see also Steele 2007b, 278–80). In this context, Lang has drawn from Morgenthau to develop a "social concept of 'agency'" (see Lang 2002, 8; see also Lang 2007; Williams 2004). As Lang explains, this concept of action "does not assume that political actors assert their identities in certainty and confidence. Instead, only when they act do they take on an identity, and not an identity that is fixed but one that is fluid and changing with each political engagement" (2002, 14). Recalling the agent-structure problem as originally formulated, this perspective acknowledges that power is not located per se in structures (with the need to socialize actors), but in the agent's own limitations and the ability to acknowledge (the agency) of other(s) (Hom and Steele 2010). When reading through the literature on the so-called "reflexive" turn of realism, one observation is just how much an engagement of classical realism's normative purpose allowed constructivists to issue normative arguments. Such arguments would have been more difficult to issue within a constructivism that had, especially after the 1990s, sought to compete against the rationalist perspectives of neoliberalism and neorealism.

What has not been adequately acknowledged, however, is the role and function of contingency in some of these moves. Put another way, the move to rationalize and scientificize constructivism in the 1990s, and then why and how constructivists in the 2000s seemed to find classical realist works so useful for engagement, can be reconfigured through an examination of the role of contingency in different constructivist works through time.

Contingency and Realism

The last section has shown the past parameters of the realism-constructivism debate that circulated in particular around power and morality. In this section, we propose a slightly different avenue to cut through the woods. Both power and morality address the question of contingency, but without making contingency a key concern for their analyses. Contingency at first only refers to the social space between the impossible and the necessary: what seems necessary (a thrown stone falls to the ground) and impossible (peace on earth) is not part of contingency. In this sense, contingency always implies a "could have been otherwise" and thus instantly refers to questions of power and morality.

Of course, contingency is best known in our scholarly work in terms of "probability." Yet this form of probability, a form that we also encounter in the economics-based decision under uncertainty literature, is based on a *single* actor facing an objectively given albeit contingent future. This literature subsequently explores how scientifically valid presumptions can be formulated in spite of the contingent reality of nature. Even though reality is contingent, science can show how to best encounter it on the basis of a priori axioms and conditions. Necessary scientific knowledge, laws, and regularities that are truly independent of time and space, in this context, then fulfills the task of leading the way to a successful encounter with contingency.

We think that classical realists have started with a different notion of contingency in mind: the contingency that arises in "intersubjective" decision-making processes, that is, the mutual taking each other into account between different actors. This *double* contingency arises through the copresence of at least two actors, where ego and alter as two actors not only realize that they are faced with the contingent decision by the other actor, but that their own position, evaluation, and expectations are contingent. Double contingency does not only imply a situation where two actors simply solve a game-theoretical decision problem, but where their positionality and the form of relationship are negotiated. This implies that mutual positionality is always subject to (potential) change.

Consider, for example, how classical realists have touched upon this problem. For example, Herz (1950) has shown that the individual strategy of maximizing security is close to nonsense in an intersubjective setting. Or consider realist concerns through time against so-called "Manichean" language, and especially concerns with the "demonological" approach to foreign policy. Morgenthau describes the workings of how the "human mind approaches reality for the purpose of taking action," and in the case of a demonological approach this consists of substituting a "fictitious reality—peopled by evil persons rather than seemingly intractable issues—for the actual one" (1948/2006, 7). The contingency here, however, rests on the notion that discourse is describing—creating a context for action within—a reality that *does not exist.* And yet notice what Morgenthau titles this in an almost oxymoronic sense: fictitious reality. The point here is not a discussion over what the world "out there" is, but rather the behavior that human subjects engage in to create the means for action, and that this action depends largely on the discourse used to construct meanings and how those are received, reinterpreted, and re-expressed by others in that space. From this perspective, the balance of power (at least in the context of Morgenthau), is a relational space where both the actions of the self/other could be considered. Oren thus rightly points to the Weberian influence in Morgenthau that emphasizes the "researcher's capacity to empathize with (if not necessarily valorize) the thinking of [the] other human being" (2009, 291).

Early constructivists share the same insight, albeit in a slightly different fashion. For example, Wendt (1999, 89) introduced the idea of an "original position" where *two* actants (Montezuma and Spaniards, aliens and earthlings) meet for the first time. Wendt thereby touches upon this very question of how that space between these two actants can be bridged, and he is firm in pointing out that the identities and cultures of anarchy only emerge through the constant interactions. And it is through the way in which *ego and alter differentiate each other* that friendship, enmity, or interest coalitions emerge. Similarly, Kratochwil and Onuf have both used *speech act theory* to address the question of intersubjectivity and double contingency. For example, Onuf proposes that rules mediate between people and societies and allow us to trace the performative power of language. Rules allow us to trace how order allocates (1) naming and relating, (2) enabling and disabling, (3) having and using. All these functions cannot be reduced to a single actor and some "individual interests" but are "intersubjective" categories. Also, Friedrich Kratochwil in his *Rules, Norms, and Decisions* argued that "our conventional understanding of social action and of the norms governing them is defective because of a fundamental misunderstanding of the function of language in social interaction, and because of the positivist epistemology that treats norms as 'causes.' Communication is therefore reduced to issues of describing 'facts' properly, i.e. to match of concepts and objects, and to the ascertainment of nomological regularities. Important aspects of *social* action such as advising, demanding, apologizing, asserting, promising, etc., cannot be adequately understood thereby" (Kratochwil 1989, 5–6).

Thus, in contrast to what later norm-based constructivists would assert, norms are not relevant because they "cause" action or make states behave in a certain way, because *norms allow us to capture the intersubjective contingency* rooted in the language of promising, advising, demanding, and apologizing.

At this point, it might appear immaterial how one treats norms (as prescriptions or as causal factors), but one needs to be aware that this has two important repercussions. The first set of repercussions is methodological. Kratochwil's recently published *The Status of Law in World Society* (Kratochwil 2014) argues that this double contingency can never really be captured in deductive or inductive reasoning. Induction and deduction are both attempts to create a hierarchical relationship between sentences and thereby create necessary knowledge. The point is not whether they produce necessity, but that in the quest for certainty, methods are invoked that leave the observer scientist outside the used conceptual framework. In the quest for certainty, one attempts to identify necessary relationships that hold true independent of who observes them.

In the context of double contingency, the quest for certainty has to give way to "practical reasoning." If different perspectives are to be acknowledged, one cannot assume one's own position to be *true*. The entire literature on reflexivity is based on this conviction. Rather, what is true or false is part of a negotiation process between actors (and, if one takes into account Actor Network Theory, also objects). The question is thus how the contingency of one's own position can be acknowledged without giving way to fatalism and anything goes.

Of course, we readily admit that much more work is needed to fully understand the methodological implications of such a contingency-based approach to the realism-constructivism debate. We certainly do not claim that the focus on double contingency "constituted" both classical realism and constructivism and hence both might be two sides of the same coin. Even though we do believe there is a sound amount of realist influence in both Kratochwil and Onuf (and hence their shared critique of both liberalism and the scientific method), Kratochwil and Onuf never made this link explicit. For, like the classical realists, Kratochwil and Onuf acknowledge the role of international law, the interplay of domestic and international politics, and the necessity to hold a firm ground in political theory for understanding political theory.

A second set of repercussions is related to the question of politics. If norms are treated as an objective force that an individual state either has to comply with or deviate from, then the intersubjectivity is encapsulated in the objectivity of norms, as liberal constructivists tend to do. The politics then observed is that of compliance, or what makes a state to comply with a norm (see dos Reis and Kessler 2016 for a discussion). In contrast, both Kratochwil and Onuf point to a politics of meaning fixation: when different perspectives are to be negotiated, then the "hegemony" of one perspective, the fixation of meaning, is the result of politics. Again, one needs to highlight the use of speech act theory in this context, which locates the politics between illocutionary intent and perlocutionary effect (Kratochwil 1989). As Kratochwil later confirms, "choosing and debating among actors is . . . quite different from solving the choice problem in the case of an individual" (Ibid., 38).

Where constructivists and classical realists differ, however, is through the concept of *power*: Classical realists here moved away from the intersubjective dimension and reduced power to the national-individual level. Equally, both Kratochwil and Onuf would defy easy political strategies to "maximize" power or security, and instead would emphasize that power relates to the "constitution" of facts as "facts," the qualitative judgments that allow us to identify something as something. A defining focus in constructivism is the intersubjective fixation or challenge of qualitative judgments. Hence in line with poststructuralist thought, power is never in the "possession" of an actor, but is relational and specific to time-spatial constellations. Even though both realism and constructivism share an interest in double contingency, they associate a *different politics* with it. Whereas classical realists propose national strategies, constructivists emphasize the politics of positioning, relating, and fixing of signs, events, and perspectives.

In the following, we propose that this position of "contingency" allows us to tackle the question of power and morality in different ways. It also allows us to provide a different account of what happened to both realism and constructivism, which in the end produced the "lock-in" effect of the "realism-constructivism as Waltz vs. Wendt" story. As the next section proposes, we argue that the common insight that constructivism suffers from a liberal bias—and that moderate constructivists have actually left the constructivist building—can be reconstructed as the result of a loss of double contingency in the name of science.

Constructivism and the Problem of Contingency

We have so far proposed a reconstruction of the realism and constructivism debate in terms of "double contingency" and suggested that both classical realists and early constructivists actually share this concern. Even though we readily admit that there are differences in how this double contingency is framed (one would not find an interest in speech act theory in classical realism for example), we think that further discussion in this regard could sharpen our understanding of these two approaches.

In this section, we suggest that double contingency was removed, and in its place a "single" contingency was offered, for "scientific reasons." The story we tell in this section thus has two parts: the loss of contingency through the advent of the neo-neo discourse on the one hand, and its loss in a 1990s liberal variant of constructivism on the other.

The first half of the story is well-known: Waltz and the neorealists who followed challenged classical realism for its unscientific approach. Through an establishment of IR as a "genuine" science alongside economics, Waltz called everything that is not linked to "anarchy" as "outside" the important questions in IR. This included not only domestic institutions and international law, but also political and legal theory. Instead, Waltz opted for "parsimony" and the quest for generality, explanation, prediction, and simplification (Hom and Steele 2010, 275). That Waltz took refuge in the economic theory of the firm has already been subject to intense scrutiny (Ashley 1984; Wendt 1987, 1999). We suggest that the question of "limited agency," positionality, and double contingency was replaced by single contingency, the individual strategy to maximize security in a "market-like" anarchical system. Here the policy contextuality of political questions, the art of diplomacy (as acknowledging the other) and the delicate (uncertainty of) balance of power are solved by assuming "rational actors."

The second half of the story unfolds in a similar manner, but roughly a decade later (1990s). Let us remember that both Kratochwil and Onuf were not interested in "norms" in themselves, but they "used" norms to open the discourse of IR to social and political theory in general and the philosophy of language in particular. They were never interested in "testing" the validity of norms empirically,[5] but to explore the kind of contingency and thus rules and rule they constituted (see also Kratochwil 1989, chap. 7).

In the 1990s debates over norms, this "double contingency" was lost. Let us focus on four particular examples. First, the seminal 1996 volume edited by Peter Katzenstein, *Cultures of National Security*, bracketed many international norms—formulated from past interaction—as structural logics (rather than contingent and uncertain spaces) shaping state behavior. Contributors to that oft-cited work analyzed, for example, chemical and nuclear weapons "taboos" (Price and Tannenwald), a norm of humanitarian intervention (Finnemore), the collective identity of NATO (Risse-Kappan), and Arab identity and Arab states (Barnett). These and the many similar works that Neumann and Sending accurately describe as seeing "norms . . . as the key 'independent variable' used to study changes in states' interests and identities" (2010, 54),[6] evinced, if not a singular focus, a more narrowly contingent and more unidirectional understanding of world politics.[7]

Consider in this context also the advent of specific models like Finnemore and Sikkink's (1998) (in)famous life-cycle model. There, norms are proposed by private norm entrepreneurs (or advocacy networks), who "persuade" states to adopt a norm once a "trigger point" is reached. The norms then "cascade" and become "the new normal," and finally the norm is internalized by states and states' behavior observed in terms of adherence/deviance (Finnemore and Sikkink 1998, 904). What is crucial here is that the ultimate goal of the model is to explain how states' behavior can be changed. They frame "norms" not in terms of contingency or "intersubjective meaning," but as necessary and sufficient conditions that provide "empirically testable criteria." The constructivist concept of norm was thereby repositioned in a neopositivist vocabulary. Hence, in line with what Sterling-Folker observed beforehand (2000), we see how some of the 1990s constructivists bought into positivist ideas in their quest to provide "necessary knowledge" that stands firm in empirical tests.

Similarly, in their follow-up "Taking Stock" article, Finnemore and Sikkink (2001) turned to Lakatos's philosophy of "research programs" to present constructivism in scientific terms and thereby answer Keohane's early critique on "reflectivist" approaches (Finnemore and Sikkink 1999; Keohane 1989. It is quite telling that they start their discussion by *presupposing* that constructivism is an "empirical" research program, as they note that "the empirical research program, on which the 'success' of this theorizing depended in the eyes of many, has received much less systematic treatment." (Finnemore and Sikkink 2001, 392). Early constructivists like Kratochwil and Onuf do not play much of a role in this "taking stock." Onuf is not mentioned a single time, while Kratochwil's 1989 *Rules, Norms and Decision* is at only one occasion summarized as to have "examined the role of legal reasoning in persuasion and other social construction processes" (Ibid., 402).

Some of the constructivists who participated in this movement still, to this day, emphasize the role they played in making constructivism more amenable to "testing," and they continue to use that language in their current studies. Looking back upon her first engagements with constructivism in the 1990s, Klotz expressed in a methods study from the late 2000s: "this [Kratochwil and Ruggie] *nascent constructivism* did not offer a specific theory to test. Indeed, it resisted the whole endeavor of testing theories in the conventional sense!" Klotz poses a counterfactual, namely, "if constructivist theory had been articulated in a *less meta-theoretical way* when I plunged into my dissertation, I might have framed it as a 'least likely' study because of the substantial amount of evidence in favor of materialist arguments" (2008, 51–52, emphases added). This dissertation would be revised into Klotz's seminal work on norms and the ending of apartheid (1995). An even more recent example comes from Ted Hopf's meticulous study on the beginning years of the Cold War (Hopf 2012). Hopf also prefers to structure his arguments within the language of neopositivism. His work is different from other constructivist studies, as it is "falsifiable" with "variables that vary" (Hopf 2012, 27). This leads to hypotheses that are then tested by Hopf in subsequent chapters.

A brief caveat here, as we are *not* claiming that the work of these eminent scholars is less useful than the work of "early constructivists" due to the former's modifications of constructivism so that their approaches were amenable to "testing." We do agree, however, with Onuf, who has since remarked that the 1990s works involve "the casual appropriation of the constructivist label by scholars who are not Kantian constructivists. In most cases they think that an interest in collective identity and informal rules (dubbed norms) instead of the legal rules means that they are somehow no longer liberal institutionalists. They are wrong" (Onuf 2012). In our terms, we would argue that by giving up "contingency" and replacing it with the "quest for necessity," these self-acclaimed constructivists have in this instance, and here we agree with Sterling-Folker and Onuf, moved themselves beyond the confines of constructivism itself.

It is may therefore not be a surprise that the more this liberal constructivism become subject to critical scrutiny by those constructivists working in the 2000s (see for example Barder and Levine 2012), classical realist works were engaged more frequently, and a double contingency re-emerged. For instance, Tjalve's (very constructivist) re-engagement of what she titles Reinhold Niebuhr's "Augustinian anthropology" led to an "epistemological skepticism." Tjalve noted how for Niebuhr the finite (temporal *and* spatial) existence of human beings meant that "human beings [had] no access to objective truth" (Tjalve 2008, 67), and therefore had to construct devices (such as narratives) to create pragmatic understandings of society and order. This will to construct acknowledged for classical realists not an "objective reality" per se but focused on the devices that actors and scholars use to make sense of a seemingly disorderly world. Such lessons became for those trained as (or familiar with, or disciplined into) constructivists/

constructivism useful lessons on contingency .and interactions from our own particular, yet still intersubjective, positions.

Another example of double contingency can be found in Sylvest's (2008) study, which revealed the "underlying constructivism" in classical realist Herz's work as being exemplified in "the importance of context, interaction and actors" (Sylvest 2008, 450). The security dilemma provides one example of a *construct* that is as much pedagogical as it is "real"; it helps teach us, and policymakers, that for all their zeal, transnational ideologies such as communism collapse back into nationalisms via the security dilemma. Thus the key is to both recognize the limits of others' agency, as well as one's own, to recognize not only these limits but their double contingency.

One of us (Steele 2007b) titled this development (which in rare cases preceded the 2000s) "reflexive realism," which sought to revive the principles and basic insights of classical realism. Such an engagement of realism, largely by those trained within constructivism and its concepts, focused on the contingency ("the limits of power," "agency of self and others") of the international political world, but it was also a recognition of the situatedness of the scholars as well, never completely apart from the world that they studied. This would include especially works on emotions (Ross 2013),[8] roles (McCourt 2014), and the identity relations (and spaces) between both democracies and nondemocracies (Hayes 2013).

Contingency and the Problem of Normative Theory:
Toward the Problem of the Third

The last section has shown how the interest in double contingency was lost, which then unfolded into more inevitable or probable understandings of possibility and the necessity to formulate those understandings into "hypotheses" and "tests" under which generalizable statements could be formulated. This of course makes sense if one sees the world being graspable with some diminishing (if not redacting) of agency, which we posit occurred with some frequency in the 1990s or via media constructivism. This move was not only ontological, it had methodological "benefits." But in the process it removed the double contingency from constructivism, the focus on the social/relational space and place between ego and alter.

Yet to do so one would need an approach that practiced what Herborth has titled a "logic of reconstruction" rather than one of externally validated "subsumption" (2012), and not only because of issues of incommensurability but because of the layered contingencies that now abound in late modernity (what we title "the problem of the third" below). Admittedly, the constructivisms of the (recent or further) past that centralized double contingency proved difficult to test against an objectively given reality, and thus in a way it will be difficult for a doubly contingent constructivism to be "tested" against other perspectives to see which one best stacks up against a static "reality."

But we should not stop here, and thus this section suggests a way forward that can grapple with an additional layer of contingency not explicitly acknowledged, a triple contingency that may be utilized in constructivist works going forward by invoking some of the referents once centralized in earlier constructivist works. For instance, recall how Onuf identifies the need for "institutionalization" of norms in order for them to count as legal norms, or when Kratochwil talks about "institutional trust," or when Wendt uses the referent "culture." Something deeper is at play. Institutionalization, institutional trust, or culture cannot be reduced to the ongoing interaction between actors. Rather, these concepts position and shape the interactions between ego and alter in the first place. Culture or institutional rules shape the conditions under which ego and alter interact, how they will interact, and what kind of social relations and identities emerge. We call this dimension *triple contingency* insofar as the structure-formation processes between ego and alter are changed in relation to "thirds" (culture, institutions, etc.).

What emerges is a focus on discourses, discursive power, and semiosis in ways that, while springboarding from the agenda of classical realism, at the same time departs from it. This problem of the "third" can thus be framed as: *ego and alter are observed from a "third" and become aware of this.* Hence their interaction and the kind of sociality changes. This third position then mirrors the "institutional facts" Kratochwil referred to (Kratochwil 1989, 22). They only exist in their continuous performance through speech acts, and they further presuppose a reflexivity about their existence: actants need to become aware of these thirds and form expectations and "trust" on them. At the same time, acknowledging this further "position," instantly requires a normative vocabulary. Here we propose that the separation of single, double, and triple contingency might help to disentangle the problem of the balance of power: the concept of balance of power is actually three combined problems with specific moves, dynamics, and reflexivity. Balance of power is a problem of individual states in their formation of strategies, the intersubjective formation of expectations between states, and an institutional fact with productive power.

Conclusion

One issue we have avoided until now is what constitutes constructivism. How one answers this question discloses not only what they think constructivism "is," but what it should be, what the field is and should be, where constructivism has been, and, perhaps most importantly, where it is (or is not) going. We would add one further loosened identifier relating to our narration of constructivism within different forms of contingency: not only *what* constructivism is but *when* it is and has been (and could be in the future). We thus, likely in a cavalier manner, take a broad understanding of constructivism as an approach to international relations that utilizes social theory (more generally) and its concepts to understand the world.[9] Even more hopefully, so long as one is familiar with "constructivism," one can engage in an extremely wide variety of conversations about world politics and its study.

The debates within constructivism can become just as heated as those between constructivists and those considered its critics, and this too has implications for the possibilities (or lack thereof) for any intervention that could serve to unify constructivists in the future. Now we think this is both a validation of constructivism's versatility, especially in its modest success breaking into a US field of IR and political science not known for fostering creative intellectual enterprises, *as well as* a testament to constructivism's passage from a period of youthful vanguardism to more cynical middle-age. Constructivism has now been around long enough to develop not only philosophical ontological debates, but intergenerational fault lines as well, lines that are as much about style and sensibility as they are about substance. But some of the fault lines that exist within constructivism, we would suggest, can be explained by typical moves one sees in the maturation (or evolution or contamination) of older research traditions (or paradigms, perspectives, or what have you), including realism.

Therefore, in this chapter, we proposed an avenue to reconstruct the relationship between constructivism and realism on the basis of contingency. Here we differentiate three different kinds of contingency. To take the balance of power problem as an example, we can see:

- **Single contingency**: every state faces contingencies in relation to the balance of power insofar as it is not sure about its own calculations.
- **Double contingency**: the balance of power provides a means to form intersubjective expectations about possible behavior of other

actants. It provides a reference point and an intersubjective foil where critique, consent, and approval can be communicated. In this context, the balance of power provides a signaling system and means for communication.

- **Triple contingency**: actors recognize the productive power of the balance and can link it to questions of identity. The balance of power has structure formation power. And it is here where constructivists and classical realists differ: classical realists were ambiguous about whether the balance of power is a natural product or a social system. They were also ambiguous on where the balance of power operated: the first, second, or third image. For a realist constructivism, we can see that the balance of power as a third is necessarily social, yet it is social in a different way as simply intersubjectivity or double contingency suggests: it forms and limits interactions, identities, and expectations. This reflexivity cannot be made within the classic realist approaches, and certainly not by the rationalists. At the same time, it is also clear that a contingency-based approach to constructivism separates realist tenets from anthropological groundings, rationalism, or second-image-reversed (Gourevitch 1978) arguments.

In this chapter, we have shown how realism and constructivism actually share some common history: even though there are differences, both shared an interest in double contingency at the beginning. Then, in the name of science, neorealism traded in this otherness for a unified theory of rationality linked to microeconomic single decision-making problems. The generation of constructivists and their works produced in the 1990s sought to advance constructivism by providing a more scientific version. Perhaps as a reaction to this move, along with geopolitical developments of a less hopeful decade of the 2000s (Barder and Levine 2012), there was a revived and renewed interest in double contingency *and* a use by constructivists of classical realist works for such a purpose. We cannot argue that this is the very reason for the realism-constructivism debate. Yet we do argue that our contingency position captures the two key moments of the debate: the importance of power and the question of normative theory.

NOTES

1. We do not engage in attempts to define realism and constructivism, that is, the view that if only rightfully defined, realism and constructivism can be made compatible or incompatible. We do in our conclusion share an understanding of

constructivism, but for a broader discussion of definitions of realism see Donnelly 2000. For a discussion of constructivism, this volume provides ample evidence. See the introduction to this volume and also Steele 2007a and Kessler 2009.

2. Constructivists have emphasized structure formation processes between ego and alter as two "actors." Be it in Wendt's formulation of the first contact situation (which is at least a "contact" between different actors) or speech act theory in Kratochwil and Onuf with its differences of illocution (ego) and perlocution (alter). For a discussion of illocution and perlocution see Austin 1962, lecture 4.

3. We refer to this dichotomy a bit more in our conclusion. The logic of subsumption means to engage with reality with an already fixed set of categories, projected onto empirical phenomena. Subsumption is contrasted with the logic of reconstruction, where the development of categories is not prior to observation but "reconstructed" through engagement with the empirical development.

4. At this point, a more elaborate discussion on critical constructivism and poststructuralist thought would be necessary. Unfortunately, we cannot deal with this question at this point but have to leave it for another occasion.

5. For Jackson (2011, 31–32), this was because it is only within a mind-world dualist philosophical ontology (the world is external to the discourses and mental states we hook into it) that one could "subject" claims to "testing." In Jackson's words, and citing Onuf and Kratochwil as exemplars, "IR constructivists have been leveling challenges at mind-world dualism for at least two decades." Yet "we persistently fail to notice the logical absurdity of the situation—obviously it makes no sense to evaluate a claim *opposing* mind-world dualism by *presuming* mind-world dualism."

6. Neumann and Sending cite the following studies characterizing this structural focus: Finnemore 1996; Gurowitz 1999; and Katzenstein 1996. In his 1998 study, Gould seemed to be one of the first to notice this trend: "The agent-structure debate has been remarkably one-sided. In IR, no self-conscious advocate of methodological individualism has taken up the debate. The nature of agency is so neglected that it is misleading even to speak of an 'agent-structure debate.'" (1998, 83).

7. To name but two examples, Risse's works suggested that through argumentation, actors could not only shift their understandings, but their interests and their identities as well (Risse 2000, 10). See also Klotz 1995 on the possibility of global "constitutive norms . . . likely lead[ing] to changes in actors' interests and identities" (26).

8. Ross's seminal article on emotions saw them as double-contingent affects; not "possessed" but rather "nonsubjective, "they do not define the self but exist as strata, alongside numerous other habits, memories and beliefs that together comprise a particular construction of the self" (2006, 213).

9. In a recent e-international relations interview, Onuf uses similar terms as a self-description: "I [have] suggested that we should think of international relations as a species of social relations and abandon IR theory for social theory." See http://www.e-ir.info/2014/05/09/interview-nicholas-onuf/.

REFERENCES

Ashley, Richard K. 1984. "The poverty of neorealism." *International Organization* 38, no. 2: 225–86.

Austin, J. L. 1962. *How to Do Things with Words*. Cambridge, MA: Harvard University Press.

Barder, Alexander, and Daniel Levine. 2012. "The World Is Too Much with Us: Reification and the Depoliticizing of Via Media Constructivist IR." *Millennium* 40, no. 3: 585–603.

Barkin, Samuel. 2003. "Realist-Constructivism." *International Studies Review* 5, no. 5: 325–42.

Barnett, Michael, and Raymond Duvall. 2005. "Power in International Politics." *International Organization* 59.1: 39–75.

Carr, Edward Hallett. 1964. *The Twenty Years' Crisis, 1919–1939: An Introduction to the Study of International Relations*. Rerinted from the earlier edition. New York: Harper and Row.

Donnelly, Jack. 2000. *Realism in International Relations*. Cambridge: Cambridge University Press.

dos Reis, Filipe, and Kessler, Oliver. 2016. Constructivism and the politics of international law. In *The Oxford Handbook of the Theory of International Law*, edited by Anne Orford and Florian Hoffmann.

Finnemore, Martha. 1996. *National Interests in International Society*. Ithaca, NY: Cornell University Press.

Finnemore, Martha, and Kathryn Sikkink. 1998. "International Norm Dynamics and Political Change." *International Organization* 52, no. 4: 887–917.

Finnemore, Martha, and Kathryn Sikkink. 2001. "Taking Stock: The Constructivist Research Program in International Relations and Comparative Politics." *Annual Review of Political Science* 4: 391–416.

Gould, Harry. 1998. "What Is at Stake in the Agent-Structure Debate?" In *International Relations in a Constructed World*, edited by Vendulka Kubalkova, edited by Nicholas Onuf and Paul Kowert, 79–100. Armonk, NY: M. E. Sharpe.

Gourevitch, Peter. 1978. "The Second Image Reversed: The International Sources of Domestic Politics." *International Organization* 32: 881–912.

Gurowitz, Amy. 1999. "Mobilizing International Norms: Domestic Actors, Immigrants and the Japanese State." *World Politics* 51, no. 3: 413–45.

Hayes, Jarrod. 2013. *Constructing National Security: US Relations with India and China*. New York: Cambridge University Press.

Herborth, Benjamin. 2012. "Theorising Theorising: Critical Realism and the Quest for Certainty." *Review of International Studies* 38, no. 1: 235–51.

Herz, John. 1950. "Idealist Internationalism and the Security Dilemma." *World Politics* 2, no. 2: 157–80.

Hom, Andrew R., and Brent J. Steele. 2010. "Open Horizons: The Temporal Visions of Reflexive Realism." *International Studies Review* 12, no. 2 (June): 271–300.

Hopf, Ted. 2012. *Reconstructing the Cold War: The Early Years, 1945–1958*. New York: Oxford University Press.

Jackson, Patrick. 2011. *The Conduct of Inquiry in International Relations*. New York: Routledge.

Jackson, Patrick, and Dan Nexon. 2004. "Constructivist Realism or Realist-Constructivism." *International Studies Review* 6: 337–41.

Katzenstein, Peter, ed. 1996. *Cultures of National Security.* Ithaca, NY: Cornell University Press.

Keohane, Robert. 1989. "International Institutions: Two Approaches." *International Studies Quarterly* 32: 379–96.

Kessler, Oliver. 2007. From Agents and Structures. https://www.academia.edu/2065699/From_Agents_and_Structures_to_Minds_and_Body.

Kessler, Oliver. 2009. Toward a Sociology of the International? International Relations between Anarchy and World Society. https://onlinelibrary.wiley.com/doi/full/10.1111/j.1749-5687.2008.00065.x?globalMessage=0&.

Klotz, Audie. 1995. *Norms and International Relations: The Struggle Against Apartheid.* Ithaca, NY: Cornell University Press.

Klotz, A. 2008. "Case Selection." In *Qualitative Methods in International Relations,* edited by A. Klotz and D. Prakash, 43–58. Palgrave Macmillan, London.

Kratochwil, Friedrich. 1989. *Rules, Norms and Decisions.* Cambridge: Cambridge University Press.

Kratochwil, Friedrich. 2006. "History, Action and Identity: Revisiting the 'Second' Great Debate and Assessing Its Importance for Social Theory." *European Journal of International Relations.* http://reinhardmeyers.uni-muenster.de/docs/GraduateT/Kratochwil2006.pdf.

Kratochwil, Friedrich. 2014. *The Status of Law in World Society.* Cambridge: Cambridge University Press

Krebs, Ronald R., and Patrick Thaddeus Jackson. 2007. "Twisting Tongues and Twisting Arms: The Power of Political Rhetoric." *European Journal of International Relations* 13, no. 1: 35–66.

Lang, Anthony F. 2002. *Agency and Ethics: The Politics of Military Intervention.* New York: SUNY Press.

Lang, Anthony F. 2007. "Morgenthau, Agency, and Aristotle." In *Realism Reconsidered: The Legacy of Hans Morgenthau in International Relations,* edited by Michael C. Williams, 18–41.

McCourt David M. 2014. *Britain and Word Power since 1945.* Ann Arbor: University of Michigan Press.

Mearsheimer, John. 1994/1995. "The False Promise of International Institutions." *International Security* 19: 5–49.

Morgenthau, Hans. 1946. *Scientific Man versus Power Politics.* Chicago: University of Chicago Press

Morgenthau, Hans. 1948/2006. *Politics Among Nations.* 7th ed. New York: McGraw Hill.

Neumann, Iver, and Ole Jacob Sending. 2010. *Governing the Global Polity.* Ann Arbor: University of Michigan Press.

Niebuhr, Reinhold. 1932. *Moral Man and Immoral Society.* New York: Scribner and Sons.

Onuf, Nicholas. 2012. The Tinos Lectures: Three Generations of International Relations. Presented at the 21st Annual Summer Seminar, Institute of International Relations, Tinos, Greece, July 4–5, 2012.

Oren, Ido. 2009. "The Unrealism of Contemporary Realism: The Tension between Realist Theory and Realists' Practice." *Perspectives on Politics* 7, no.2: 283–301.

Risse, Thomas. 2000. "'Let's Argue!': Communicative Action in World Politics." *International Organization* 54, no.: 1–39.

Ross, Andrew A. G. 2006. "Coming in from the Cold: Constructivism and Emotions." *European Journal of International Relations* 12, no. 2: 197–222.

Ross, Andrew A. G. 2013. *Mixed Emotions*. Chicago: University of Chicago Press.

Steele, Brent. 2007a. "Liberal-Idealism: A Constructivist Critique." *International Studies Review* 9, no. 1 (Spring): 23–52.

Steele, Brent. 2007b. "'Eavesdropping on Honored Ghosts': From Classical to Reflexive Realism." *Journal of International Relations and Development* 10, no. 3: 272–300.

Steele, Brent. 2010. *Defacing Power: The Aesthetics of Insecurity in Global Politics*. Ann Arbor: University of Michigan Press.

Steele, Brent J. 2013. "Context and Appropriation: The Risks, Benefits and Challenges of Reinterpretive Expression." *International Politics* 50: 739–52.

Steele, Brent J., and Oliver Kessler. 2016. "Constructing the Next Generation of Constructivism in IR." Introduction to the "Next Generation in Constructivist Scholarship." Special issue. *European Review of International Studies* 3, no. 3: 7–13.

Sterling-Folker, Jennifer. 2000. "Competing Paradigms or Birds of a Feather? Constructivism and Neoliberal Institutionalism Compared." *International Studies Quarterly* 44, no. 1: 97–119.

Sylvest, Casper. 2008. "John H. Herz and the Resurrection of Classical Realism." *International Relations* 22, no. 4: 441–55.

Tjalve, Vibeke Schou. 2008. *Realist Strategies of Republican Peace: Neibuhr, Morgenthau and the Politics of Patriotic Dissent*. New York: Palgrave.

Waltz , Kenneth. 1979. *Theory of International Politics.*. Reading: Addison Wesley.

Wendt, A. E. 1987. "The Agent-Structure Problem in International Relations Theory." *International Organization* 41, no. 3: 335–70.

Wendt, Alexander. 1999. *Social Theory of International Politics*. Cambridge: Cambridge University Press.

Williams, Michael C. 2004. *The Realist Tradition and the Limits of International Relations*. Cambridge: Cambridge University Press.

FIVE

Constructivism and the Logic of Legitimation

Stacie E. Goddard
Ronald R. Krebs

Over the past decade scholars associated with diverse research traditions increasingly have agreed that legitimacy matters to the theory and practice of world politics. It is not surprising that constructivists, sensitive to the social fabric of international life, would see legitimacy as central even to the high politics of diplomacy and threat assessment. We would expect constructivists to highlight how states strive to frame even their deviant foreign policy behaviors as consistent with dominant norms and how norm violators seem especially menacing.[1] But it is more surprising that realists and liberal rationalists too now argue that states generally value their reputation for being upstanding, rule-following members of the international community. Realists acknowledge that hegemony that rests on coercion alone is expensive and that legitimacy greases the wheels of global rule.[2] Liberal rationalists similarly argue that insofar as abiding by or violating global norms can be costly, legitimate and illegitimate behavior potentially reveal a state's "type."[3]

Despite the field's embrace of legitimacy, scholars of international relations have shown less interest in the politics of *legitimation*: how political actors publicly justify policy stances before concrete audiences, seeking to secure audiences' assent that their positions are indeed legitimate and thus potentially to garner audiences' approval and support.[4] Even scholars who see legitimacy as integral to world politics often pay little attention to the rhetoric that gives rise to it. Some dismiss such rhetoric as meaningless posturing, as mere window dressing masking interests and power. For realists, leaders deploy rhetoric to manipulate and mobilize the credulous masses, who seem always to fall for the ethnic cards they play and for the myths of empire they propagate.[5] For liberal rationalists, leaders' public rhetoric might help overcome secrecy's deleterious consequences, but only if uttering the words or eventually violating those commitments is sufficiently costly that it reveals true interests and actual will.[6] Even mainstream constructivists have shown more interest in how already legitimate norms and ideas drive and constrain foreign policy than in how actors go about rendering particular policies legitimate.[7]

The field's legitimation blind spot is puzzling. If legitimacy matters, so too must legitimation: action can be legitimate only if actors claim legitimacy and only if audiences grant those claims. Moreover, much of the empirical substance of world politics revolves around legitimation contests: dizzying public claims, counterclaims, and counter-counterclaims with respect to the legitimacy, and not merely the wisdom or advisability, of policy. Political actors the world over—from politicians to pundits to activists—devote substantial resources, energy, and political capital to rhetorical battle. They implicitly recognize that legitimation shapes the fate of political projects, from the welfare state to national security. To overlook legitimation is to overlook much of global politics. For these reasons, this chapter urges constructivists to take a public rhetorical turn and to make legitimation central to the study of international relations and foreign policy.

As we have already suggested, card-carrying social constructivists are not the only ones who should be attentive to legitimation. It should be a concern for all scholars of international relations who invoke notions of legitimate action. But that, in our view, is because any account that takes legitimacy seriously—in that it refuses to reduce standards of legitimacy to the interests, resources, and beliefs of individual actors and further that it sees those standards as shaping the behavior of even the materially and institutionally powerful—rests on social constructivist premises about the nature of the world, or ontology. A constructivist perspective sees politics as a contest not just over the distribution of material resources, but over social meaning, over how we make public sense of events and action. Constructivist accounts normally invoke social phenomenona—norms, identities, rules—that embody specific constellations of meaning and define the boundaries of legitimate political action. When these contingent constellations become sufficiently institutionalized and sedimented, they acquire the status of background common sense, to the point that they seem natural, timeless, and beyond the political realm; that is, they become social facts.[8] When realists and liberal rationalists invoke legitimacy as an independent causal force in international relations and foreign policy, they are at the very least smuggling in, if not openly conceding, social constructivist insights. As will become clear below, however, we do not see constructivism as at odds with either strategic action or the operation of power. On the one hand, the social processes that give rise to the boundaries of legitimation necessarily entail power, albeit in a constitutive and sometimes indirect form.[9] On the other hand, we oppose the common effort to assign human action to either the logic of instrumentalism or the logic of appropriateness and to associate the former with constructivism. Such an analytical move obscures how social standards are intertwined with, make possible, and confine rational action.[10]

The rest of this chapter proceeds in three sections. First, we define legitimation and clarify how a legitimation perspective differs from other approaches to public rhetoric in the field. Second, we specify the conditions under which legitimation affects political processes and outcomes: that is, when students of global politics should be particularly attentive to legitimation. Third, we conclude by laying out an agenda for future constructivist research on legitimation in international relations.

Legitimation as Concept and Perspective

By legitimation, we mean how political actors publicly justify their policy stances before concrete audiences. Our argument for making legitimation central to international relations theory derives from two premises regarding human nature: that human beings are both meaning-making and deeply social animals. A long line of research in the social sciences and humanities affirms that humans are compelled, perhaps even by nature, to imbue their own actions and those of others with meaning. That is why the human mind readily imposes an interpretive framework on disparate pieces of data, seeing order even when there is none.[11] And that is why human beings are driven not only to describe what they have done but to explain why they have done it. Philosophers debate whether reasons are properly understood as causes for action, but providing reasons for our own actions, and making sense of others' actions, is central to our existence.[12] A more social imperative complements this internal one. Living in communities and craving their fellows' approval, human beings are governed by what Elster has termed "the civilizing force of hypocrisy": when we speak in public, we must offer socially acceptable reasons or face the censure of our peers.[13]

Moreover, there are few social settings in which legitimation does not prominently feature. Although exasperated parents may eventually command their children to "do as I say!" at even a fairly young age, children resist parental orders they think morally wrong or otherwise illegitimate.[14] In hierarchical societies, the dominated—whether on the basis of class, ethnicity, caste, religion, or gender—refuse to grant legitimacy to their subordination.[15] Superiors in a bureaucracy do at times issue orders without explaining themselves, but they too typically justify their decisions, to secure their underlings' buy-in. Certainly the powerful, more often than the weak, can say patently absurd or contradictory things and still get their way. But in most social circumstances, even the powerful must explain themselves in terms that others comprehend and find acceptable. Those who do not care to legitimate their claims are rejected or ignored. At the extreme such an individual "is quickly regarded as a fanatic, the prey of interior demons, rather than as a reasonable person seeking to share his convictions."[16]

It is because language imbues events and actions with meaning that legitimation is an imperative, not a mere nicety, of global politics.[17] There are of course brute facts in the world. "The rise of China" is a prevalent trope in elite and popular discourse, but it does not exist solely in the linguistic realm: it encapsulates that nation's rapid economic growth, urbanization, and military modernization.[18] But processes of legitimation impart meaning to those material developments and thus shape how other nations respond. If China's rise spoke for itself, as both defenders and critics of US foreign policy often imply, there would not be a vigorous debate over the implications of its rise for international and regional order. Because the meaning of global events and material structures is not self-evident—they "do not come with an instruction sheet," as Blyth has put it—they cannot be treated as objective inputs into strategy.[19] This is where legitimation comes in.

In arguing that legitimation should be front and center in constructivist theorizing, we are clearly indebted to and inspired by an earlier, critical linguistic turn in international relations that deconstructed authoritative texts to unearth the unarticulated "commonsense" assumptions that inform and structure policy. That literature rightly argued that the social could not be understood outside of language and that language is both the product of and productive of power. It insightfully placed the analysis of discourse at its center to reveal the exclusions and incoherence that are constitutive of identity.[20] But, like many constructivists, we have found the critical linguistic turn unsatisfying in its refusal to engage causal dynamics and in its static presentation of dominant discursive structures that strip agency and politics out of the analysis. We thus opt for a "pragmatic" model of rhetorical politics that centers on specific rhetorical deployments in particular political and social contexts.[21] This approach rests on four analytical wagers: that actors are both strategic and social, that legitimation works by imparting meaning to political action, that legitimation is laced through with contestation, and that the power of language emerges through contentious dialogue. In combination, these four wagers distinguish our pragmatic model from other approaches to language—critical and neopositivist, materialist and constructivist—common in the study of politics and international relations.

First, while we agree that political actors are often strategic, this does not mean that legitimation can be reduced to self-interest. Actors are embedded in a social environment that simultaneously makes possible and confines strategic action. Even scheming elites cannot stand outside structures of discourse. As these elites too are products of a given social milieu, the schemes they design must necessarily draw on their inherited "cultural tool-kit," in Swidler's words, which includes rhetorical resources.[22] To conceive of speakers and audiences as social creatures is not to imagine them as cultural dopes, mindlessly following culture's purported dictates. Rather, as they seek to make sense of their world, and as they respond to others' meaning-making efforts, they are equally subject to, and empowered by, the shared resources embedded in their culture. This stands in contrast to the many realists who see public rhetoric as a mere fig leaf covering the naked pursuit of interest and who assume that elites easily bend the masses to their ends. It is not the case then that where there is a will, there must always be a rhetorical way.

Second, legitimation exerts effects on politics by imparting *meaning* to action. This model thus departs significantly from rationalist approaches to public rhetoric, which flatten language to a medium for the communication of information that, when costly, reveals such information to be credible. Rationalists thereby overlook the care with which speakers construct public arguments, audiences' attention to rhetorical contest, and the ensuing intense debates over the interpretation of legitimation, over what a given speaker means and what it portends. A pragmatic approach emphasizes that whether public claims making is legitimate renders a signal meaningful, even if it does not entail material costs. How a nation's central economic policymakers legitimate their policy stances demonstrates their competence to the global financial community, serves as a meaningful guide to their future behavior, or index,[23] and shapes patterns of lending—even when their appointment or their articulation of policy is not especially costly.[24] More important, by shaping public expectations, defining the issues at stake, distinguishing signals from noise, and laying the basis for debate, legitimation has constitutive effects in world politics. Whether leaders make legitimate sense of their nations' actions affects whether other states deem them benign or aggressive: security threats are constructed, not merely revealed, in the course of legitimation. Whether actors succeed in legitimating their private agendas affects whether their aims are thought cosmopolitan (that is, in the interest of the global community), parochial (that is, in the interests of domestic groups), or in the service of the nation's long-term welfare. Legitimation is thus essential to the production of the national interest. The rationalist bargaining model has seized upon one aspect of the dynamics of public rhetoric, while overlooking its much more fundamental role in the making of meaning in global politics.

Third, compared to many constructivist accounts, we conceive of political actors as less socialized and more strategic. Constructivists informed by the discourse ethics of Habermas have viewed persuasive rhetoric as central to normative change in international relations, and they have argued that persuasion is most likely when speakers and listeners are both committed to the open exchange of ideas.[25] While Habermas recognizes that politics is often a site of strategic action, he envisions and directs humanity toward a politics in which power and rank are left at the door, in which agonistic competition is replaced by deliberation and ultimately by consensus. Our pragmatic model, in contrast, theorizes language use as necessarily deeply shot through with power and marked by contest. Moreover, we do not presuppose universal standards by which audiences judge arguments persuasive. In Habermas's account, actors can be moved by the "unforced force of the better argument," but this presumes that they are already in agreement on fundamentals, that they have already attained substantial zones of consensus.[26] We, however, see legitimation as taking place before particular, not universal, audiences, and claimants adapt to the audience's "distinctive and particular passions and their particular commitments, sentiments, and beliefs."[27]

Finally, a pragmatic model of legitimation rests on a *dialogical* view of politics, in which various articulations compete for dominance. Scholars associated with the aforementioned critical linguistic turn in international relations point out, following Foucault, how discursive formations define the key categories of social and political life and thus constitute the range of legitimate politics. We concur with their foundational insight that discourse is both the product of, and productive of, power. But we take issue with their implicit assertion, in Neumann's formulation, that "there is nothing outside of discourse and, for this reason, the analysis of language is *all* that we need in order to account for what is going on in the world."[28] Rather, legitimation proves powerful through a complex interplay between text and context, between what is said and where and when it is said. Existing discursive formations do not eliminate all space for choice and contingency, and thus agency.

Scholars of international relations routinely treat legitimation as a mask for power and interests, cast legitimation as an idealized alternative to power, reduce public rhetoric's effects to revealing information, or see public rhetoric as an exercise in manipulation. To place one's analytical bets on legitimation as pragmatic performance is not to deny that rhetorical exchange takes place in the shadow of material power, reflects elite strategizing, or involves the communication of information. It is, however, to insist that legitimation is a form of power, that strategizing elites cannot escape the bonds of legitimacy, that rhetorical exchange goes beyond signaling resolve and reservation values, and that the outcome of rhetorical contestation cannot be boiled down to the distribution of material power alone. Legitimation, in our view, neither competes with nor complements power politics: it *is* power politics.[29] Triumph in the public contest over social meaning affects the distribution of capabilities, actor identities, and even their visions of political possibilities. It marginalizes some voices, rendering them effectively silent, while it empowers others to effect political change. Those who cannot legitimate their preferred strategy are, as Hans Morgenthau long ago argued, "at a great, perhaps decisive, disadvantage in the struggle for power."[30]

When Legitimation Matters

Legitimation is so commonplace that we might be tempted to conclude that it is of little consequence in accounting for variation in political processes and outcomes. Part of the analytical challenge is to ascertain when legitimation matters: when must global actors attempt to legitimate their actions to domestic or international audiences, and when do their efforts at legitimation, and their diverse strategies, have powerful effects, both causal and constitutive? At the most basic level, we contend that legitimation is necessary whenever publics, be they domestic or global, must be mobilized, and it lurks in the background wherever there is a reasonable chance that the glare of attention will turn. Put differently, the political impact of legitimation lies at the intersection of two demands: some important public's demand for legitimation, or the visibility of a policy domain, and the government's demand for some public's contribution, or the need for mobilization.

Audiences' insistence that officials explain themselves is a key driver of legitimation. If relevant publics are inattentive, if they are unlikely to be made to pay attention, and if the policy in question can be hidden from public view, legitimation is not necessary. Much escapes public scrutiny in large bureaucratic nation-states thanks to the public's and the media's wavering attention, the technical sophistication of policy, legislatures' inclination to delegate, the broad scope of state activity, and the sheer size of the bureaucracy. Yet policy must generally be capable of legitimation: policies that domestic and global publics at first ignore may subsequently come into their crosshairs, and even those policies that government officials go to lengths to keep secret may eventually come to light and prove highly controversial—as recent scandals over National Security Agency spying in the United States and over CIA-led torture of terrorist suspects have reminded us. Politicians prefer covert means when they cannot offer a rationale that audiences would deem legitimate, but covert actions rarely remain covert forever, and sometimes not for long at all, and they then require justification after the fact. Russia's denial that its forces secretly had intervened in the Ukrainian civil war in 2014 was unusual only in its audacity. With the world's, and notably NATO's, attention fixed on the Ukraine crisis, Russia's steadfast refusal to acknowledge the full extent of its involvement and to provide public justification for its seeming violation of international norms ensured that its activities enjoyed little legitimacy outside Russia.

Government officials, however, do not have incentives to keep invisible as much of the policy space as possible. Governments often need to mobilize domestic publics, for both tangible resources and symbolic support, and they would rather people willingly contribute the needed resources. That requires engaging relevant publics, not shutting them out of the policymaking process, and thus legitimation, not coercion. The more extensive and regular the government's needs, the more institutionalized legitimation becomes. Thus the roots of representative parliamentary institutions and the machinery of liberal politics lie, Tilly argues, in European states' need to mobilize resources for war making.[31] The greater government's demand for resources, the greater its need to engage in legitimation.

This same logic extends, albeit incompletely, to international relations, where the grounds for legitimation are often more uncertain and contested. Insofar as states require international cooperation, they must engage in legitimation to some foreign audience, whether other state leaders or mass publics. International institutions, in particular, can increase the demand for legitimation and thus exert effects on behavior, even when their powers of punishment and socialization are weak. This was true, Mitzen argues, of the Concert of Europe, which required European statesmen to legitimate their stances in the language of shared European norms, made it less likely they would openly invoke self-interest, and thereby compelled them to act contrary to their interests and even helped them to redefine their interests; via the logic of legitimation, the Concert forestalled Russian intervention in the Greek Revolt.[32] It was even true of the League of Nations, which, despite being a notoriously weak organization, sustained the international community's demand that Japan legitimate its invasion of Manchuria; when its answers proved unsatisfactory, Japan left the League of Nations. The more extensive and regular are states' needs for international cooperation, the more institutionalized legitimation becomes, as reflected in NATO's governing arrangements that provided for deep consultation among the allies and that, to an extent, mitigated inequalities of power.[33] At times, state leaders may even attempt to justify their behavior to the foreign masses, as Russia's Vladimir Putin sought in a *New York Times* op-ed in September 2013.

In figure 5.1, we combine these two dimensions to generate claims about when legitimation matters. Legitimation is obviously crucial in the upper-right cell, when policies are highly visible and when the government must mobilize public support. We then should observe substantial government-led efforts to legitimate its preferred policy, and the success of those efforts will have real consequences, or the government would not have expended resources on legitimation in the first place. These dynamics are, for instance, typical of the years of rivalry and crisis that precede major interstate war, and they affect whether, and how effectively, the home front is mobilized and alliances are brought to bear. But the government's success is not assured. When policy is highly visible, it is then also more likely that political forces are arrayed in opposition and that alternative legitimations are present in the public sphere.

In contrast, legitimation matters little in the lower-left cell, when policies are relatively invisible and when government has little incentive to

Government Need for Mobilization

		Low	High
Visibility of Policy	*High*	Legitimation (potentially) matters *Potential Legitimation*	Legitimation Matters *Substantial Legitimation*
	Low	Legitimation Irrelevant *Little Legitimation*	Legitimation Matters *Substantial Legitimation*

Figure 5.1. When legitimation matters

mobilize public resources. With audiences inattentive or unaware, and with government not requiring overt expressions or manifestations of legitimacy, government-led efforts to legitimate policy are expected to be minimal. In relatively open polities and international regimes, challenges are inevitable, but under circumstances of low visibility and mobilization, these are fewer in number and lower in intensity and hail from the margins, and officials, feeling little pressure to take critics seriously, respond in relatively perfunctory fashion. Think, for instance, of the spare efforts among US officials to legitimate the establishment and maintenance of hundreds of military installations around the world: US ambassadors exert far more energy defending these bases to host audiences than their domestic counterparts must at home. Or consider covert operations, from the arming of rebels to the assassination of foreign leaders, for which public legitimation is irrelevant, at least temporarily. But this zone, we argue, is fairly small because government must always account for the possibility that outside actors—from domestic and transnational nongovernmental organizations to foreign and opposition politicians—will work to increase an issue's visibility and thus that newly attentive publics will demand legitimation in retrospect.

Many policy issues, however, fall into the other two cells of figure 5.1. In the lower-right cell, the public is not focused on a given issue, yet the government requires major public contributions for policy to succeed. The purpose of legitimation under these conditions is to set the public agenda, to get people to pay attention. Consider, for instance, the strategic efforts of governments, and sometimes groups in national and transnational civil society, to raise the profile of particular threats. This is as true of routine threat construction as it is of so-called threat inflation. There are numerous ways to render a policy domain publicly visible, but it is hard to imagine doing so without a sustained campaign of legitimation, as Dean Acheson understood early in the Cold War when he helped craft Harry Truman's case for aid to Greece and Turkey in dramatic terms; as environmentalists understood when they sought to awaken mass publics and policymakers to the dangers of climate change; and as transnational activists aiming to ban chemical arms and landmines understood when they profiled these weapons' innocent and unintended victims. The strategy and style of legitimation during this agenda-setting phase sets boundary constraints for subsequent legitimation once the issue has already seized the public's attention. Whether there are powerful rhetorical "consistency constraints" at work in the political arena is much debated, and indeed the empirical jury is still out, but they would seem most likely to operate in the wake of a concerted campaign to shape the national conversation. This cell then is usually not a stable equilibrium. As an issue's visibility rises, politics migrates toward the upper-right cell.

In the upper-left cell of figure 5.1—when the visibility of an issue is high, yet the government's demand for public contribution is low—the degree of observed legitimation is contingent. Not needing much public mobilization, the government has no incentive to engage in regular legitimation. Many episodes of coercive diplomacy fall into this category. So too has the US drone strike campaign of recent years in such places as Pakistan and Yemen. But often policy opponents will choose to make this a site of challenge, whether out of principle or because they see potential for political profit, as has been the case with respect to drone warfare. Moreover, under the watchful eye of civil society, officials must be ready to justify policy and thus have strong incentives to avoid flagrantly illegitimate behavior. Policies in this zone may then not be the subject of active official legitimation, but they must always be capable of legitimation.

While legitimation is nearly ubiquitous, it does not always play a signal causal role in foreign policy and international relations. It matters most, we maintain, when officials need to mobilize resources—from either domestic or foreign audiences, whether mass or elite—and when relevant publics are attentive. Much of the politics of foreign policy thus revolves around the politics of visibility, as government officials and their opponents seek to define the scope of the audience for legitimation. Officials seek to confine issue awareness to public audiences before whom legitimation is possible and to keep issues out of the public eye when their legitimation would be difficult. Opponents in both the halls of power and civil society seek to broaden the audience to the point that legitimation becomes challenging. By rendering policy visible, they hope to compel officials to justify what cannot be justified and ideally force government into a rhetorical vise.[34]

Legitimation and the Future of Constructivism

While scholars across the field of international relations have acknowledged the power of legitimacy, the concept is most central to the constructivist tradition. Legitimacy refers to the boundaries of the acceptable within a given social community, and it therefore sets out the limits of sustainable social practice. Among international relations' diverse research traditions, constructivists most fully trace the implications of the international as a social realm, and it is thus no surprise that constructivists would see legitimacy as especially important. But, perhaps because constructivists have emphasized ideas and norms, they have devoted less attention to *legitimation*— that is, to the public rhetorical practices through which actors seek to cultivate legitimacy, to draw and redraw its boundaries, and to produce political effects. We have only a dim understanding of how political actors engage in legitimation, and with what consequences, in different domains. And we have even less understanding of how *contests* of legitimation play out, why political debate is sometimes wide-ranging and sometimes proceeds on a narrow foundation, why certain rhetorical formulations are transformed into background common sense while others remain subject to open challenge.[35] This chapter's ambition has been less to resolve long-standing questions and summarize the existing scholarly wisdom than to open a conversation and invite new lines of research.

This chapter has left at least three significant questions unanswered, which point to starting points for future constructivist research into the politics of legitimation. First, in the section above, we treated the model's two dimensions—the visibility of policy and the government's need for mobilization—largely as untheorized, exogenous inputs. If constructivists are to understand when legitimation shapes political processes and outcomes, this requires determining the concrete circumstances under which policies are likely to become visible and when publics must be mobilized. For instance, the broader the scope of policy, the more important legitimation is for its success. Officials can, and often seek to, keep fine-grained matters out of the public eye, but that is not possible when it comes to policies of broad scope, which are intrinsically visible because they impact so many constituencies and often require substantial mobilization. This implies that officials are more likely to have to legitimate, say, grand strategy than more mundane areas of policy, domestic or foreign. Even more counterintuitively, it further follows that the more private interests stand to gain or lose from the adoption of a particular policy, the more legitimation determines actors' success. The more clearly interests are at stake in foreign policy, and the more substantial those interests are, the more others expect these private interests to seek to turn the machinery of government to their own ends, and the greater the scrutiny to which they subject policy proposals. The more divided the contending interests, the greater the need to mobilize the public, and the more political success hinges on a resonant rhetoric that can mobilize a winning coalition. This line of reasoning might be followed to explore how the threat environment, regime type, density and strength of international institutions, and other factors shape the significance of legitimation in particular domains of world politics.[36]

Second, we have alluded to, but not theorized, the *outcome* of legitimation contests. If legitimation is a war of words, what distinguishes the winners from the losers of a rhetorical battle? Why are some efforts more successful than others in specific policy domains? While processes of legitimation are in principle open—anyone can attempt to legitimate using whatever language they would like—a pragmatic model of legitimation suggests, as Williams argues, that "in practice [they are] structured by the differential capacity of actors to make socially effective claims[,] . . . by the forms in which these claims can be made in order to be recognized and accepted as convincing by the relevant audience, and by the empirical factors or situations to which these actors can make reference."[37] In other words, explaining rhetorical power cannot just be a matter of conforming to the linguistic rules of a given domain, as seminal work on securitization emphasized.[38]

Broadly speaking, and drawing from more recent agenda-setting work on securitization, it seems that five factors shape which legitimation attempts succeed and which fail: (1) who speaks, (2) where and when they say it, (3) to whom they say it, (4) what they say, and (5) how they say it.[39] (1) Some *speakers* have authority to legitimate policy, while others shout from the sidelines. Some enjoy credibility as spokespersons for the public interest, while others are dismissed as self-serving. (2) *Context* matters as well to whether legitimation is required and is politically significant and to how legitimation contests play out. On the one hand, institutional rules may shape the authority and capacity of speakers. On the other hand, discursive structures can be so tight that all legitimation is confined to a dominant discourse, which renders some policy stances indefensible, or they can permit a far broader range of legitimation strategies and policy stances. (3) *Audiences* are central to rhetorical battle, for it is they who determine the victor. Contestants' capacity to craft resonant legitimations presumably depends on various features of relevant audiences: the nature of their interests, their unity or diversity, their education and political sophistication. (4) The *content* of legitimating appeals affects their persuasiveness. It is well established that when deployed frames draw on and are consistent with common rhetorical formulations, they are more likely to resonate than when these frames sit in tension with audiences' rhetorical priors. (5) The fate of legitimation rests also on rhetorical *technique*. Speakers strike audiences as skilled based in part on what metaphors, analogies, figures of speech, and tone they choose, as well as how they conform to the rhetorical conventions associated with particular forms of public address or genres. Audiences respond differently under different circumstances and to different rhetorical modes, whether speakers offer argument or whether they tell compelling stories.[40]

These five baskets of factors shape the outcome of legitimation contests, but the literature lacks many well-limned causal claims with well-conceptualized variables and appropriate scope conditions. Future research has far to go in unpacking these broad baskets, specifying the conditions under which particular factors operate, and spelling out what effects they produce.

Third, and finally, the effects of legitimation are not constant through time and space. They vary along with developments in technologies of communications and information, which in turn bolster (or undermine) authority, enlarge (or shrink) audiences, polarize (or unify) those audiences, make policy more (or less) visible, and increase (or diminish) the demand for legitimation. Theorizing and examining empirically how recent and historical changes in the material and social context of communication have shaped the intensity and dynamics of legitimation is a tall order for future research, but an essential one if we are to make sense of leadership in the contemporary age.[41]

NOTES

Portions of this chapter draw from our contribution to a special issue on "Rhetoric and Grand Strategy." Stacie E. Goddard and Ronald R. Krebs, "Rhetoric, Legitimation, and Grand Strategy," *Security Studies* 24, no. 1 (Jan.–March 2015): 5–36.

1. Ian Hurd, *After Anarchy: Legitimacy and Power in the United Nations Security Council* (Princeton, NJ: Princeton University Press, 2007); Christian Reus-Smit, *American Power and World Order* (Cambridge: Polity Press, 2004), 102; Mlada Bukovansky, *Legitimacy and Power Politics: The American and French Revolutions in International Political Culture* (Princeton, NJ: Princeton University Press, 2002). On legitimacy and global politics, see generally Ian Clark, *Legitimacy in International Society* (New York: Oxford University Press, 2007); and Ian Hurd, "Legitimacy and Authority in International Politics," *International Organization* 53, no. 2 (Spring 1999).

2. Stephen G. Brooks and William C. Wohlforth, *World Out of Balance: International Relations and the Challenge of American Primacy* (Princeton, NJ: Princeton University Press, 2008), 207.

3. On rhetoric and signaling, see Jack L. Goldsmith and Eric A. Posner, "Moral and Legal Rhetoric in International Relations: A Rational Choice Perspective," *Journal of Legal Studies* 31, no. 1 (January 2002): esp. 123–25.

4. On the distinction between legitimacy and legitimation, see Rodney Barker, *Legitimating Identities: The Self-Presentations of Rulers and Subjects* (Cambridge: Cambridge University Press, 2001), 1–29.

5. Jack L. Snyder, *Myths of Empire: Domestic Politics and International Ambition* (Ithaca, NY: Cornell University Press, 1991); Jack L. Snyder and Karen Ballentine, "Nationalism and the Marketplace of Ideas," *International Security* 21, no. 2 (Fall 1996): 5–40; and John J. Mearsheimer, *Why Leaders Lie: The Truth about Lying in International Politics* (New York: Oxford University Press, 2011). For a neoclassical realist exception, see Randall L. Schweller, *Unanswered Threats: Political Constraints on the Balance of Power* (Princeton, NJ: Princeton University Press, 2006).

6. On public commitments, credibility, and audience costs, see, among a very large literature, James D. Fearon, "Domestic Political Audiences and the Escalation of International Disputes," *American Political Science Review* 88, no. 3 (1994): 577–92; Anne E. Sartori, "The Might of the Pen: A Reputational Theory of Communication in International Disputes," *International Organization* 56, no. 1 (Winter 2002): 121–49; and Charles Lipson, *Reliable Partners: How Democracies Have Made a Separate Peace* (Princeton, NJ: Princeton University Press, 2005).

7. However, on normative change, see Neta Crawford, *Argument and Change in World Politics: Ethics, Decolonization, and Humanitarian Intervention* (Cambridge: Cambridge University Press, 2002); Martha Finnemore, *The Purpose of Intervention: Changing Beliefs About the Use of Force* (Ithaca, NY: Cornell University Press, 2003); Richard Price, "Reversing the Gun Sights: Transnational Civil Society Targets Land Mines," *International Organization* 52, no. 3 (Summer 1998): 613–44; Nina Tannenwald, *The Nuclear Taboo: The United States and the Non-Use of Nuclear Weapons Since 1945* (Cambridge: Cambridge University Press, 2007). There is also a large, relevant literature on the legitimation of global institutions: see, among others, Jens Steffek, "The Legitimation of International Governance: A Discourse Approach," *European Journal of International Relations* 9, no. 2 (June 2003): 249–75; Achim Hurrelmann et al., eds., *Legitimacy in an Age of Global Politics* (Basingstoke: Palgrave Macmillan, 2007); Dominik Zaum, ed., *Legitimating International Organizations* (Oxford: Oxford University Press, 2013).

8. On social facts, see Emile Durkheim *The Rules of Sociological Method*, ed. Ste-

ven Lukes (New York: Free Press, 1982); John R Searle, *The Construction of Social Reality* (New York: Free Press, 1995).

9. This is the form of power that Michael N. Barnett and Raymond Duvall term "productive." See Barnett and Duvall, "Power in International Politics," *International Organization* 59, no. 1 (Winter 2005), 39–76.

10. On these logics, see James G. March and Johan Olsen, *Rediscovering Institutions: The Organizational Basis of Politics* (New York: Free Press, 1989); and for an application to international relations, see Martha Finnemore and Kathryn Sikkink, "International Norm Dynamics and Political Change," *International Organization* 52, no. 4 (1998): 887–917. For a critique, see Ole Jacob Sending, "Constitution, Choice and Change: Problems with the 'Logic of Appropriateness' and Its Use in Constructivist Theory," *European Journal of International Relations* 8, no. 4 (2002): 443–70.

11. On the human penchant for imposing cognitive order, see Thomas Gilovich, *How We Know What Isn't So: The Fallibility of Human Reason in Everyday Life* (New York: Free Press, 1991), esp. 9–28; Arie W. Kruglanski, *The Psychology of Closed Mindedness* (New York: Psychology Press, 2004); Leonid Perlovsky, "Language and Cognition," *Neural Networks* 22, no. 3 (April 2009): 247–57; Richard M. Sorrentino and Christopher J. R. Roney, *The Uncertain Mind: Individual Differences in Facing the Unknown* (Philadelphia: Psychology Press, 2000).

12. The seminal philosophical work is Donald Davidson, "Actions, Reasons, and Causes," *Journal of Philosophy* 60, no. 23 (November 1963): 685–700. On the centrality of reason giving in practice, see Charles Tilly, *Why? What Happens When People Give Reasons . . . and Why* (Princeton, NJ: Princeton University Press, 2008).

13. Jon Elster, "Deliberation and Constitution-Making," in *Deliberative Democracy*, ed. Jon Elster (Cambridge: Cambridge University Press, 1998), 104.

14. Serena A. Perkins and Elliot Turiel, "To Lie or Not to Lie: To Whom and Under What Circumstances," *Child Development* 78, no. 2 (March–April 2007): 609–21; Elliott Turiel, *The Culture of Morality: Social Development, Context, and Conflict* (Cambridge: Cambridge University Press, 2002), esp. 107–18; Elliott Turiel, "Moral Development," in *Handbook of Child Psychology and Developmental Science, Volume 1: Theory & Method*, ed. William F. Overton and Peter C. Molenaar (Hoboken, NJ: Wiley, 2014).

15. See James C. Scott, *Weapons of the Weak: Everyday Forms of Peasant Resistance* (New Haven, CT: Yale University Press, 1985): for a psychological perspective, Turiel, *The Culture of Morality*, esp. 67–93.

16. Chaïm Perelman, *The Realm of Rhetoric* (Notre Dame, IN: University of Notre Dame Press, 1982), 16.

17. Generally, on the imperative to legitimation, see Jon Elster, "Strategic Uses of Argument," in *Barriers to Conflict Resolution*, ed. Kenneth Arrow et al. (New York: Norton, 1995), 244–52; Mark C. Suchman, "Managing Legitimacy: Strategic and Institutional Approaches," *Academy of Management Review* 20, no. 3 (July 1995): 571–610.

18. Though those too are bulky concepts, resting on layers of sedimented meanings. They are, however, shorthand for concrete processes: goods being manufactured and sold, people moving from villages to cities, capital-intensive weaponry being acquired.

19. Mark Blyth, "Structures Do Not Come with an Instruction Sheet: Interests, Ideas, and Progress in Political Science," *Perspectives on Politics* 1, no. 4 (December 2003): 695–706.

20. See, among many others, Michael J. Shapiro, *Language and Political Understanding: The Politics of Discursive Practices* (New Haven, CT: Yale University Press, 1981); James Der Derian and Michael J. Shapiro, eds., *International/Intertextual Relations: Postmodern Readings of World Politics* (Lexington, MA: Lexington Books, 1989); David Campbell, *Writing Security: United States Foreign Policy and the Politics of Identity*, rev. ed. (Minneapolis: University of Minnesota Press, 1998); Roxanne Lynn Doty, *Imperial Encounters: The Politics of Representation in North-South Relations* (Minneapolis: University of Minnesota Press, 1996).

21. See similarly Marie-Laure Ryan, "Toward a Definition of Narrative," in *The Cambridge Companion to Narrative*, ed. David Herman (Cambridge: Cambridge University Press, 2007), 25; Tine Hanrieder, "The False Promise of the Better Argument," *International Theory* 3, no. 3 (November 2011): 409–10. On pragmatism and international relations, see Gunther Hellmann, "Pragmatism and International Relations," *International Studies Review* 11, no. 3 (September 2009): 638–62; Jörg Friedrichs and Friedrich Kratochwil, "On Acting and Knowing: How Pragmatism Can Advance International Relations Research and Methodology," *International Organization* 63, no. 4 (Fall 2009): 701–31.

22. Ann Swidler, "Culture in Action," *American Sociological Review* 51, no. 2 (April 1986): 273–86.

23. Robert Jervis, *The Logic of Images in International Relations*, Morningside ed. (New York: Columbia University Press, 1989 [1970]).

24. For related supportive evidence, see Stephen C. Nelson, "Playing Favorites: How Shared Beliefs Shape the IMF's Lending Decisions," *International Organization* 68, no. 2 (May 2014): 297–328.

25. Thomas Risse, "'Let's Argue!': Communicative Action in World Politics," *International Organization* 54, no. 1 (Winter 2000): 1–39; Harald Müller, "International Relations as Communicative Action," in *Constructing International Relations: The Next Generation*, ed. Karin M. Fierke and Knud Erik Jorgensen (Armonk, NY: M. E. Sharpe, 2001); Marc Lynch, "Why Engage? China and the Logic of Communicative Engagement," *European Journal of International Relations* 8, no. 2 (June 2002): 187–230. On the centrality of persuasion to much constructivist international relations scholarship, see Crawford, *Argument and Change*; Martha Finnemore, *National Interests in International Society* (Ithaca, NY: Cornell University Press, 1996), 141; Martha Finnemore and Kathryn Sikkink, "International Norm Dynamics and Political Change," *International Organization* 52, no. 4 (Fall 1998): 914; Rodger A. Payne, "Persuasion, Frames and Norm Construction," *European Journal of International Relations* 7, no. 1 (March 2001): 37–61.

26. Hanrieder, "The False Promise of the Better Argument."

27. Bryan Garsten, *Saving Persuasion: A Defense of Rhetoric and Judgment* (Cambridge, MA: Harvard University Press, 2006), 5. See also Clark, *Legitimacy in International Society*, 254.

28. Iver B. Neumann, "Returning Practice to the Linguistic Turn: The Case of Diplomacy," *Millennium: Journal of International Studies* 31, no. 3 (July 2002): 629.

29. Janice Bially Mattern, "The Concept of Power and the (Un)Discipline of

International Relations," in *The Oxford Handbook of International Relations*, ed. Christian Reus-Smit and Duncan Snidal (Oxford: Oxford University Press, 2009), 691–98.

30. Hans Morgenthau, *Politics Among Nations: The Struggle for Power and Peace*, 2nd ed. (New York: Knopf, 1954), 61–63.

31. Charles Tilly, *Coercion, Capital, and European States, AD 990–1992* (Cambridge: Blackwell, 1992); Tilly, The Emergence of Citizenship in France and Elsewhere, *International Review of Social History* 40, supplement 3 (1995): 223–36. See also Stephen Holmes, "Lineages of the Rule of Law," in *Democracy and the Rule of Law*, ed. José María Maravall and Adam Przeworski (Cambridge: Cambridge University Press, 2003), 19–61.

32. Jennifer Mitzen, *Power in Concert: The Nineteenth-Century Origins of Global Governance* (Chicago: University of Chicago Press, 2013); Mitzen, "Illusion or Intention? Talking Grand Strategy into Existence," *Security Studies* 24, no. 1 (Jan.–March 2015), 61–94.

33. Thomas Risse-Kappen, *Cooperation Among Democracies: The European Influence on U.S. Foreign Policy* (Princeton, NJ: Princeton University Press, 1995).

34. On the mechanism of rhetorical coercion, see Ronald R. Krebs and Patrick T. Jackson, "Twisting Tongues and Twisting Arms: The Power of Political Rhetoric," *European Journal of International Relations* 13, no. 1 (March 2007): 35–66; and Ronald R. Krebs, *Fighting for Rights: Military Service and the Politics of Citizenship* (Ithaca, NY: Cornell University Press, 2006); Stacie E. Goddard, "When Right Makes Might: How Prussia Overturned the Balance of Power," *International Security* 33, no. 3 (Winter 2008/2009): 110–42.

35. A wide range of scholarly traditions, despite differences in epistemological orientation and substantive concern, recognizes that some premises are unquestioned and strike participants and observers as common sense but are actually the product of human agency. See, among many others, Schattschneider's classic insights into agenda setting, sociological accounts of political competition over the "definition of the situation," Barthes's efforts to demystify the naturalness that seemed to surround social myths, Bourdieu's *habitus* that structures the everyday cultural forms through which subjects express themselves, Laclau's writings on the establishment and disruption of *doxa*, and Foucault's genealogies of institutional and disciplinary discourses.

36. We have done so with respect to legitimation and grand strategy in Goddard and Krebs, "Rhetoric, Legitimation, and Grand Strategy."

37. Michael C. Williams, "Words, Images, Enemies: Securitization and International Politics," *International Studies Quarterly* 47, no. 4 (December 2003): 514.

38. In his seminal theory of speech acts, Austin pointed out, rightly, that some utterances—such as saying "I do" at a wedding or making a promise—were themselves actions, and he argued that the key to their productive effect was their conformity to linguistic rules. This has found its way into international relations via theories of securitization. See John L. Austin, *How To Do Things with Words*, 2nd ed. (Cambridge, MA: Harvard University Press, 1975). On securitization, see Barry Buzan et al., *Security: A New Framework for Analysis* (Boulder, CO: Lynne Rienner, 1998); Thierry Balzacq, ed., *Securitization Theory: How Security Problems Emerge and Dissolve* (Abingdon, UK: Routledge, 2011).

39. See, similarly, Holger Stritzel, "Towards a Theory of Securitization: Copenhagen and Beyond," *European Journal of International Relations* 13, no. 3 (September 2007): 357–83; Thierry Balzacq, "The Three Faces of Securitization: Political Agency, Audience and Context," *European Journal of International Relations* 11, no. 2 (June 2005): 171–201.

40. For exploration of these dynamics, see Ronald R. Krebs, *Narrative and the Making of U.S. National Security* (Cambridge: Cambridge University Press, 2015); Krebs, "How Dominant Narratives Rise and Fall: Military Conflict, Politics, and the Cold War Consensus," *International Organization* 69, no. 4 (Fall 2015): 809–45; Krebs, "Tell Me a Story: FDR, Narrative, and the Making of the Second World War," *Security Studies* 24, no. 1 (January–March 2015): 131–70; Stacie E. Goddard, *When Right Makes Might: Rising Powers and World Order* (Ithaca, NY: Cornell University Press, forthcoming).

41. For preliminary efforts along these lines, see Ronald R. Krebs, "Pity the President," *The National Interest* 148 (March/April 2017): 34–42; and Krebs, "The Politics of National Security," in *The Oxford Handbook of International Security*, ed. Alexandra Gheciu and William C. Wohlforth (Oxford: Oxford University Press, 2018), 259–73.

SIX

The Power of Prejudice

The Race Gap in Constructivist International
Relations Scholarship

Audie Klotz

Nearly two decades ago, Locher and Prügl (2001) diagnosed a serious gender gap in constructivist international relations (IR). Pointing to decades of feminist research that had already thoroughly probed diverse issues surrounding social construction as an ontological and epistemological framework, their article supplemented Tickner's (1992) trenchant critique of mainstream paradigms for ignoring feminist insights. They also viewed the rising salience of constructivism within IR as a new opportunity for more balanced dialogue that merited pursuit (Locher and Prügl 2001, 112–13).[1] Unfortunately, that potential for bridge building has yet to be fully realized, even though including a separate chapter on gender or feminism has become convention in most constructivist-friendly efforts to define the discipline (e.g., Carlsnaes, Risse, and Simmons 2002; Barnett and Duvall 2005; Dunne, Kirke, and Smith 2007; Reus-Smit and Snidal 2008).

An even bigger gap—also with unrealized potential for dialogue— exists for race, which has received minimal attention even in constructivist analyses and nary a mention in those same volumes seeking to survey the whole field.[2] Indeed, many scholars of what is now called the Global South simply abandoned IR as a field many decades ago, precisely because of its perceived conceptual irrelevance (Inayatullah and Blaney 2004). In contrast, Doty (1993, 1996) drew explicit attention to race from a postcolonial perspective, while other scholars with similar concerns were shunted aside into marginalized fields such as development studies. With the subsequent mainstreaming of constructivist and critical theories, more scholars have raised concerns about biases and blind spots (e.g., contributors to Anievas, Manchada, and Shilliam 2015). Yet no one to my knowledge has undertaken a thorough critique regarding the race gap in IR theory, comparable to Tickner (1992) on gender.

In this chapter, I take up only one aspect of this challenge by exploring the race gap specifically within constructivist IR. First, I discuss what it even means to have such a gap, empirically and epistemologically. Along the way, I challenge the common conflation of constructivism and liberalism. Then, to illustrate some promising avenues for research, I build on a smattering of exemplary works that have pushed constructivism to be more thoroughly constructivist in its two core areas: norm diffusion and state identity. Finally, I underscore potential synergies that might push constructivists within IR to be more innovative.

Why These Gaps Matter

Based on decades of constructivist theorizing and detailed analyses, the gender literature helps us to avoid reinventing the wheel in discussions of race, starting with the basic distinction between empirical and epistemological gaps. On the empirical side, overcoming omitted variable bias by adding gender—often called the "add women and stir" approach—accepts the epistemological assumptions that underpin hypothesis-testing research. In this empirical sense, more and more studies within IR, constructivist or not, have been incorporating gender. Goldstein's *War and Gender* (2001) is perhaps the most extensive testing of gender-based hypotheses, but it is hardly the only example (Peterson and Runyon 1993).

Analyses of race in IR, albeit fewer in number, have an equivalent of "add women and stir." A few mainstream researchers did take up race issues in the late 1960s (Doty 1993, 445–48). For instance, Rosenau (1970) made suggestions for race-based variables that could fit into standard comparative foreign policy frameworks. Yet that agenda did not make lasting inroads, perhaps because many of these efforts reflected foreign policy issues of the day, or perhaps due to the difficulty of reducing race to variables (Rosenau 1970, 61; Doty 1993, 446). I also would place my work on antiapartheid sanctions in this category. Although I eschewed terminology of variables and hypotheses, I distinguished between three identities (global, imperial, and African) in order to gauge variation in multilateral settings (Klotz 1995, 27–31, 35). And at other times, I held each of these identities constant in order to distinguish between multilateral and bilateral relationships (Klotz 1995, 32–35).

While I still do not go so far as to say that variables such as norms or identity need to be measured, I do not reject outright the notion that some quantitative proxies, with appropriate caveats, might be useful. Kratochwil and Ruggie (1986, 767) rightly pointed out in their influential critique of 1980s regime theory that norms cannot be falsified. Although failing to engage their concerns directly, Goertz and Diehl (1992, 638) did make a reasonable claim in setting up a quantitative analysis that norm-driven (or inspired or constrained, call it what you want) behavior ought to exhibit fairly high consistency. Their caveats, echoing constructivist concerns, included the need for understanding context and history (Goertz and Diehl 1992, 645).

Kratochwil and Ruggie (1986, 768) also underscored that responses to norm violation are a crucial component of comprehending the norm, as well as its strength. Similarly, Goertz and Diehl (1992, 638, 646, 654) concentrated on sanctions as just one indicator of a response to norm violation. I leave aside any debate over their specific study of decolonization except to note its disappointing lack of engagement with the trajectory of (anti-)racism as a possible explanatory factor (Goertz and Diehl 1992, 647, 652, 660; cf. Crawford 2002). Obviously I agree about the relevance of sanctions for gauging the meaning and strength of an international norm (Klotz 1995, 14).

My point is not that adopting any particular methodologies would suddenly transform constructivism into an approach that thoroughly incorporates gender or race, but rather that some techniques are well-suited to probing process-oriented claims. For example, Hoffmann (2005, 55–56) employed agent-based modeling to experiment with dynamics of norm diffusion as a complement to a traditional qualitative case-study analysis and other methods. Also using agent-based modeling, Rousseau (2006, 121–22) compared realist, liberal, and constructivist claims about identity in foreign policy, triangulating his claims using additional tools. The lesson is simply that methodologies are not to blame for the dearth of gender and race in IR scholarship. Having or not having variables, quantifying or not quantifying, are not the crucial choices.

A stronger criticism arises from another strand of feminist analysis, sometimes called standpoint theory, which points to limitations in variable-testing social science. The commonplace distinction between conventional and critical constructivism in IR follows a similar trajectory (Price and Reus-Smit 1998). In this vein, Locher and Prügl emphasize how gender highlights aspects of power that constructivists in IR typically overlook. Specifically, they assert that "constructivists lack the tools to explain how gender and power reproduce, how and why certain constructs emerge as more influential than others" (Locher and Prügl 2001, 113). Doty (1993, 448–50) makes a similar claim in her call for greater attention to representations of identity and difference, warning in particular against naturalizing race into a politically neutral concept.

Yet analyses that *overlook* a focus of inquiry do not necessarily *lack tools*. As was widely acknowledged even back when Locher and Prügl wrote their article, the primary problem is that typical variable analysis is not well-suited to capturing recursive relationships (Goertz and Diehl 1992, 646, 656; Guzzini 2000, 149–50; Finnemore and Sikkink 2001, 400; Cederman and Daase 2003, 6–7). In contrast, Guzzini explicitly tackled some of these barriers by placing the concept of power front and center in defining a constructivist approach. Specifically, he characterized constructivism as a perspective that concentrates on the reflexive relationship between historically embedded knowledge and social reality, where "institutional facts" are the focal point of analysis (Guzzini 2000, 150, 160; Guzzini 2005, 496, 507).

Consequently, acceptable muses for constructivists vary from Weber or Searle to Foucault or Bourdieu—but not Derrida (cf., Doty 1993, 1996; Zehfuss 2002)—with corresponding "institutional facts" ranging from bureaucracies, speech acts, discourses, or practices (Finnemore and Sikkink 2001, 395; Ackerly, Stern, and True 2006; Klotz and Prakash 2008; Lynch 2014, 4–6). Yet even such an embarrassment of riches at our analytical disposal does not resolve the challenges of designing research to capture recursive relationships without depoliticizing gender or race. Bracketing strategies and process tracing of feedback loops are typically employed, each of which exhibits distinctive strengths and weaknesses.

Therefore, I rephrase Locher and Prügl's critique into a question: *How can analysts conceptualize power in ways that better grasp the inherently recursive nature of racial dynamics?*

A huge hurdle is that most contemporary IR theories, including constructivism, suffer from what Vitalis (2000, 333), drawing on the renowned novelist Toni Morrison, calls the "norm against noticing." His point is subtly distinct from a charge of simply ignoring race. Although historical retrospectives have no trouble finding evidence of racism in theorizing as well as in practice (e.g., Vitalis 2005, 2015; Lake and Reynolds 2008; Hobson 2012; Klotz 2017), the contemporary literature treats that racist past as past. With rare exceptions (e.g., Klotz 1995; Vucetic 2011), IR treats American hegemony since 1945 as the launch of a new era of democracy and human rights, even though its race politics clearly tell a different story (e.g., Doty 1996; von Eschen 1997; Layton 2000; King and Smith 2005; Fitzgerald and Cook-Martín 2014; Jung 2015). In essence, the whole field of IR, including most of constructivism, actively *denies* the salience of race, rather than passively ignoring it (Henderson 2015a).

One of the most ambitious attempts to counter this silence is Hobson's magisterial survey of Eurocentrism in IR theories across the past two centuries. He uses this expansive term to mean a "polymorphous, multivalent discourse" based on assumptions that diminish the role of people outside of the "West" (Hobson 2012, 1). In particular, Hobson seeks to disentangle Eurocentrism and imperialism, which he argues have been inappropriately conflated by postcolonial theorists (2012, 3–5). To do so, he categorizes scholars, public intellectuals, and politicians within complex typologies and flowcharts to track their innumerable similarities and differences (e.g., Hobson 2012, 260, 314).

Any sweeping analysis inevitably overstates its case, and Hobson's is no exception. Once he distinguishes between so-called manifest and subliminal Eurocentrism, almost anything can then be tarred. And pervasive terminological ambiguities prove problematic. For instance, he uses but never defines Eurocentric institutionalism, even though the term implies causal connections between the past and present. Furthermore, Hobson sometimes conflates or concatenates racism and Eurocentrism, while at other times he makes a point to isolate scientific racism as a separate strand that sometimes intersects with Eurocentrism. By the end, Hobson (2012, 344) merely concludes that IR theory is not as value-free as many epistemologically mainstream proponents argue, an obvious point to any constructivist.

Unfortunately, Hobson leaves us with little advice on how to avoid Eurocentrism, especially its insidious subliminal variant, because he fails to engage contributions (constructivist or otherwise) that do offer alternative exemplars. Indeed, Hobson's discussion of constructivism is woefully inadequate. In a mere three pages, he simply highlights how some contemporary constructivist-liberal analysts replicate nineteenth-century hierarchies, minus racist language (Hobson 2012, 302–4).[3] In contrast, he could have discussed how Crawford (1994) integrated indigenous practices into her critique of collective security. More recently, Lightfoot (2016) has placed indigenous perspectives into major theoretical and methodological debates. Also drawing on experiences of people on the presumed periphery,

I have used migration history to subvert embedded Eurocentrism in the "security communities" literature (Klotz 2012, 100).

Although Hobson replicates a common—debated—conflation of constructivism with liberalism (e.g., Barkin 2003; Steele 2007), its liberal variants do merit greater scrutiny. In particular, the human rights literature offers many examples of the norm against noticing race, even as gender analysis has made inroads. Notably, Risse, Ropp, and Sikkink organized *The Persistent Power of Human Rights* (2013) thematically, with a chapter related to gender but nothing on race. That omission is especially striking given Black's chapter on apartheid South Africa in their iconic first volume, *The Power of Human Rights* (Black 1999; Risse, Ropp, and Sikkink 1999). Similarly, Simmons' award-winning *Mobilizing for Human Rights* (2009), while exemplary for its high-profile inclusion of both women and children, pays little attention to race.

Given liberalism's privileging of ideational factors, and given the extent to which an ancient "realism versus idealism" framing of the field still lingers, constructivists routinely but unfairly get derided for concentrating on "good" causes (Finnemore and Sikkink 2001, 403–4). Nothing inherent in the constructivist theoretical toolkit precludes attention to "bad" ideas. After all, in the nineteenth century, white supremacy was widely accepted as a norm, the "good" foundation of British liberal hegemony (Vitalis 2000, 332, 337–38; Lake and Reynolds 2008; Vucetic 2011, chap. 2; Klotz 2013, chap. 2). And bureaucracies can have a range of effects, not always the diffusion of "good" policies (Barnett and Finnemore 2004).

In sum: taking race seriously requires significant conceptual shifts. Thus far, much of constructivism in IR has reinvented insights that feminists and postcolonial scholars already have debated extensively. One result of this missed engagement has been insufficient attention to major problems that result from grafting constructivist IR onto existing interparadigm debates. The key is to replace easy dichotomies with multivalent hierarchies. In the following two sections, I illustrate with exemplars of recent research in norm diffusion and state identity.

Norm Diffusion

Constructivists made their first inroads into the field of IR by challenging dominant materialist assumptions. Notably, Ruggie's (1986) response to neorealism served as a call to action, because he hammered home that a seemingly unassailable set of assumptions about both the international system and the very nature of social research were severely limiting, conceptually and historically. Thus, initially, attention to institutions and processes of institutionalization retained a structural focus. By grafting onto state-centric notions of an anarchical society, for instance, Reus-Smit (1999) concentrated on demonstrating the sociohistorical origins of state sovereignty as a foundational principle. In keeping with an interparadigm framework of debate, and its straitjacket of Eurocentric assumptions, much of what would later be categorized as conventional constructivism missed opportunities to push deeper on the nature of the state (cf. Cooper 2005).

Only recently has a growing literature challenged more fundamentally the myth of Westphalia and other Eurocentric staples (e.g., Branch 2014; Glanville 2014; Lightfoot 2016). These more nuanced histories also open up analytical space to recognize multiple layers of institutionalization, which is essential for comprehending legacies of racism. Once again, parallels with gender analysis help, as both the field of IR generally and constructivism specifically are catching up in their recognition of hierarchies. For example, Towns (2010: 24) challenged the presumption that normative change starts with the great powers and then diffuses (with or without adaptation) to the periphery by showing that women's suffrage initially advanced at the turn of the twentieth century in the semi-periphery: New Zealand, Australia, Finland, and Norway. The putative liberal leaders, the United States and Britain, did not adopt universal franchise until the early 1920s, along with many other European countries, followed by another wave in the 1930s that included Latin America. Only once decolonization took hold after 1945 was female franchise taken for granted, even while women in leadership roles have lagged (Towns 2010, table 5.1).

Still, despite wide-ranging scope and refreshing insights, even Towns did not overcome the implicit racial hierarchy embedded in IR theories. For instance, the story of women's right to vote in South Africa tells a more complicated story where gender and race are intricately intertwined. First, at the conclusion of the Boer War in 1902, negotiators rejected the Australian model, which included female franchise, because it would have complicated the already tendentious issues surrounding Anglo versus Afrikaner (white male) representation. At Union in 1909, negotiators again rejected female franchise, since it would complicate disagreements about whether to extend the Cape system of educational and financial qualifications. In 1930, the government finally agreed to include women at the polls, not as a matter of principle but as a way to reduce the salience of an already small African electorate (Walker 1990, 314). Not surprisingly, the place of women remained contested in South Africa throughout the next six decades, until the adoption of universal suffrage in 1994 (Seidman 1993).

While the intersection of race and gender may be exceptionally visible in those South African debates, similar dynamics are equally relevant in Australia, one of Towns' major innovators. There, the popular aim to exclude Asian migrants was one of the key concerns that bolstered arguments for enfranchising women (Lake and Reynolds 2008, 35–36; Klotz 2012, 81–82; Klotz 2013, 236–37). Thus racial solidarity again trumped gender hierarchy, even though the policy outcome was exactly the opposite in South Africa.

Although friendly in intent, these criticisms harbor serious analytical implications. For Towns to describe Australia as on the "outskirts" of civilization is an empirical overstatement, when its representatives routinely attended influential imperial conferences. Crucial issues at stake ranged from citizenship policies to military strategy. Indeed to label Australia a "state" is inappropriate, because it was a self-governing colony within the British Empire. As such, it enjoyed relative autonomy in domestic politics but not foreign affairs. Crucially, London retained the power to declare war on behalf of the empire, which obligated the Dominions, including Australia as well as India and the other colonies, to participate. This anomalous situation provides just one illustration of a fundamentally hierarchical nineteenth-century international system that bears little resemblance to a theoretical assumption of anarchy.

Further scrutiny of Britain—the putative liberal hegemon—demonstrates why race should be taken more seriously, historically and analytically. For example, much ink has been spilled on the topic of democratic peace theory, but few attempt to test race-based variables. In particular, both Lemke (2003) and Henderson (2015b) have criticized the failure of democratic peace theorists to explain the prevalence of peaceful dyads on the African continent. Instead, the traditional democratic peace narrative typically starts with the American Revolutionary War, despite the presence of slavery and the absence of universal suffrage. In response to criticism about discounting slavery and other limits on electoral participation, some analysts have claimed that institutions, such as freedom of speech and competitive elections, should instead be the defining standard of a democratic regime.

Still, the historical narrative quickly runs into trouble as early as the War of 1812, since both Britain and the United States were arguably democracies. One escape route, employed by Owen, was to concentrate on perceptions, specifically skepticism in the United States about the democratic qualities of the British monarchy (Owen 1994, 90, 97, 108–10). But at what point did the monarchy in Britain no longer preclude its being a democracy in American eyes? Unintentionally illustrating the difficulties of pinning down any consensus in elite perceptions, Owen suggests either the 1860s (1994, 104, 111) or the 1890s (1994, 114–15). On the flip side, during the Civil War, did Britain perceive either the Union (which employed wartime limits on some civil liberties) or the Confederacy (unabashedly defending slavery) as democracies? Even within the cabinet, views differed sharply.[4]

And what about overlooked Canada, location of many battles?[5] In 1774, London granted Catholics a range of civil rights that they did not yet enjoy elsewhere in the empire. Then violent unrest in the 1840s led London to grant Canadians unprecedented legislative powers, again wider than what were enjoyed by imperial subjects anywhere else. Apparently, London was dragged into deepening democracy, in contrast to its presentation in IR theories as an exporter of liberalism (but consistent with the stress Towns places on normative innovations originating from outside the core). This alternative imperial storyline is familiar to those who have followed British colonial policy, among the Dominions and beyond. Yet these tend to be precisely postcolonial theorists, who have typically been marginalized by the mainstream, including by constructivists.

A similar conclusion emerges from closer consideration of race within the United States. Long after the Civil War, legacies of slavery continued to affect US institutions, including Congress and the bureaucracy (King and Smith 2005, 84–89). For instance, during the so-called Jim Crow era, President Woodrow Wilson, renowned liberal internationalist, extended segregation within the federal government. And a century of exclusionary immigration policies kept out many darker-skinned people until the 1960s. Indeed, the gap between the analysis of contemporary American foreign policy, which ignores race, and the subfield of American Political Development, which confronts race, is striking. Even constructivists, generally attuned to historical context, remain surprisingly silent on such obvious race issues.

State Identity

Constructivists do have the tools to break this silence. In particular, the concept of state identity positions them to take more seriously the role of race. Following Wendt (1992, 1994), constructivism distinguishes two components of state identity: social and corporate. The bulk of the literature, however, concentrates on social identities as variable while treating corporate identities as constant (Wendt 1994, 385). Unfortunately, this bracketing is precisely how many of the most profound effects of race get sidelined (Sampson 2002). Instead, corporate identity can and should be more thoroughly analyzed. Once again, I will illustrate with the democratic peace debate.

The first step is to disentangle constructivist from liberal versions of ideational arguments. For example, in assessing the democratic peace debate, Vucetic (2011, 140–42) makes the key distinction between racial identity (constructivist) and regime type (liberal) as the driving causal force. And in contrast to Rosenau (1970), who asked how individual attitudes and domestic tensions might affect interstate conflicts, Vucetic (2011, 140) allows for racial solidarity to further cooperation. Empirically, the centerpiece of his analysis is the so-called Anglosphere: the United States, Britain, Australia, and Canada.

To trace the evolution of Anglo-American strategic ties over the past century, Vucetic maps out a three-step methodological strategy to tease apart conventional wisdoms of the time from specific policy decisions. Admittedly, this bracketing approach might draw criticism for underemphasizing the recursive dynamics that link social discourse and individual beliefs. But for understanding race, which is often implicit in the policy-making phase, the benefits outweigh the limitations. In particular, Vucetic shows the transformation of race-based arguments into cultural or ethnic terminology as the larger sociopolitical context shifts. This tendency to couch racial claims in cultural terms is also evident, he notes, in contemporary debates over multiculturalism (Vucetic 2011, 132).

Unlike Towns, Vucetic places British imperial networks at the center of his analysis. Yet he too overlooks the significance of South Africa within this cluster, both historically and analytically. Ironically, he thereby naturalizes a partial reading of the very white solidarity that he aims to de-naturalize. By accepting without question post-1945 marginalization of South Africa within the Anglosphere, he erases its significance in the previous period. For example, treating the Boer War of 1899–1902 as merely a shadow case in his analysis of Venezuela and Anglo-American rapprochement (2011, 39–42) overlooks the Cape's ontological significance as part of the empire rather than merely a distant arena of potential rivalry. Indeed the Boer War shaped the very nature of Anglo-imperial identity, with long-lasting implications for British foreign relations (Klotz 2012, 86–91).

This friendly critique demonstrates the value of employing race as a distinctive lens through which we can reread diplomatic history. Similarly, two studies (paired in a recent issue of *Security Studies*) have paid closer attention to Japan in the interwar period, and each offers additional conceptual tools. Búzás (2013) links race to threat perception. Specifically, he argues that racial similarities deflate perceptions of threat, and vice versa. Drawing on a mix of psychological and sociological theories, Ward (2013, 615–18) makes a parallel argument that perceptions of status, and not solely capabilities or cost-benefit calculations, affect the grand strategies of rising powers.

Their emphases on perception and related questions of how to scale up from the individual to collective mechanisms echo earlier liberal claims about the democratic peace, but concentrated on identity rather than ideology. While Búzás (2013, 579) draws on cognitive psychology and social cues as mechanisms, securitization theory offers a potentially complementary approach (e.g., Hayes 2009, 981; Ilgit and Klotz 2014). And, circling back to where I started with norm diffusion, Ward's (2013, 308) framework, which posits status immobility as one international variable driving demands for systemic reforms, might be applied to provide causal mechanisms for the largely descriptive claims that Towns has made about the gendered nature of hierarchy.

Analyzing state identity is neither a magic fix nor the sole solution to the silence that shrouds race in IR. All concepts privilege certain types of evidence and downplay others. What I have found most shocking over the years is the extent to which IR theories, constructivism included, have filtered out a wide swath of historical evidence that does not conform to state-centric premises. Fortunately, historians increasingly adopt global or transnational perspectives, which provide more secondary literature upon which IR scholars can rely. Eurocentrism, racism, and other forms of prejudice will not be toppled quickly, but I am reassured that diverse perspectives are gradually gaining more attention and, occasionally, even accolades.

Future Pathways

In the 1980s, constructivism opened many possibilities for asking previously silenced questions, including those about gender, but over the years that momentum has tempered into a plethora of mundane studies. In a small way, I have tried in this chapter to rejuvenate that potential for generating path-breaking insights with two ambitious suggestions:

- IR must move beyond the interparadigm debates to topple the anarchy assumption and debunk the myth of Westphalia.
- IR must expand its historical scope to grasp patriarchal and paternalist parameters, even venturing to learn lessons from indigenous societies.

Finally, I would like to see the field, of which constructivism is now a major part, become more attuned to race gaps within academia. The recently publicized issue of a "gender citation gap" (Maliniak, Powers, and Walter 2013) is but one example of a pervasive problem. I suspect that a similar analysis of a diversity citation gap (admittedly much harder to do, without easy-to-code author names) would be even more depressing. Easier to achieve: each of us can become more mindful of what we cite in our writing and assign in our courses. Initiatives such as #womenalsoknow and #POCalsoknow offer essential resources and networking infrastructure to achieve these goals.

NOTES

1. Cf. Adler (1997, 332–33) who underscores division in order to map out a middle ground.

2. Among the surveys, Rupert 2005 (in Barnett and Duvall 2005) is notable for at least flagging the intersection of race and gender with class, his primary focus.

3. Vitalis (2000, 336–43) offers a more trenchant critique.

4. Owen (1994: 104, 111–13, 115) proclaims late 1862 as the turning point, a result of the Emancipation Proclamation.

5. How to define Canadian independence is a complicated question. Confederation occurred in 1867. The Dominions received substantial autonomy including foreign affairs in 1927, yet London retained the power to amend the Canadian constitution until 1982, and the monarchy remains the formal head of state.

REFERENCES

Ackerly, Brooke, Maria Stern, and Jacqui True, eds. 2006. *Feminist Methodologies for International Relations*. Cambridge: Cambridge University Press.

Adler, Emanuel. 1997. "Seizing the Middle Ground: Constructivism in World Politics." *European Journal of International Relations* 3, no. 3: 319–63.

Anievas, Alexander, Nivi Manchanda, and Robbie Shilliam. 2015. *Race and Racism in International Relations: Confronting the Global Colour Line*. London: Routledge.

Barkin, J. Samuel. 2003. "Realist-Constructivism." *International Studies Review* 5: 325–42.

Barnett, Michael, and Robert Duvall, eds. 2005. *Power in Global Governance*. Cambridge: Cambridge University Press.

Barnett, Michael, and Martha Finnemore. 2004. *Rules for the World: International Organizations in Global Politics*. Ithaca, NY: Cornell University Press.

Black, David. 1999. "The Long and Winding Road: International Norms and Domestic Political Change in South Africa." In *The Power of Human Rights: International Norms and Domestic Change*, edited by Thomas Risse, Stephen Ropp, and Kathryn Sikkink, 78–108. Cambridge: Cambridge University Press.

Branch, Jordan. 2014. *The Cartographic State: Maps, Territory and the Origins of Sovereignty*. Cambridge: Cambridge University Press.

Búzás, Zoltán. 2013. "The Color of Threat: Race, Threat Perception, and the Demise of the Anglo-Japanese Alliance (1902–1923)." *Security Studies* 52: 573–606.

Carlsnaes, Walter, Thomas Risse, and Beth Simmons. 2002. *Handbook of International Relations*. Thousand Oaks, CA: Sage.

Cederman, Lars-Erik, and Christopher Daase. 2003. "Endogenizing Corporate Identities: The Next Step in Constructivist IR Theory." *European Journal of International Relations* 9, no. 1: 5–35.

Cooper, Frederick. 2005. "States, Empires, and Political Imagination." In *Colonialism in Question: Theory, Knowledge, History*. Berkeley: University of California Press.

Crawford, Neta. 1994. "A Security Regime among Democracies: Cooperation among Iroquois Nations." *International Organization* 48, no. 3: 345–85.

Crawford, Neta. 2002. *Argument and Change in World Politics: Ethics, Decolonization, and Humanitarian Intervention*. Cambridge: Cambridge University Press.

Doty, Roxanne. 1993. "The Bounds of 'Race' in International Relations." *Millennium* 22, no. 3: 443–61.

Doty, Roxanne. 1996. *Imperial Encounters: The Politics of Representation in North-South Relations*. Minneapolis: University of Minnesota Press.

Dunne, Tim, Milja Kurki, and Steve Smith. 2007. *International Relations Theories: Discipline and Diversity*. Oxford: Oxford University Press.

Finnemore, Martha, and Kathryn Sikkink. 2001. "Taking Stock: The Constructivist Research Program in International Relations and Comparative Politics." *Annual Review of Political Science* 4: 191–216.

Fitzgerald, David, and David Cook-Martín. 2014. *Culling the Masses: The Democratic Origins of Racist Immigration Policy in the Americas*. Cambridge, MA: Harvard University Press.

Glanville, Luke. 2014. *Sovereignty and the Responsibility to Protect: A New History*. Chicago: University of Chicago Press.

Goertz, Gary, and Paul Diehl. 1992. "Toward a Theory of International Norms." *Journal of Conflict Resolution* 36, no. 4: 634–64.

Goldstein, Joshua. 2001. *War and Gender: How Gender Shapes the War System and Vice Versa*. New York: Cambridge University Press.

Guzzini, Stefano. 2000. "A Reconstruction of Constructivism in International Relations." *European Journal of International Relations* 6, no. 2: 147–82.

Guzzini, Stefano. 2005. "The Concept of Power: A Constructivist Analysis." *Millennium* 33, no. 3: 495–521.

Hayes, Jarrod. 2009. "Identity and Securitization in the Democratic Peace: The United States and the Divergence of Response to India and Iran's Nuclear Programs." *International Studies Quarterly* 53: 977–99.

Henderson, Errol. 2015a. "Hidden in Plain Sight: Racism in International Relations Theory." In *Race and Racism in International Relations: Confronting the Global Colour Line*, edited by Alexander Anievas, Nivi Manchanda, and Robbie Shilliam, 19–43. London: Routledge.

Henderson, Errol. 2015b. *African Realism? International Relations Theory and Africa's Wars in the Postcolonial Era*. Lanham, MD: Rowman & Littlefield.

Hobson, John A. 2012. *The Eurocentric Conception of World Politics: Western International Theory, 1760–2010*. Cambridge: Cambridge University Press.

Hoffmann, Matthew. 2005. *Ozone Depletion and Climate Change: Constructing a Global Response*. Albany: State University of New York Press.

Ilgit, Asli, and Audie Klotz. 2014. "How Far Does Societal Security 'Travel'? Securitization in South African Immigration Policies." *Security Dialogue* 45, no. 2: 137–55.

Inayatullah, Naeem, and David Blaney. 2004. *International Relations and the Problem of Difference*. New York: Routledge.

Jung, Moon-Kie. 2015. *Beneath the Surface of White Supremacy: Denaturalizing U.S. Racisms Past and Present*. Stanford, CA: Stanford University Press.

King, Desmond, and Rogers Smith. 2005. "Racial Orders in American Political Development." *American Political Science Review* 99, no. 1: 75–92.

Klotz, Audie. 1995. *Norms in International Relations: The Struggle against Apartheid*. Ithaca, NY: Cornell University Press.

Klotz, Audie. 2012. "The Imperial Self: A Perspective on Anglo-America from South Africa, India, and Ireland." In *Anglo-America and Its Discontents: Civilizational Identities beyond East and West*, edited by Peter Katzenstein, 81–104. New York: Routledge.

Klotz, Audie. 2013. *Migration and National Identity in South Africa, 1860–2010*. New York: Cambridge University Press.

Klotz, Audie. 2017. "Racial Inequality." In *The Globalization of International Society*, edited by Tim Dunne and Christian Reus-Smit, 362–79. Oxford: Oxford University Press.

Klotz, Audie, and Deepa Prakash, eds. 2008. *Qualitative Methods in International Relations—A Pluralist Guide*. Basingstoke: Palgrave Macmillan.

Kratochwil, Friedrich, and John Gerard Ruggie. 1986. "International Organization: A State of the Art on an Art of the State." *International Organization* 40, no. 4: 753–75.

Lake, Marilyn and Henry Reynolds. 2008. *Drawing the Global Colour Line: White Men's Countries and the International Challenge of Racial Equality*. Cambridge: Cambridge University Press.

Layton, Azza. 2000. *International Politics and Civil Rights Policies in the United States, 1941–1960*. New York: Cambridge University Press.

Lemke, Douglas. 2003. "African Lessons for International Relations Research." *World Politics* 56: 114–38.

Lightfoot, Sheryl. 2016. *Global Indigenous Politics: A Subtle Revolution*. London: Routledge.

Locher, Birgit, and Elisabeth Prügl. 2001. "Feminism and Constructivism: Worlds Apart or Sharing the Middle Ground?" *International Studies Quarterly* 45, no. 1, 111–29.

Lynch, Cecelia. 2014. *Interpreting International Politics*. New York: Routledge).

Maliniak, Daniel, Ryan Powers, and Barbara Walter. 2013. "The Gender Citation Gap in International Relations." *International Organization* 67, no. 4: 889–922.

Owen, John. 1994. "How Liberalism Produces Democratic Peace." *International Security* 19, no. 2: 87–125.

Peterson, V. Spike, and Anne Sisson Runyan. 1993. *Global Gender Issues*. Boulder, CO: Westview Press.

Price, Richard, and Christian Reus-Smit. 1998. "Dangerous Liaisons? Critical International Relations Theory and Constructivism." *European Journal of International Relations* 4, no. 3: 259–94.

Reus-Smit, Christian. 1999. *Moral Purpose of the State: Culture, Social Identity and Institutional Rationality in International Relations*. Princeton, NJ: Princeton University Press.

Reus-Smit, Christian, and Duncan Snidal, eds. 2008. *The Oxford Handbook of International Relations*. Oxford: Oxford University Press.

Risse, Thomas, Stephen Ropp, and Kathryn Sikkink. 1999. *The Power of Human Rights: International Norms and Domestic Change*. Cambridge: Cambridge University Press.

Risse, Thomas, Stephen Ropp, and Kathryn Sikkink. 2013. *The Persistent Power of Human Rights: From Commitment to Compliance*. Cambridge: Cambridge University Press.

Rosenau, James. 1970. "Race in International Relations: A Dialogue in Five Parts." In *Race Among Nations: A Conceptual Approach*, edited by George Shepherd Jr. and Tilden LeMelle, 61–122. Lexington, MA: Heath Lexington.

Rousseau, David. 2006. *Identifying Threats and Threatening Identities: The Social Construction of Realism and Liberalism*. Stanford, CA: Stanford University Press.

Ruggie, John Gerard. 1986. "Continuity and Transformation in the World Polity: Toward a Neorealist Synthesis." In *Neorealism and Its Critics*, edited by Robert Keohane, 131–57. New York: Columbia University Press.

Rupert, Mark. 2005. "Class Powers and the Politics of Global Governance." In *Power in Global Governance*, edited by Michael Barnett and Robert Duvall, 205–28. Cambridge: Cambridge University Press.

Sampson, Aaron. 2002. "Tropical Anarchy: Waltz, Wendt, and the Way We Imagine International Politics." *Alternatives* 27, no. 4: 429–57.

Seidman, Gay. 1993. "'No Freedom without the Women': Mobilization and Gender in South Africa, 1970–1992." *Signs: Journal of Women in Culture and Society* 18, no. 2: 291–320.

Simmons, Beth. 2009. *Mobilizing for Human Rights: International Law in Domestic Politics*. New York: Cambridge University Press.

Steele, Brent. 2007. "Liberal-Idealism: A Constructivist Critique." *International Studies Review* 9: 23–52.

Tickner, J. Ann. 1992. *Gender in International Relations: Feminist Perspectives on Achieving Global Security*. New York: Columbia University Press.

Towns, Ann. 2010. *Women and States: Norms and Hierarchies in International Society*. New York: Cambridge University Press).

Vitalis, Robert. 2005. "Birth of a Discipline." In *Imperialism and Internationalism in the Discipline of International Relations*, edited by David Long and Brian Schmidt, 159–81. Albany: State University of New York Press.

Vitalis, Robert. 2000. "The Graceful and Generous Liberal Gesture: Making Racism Invisible in American International Relations." *Millennium* 29, no. 2: 331–56.

Vitalis, Robert. 2015. *White World Order, Black Power Politics: The Birth of American International Relations.* Ithaca, NY: Cornell University Press.

Von Eschen, Penny. 1997. *Race Against Empire: Black Americans and Anti-colonialism, 1937–1957.* Ithaca, NY: Cornell University Press.

Vucetic, Srdjan. 2011. *The Anglosphere: A Genealogy of a Racialized Identity in International Relations.* Stanford, CA: Stanford University Press.

Walker, Cherryl. 1990. "The Women's Suffrage Movement: The Politics of Gender, Race and Class." In *Women and Gender in Southern Africa to 1945,* edited by Cherryl Walker, 315–45. Cape Town: David Philip.

Ward, Steven. 2013. Race, Status, and Japanese Revisionism in the Early 1930s. *Security Studies* 22: 607–39.

Wendt, Alexander. 1992. "Anarchy Is What States Make of It." *International Organization* 46, no. 2: 391–425.

Wendt, Alexander. 1994. "Collective Identity Formation and the International State." *American Political Science Review* 88, no. 2: 384–96.

Zehfuss, Maja. 2002. *Constructivism in International Relations: The Politics of Reality.* Cambridge: Cambridge University Press.

SEVEN

Technology and Constructivism

Interrogating the Material-Ideational Divide

Jordan Branch

Constructivism in international relations (IR) originated out of many strands of theorizing about international politics, but one of the most central was a shared emphasis on ideational factors, in opposition to the then-dominant focus on material interests and drivers (in theories such as structural realism or neoliberal institutionalism). Ideas, it was argued, matter as much as—or perhaps more than—material power capabilities or economic interests. Since then, the material-ideational relationship has been interrogated extensively, by constructivist IR scholars and by others outside of this tradition. This occurs both in terms of suggesting different interpretations of the relationship between the two and by questioning the dichotomy as a useful framing to begin with. Yet the tension between material and ideational factors remains an important touchstone in how we think about explaining and understanding the processes and outcomes of international politics, thanks largely to the emphasis placed on it by early constructivist theorizing.

This chapter examines the material-ideational intersection, and how it has informed constructivist IR scholarship, by focusing on one empirical domain: technology and technological change. Technologies are unquestionably central to international politics, from weapons systems to communication capabilities. Moreover, because they are created artifacts, technologies are material, but they are also socially constructed by the ideas that give them meaning. This dual nature makes technology a useful lens for thinking about what constructivism has contributed to our understanding of international politics.

In this chapter's first section, I briefly review how constructivism has approached the ideational-material divide, noting in particular the way this dichotomy has been framed—and critiqued—in constructivist scholarship. The next section considers the role of technology and technological change, first in IR scholarship in general and then in constructivism specifically. How have constructivist theories approached technology and technological change? What is revealed by empirical constructivist IR studies that have incorporated technology as a major component of their arguments? The third section then brings to bear arguments from science and technology studies (STS), a field outside of IR that has specifically dealt with the complex relationship between technological change and social and political processes. Applying insights from STS gives us some new ways to think about the role of technology in international politics and the implications of that role for the material-ideational division. Finally, the conclusion builds on these points to suggest new theoretical, empirical, and methodological areas for constructivist IR scholarship on technology, technological change, and the material-ideational intersection.

The Material and the Ideational in Constructivism

The various strands of constructivist IR do share certain common features, but they also disagree on a wide range of theoretical and methodological points. This results from the way in which constructivism is not a theory of politics, like realism or Marxism, but a broader approach or "social theory." As Guzzini notes, constructivist scholarship can be framed in terms of both epistemological and ontological features, focusing on the social construction of knowledge and of social reality, respectively.[1] Part of that ontological commitment to the socially constructed nature of political life involves a broadly—though not universally—shared notion that ideas "matter" in some capacity for international outcomes.

Even on the issue of material versus ideational factors, however, there is no single view. As will be discussed below, a number of scholars also question the entire framing of ideational versus material as a dichotomy. Yet in what might be labeled "mainstream" constructivism,[2] there are relatively straightforward statements about this relationship. As one review essay argues, one of constructivism's central assertions is that "human interaction is shaped primarily by ideational factors, not simply material ones."[3] Combined with other key assumptions about the intersubjective nature of these norms and beliefs and the importance of identities, this view of the ideational nature of political structures and outcomes defines constructivism.

We can see this focus on demonstrating the importance of ideational factors in a variety of influential constructivist texts, many of which are explicitly oriented toward challenging the then dominant realist or neoliberal institutionalist analyses.[4] To take one specific example, consider Ruggie's reflections on the origins of statehood, the international system, and territoriality.[5] Part of his argument concerns the important, and distinct, impact of changing "social epistemes" alongside material and strategic drivers of state formation; on the effects of ideational factors, "the breadth and depth of these changes argue, at the very least, in favor of a relative autonomy for the realm of social epistemology."[6] Similarly, constructivist scholarship that has focused on the various effects of norms on international politics also builds on the notion that this category of ideas has an impact distinct from material forces.[7]

Perhaps the most influential single statement—or summary—of the mainstream constructivist approach is Wendt's *Social Theory of International Politics*.[8] This book argues that ideas give meaning to material facts, and those material facts on their own explain little of interest in international relations. Building on the tradition of scientific realism—the notion that the world exists out there, independent of our perceptions of it—Wendt argues for the reality of both material and social facts, including political institutions and structures such as the organization of the international system. Although this does support an emphasis on the ideational character of the international system, it also leads him to argue for a "rump materialism": ideas constitute interests and shape outcomes, but it is *not* "ideas all the way down." He sees "brute material forces" at the bottom, constraining and driving—but not necessarily determining—the ideational layers that do most of the work in his theory. This theory thus explicitly incorporates *both* ideational and material factors, but it does so in a specific way: at any given analytical or theoretical level, the emphasis is on either the material or the ideational.[9]

From the beginning, of course, constructivists and their critics have pointed out that the framing of ideational *versus* material can be problematic.[10] Early constructivist theory, in fact, did not make this distinction particularly central.[11] More recent work within or close to constructivism has continued to critique or rethink the ideational-material intersection, often by trying to bring them together as two simultaneous aspects of a single concept or framework, rather than in the one-layer-over-another from Wendt. For example, the application of the "logic of practice" to IR sees important processes and outcomes as practices, patterned performances that are both material and meaningful (i.e., ideational).[12] The logic of habit, likewise, combines material and ideational in a single framework.[13] Habits are background to purposive actions (whether those actions are carried out in terms of consequences or appropriateness), but they are unthinking and unreflective, so even if habits can be thought of as ideas, they are very different from the concept of norms in mainstream constructivism. Habit also suggests an additional means of connecting the material to IR decisions and outcomes: there is a material basis in neuroscience, since habits are "physiological features of the brain."[14] Finally, theorists continue to point out that material versus ideational is a "flawed dichotomy," since important IR outcomes (such as foreign policy decision making) are shaped by both material and ideational interests. What we need is a "hybrid explanation" rather than an effort to assert the dominance of one theory (realism versus constructivism, for example) or one category of driving factor (ideational versus material).[15] Maybe neither ideational nor material has to be treated as the foundation for the other.

Technology and (Constructivist) IR

One empirical domain that particularly demands hybrid explanations is the role of technology in international politics (technology understood broadly as the application of knowledge to specific practical purposes). Technologies and technological systems, in fact, are themselves both ideational and material, in two ways. First is that there are not only material technologies, such as mechanical tools, artifacts, and so on, but also what can be thought of as "social technologies," ideas about organization that similarly function as tools for achieving ends. In the military domain, for example, weapons technologies are material artifacts, but there are also organizational technologies, such as drilling procedures, tactical innovations, or even ideas like the *levée en masse*. Second is the way in which all technologies, even those involving material artifacts and their use, are simultaneously material and social; this is one of the important insights of the field of STS, discussed below.

Although technology is clearly seen as a central feature of international politics by most if not all mainstream IR theories, it has often been neglected as a distinct focus for study.[16] If technology is addressed at all, it has been incorporated as an exogenous driver of change or as an underlying condition for political action (although rarely in a purely deterministic way). As one of the few studies to focus explicitly on technology in IR notes, it is most useful to plot a middle course between technologies as deterministic and technologies purely as outcomes of social or political forces: "technologies have both social origins (constructionism) and social effects (determinism); are shaped by human intent and interest (constructionism) and resist such intentions (determinism)."[17]

How has technology been approached in explicitly constructivist IR theorizing and empirical studies?[18] In Wendt's constructivist theory of IR, technology is one of the three "brute material forces" at the foundation of his theory.[19] Moreover, although Wendt does acknowledge the role of ideas in creating technologies, his theory again separates out ideational and material aspects at different theoretical levels: a material technology "is created by purposeful agents and embodies the state of their technical knowledge (ideas) at that time. To be sure. But once in existence, a technological artifact has intrinsic material capacities."[20] More broadly, constructivist studies tend to acknowledge that ideational and material aspects exist simultaneously, but then a given study will privilege whichever side of the dichotomy is seen as fundamental to the overall theory. Thus Wendt highlights the material at the foundation, while more norm-focused constructivist scholars sometimes "underestimate material/structural variables and their constraints on human agency."[21]

While there are many examples of constructivist scholarship incorporating technological change, or even focusing directly on a technology, the following discussion looks in more detail at two illustrative examples: one military technology (nuclear weapons) and one communication technology (mapping). Tannenwald's research on the "nuclear taboo"—the norm favoring the nonuse of nuclear weapons—explicitly frames its argument as showing the importance of ideational rather than material drivers of foreign policy decision making.[22] Nuclear weapons came to be seen as a qualitatively different type of weapon, based not just on their material technology and destructive power but also on a norm that developed around them as being a particularly illegitimate weapon to use. In other words, a technology not only represented a new material capability but also was structured by norms surrounding it. Now this does not go so far as to say that the technology is entirely ideational, but it does point out how material "brute facts" are only given meaning and consequence by ideas. As Guzzini points out, "Constructivism does not deny the existence of a phenomenal world, external to thought. This is the world of brute (mainly natural) facts. It does oppose, and this is something different, that phenomena can constitute themselves as objects of knowledge independently of discursive practices."[23]

Another intersection between technological and political change, on which my research has focused, is the role played by mapping in the emergence of the territorial state in early modern Europe.[24] Mapping technologies played a key role in enabling and driving the assertion of boundary-defined territorial rule, eventually leading to the consolidation of the sovereign territorial state as we know it. Particularly in terms of the *territorial* nature of modern statehood, maps were an essential component in the complex process that constructed this particular form of political organization. In the ongoing constitutive relationship between actors' ideas about political rule and organization and their authoritative political practices—which put those ideas into action—techniques such as mapping served to shape and instantiate ideas about rule. Changes in those technologies were therefore constitutive of changes in political practices, while changing political ideas could also lead to new representations and new demands for technological capabilities, such as the interest in increasing cartographic coverage and accuracy by rulers as they tried to assert ever closer and more direct rule over their domains.

Comparing mapping as a contributing factor in the origins of territorial statehood to parts of Ruggie's argument about the transition to modernity,[25] we can see the benefits of focusing on a technology while simultaneously applying the constructivist insight that the international system is itself constituted by ideas. While Ruggie examines corollaries to sovereign statehood in visual arts (single-point perspective) and linguistic usage (the "I-form" in speech), bringing in a materially instantiated technology like mapping provides a mechanism to connect ideas to practices. These were artifacts, *things*, that were used by the actors whose ideas, behaviors, and interactions constituted political organization and rule, and whose changing practices led to the transformation to the modern state system. Yet this is not an example of the "rump materialism" discussed above; the technology was only consequential because of the uses it was put to and the ideas it supported, and its importance was further shaped by political goals.

Science and Technology Studies (STS) and Constructivist IR

Focusing on technology and technological change offers the opportunity to bring in some useful arguments and insights from the field of science and technology studies (STS), a relatively wide category of approaches sharing a few key characteristics.[26] For one, scientists and engineers are recognized to be members of communities, which shapes their actions and the technological or scientific outcomes of their work. Science and technology are actively constructed in a social process, in other words, but they are also materially present. The so-called "strong program" in STS also provided a methodological framework: first, be impartial about the truth or falsity of scientific theories (or the success or failure of technologies) and thus, symmetrically, apply the same arguments to both success and failures; and, second, be reflexive, applying the same methods to STS itself.

The benefits of bringing STS to bear on constructivist IR are several. First, it can provide a set of theoretical and methodological tools that are equally applicable to traditional material technologies (artifacts, weapons, etc.) and to more institutional or symbolic technologies (organizational ideas, etc.). In addition, in an interesting example of shared foundations, some strands of STS and constructivism in IR have built on the same early work on social construction.[27] Those early studies focused on social relations rather than on material artifacts or scientific knowledge. Scholars in STS have then gone on to argue that social and material features of our world rely on ongoing processes of active construction. Thus, although STS and constructivist IR started with some of the same foundations, they have focused on different drivers, processes, and outcomes, giving us the opportunity to bring some insights from STS usefully into IR.[28] Among the multiple approaches within STS, I will consider in more detail two with particular relevance for constructivist IR: the social construction of technology and actor-network theory.[29]

The approach known as the social construction of technology and technological systems (SCOT) argues that technologies are, in practice, entirely social and are actively constructed in their creation and use.[30] One of the key concepts introduced is that of the "technological frame": the set of concepts and techniques employed by a community in its problem solving, combining current theories, tacit knowledge, engineering practices, and goals.[31] This frame gives new technologies certain meanings and prevents other meanings—or applications—from emerging. This approach has been challenged by realism, which "typically amounts to an intuition that truths are more dependent upon the natural world than upon the people who articulate them."[32] What could be useful about thinking through technologies in IR in these terms of social construction, however, is not to argue that there is no natural world out there within which political actors work, but instead to see technologies as *simultaneously* material and ideational, rather than material at the bottom and ideational layered on top. This actually reflects the constructivist notion of the "co-constitution" of agents and structures, which has been widely discussed[33] but rarely applied to the specific issue of technological artifacts and systems.

With nuclear weapons or other military technological systems, therefore, it is important to look simultaneously at their ideational and material features, rather than starting with a set of material constraints and possibilities afforded by a technology and then looking for political and social processes layered on top of that. The development of these technological systems, after all, is a political and social process in itself, and thus the "base material constraints" do not emerge out of nature. Likewise with the argument connecting mapping to state formation. Reframing that based on social construction of technology (SCOT) would involve treating the technological changes of mapping less as exogenous, "non-political" drivers of change and more as one aspect of a single social and technological process: the description, depiction, and rule over space.

Another approach from STS that provides a very different take on the ideational-material question in IR is actor-network theory (ANT), which came out of the work of Bruno Latour and others, initially about scientific discovery in the laboratory and then later applied to a wide variety of domains.[34] The key element for ANT is the *network*, which can incorporate both human and nonhuman actors, enrolled in the network in pursuit of a goal. The products of those networks can be material artifacts, such as technological systems or machines, but they also include social relations and groups. In a sense, ANT "expressly abandons the dichotomy between the semiotic and the material"[35] by reducing the social almost entirely to the material, but materiality in the context of networks of relations (which are themselves not observably material). When the products of those networks become stable and accepted, they are treated as "black boxes," taken for granted without acknowledging their contested origins.

What might ANT contribute to constructivist IR?[36] For one, by sidestepping the "pathology" of opposing the material to the ideational,[37] ANT shifts the focus to looking for the relevant actors (both human and nonhuman) and the networks they create. There is a growing interest in applying a variety of relational theories to IR (including the logic of practices or social network analysis, for example), and ANT provides a distinct means of doing this. If we think about large IR outcomes such as wars, states, or trade as network projects, we can look for the actors in those networks and the allies enrolled toward the project.[38] One problem that has been raised, however, is that ANT is predominantly focused on micro processes (networks of individual scientists in laboratories and their actions, for example), while many of the outcomes IR is most interested in are at the macro level: systemic change, major war, and so on.[39] Yet that might be where constructivist IR theory works well: scaling up from micro processes to macro-level outcomes based on the constraining and driving effects of ideas that emerge and are reproduced through networks. For example, in considering the outbreak of interstate war, one study applies a social network analysis of the power relations among states to improve upon the standard focus on the role of geography and proximity in conflict.[40] This could be further expanded upon by combining the network-centered analysis of ANT with constructivism's interest in actor identities and the role of ideas in constituting power relations.

Further Directions for Technology and Constructivism

While there has been limited interchange between STS and constructivist IR so far, I would like to conclude by suggesting two routes for further conversation: first, looking at more empirical and theoretical domains that might benefit from this interchange, and second, considering the way an STS approach might analyze some of the ways we are *using* technologies in constructivist—and other—IR research.

For example, the possible interaction between information technology and international relations could be studied through the application of STS theories, again allowing for an approach that goes beyond asking what the effects of new technologies are. Digital mapping, to take one example, can be understood from an approach that captures the way these systems do not prefigure the political practices that use them, but are instead "always coming into being" alongside the relationships and actors to which they are connected.[41] How are digital mapping tools used in territorial disputes? Who are the actors enrolled in the relevant networks: negotiating parties, mediators, technology providers like Google? Focusing on continuing network creation (from ANT) or the social construction of these systems (from SCOT) would go beyond a basic framework in which political actors have goals and use technological tools to achieve them.

In addition, applying STS to constructivism might make it easier to incorporate other *types* of technologies, using the same frameworks and arguments as material technologies. For example, ideas have been framed as "symbolic technologies" that can be used to enable or constrain action.[42] Likewise, Elden's conceptualization of modern territorial rule itself as a "political technology" could be incorporated, using STS framings, alongside the material technologies that give territoriality its physical instantiation: boundary demarcation, mapping, and so on.[43]

Finally, the methodological principle of reflexivity suggests that we should think carefully about our research methods and tools, using the same concepts and theoretical arguments that we apply to the subjects of our study. In terms of technologies, this suggests that we should look carefully at the application of high-tech computer-based analysis tools, such as geographic information systems (GIS), agent-based modeling, or the analysis of so-called "big data."[44] What are the networks and goals toward which these tools are put? How are their means and ends socially constructed in the process?

Technology, in short, continues to play an ever-larger role in our theories and methodologies, as well as in international politics itself. Thinking clearly about this—building on the insights of decades of studies of technology from STS and other fields—will help constructivism, and other IR approaches, continue to generate useful knowledge about international politics.

NOTES

1. Guzzini 2000, 147.

2. This designation of some constructivist theories as "mainstream" is, of course, problematic for such a disparate set of approaches. I attach this label merely in recognition of the importance given to these strands of constructivism in expositions such as introductory IR textbooks, review essays, and so on.

3. Finnemore and Sikkink 2001, 393.

4. E.g., Katzenstein 1996; Goldstein and Keohane 1993.

5. Ruggie 1993.

6. Ruggie 1993, 160.

7. Finnemore and Sikkink 1998.

8. Wendt 1999.

9. Even when these are conceptualized as two ends of a continuum, this type of analysis still tends to shift back and forth between the two extremes.

10. For example, Wendt himself has noted that this distinction is not necessarily useful (Fearon and Wendt 2002).

11. E.g., Onuf 1989.

12. Adler and Pouliot 2011.

13. Hopf 2010.

14. Hopf 2010, 543.

15. Hayes and James 2014, 427.

16. Fritsch 2011.

17. Herrera 2006, 34.

18. This chapter leaves aside the role played by technology in other approaches to IR, but it has been a central—though not determining—component in many influential arguments in IR, especially those concerning large-scale historical change, such as the "bellicist" model of state formation (e.g., Tilly 1992). Likewise, technological change provides an independent variable for research framed in quantitative terms. See, for example, the special issue of the *Journal of Peace Research* (52, no. 3) on "Communication, Technology and Political Conflict."

19. Wendt 1999, 111.

20. Wendt 1999, 111.

21. Fritsch 2011, 39.

22. Tannenwald 1999.

23. Guzzini 2000, 159.

24. Branch 2014. See also Biggs 1999; Strandsbjerg 2008.

25. Ruggie 1993.

26. Much of the following overview of STS relies on the very helpful text by Sismondo 2010.

27. E.g., Berger and Luckmann 1966.

28. Being aware, of course, of the danger of falling into the "import syndrome" for which IR has been criticized, constantly importing frameworks from other disciplines such as economics (Best and Walters 2013, 333). See Mayer, Carpes, and Knoblich 2014 for a recent effort to bring together STS and IR.

29. There are other approaches to STS that could prove fruitful for constructivist IR, including the critical theory of technology (e.g., Feenberg 1991), among others.

30. Key texts of this tradition include Pinch and Bijker 1984 and Bijker, Hughes, and Pinch 1987.

31. Bijker 1987.

32. Sismondo 2010, 58.

33. E.g, Wendt 1987, among many others.

34. Key ANT texts include Latour 1987 and Latour 2005, among many others. Sismondo 2010, chap. 8, provides an excellent overview.

35. Nexon and Pouliot 2013, 344.

36. A question explicitly taken up by Best and Walters 2013 and Nexon and Pouliot 2013.

37. Nexon and Pouliot 2013, 343.

38. As Schouten 2013 does with regard to state failure.

39. Nexon and Pouliot 2013, 344.

40. Flint et al. 2009.

41. Kitchin, Gleeson, and Dodge 2012.

42. Laffey and Weldes 1997.

43. Elden 2013, 322–30.

44. On GIS in IR, see Gleditsch and Weidmann 2012 and Branch 2016; for an example of constructivist agent-based modeling, see Lustick, Miodownik, and Eidelson 2004; and for one of the many examples of large-scale dataset creation (particularly with regard to "event data"), see http://gdeltproject.org/.

REFERENCES

Adler, Emanuel, and Vincent Pouliot, eds. 2011. *International Practices*. Cambridge: Cambridge University Press.

Berger, Peter L., and Thomas Luckmann. 1966. *The Social Construction of Reality: A Treatise in the Sociology of Knowledge*. New York: Penguin.

Best, Jacqueline, and William Walters. 2013. "'Actor-Network Theory' and International Relationality: Lost (and Found) in Translation." *International Political Sociology* 7: 332–34.

Biggs, Michael. 1999. "Putting the State on the Map: Cartography, Territory, and European State Formation." *Comparative Studies in Society and History* 41, no. 2: 374–405.

Bijker, Wiebe E. 1987. "The Social Construction of Bakelite: Toward a Theory of Invention." In *The Social Construction of Technological Systems: New Directions in the Sociology and History of Technology*, edited by Wiebe E. Bijker, Thomas P. Hughes, and Trevor J. Pinch. Cambridge, MA: MIT Press.

Bijker, Wiebe E., Thomas P. Hughes, and Trevor J. Pinch, eds. 1987. *The Social Construction of Technological Systems: New Directions in the Sociology and History of Technology*. Cambridge, MA: MIT Press.

Branch, Jordan. 2014. *The Cartographic State: Maps, Territory, and the Origins of Sovereignty*. Cambridge: Cambridge University Press.

Branch, Jordan. 2016. "Geographic Information Systems (GIS) in International Relations." *International Organization* 70, no. 4: 845–69.

Elden, Stuart. 2013. *The Birth of Territory*. Chicago: University of Chicago Press.

Fearon, James, and Alexander Wendt. 2002. "Rationalism v. Constructivism: A Skeptical View." In *Handbook of International Relations*, edited by Walter Carlsnaes, Thomas Risse, and Beth A. Simmons. London: Sage.

Feenberg, Andrew. 1991. *Critical Theory of Technology*. Oxford: Oxford University Press.

Finnemore, Martha, and Kathryn Sikkink. 1998. "International Norm Dynamics and Political Change." *International Organization* 52, no. 4: 887–917.

Finnemore, Martha, and Kathryn Sikkink. 2001. "Taking Stock: The Constructivist Research Program in International Relations and Comparative Politics." *Annual Review of Political Science* 4: 391–416.

Flint, Colin, Paul Diehl, Juergen Scheffran, John Vasquez, and Sang-hyun Chi. 2009. "Conceptualizing ConflictSpace: Toward a Geography of Relational Power and Embeddedness in the Analysis of Interstate Conflict." *Annals of the Association of American Geographers* 99, no. 5: 827–35.

Fritsch, Stefan. 2011. "Technology and Global Affairs." *International Studies Perspectives* 12: 27–45.

Gleditsch, Kristian Skrede, and Nils B. Weidmann. 2012. "Richardson in the Information Age: Geographic Information Systems and Spatial Data in International Studies." *Annual Review of Political Science* 15: 461–81.

Goldstein, Judith, and Robert O. Keohane. 1993. *Ideas and Foreign Policy: Beliefs, Institutions, and Political Change*. Ithaca, NY: Cornell University Press.

Guzzini, Stefano. 2000. "A Reconstruction of Constructivism in International Relations." *European Journal of International Relations* 6, no. 2: 147–82.

Hayes, Jarrod, and Patrick James. 2014. "Theory as Thought: Britain and German Unification." *Security Studies* 23, no. 2: 399–429.

Herrera, Geoffrey L. 2006. *Technology and International Transformation: The Railroad, the Atom Bomb, and the Politics of Technological Change.* Albany: State University of New York Press.

Hopf, Ted. 2010. "The Logic of Habit in International Relations." *European Journal of International Relations* 16, no. 4: 539–61.

Katzenstein, Peter J., ed. 1996. *The Culture of National Security: Norms and Identity in World Politics.* New York: Columbia University Press.

Kitchin, Rob, Justin Gleeson, and Martin Dodge. 2012. "Unfolding Mapping Practices: A New Epistemology for Cartography." *Transactions of the Institute of British Geographers* 38: 480–96.

Laffey, Mark, and Jutta Weldes. 1997. "Beyond Belief: Ideas and Symbolic Technologies in the Study of International Relations." *European Journal of International Relations* 3, no. 2: 193–237.

Latour, Bruno. 1987. *Science in Action: How to Follow Scientists and Engineers Through Society.* Cambridge, MA: Harvard University Press.

Latour, Bruno. 2005. *Reassembling the Social: An Introduction to Actor-Network-Theory.* Oxford: Oxford University Press.

Lustick, Ian S., Dan Miodownik, and Roy J. Eidelson. 2004. "Secessionism in Multicultural States: Does Sharing Power Prevent or Encourage It?" *American Political Science Review* 98, no. 2: 209–29.

Mayer, Maximilian, Mariana Carpes, and Ruth Knoblich, eds. 2014. *The Global Politics of Science and Technology.* Heidelberg: Springer.

Nexon, Daniel H., and Vincent Pouliot. 2013. "'Things of Networks': Situating ANT in International Relations." *International Political Sociology* 7: 342–45.

Onuf, Nicholas. 1989. *World of Our Making: Rules and Rule in Social Theory and International Relations.* Columbia: University of South Carolina Press.

Pinch, Trevor J., and Wiebe E. Bijker. 1984. "The Social Construction of Facts and Artefacts: or How the Sociology of Science and the Sociology of Technology might Benefit Each Other." *Social Studies of Science* 14: 399–441.

Ruggie, John G. 1993. "Territoriality and Beyond: Problematizing Modernity in International Relations." *International Organization* 47, no. 1: 139–74.

Schouten, Peer. 2013. "The Materiality of State Failure: Social Contract Theory, Infrastructure and Governmental Power in Congo." *Millennium* 41, no. 3: 553–74.

Sismondo, Sergio. 2010. *An Introduction to Science and Technology Studies, Second Edition.* Malden, MA: Blackwell.

Strandsbjerg, Jeppe. 2008. "The Cartographic Production of Territorial Space: Mapping and State Formation in Early Modern Denmark." *Geopolitics* 13, no. 2: 335–58.

Tannenwald, Nina. 1999. "The Nuclear Taboo: The United States and the Normative Basis of Nuclear Non-Use." *International Organization* 53, no. 3: 433–68.

Tilly, Charles. 1992. *Coercion, Capital, and European States, AD 990–1992.* London: Blackwell Publishers.

Wendt, Alexander. 1987. "The Agent-Structure Problem in International Relations Thoery." *International Organization* 41, no. 3: 335–70.

Wendt, Alexander. 1999. *Social Theory of International Politics.* Cambridge: Cambridge University Press.

EIGHT

Integrating Social Psychological Insights into Constructivist Research

Jennifer M. Ramos

Constructivism offers a broad approach with which to interrogate the social world, yet it lacks the specificity of a theory.[1] One of the most promising directions to further our understanding of how the sociopolitical world works is found in the intersection of social psychology and constructivism. In this chapter, I assert that social psychology can be useful in furthering constructivist research. Specifically, social psychology provides the key to establishing an empirical foundation for constructivism.[2] While the marriage of the two is not perfect, the gains we can make in our understanding of the social world by adopting social psychological insights into the constructivist paradigm outweigh the limitations.

To illustrate the value of incorporating social psychology into constructivism, I conduct a plausibility probe. In it, I ask a classic constructivist-type question: How do norms emerge? In particular, how is it possible that preventive self-defense, once seen as illegal and illegitimate by international standards, emerged as a norm? One theory within social psychology offers particularly novel insights to supplement my study: cognitive dissonance theory. Its key insight about individuals' desire for cognitive consistency can provide the microfoundational mechanism of norm emergence—in this case, for the initial emergence of the norm of preventive self-defense—within a social constructivist approach.

In the following section, I first discuss why social psychology might be useful in supplementing the constructivist approach. Next I apply social psychology's cognitive dissonance theory to better understand how it became possible for the preventive self-defense norm to emerge. I propose that this was, in part, due to the narrative established in the Bush Doctrine that allowed the US public to maintain cognitive consistency between their policy interests and values. I then review the main points of the chapter and conclude with some final thoughts.

Why Social Psychology and Constructivism?

Constructivism as we know it in international relations is a product of multiple and evolving disciplines.[3] As scholars continue to construct and deconstruct constructivism, I suggest that one avenue forward can be found in social psychology, "the study of how individuals affect and are affected by other people and by their social and physical environments" (APA.org, 2018).[4] At their cores, both social psychology and constructivism share an interest in understanding ideas, beliefs, and norms within a social context. Indeed, bridging constructivism with *social* psychological theories, which emphasize the importance of the *social* in the development of attitudes, behaviors, and norms (in contrast to psychology's focus not only on the individual but on an individual detached from her environment)[5] can yield important insights for scholars and policymakers alike.

Fortunately, social psychologists have produced a rich body of theories from which constructivists may draw for their empirical research (Houghton 2007). In broad terms, these include evolutionary, cognitive, motivational/affective, interpersonal, and group/cultural theories that help us explain a number of social phenomena such as intergroup bias, aggression, and imitation (van Lange, Kruglanski, and Higgins 2011). Not only does this research help us better understand social events and experiences, it also helps us to formulate better policies to address social problems.

One of the most fruitful theories in social psychology has been social identity theory (Tajfel and Turner 1979), which offers insights into identity formation and change. This theory suggests that individuals seek a positive sense of self, and one way to achieve this is to emphasize the desirability of one's own social group (the "in-group"), while distinguishing one's group from the lesser "out-group." This proposition is particularly pertinent to international relations scholars working from a constructivist approach. For example, Larson (2012) demonstrates how constructivism's lack of attention to the mechanisms of change can be ameliorated by incorporating social identity theory. In doing so, she argues that we can better understand important changes in international politics, such as the motivating factors behind China's and Russia's identity changes after the Cold War. In understanding these motivations, countries, like the United States, are better prepared to succeed in their foreign relations. Other work integrating social identity theory into constructivism also has been important in suggesting how states and their leaders manage multiple, if at times conflicting, identities (Anstee 2012). These are but a few examples of where supplementing constructivism with social identity theory better reflects the complexity of the real world not captured by constructivism's often simplistic and static view of identity (see also Shannon and Kowert 2012; Hopf 1998, 2002).

Norm Development and Evolution

With regard to the question of interest in this chapter, one of the weaknesses in some strands of constructivism concerns international norms. Norms "are intersubjectively shared understandings about the obligations of international actors to behave in specified ways" (Kegley and Raymond 2003, 390). Most constructivist scholars agree that international norms evolve according to constant negotiation of actors with one another regarding what the social standards are within the current social system.[6] Through an ongoing process of socialization, states and other actors both influence norms and are affected by them.[7] Constructivists, however, tend to underspecify the mechanisms of norm development and evolution (for exceptions, see Onuf 1989). This is especially true in the Wendtian (1999) constructivist view, which reads as overly structural (Jepperson, Wendt, and Katzenstein 1996, 44 n. 30; Price and Reus-Smit 1998; Weldes 1996, 280). That is, despite the constructivist proposition that structures and agents are coconstituted, the structure tends to dominate in explanations. While certainly there are conditions at the structural level that must be met for change to occur, actors are key to any transformation. The normative structure sets the stage for an actor in that it both guides and is shaped by the actor, but a structural explanation alone does not take into account actors' behavior, and it therefore provides only a partial explanation of norm change (Adler 1997; Hay 2002).

Social psychology's attention to actors within a social context can help fill this gap. Indeed, some scholars already have suggested as much. For example, Goldgeier and Tetlock (2001) specifically propose that constructivists draw on advances in cross-cultural social psychology to hone our understanding of how the international social structure is created and maintained. Recent research asserts that there may be cultural differences in cognitive processes (Nisbett and Norenzayan 2002; see also Markus and Katayama 1991), though psychologists remain engaged in trying to better understand the interdependent relationship between culture and cognition. Such findings have implications for how international (and local) norms develop.

Indeed, there are a number of constructivist works on international norm development and evolution (Acharya 2004; Checkel 1998; Cortell and Davis 1996, 2000; Legro 1997; Klotz 1995; Nadelmann 1990; Price and Tannenwald 1996; Sandholtz and Stiles 2008; Zartner and Ramos 2011). Among them is Finnemore and Sikkink's (1998) norm "life cycle," which identifies three stages of norm development and diffusion. Other prominent stage models include Risse, Ropp, and Sikkink's (1999) "spiral model" of human rights transnational advocacy, which further refines the five-stage "boomerang" model of transnational advocacy network influence by Keck and Sikkink (1998). With attention to the various roles actors play in norm evolution, their various motivations for their social behavior, the comparisons the actors make vis-à-vis one another, and their social identities, these models seem to draw on ideas from social psychological frameworks, and thus it seems hardly a stretch to make the use of social psychological theories more explicit and foundational as scholars continue to examine the evolution of norms.

Even when social psychology is acknowledged, it begs further development, especially given the vast array of social psychology research to draw on. For example, in Finnemore and Sikkink's (1998) three-stage model, they do point to the social psychological need of individuals and states to legitimately belong to groups. They suggest that the way states can signal their legitimacy and feel a sense of belonging is to adopt and follow social norms. To further augment this idea, one might borrow from the extensive research on social comparison theory in social psychology to understand why states follow social norms (Festinger 1954; Kruglanski and Mayseless 1990; Suls and Wheeler 2002). Social comparison theory asserts that individuals have a need for self-evaluation and they meet this need by comparing themselves to others. Incorporating this into models of norm diffusion, for instance, could provide one way to ground the micro-level motivations of states, since states may be seeking to enhance their self-esteem by competing to meet the new international standard of behavior before their "inferior" peers do or to distinguish themselves from those that do not adopt the norm (Garcia and Tor 2007). And social comparison theory is just one that might be applicable here. The main point here is to show that social psychological theories can help constructivists provide the empirical microfoundations for their theories.

Initial Emergence of Preventive Force Norm: Applying Social Psychology

Having reviewed why social psychology might be useful and even compatible with constructivism, let us turn back to the question at hand regarding the emergence of international norms. Though there are a number of works that address the emergent stage of norms (e.g. Finnemore and Sikkink 1998; Cortell and Davis 1996; Price and Tannenwald 1996), this traditionally has been an area in the norms literature that has been "undertheorized" (Gest et al. 2013).[8] One route to remedying this issue, however, is by utilizing social psychological theories.

In the remaining portion of this chapter, I will illustrate how insights from social psychology's cognitive dissonance provide at least one way for us to better understand *how* it became possible for the preventive force norm to emerge in the United States. After all, cognitive dissonance is "one of the most classic social psychological phenomena," and I believe it offers one way—certainly not the only way—to understand how a norm may emerge (Miyamoto and Eggen 2013, 602). In addition, though it has not been explored in great depth in this way (but see Cortell and Davis 2000), previous scholars have suggested cognitive dissonance as a useful direction for constructivist research. For example, Martha Finnemore writes that "social psychological mechanisms, such as *cognitive dissonance*," contribute to changes in social purpose, and thereby shifts in normative understandings (2003, 67, italics added).

In order to understand how a previously taboo behavior emerges as something acceptable, I will conduct a plausibility probe focused on the initial emergence of the preventive force norm (or, preventive self-defense) within the United States. In other work (Fisk and Ramos 2014, 2016, 2018), I have argued that the preventive self-defense norm, formerly seen as illegal and illegitimate, is diffusing in the international system, with the United States acting as the norm entrepreneur (Fisk and Ramos 2014). That is, preventive force has come to be seen as legitimate behavior by major states such as India and Russia, among others (Fisk and Ramos 2014,

2018). I now focus, however, on the step prior and address the question of how the preventive force norm became possible in the context of the United States.

Developing Expectations

Cognitive dissonance was first developed by social psychologist Leon Festinger (1957) and is premised on the fact that humans—whether as individuals or in groups—seek cognitive consistency.[9] It begins with the observation that relevant thoughts, beliefs, or attitudes can either be consonant or dissonant. If consonant, they create no psychological tension because they are mutually implied. But if the beliefs clash, they create psychological discomfort for the person. She or he will seek to lessen this discomfort by avoiding information that emphasizes the dissonance or by changing one of the beliefs so that it aligns with the other. Other research along these lines proposes that with regard to decision making, if an individual is choosing among a range of actions, that individual may alleviate the mental discomfort by exaggerating the benefits of the chosen decision and downplaying the drawbacks, while applying the reverse to the alternatives not chosen (Shultz and Lepper 1996). Festinger's initial study has since inspired a plethora of similar studies and derivatives (for review, see Metin and Camgoz 2011), and cognitive dissonance theory remains one of the most influential theories in social psychology for explaining changes in, and the maintenance of, attitudes and beliefs, with the most important principle being that individuals seek cognitive consistency.[10]

I propose that cognitive dissonance is especially applicable to the emergence of norms regarding the use of force because the decision to intervene is not made lightly. Most state leaders and their publics are reluctant to use force abroad, even under the best of conditions. It is an incredibly serious decision in which individuals may very well be faced with competing thoughts or beliefs about the right course of action that has life-or-death consequences. In short, cognitive dissonance has important implications for how state leaders and their publics weigh how to best pursue their values and national security interests. Cognitive dissonance theory suggests that they are more likely to support a "new" norm (and a thus a policy based on that norm) that is consistent with their beliefs and attitudes so as to avoid any psychological discomfort.

One may note that in explaining how the preventive force norm initially emerged in the United States, I am assuming an elite-driven process, one in which leaders shape the content of public information (Converse 1964;

Zaller 1990, 1992). As Converse asserted, beliefs systems diffuse from elites to the masses since elites often serve as the source of ideologies (1964). Moreover, the masses are not likely to hold readily accessible knowledge or opinions on any given topic, and so they rely on cues from elites (Zaller 1992). This is especially likely to occur when these topics involve matters "out of reach, out of sight" like foreign policy (Zaller 1992, 8). Though historical details of the norms regarding the use of force do not directly interest the average citizen, the actual prospect of military intervention and its related policy do. Therefore, elites are charged with constructing a compelling and legitimizing narrative for their actions (e.g. Jackman 1993).

Constructing this narrative is critical to obtaining public support: "language is not just a social mechanism that creates and reinforces meaning and identity; it can be manipulated by speakers" to their own ends (Kowert 1998, 105). In doing so, leaders want to minimize cognitive dissonance for their publics in the rationale for their policies. The constant reiteration of the justification for a state's policy that yields *cognitive consistency* for the public, such as a new doctrine on the use of force like the Bush Doctrine, will enable a norm-like preventive self-defense to be accepted by a public, and perhaps beyond.[11]

In the following section, I provide preliminary evidence for the utility of social psychology's cognitive dissonance in understanding how the preventive force norm came to be seen as legitimate, with its origins in the narrative of the Bush Doctrine. In short, the framing of the practice of preventive force with the language of "pre-emptive" use of force enabled the public to maintain cognitive consistency because it allowed the United States to pursue its foreign policy goals while seemingly upholding its commitment to American ideals and international law (even if the latter was not a primary concern of the Bush administration).

Norm Emergence: Preventive Self-Defense as "Preemptive Force"

The norm against preventive force had been long-standing in the international system until recently (Fisk and Ramos 2014; Silverstone 2009). For many years, the dominant understanding of legitimate anticipatory self-defense relied on the "*Caroline* standard," established in 1837. The "*Caroline* standard" is derived from an incident in which the British attacked a US ship near the US-Canadian border. The United States considered the attack an unjustified use of force, outside the bounds of what could be reasonably considered anticipatory self-defense. Conditions were thus established via customary international law by which pre-emptive self-defense was justified. It should be "(i) 'overwhelming' in its necessity; (ii) leaving 'no choice of means'; (iii) facing so imminent a threat that there is 'no moment for deliberation'; and (iv) proportional" (secretary of state Daniel Webster quoted in Doyle 2008, 12). This *pre-emptive* use of force lies in stark contrast to *preventive* self-defense, in which an actor strikes first to target someone for a potential threatening act he or she might commit sometime in the future. The legality and legitimacy of pre-emptive use of force largely stems from the high level of certainty in such circumstances. Preventive self-defense, as the United States perceived the British attack on the *Caroline* to be, has thus been internationally regarded as both illegal and illegitimate.

Yet despite public claims from President Truman that preventive wars are the "weapons of dictators, not of free democratic countries like the United States"[12] and under the Eisenhower administration that they "never will be any part of United States foreign policy,"[13] preventive force was sometimes pushed as a serious option during the Cold War.[14] After the Cold War, though President Clinton eventually rejected the idea, US defense secretary William Perry had argued for the United States to conduct a preventive strike against North Korea when it threatened to withdraw from the NPT in 1993. Such a strike could not only have led to another tragic war, it would have also gone against international law and norms, which the United States, as the leader of the liberal global order, had a key interest in maintaining. Still, the possibility had been privately considered.[15] It would be years later, under a different president, before the idea of preventive self-defense would be presented not just for a specific crisis, but as a guiding strategy, to the public and accepted.

The public legitimation for the use of preventive self-defense in the United States took root under the Bush administration after 9/11 and in the lead-up to the Iraq war. In President Bush's speeches in 2002 prior to the release of the National Security Strategy (NSS), he highlights the possibility that the United States could strike first if a threat is perceived. In his first State of the Union address (2002), President Bush declares, "We'll be deliberate, yet time is not on our side. I will not wait on events while dangers gather. I will not stand by as peril draws closer and closer."[16] In this speech, President Bush is clearly suggesting an opening for preventive self-defense in US foreign policy, with an eye toward garnering support for a preventive war in Iraq. Later in June 2002 at West Point, President Bush begins to use the language of "pre-emptive" force. In his commencement speech, he declares, "And our security will require all Americans to be for-ward looking and resolute, to be ready for preemptive action when neces-sary to defend our liberty and to defend our lives."[17] From these speeches, one begins to get a sense that it is actually the *preventive* self-defense option that is going to be a hallmark of the Bush presidency.

The release of the NSS in September of 2002, amidst debate about a possible invasion of Iraq, helped to clarify the strategic vision of the Bush administration to meet the global challenges. It also provided insight into what exactly President Bush and his administration meant by "pre-emptive" action. The NSS, or the "Bush Doctrine," asserts, "The greater the threat, the greater is the risk of inaction—and the more compelling the case for taking anticipatory action to defend ourselves, even if uncer-tainty remains as to the time and place of the enemy's attack. To forestall or prevent such hostile acts by our adversaries, the United States will, if necessary, act *preemptively*"[18] (italics added). The NSS pointed out that in the new global threat context, the United States had a right to use uni-lateral force. Here we begin to see the slippage between preventive self-defense and pre-emptive use of force. The administration says that it will "act preemptively," which is lawful and legitimate, and acknowledges that "[f]or centuries, international law recognized that nations need not suffer an attack before they can lawfully take action to defend themselves" (NSS 2002, 15). But at the same time, without using the language of "preventive self-defense," the administration is identifying practices that are wholly associated with preventive self-defense. In the introduction to the NSS, it states that the United States will engage in attacks "against emerging threats before they are fully formed," which runs counter to international law and norms (NSS 2002).

It is well known that the Bush's advisors, who were neoconservatives and Republican nationalists, were not interested in whether or not the United States complied with international law in its foreign policy (Daalder and Lindsay 2003). President Bush also had little affection for the constraints of international law and institutions, though he did place a high value on law and order domestically. As mentioned earlier, though, a key consider-ation in framing a foreign policy, particularly one with such consequence, is gaining the approval of the American public. Recall that cognitive disso-nance theory suggests that the policy must minimize any dissonance in the public's mind between their values and the policy. The Bush administra-tion could not declare "preventive self-defense," a long-established inter-national taboo and a violation under customary international law (which the United States had helped to establish), as the new foreign policy of

Americans in those terms. Rather, I argue that the term "pre-emption" was necessary for the Bush administration to use for the American public since it was consistent with Americans' respect for the rule of law: "A defining attribute of American political culture is its veneration for law" (Gibson 2007, 599).

Among the many values that Americans hold dear, besides democracy, freedom, and equality, is the rule of law. Some might find this surprising. But in an analysis of public opinion from 1995 to 2005, James Gibson (2007) finds that American citizens exhibit consistent and strong support for the rule of law, including their aversion to allowing the government to "bend the law" to solve pressing problems, including terrorism (2007, 604). In terms of how this translates to the international arena, support for international law is also high. The Chicago Council on Foreign Relations reports that in 2002, 49 percent of Americans surveyed viewed strengthening international law and institutions as a very important US foreign policy goal, and 42 percent agreed that it was somewhat important. Only 9 percent stated that it was not at all important.[19] It thus is clear that Americans are committed, by and large, to the rule of law. They are not disconnected from, nor dispassionate about, this long-standing democratic value, even in the face of elites who may seek to circumvent the rule of law in times of national security.

From a social psychological viewpoint, by attending to the cognitive consistency principle in constructing the Bush Doctrine, the administration was not only able to go on to sell the Iraq war and institute preventive self-defense drone strikes, it was able (perhaps unintentionally) to bring into being a norm that heretofore had been seen as illegal and illegitimate.[20] Using the term "pre-emptive" instead of "preventive" force highlights the power of language: "language is not simply the repository of what exists. It is also the means through which things are brought into and out of existence" (Kowert 1998, 105). By defining pre-emptive self-defense as preventive actions, the Bush administration was able to further its own goals, one being going to war in Iraq, with public support under the auspices of a seemingly legal and legitimate strategy.[21] But what was also occurring, through the power of that linguistic sleight of hand, was the emergence of the preventive self-defense norm.

Repeating the legitimizing discourse only served to further embed the emergent norm, since the refrain of its legality allowed citizens to maintain cognitive consistency. For example, National security advisor Condoleezza Rice affirmed in an interview that "the strategy of preemptive strikes" the president mentioned in his West Point speech fell in line with the UN

Charter and thus was legal under international law.[22] Yet the action under discussion is decidedly preventive, not meeting the imminence standard set under international law. With regard to Iraq, the United States's own National Intelligence Estimate (October 2002) stated that Saddam Hussain would likely develop a nuclear weapon *"within a decade."*[23] This was a far stretch from the *Caroline* standard. President Bush, however, still reasoned in his national speech in October 2002, "If we know Saddam Hussein has dangerous weapons today, and we do, does it make any sense for the world to wait to confront him as he grows stronger and develops even more dangerous weapons?"[24]

President Bush's argument for "pre-emptive" force ultimately prevailed: "At no time did the administration face a broad public backlash for advocating preventive war" (Silverstone 2007, 187). Indeed, when we look at public opinion polls (see figure 8.1), a majority of Americans agree that military force can be justified against a country that seriously threatens the United States, but has not yet attacked.[25] What is all the more interesting is that preventive force proves to be a reasonable course of action for a majority of citizens, even when a particular country or situation was not specified.

The fact that the Iraq war, a preventive war begun under President Bush, embroiled the United States in an unexpectedly long-term fiasco, seems to have done little to undermine the emerging norm of preventive use of force. Under the Obama administration, the limited use of preventive force using armed drones against suspected terrorists skyrocketed, with total strikes in Pakistan at 353 (Bush at 48).[26] Despite this heavy reliance on the logic of preventive force, the American public remained supportive, despite rising scholarly and political debates.[27] With regard to preventing countries from acquiring weapons of mass destruction, President Obama seemed to continue in the spirit of the Bush Doctrine. In remarks at an AIPAC policy conference in 2012, he stated, "I have said that when it comes to preventing Iran from obtaining a nuclear weapon, I will take no options off the table, . . . and, yes, a military effort to be prepared for any contingency. . . . Iran's leaders should understand that I do not have a policy of containment; I have a policy to prevent Iran from obtaining a nuclear weapon. . . . I will not hesitate to use force when it is necessary to defend the United States and its interests."[28] And the American public was willing to back President Obama: 58 percent of its citizens said they were willing to use military force to prevent Iran from acquiring nuclear weapons.[29]

What is striking is that politicians continue to refrain from actually calling their strategy what it is. The language of "pre-emption" continues, as

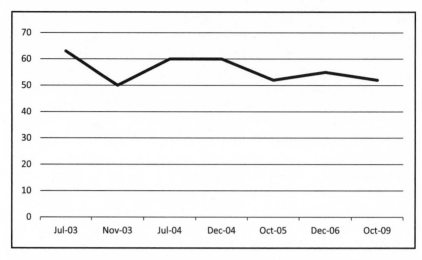

Figure 8.1. US public support for preventive war, 2003–2009 (%)

does its preventive force meaning until today.[30] The current Trump administration has considered the "pre-emptive option" against North Korea as a possible response to the testing of a nuclear weapon.[31] Vice President Pence warns, "[A]ll options are on the table as we continue to stand shoulder to shoulder with the people of South Korea."[32] Once again, according to some polls, the American public is willing to support preventive military action against North Korea should it become necessary.[33]

Indeed, the United States is not alone in this thinking, though it is likely that the Bush administration did not intend to set such a precedent for other countries (Fisk and Ramos 2014). In looking at the rise of the preventive self-defense norm more broadly, scholars note,

> More and more states and international organisations seem now to support the idea of revising long held international understandings about when force might be used. The views expressed by other states do not align perfectly with the positions held by US officials, but they do suggest that the international community is beginning to embrace some of the Bush Doctrine's underlying logic. A sizeable number seem to agree that the risk of calamitous surprise attacks, especially with chemical, biological or nuclear weapons, might well justify *preventive* strikes against terrorists or *preventive* wars against their state sponsors. (Dombrowski and Payne 2006, 115, emphasis added)

What is all the more interesting is that states continue to refrain from identifying such actions as "preventive," though they would now quietly agree that such standards of behavior are appropriate.[34]

Conclusion

In this chapter, I have tried to illustrate how the principle of cognitive consistency, upon which cognitive dissonance theory is based, helps provide a plausible explanation for how the preventive self-defense norm of sovereignty gained hold within the American public. By using the term "preemptive" force for what it clearly meant as preventive self-defense actions, the Bush administration was able to appeal to the value US citizens place in following the law. From a social psychological point of view, had the Bush administration used the correct term "preventive self-defense" throughout its rhetoric in justifying its national security strategy, the public would have experienced cognitive dissonance; it could not support any policies that derived from a strategy that would compromise its values. Here I have highlighted Americans' veneration for the law, since the use of the term "pre-emptive" self-defense seemed to be a purposeful move by the Bush administration to not just muddy the definition, but blatantly disregard international law and norms. In doing so, the preventive self-defense norm (though still called "pre-emptive force" by politicians and media) is alive and well today in the United States and abroad. The constant iteration of "pre-emptive force" for what is actually preventive force reflects the fact that leaders, especially from powerful states, can contribute to the shaping and maintenance of the normative structure, as the norm they originate takes hold first within their home state and then reverberates (or not) throughout the international system.

In proposing the utility of social psychological insights to supplement the constructivist approach, I sought to address one of the weaknesses of constructivism: a lack of a micro-level foundation that enables understandings of social change. While I drew on cognitive dissonance theory and its principle of cognitive consistency, it is only one of many social psychological theories that might prove useful in furthering empirical constructivist research in international relations (see also Tetlock 1998). Though largely relying on different analytical tools, constructivism and social psychology share some of the same basic assumptions: all behavior is social and that people's behavior is both impacted by social structure (or "social arrangements" using Onuf's preferred term) as well as other individuals. Still there are some considerations to keep in mind. Many of the social psychological insights, while robust, may have limited generalizability outside the laboratory and, indeed, across cultures. Nonetheless, a mutually beneficial relationship between constructivism and social psychology may yet be achieved.

NOTES

1. For more on constructivism and its variants, see the introductory chapter in this volume.

2. This concerns primarily empirical constructivism, such as that advanced by Wendt (1999), and not necessarily all variants of social constructivism.

3. Let me note that while the focus of this volume is on constructivism, it is not the only approach that can benefit from social psychological insights.

4. Social psychology is rooted in the disciplines of both sociology and psychology (See Cook, Fine, and House 1995).

5. Note social psychologist Allport's assertion that "there is no psychology of groups which is not essentially and entirely a psychology of individuals" (1924: 4).

6. According to Kegley and Raymond (2003), norms "express a collective, socially sanctioned set of perspectives on what ought to be done, a collective expectation as to what will be done, and pronouncements about the costs of compliant versus noncompliant behavior with respect to potential norms violations." Norms may also be thought of as informal rules (Onuf 1989, 1998).

7. Scholars have identified several different types of norms (Searle 1995). Some norms are regulative and reflect permissions, prohibitions, and obligations. Other norms are constitutive in that they define the identity of actors.

8. For an excellent systematic study of norm emergence, see Gest et al. 2013.

9. For more on cognitive dissonance, see Brehm 1956; Shultz and Lepper 1996; Burris, Harmon-Jones, and Tarpley 1997; Festinger, Riecken, and Schachter 1956; Beauvois and Joule 1996; Aronson and Mills 1959; Harmon-Jones and Mills 1999; Festinger and Carlsmith 1959.

10. Examples of cognitive dissonance abound in political life: many US legislators who initially supported the Iraq war and then were faced with a series of military battle defeats reacted in different way. Some withdrew their support, admitting a "mistake" had been made, while others intensified their efforts in justifying the war through new rationales.

11. As mentioned earlier, I illustrate in other works how the preventive self-defense norm is diffusing in the international system (Fisk and Ramos 2014).

12. Radio and Television Report to the American People on the Situation in Korea. September 1, 1950. Available at http://trumanlibrary.org/publicpapers/index.php?pid=861&st=&st1=.

13. As stated by Secretary Dulles in Silverstone 2009, 84. In fact, in the National Security Strategy of 1955, the Eisenhower administration specifically declares that "[t]he United States and its allies must reject the concept of preventive war."

14. That the US military would suggest preventive options was not new, and may have come as early as September 1945 in calls to prevent the Soviet Union from

obtaining the atomic bomb. See Mueller, Karl, et al. 2006. "Striking First: Preemptive and Preventive Attack in U.S. National Security Policy," RAND, http://www.rand.org/content/dam/rand/pubs/monographs/2006/RAND_MG403.pdf.

15. For an assessment of twenty-four preventive attacks in the twentieth century, see Reiter 2006.

16. "Bush State of the Union." January 29, 2002. CNN, http://edition.cnn.com/2002/ALLPOLITICS/01/29/bush.speech.txt/.

17. "Text of Bush's speech at Westpoint." June 6, 2002. *New York Times*, http://www.nytimes.com/2002/06/01/international/text-of-bushs-speech-at-west-point.html.

18. The National Security Strategy of the United States of America, September 2002, 15, https://www.state.gov/documents/organization/63562.pdf.

19. American Public Opinion and U.S. Foreign Policy, 2002. General Population Data. Chicago Council on Foreign Relations. The German Marshall Fund of the United States. June 1–30. Data available at Inter-university Consortium for Political and Social Research (ICPSR)3673, Icpsr.umich.edu.

20. Obviously, other factors such as level of threat come into play in selling specific policies under the strategy of preventive self-defense. In Gallup 2002 polls in June-October, a majority of Americans (ranging from 61–53 percent) supported an invasion of Iraq. In a Gallup poll just prior to the Iraq war (March 14–15, 2003), 64 percent of Americans agreed with going to war in Iraq. This figure rose to 71 percent on the day of the attack, March 20, 2003.

21. This is not to say that the preventive force norm went without contestation, as an emergent norm usually does.

22. CNN, "Late Edition with Wolf Blitzer: Interview with Condoleezza Rice," September 8, 2002, http://transcripts.cnn.com/TRANSCRIPTS/0209/08/le.00.html.

23. "Iraq's Continuing Programs for Weapons of Mass Destruction," National Intelligence Council, October 2002.

24. CNN, "Bush: Don't Wait for Mushroom Cloud." October 8, 2002, http://edition.cnn.com/2002/ALLPOLITICS/10/07/bush.transcript/.

25. Surveys by Pew Research Center for the People and the Press. Question wording: "Do you think that using military force against countries that may seriously threaten our country, but have not attacked us, can often be justified, sometimes be justified, rarely be justified, or never be justified?" Reporting "often be justified" or "sometimes be justified."

26. New America, "Drone Strikes: Pakistan," https://www.newamerica.org/indepth/americas-counterterrorism-wars/pakistan/. This is but one country in which such drone strikes occurred.

27. See Pew Research Center for the People and the Press, for example, for continuous polling on the issue of drone strikes. These polls show majority support for targeting suspected extremists outside of officially declared war zones.

28. President Obama, "Remarks by the President at AIPAC." March 4, 2012, https://obamawhitehouse.archives.gov/the-press-office/2012/03/04/remarks-president-aipac-policy-conference-0.

29. Pew Research Center for the People and Press. Feb. 15, 2012. "Public Takes Strong Stance Against Iran's Nuclear Program," http://www.people-press.org/2012/02/15/public-takes-strong-stance-against-irans-nuclear-program/.

30. What is also noteworthy is that the media continues the use of the term "preemption," which serves to further perpetuate the preventive force norm. None of the mainstream outlets corrects the misuse of the term by elites.

31. William M. Arkin, Cynthia McFadden, and Kenzi Abou-Sabe, "US may launch strike if North Korea Reaches for nuclear Trigger." April 13, 2017, *NBC News*, http://www.nbcnews.com/news/world/u-s-may-launch-strike-if-north-korea-reaches-nuclear-n746366.

32. "Mike Pence Warns 'All Options Are on the Table." Al Jazeera. April 16, 2017, http://www.aljazeera.com/news/2017/04/mike-pence-warns-north-korea-options-table-170417043047338.html.

33. 53 percent say they support military action to stop North Korea's nuclear program. Fox News Poll. April 27, 2017, http://www.foxnews.com/politics/2017/04/27/fox-news-poll-53-percent-favor-military-action-to-stop-north-korea-nukes-program.html. In a March 2017 poll by Rasmussen, 37 percent of Americans were apparently ready to take action, http://www.rasmussenreports.com/public_content/politics/current_events/north_korea/37_ready_to_take_military_action_against_north_korea.

34. Regarding the preventive self-defense norm, there tends to be more agreement among elites than between elites and publics. See Germany, for example.

REFERENCES

Acharya, Amitav. 2004. "How Ideas Spread: Whose Ideas Matter? Norm Localization and Institutionalization in Asian Regionalism." *International Organization* 58, no. 2: 239–75.

Adler, Emanuel. 1997. "Seizing the Middle Ground: Constructivism in World Politics." *European Journal of International Relations* 3: 319–63.

Allport, Gordon. 1924. *Social Psychology*. Boston: Houghton Mifflin.

American Psychological Association (APA). 2018. "All About Social Psychology." http://www.apa.org/action/science/social/education-training.aspx.

Anstee, Jodie. 2012. "Norms and the Management of Identities: The Case for Engagement between Constructivism and the Social Identity Approach." In *Psychology and Constructivism in International Relations: An Ideational Alliance*, edited by Vaughn P. Shannon and Paul A. Kowert, 76–91. Ann Arbor: University of Michigan Press.

Aronson, Elliot and Mills, Judson. 1959. "The Effect of Severity of Initiation on Liking For a Group." *Journal of Abnormal Social Psychology* 59: 177–81.

Beauvois, Jean-Leon, and Robert-Vincent Joule. 1996. *A Radical Dissonance Theory*. London: Taylor and Francis.

Brehm, Jack W. 1956. "Postdecision Changes in the Desirability of Alternatives." *Journal of Abnormal and Social Psychology* 52: 384–89.

Burris, C. T., Eddie Harmon-Jones, and W. R. Tarpley. 1997. "By Faith Alone: Religious Agitation and Cognitive Dissonance." *Basic and Applied Social Psychology* 19: 17–31.

Checkel, Jeffrey. 1998. "The Constructivist Turn in International Relations Theory." *World Politics* 50: 324–48.

Converse, Philip E. 1964. "The Nature of Belief Systems in Mass Publics." In *Ideology and Discontent*, edited by D. E. Apter. London: Free Press of Glencoe.

Cook, Karen S., Gary Alan Fine, and James S. House, eds. *Sociological Perspectives on Social Psychology*. 1995. Boston: Allyn and Bacon.

Cortell, Andrew, and James Davis, Jr. 1996. "How Do International Institutions Matter? The Domestic Impact of International Rules and Norms." *International Studies Quarterly* 40, no. 4: 451–78.

Cortell, Andrew, and James W. Davis, Jr. 2000. "Understanding the Domestic Impact of International Norms: A Research Agenda." *International Studies Review* 2, no. 1: 65-87.

Daalder, Ivo, and James Lindsay. 2003. "American Unbound: The Bush Revolution in Foreign Policy." September 1. Brookings Institution. https://www.brookings.edu/articles/america-unbound-the-bush-revolution-in-foreign-policy/.

Dombrowski, Peter, and Roger A. Payne. 2006. "The Emerging Consensus for Preventive War." *Survival* 48, no. 2: 115–36.

Doyle, Michael. 2008. *Striking First: Preemption and Prevention in International Conflict*. Princeton: Princeton University Press.

Festinger, Leon. 1954. "A Theory of Social Comparison Processes." *Human Relations* 7, no. 2: 117–40.

Festinger, Leon. 1957. *A Theory of Cognitive Dissonance*. Evanston, IL: Row, Peterson.

Festinger, Leon, and J. M. Carlsmith. 1959. "Cognitive Consequences of Forced Compliance. *Journal of Abnormal and Social Psychology* 58: 203–10.

Festinger, Leon, Henry W. Riecken, and Stanley Schachter. 1956. *When Prophecy Fails: A Social and Psychological Study of a Modern Group That Predicted the Destruction of the World*. New York: Harper and Row.

Finnemore, Martha. 2003. *The Purpose of Intervention: Changing Beliefs about the Use of Force*. Ithaca, NY: Cornell University Press.

Finnemore, Martha, and Kathryn Sikkink. 1998. "International Norm Dynamics and Political Change." *International Organization* 52: 887–918.

Fisk, Kerstin, and Jennifer M. Ramos. 2014. "Actions Speak Louder than Words: Preventive Self-Defense as a Cascading Norm." *International Studies Perspectives* 15, no. 2: 163–85.

Fisk, Kerstin, and Jennifer M. Ramos, eds. 2016. *Preventive Force: Drones, Targeted Killing and the Transformation of Contemporary Warfare*. New York: New York University Press.

Fisk, Kerstin, and Jennifer M. Ramos. 2018. "Making the World Safe for Preventive Force: India, South Korea and Preventive Force." In *The Ethics of War and Peace Revisited: Moral Challenges in an Era of Contested and Fragmented Sovereignty*, edited by Daniel Brunstetter and Jean-Vincent Holeindre. Washington, DC: Georgetown University Press.

Garcia S. M., and Tor A. 2007. "Rankings, Standards, and Competition: Task vs. Scale Comparisons." *Organizational Behavior and Human Decision Processes* 102, no. 1: 95–108.

Gest, Justin, Carolyn Armstrong, Elizabeth Carolan, Elliot Fox, Vanessa Holzer, Tim McLellan, Audrey Cherryl Mogan, and Meher Talib. 2013. "Tracking the Process of International Norm Emergence: A Comparative Analysis of Six Agendas and Emerging Migrants' Rights." *Global Governance* 19: 153–85.

Gibson, James. 2007. "Changes in American Veneration for the Rule of Law." *DePaul Law Review* 56, no. 2: 593–614.

Goldgeier, James, and Philip Tetlock. 2001. "Psychology and International Relations Theory." *Annual Review of Political Science* 4: 67–92.

Harmon-Jones, Eddie, and Judson Mills, eds. 1999. *Cognitive Dissonance: Progress on a Pivotal Theory in Social Psychology*. Washington, DC: American Psychological Association.

Hay, Colin. 2002. *Political Analysis*. New York: Palgrave.

Hopf, Ted. 1998. "The Promise of Constructivism in International Relations Theory." *International Security* 23, no. 1: 171–200.

Hopf, Ted. 2002. *Social Construction of International Politics: Identities and Foreign Policies, Moscow 1955 and 1999*. Ithaca, NY: Cornell University Press.

Houghton, David Patrick. 2007. "Reinvigorating the Study of Foreign Policy Decision-Making: Toward a Constructivist Approach." *Foreign Policy Analysis* 3, no. 1: 24–45.

Jackman, Robert W. 1993. *Power Without Force*. Ann Arbor: University of Michigan Press.

Jepperson, Ronald, Alexander Wendt, and Peter Katzenstein. 1996. "Norms, Identity, and Culture in National Security." In *The Culture of National Security*, 33–78. New York: Columbia University Press.

Keck, Margaret, and Kathryn Sikkink. 1998. *Activists Beyond Borders: Advocacy Networks in International Politics*. Ithaca, NY: Cornell University Press.

Kegley, Charles W. Jr., and Gregory A. Raymond. 2003. "Preventive War and Permissive Normative Order." *International Studies Perspectives* 4, no. 4: 385–94.

Klotz, Audie. 1995. *Norms in International Relations: The Struggle against Apartheid*. Ithaca, NY: Cornell University Press.

Kowert, Paul. 1998. "Agent versus Structure in the Construction of National Identity." In *International Relations in a Constructed World*, edited by Vendulka Kubalkova, Nicholas Onuf, and Paul Kowert, 101–22. London: M. E. Sharpe.

Kruglanski, Arie W., and Ofra Mayseless. 1990. "Classic and Current Social Comparison Research: Expanding the Perspective." *Psychological Bulletin* 108, no. 2: 195–208.

Larson, Deborah Welch. 2012. "How Identities Form and Change: Supplementing Constructivism with Social Psychology." In *Psychology and Constructivism in International Relations: An Ideational Alliance*, edited by Vaughn P. Shannon and Paul A. Kowert, 57–75. Ann Arbor: University of Michigan.

Legro, Jeffrey. 1997. "Which Norms Matter? Revisiting the 'Failure' of Internationalism." *International Organization* 51, no. 1: 31–64.

Markus, Hazel, and Shinobu Katayama. 1991. "Culture and the Self: Implications for Cognition, Emotion, and Motivation." *Psychological Review* 98, no. 2: 224–53.

Metin, Irem, and Selin Camgoz. 2011. "Advances in the History of Cognitive Dissonance Theory." *International Journal of Humanities and Social Science* 1, no. 6: 131–36.

Miyamoto, Yuri, and Amanda Eggen 2013. "Culture Perspectives." In *Handbook of*

Social Psychology, edited by J. D. Delamater and A. Ward, 595–624. New York: Springer.

Mueller, Karl, Jasen J. Castillo, Forrest E. Morgan, Negeen Pegahi and Brian Rosen. 2006. "Striking First: Preemptive and Preventive Attack in U.S. National Security Policy," RAND, http://www.rand.org/content/dam/rand/pubs/mono graphs/2006/RAND_MG403.pdf

Nadelmann, Ethan A. 1990. "Global Prohibition Regimes: The Evolution of Norms in International Society." *International Organization* 44, no. 4: 479–526.

National Security Strategy of the United States of America. 2002. https://www.state.gov/documents/organization/63562.pdf.

Nisbett, Richard E., and Ara Norenzayan. 2002. "Culture and Cognition." In *Stevens' Hanbook of Experimental Psychology*, 3rd ed., edited by Harold E. Pashler, 561–97. New York: Wiley.

Onuf, Nicholas. 1989. *World of Our Making: Rules and Rule in Social Theory and International Relations*. Columbia: University of South Carolina Press.

Onuf, Nicholas. 1998. "Constructivism: A User's Manual." In *International Relations in a Constructed World*, edited by Vendulka Kubalkova, Nicholas Onuf, and Paul Kowert, 58–78. London: M. E. Sharpe.

Price, Richard, and C. Reus-Smit. 1998. "Dangerous Liaisons? Critical International Relations Theory and Constructivism." *European Journal of International Relations* 4: 259–94.

Price, Richard, and Nina Tannenwald. 1996. "Norms and Deterrence: The Nuclear and Chemical Weapons Taboos." In *The Culture of National Security: Norms and Identity in World Politics*, edited by Peter J. Katzenstein, 114–52. Ithaca, NY: Cornell University Press.

Reiter, Dan. 2006. "Preventive Attacks Against Nuclear, Chemical and Biological Weapons Programs: The Track Record." In *Hitting First*, edited by William Walton Keller and Gordon R. Mitchell, 27–44. Pittsburgh: University of Pittsburgh Press.

Risse, Thomas, Stephen Ropp and Kathryn Sikkink. 1999. *The Power of Human Rights: International Norms and Domestic Change*. Cambridge: Cambridge University Press.

Sandholtz, Wayne, and Kendall Stiles. 2008. *International Norms and Cycles of Change*. Oxford: Oxford University Press.

Searle, John. 1995. *The Construction of Social Reality*. New York: Free Press.

Shannon, Vaughn P., and Paul A. Kowert, eds. 2012. *Psychology and Constructivism in International Relations: An Ideational Alliance*. Ann Arbor: University of Michigan Press.

Shultz, Thomas. R., and Mark R. Lepper. 1996. "Cognitive Dissonance Reduction as Constraint Satisfaction." *Psychological Review* 103: 219–40.

Silverstone, Scott. 2007. *Preventive War and American Democracy*. New York: Routledge.

Silverstone, Scott. 2009. "Chinese Attitudes on Preventive War and the 'Preemption Doctrine'." Institute for National Security Studies, US Air Force Academy. Available at http://www.dtic.mil/cgi-bin/GetTRDoc?AD=ADA535951.

Suls, J., R. Martin, and L. Wheeler. 2002. "Social Comparison: Why, with Whom, and with What Effect?" *Current Directions in Psychological Science* 11, no. 5: 159–63.

Tajfel, Henri, and John Turner. 1979. "An Integrative Theory of Intergroup Conflict." In *The Social Psychology of Intergroup Relations*, edited by W. G. Austin and S. Worchel, 33–47. Monterey, CA: Brooks/Cole.

Tetlock, Philip. 1998. "Social Psychology and World Politics." In *Handbook of Social Psychology*, vol. 2 (4th ed.), edited by By Daniel Gilbert, Susan Fiske, and Gardner Lindsey, 868–912. Boston: McGraw-Hill.

Van Lange, Paul A. M., Arie W. Kruglanski, and E. Tory Higgins, eds. 2011. *Handbook of Theories of Social Psychology*. Thousand Oaks, CA: Sage Publishing.

Wendt, Alexander. 1999. *Social Theory of International Politics*. Cambridge: Cambridge University Press.

Zaller, John R. 1990. "Political Awareness, Elite Opinion Leadership, and the Mass Survey Response." *Social Cognition* 8, no. 1: 125–53.

Zaller, John R. 1992. *The Nature and Origins of Mass Opinion. Cambridge.* Cambridge University Press.

Zartner, Dana, and Jennifer M. Ramos. 2011. "Human Rights as Reputation Builder: Compliance with the Convention Against Torture." *Human Rights Review* 12, no. 1: 71–92.

NINE

New Wine into a (Not So) Old Bottle? Constructivism and the Practice Turn

Jérémie Cornut

Whether one considers epistemology, ontology, or methods to matter most when mapping the discipline of international relations (IR), there is no doubt that constructivism and practice theory (PT) will be placed close to one another. They share an origin in social theory, with identical founding figures among theorists like Giddens and Bourdieu; they have a similar ontology and see the world as socially constructed; they both focus on norms, identity, and beliefs; they adopt the same interpretive epistemology; and they both tend to rely on qualitative methodologies. In this context, many practice turners are recognized as—and sometimes even claim to be—constructivists (e.g. Adler 2008; Leander 2011; Pouliot 2007; Kratochwil 2011; Brown 2012; Guzzini 2013; Williams 2007; Faizullaev and Cornut 2017).

In this chapter, I focus on the contribution of PT to constructivism. Constructivism here is broadly defined as an approach focusing on the social construction of international politics, both as a bundle of intersubjective processes (when constructivists answer "how" questions) and as an outcome of these processes (when they answer "why" questions) (see Bertucci, Hayes, and James in this volume). I show that PT is a form of constructivism that studies international politics by scaling down analyses of social construction to the micro level.

IR scholars have different views on PT's contributions to constructivism. Some consider that constructivists have been at the "forefront" of the study of international practices (Adler 2013: 126). More critical scholars emphasize its similarities with constructivism and consider PT to be simply old wine in new bottles. For Ringmar, "Practices were always what the theory of structuration was about, and the first generation of international relations scholars to write on the agency/structure problem [Wendt in particular] were thus nothing if not the first practice theorists" (2014: 15; also see McCourt 2016). On the contrary, proponents of PT often consider a focus on practice to be a groundbreaking innovation that leads to a paradigm shift in the discipline. For Bueger and Gadinger, even though constructivism "share[s] many concerns with practice theories" and "turf wars have to be avoided," PT "involves quite substantial shifts in thinking about the world and the nature and purpose of social science. These shifts involve epistemology, ontology, methodology, methods, and indeed also to rethink how social science, and IR, relates to and is situated in the world" (2014, 9–10). IR scholars who feel the study of practices delineates a *turn* often echo this claim that the study of practices brings something profoundly new to the discipline.

In this chapter, I suggest another way to think about the relationship between constructivism and PT. The symmetrical questions on the future of constructivism and the contribution of PT to IR are reframed into one unique question: what exactly does PT bring to constructivism? I show that PT supplements constructivism by providing new ways to think about agency, materiality, power, data collection, epistemology, and reflexivity. By shifting constructivism' center of gravity it brings new wine into the (not so) old constructivist bottle. Whether PT also supplements other IR paradigms—the contention of some practice turners like Adler and Pouliot (2011)—will not be explored here.

As a first approach, we can define practices as "socially meaningful patterns of action, which, in being performed more or less competently, simultaneously embody, act out, and possibly reify background knowledge and discourse in and on the material world" (Adler and Pouliot 2011, 4). Sharpening their definition, Adler and Pouliot build on Cook and Brown (1999) and distinguish between behavior, action, and practice. Sitting at a desk is a behavior, sitting at a desk and checking a passport in an airport is an action, checking passports in airports is a (security) practice. There is a progressive gradation between the three concepts: behaviours are constitutive of actions, which are constitutive of practices (Adler and Pouliot 2011, 5). Practices are generated by habits/habitus: individuals will do certain things and avoid others based on their mental dispositions.[1] As Hopf (2010, 541) explains, "Habits both evoke and suppress actions. They imply actions by giving us ready-made responses to the world." Approaching the social world in terms of practices is thus an invitation to look at the daily activities of international actors, their ways of doing things, their mental habits, their repertoire of actions, and their networks (Pouliot and Cornut 2015).

This chapter aims to recount PT's contribution to constructivism from this starting point. The first section introduces PT's contributions to constructivism at an ontological level. The next three sections do the same at a conceptual, methodological, and epistemological level, respectively.

Broadening Constructivism's Ontology

Constructivism was introduced in the discipline to counter the tendency of many IR scholars to overemphasize material interests; its ideationalism "challenge[s] exogenous or imputed preferences with an examination of the beliefs and identities that situate people in a political context" (Shannon 2012, 7). Constructivists thus emphasize ideas, identities, norms, and culture, all located in the human mind. The logic of appropriateness tends to acknowledge the role of materiality only indirectly; it is recognized when filtered by cognitive and ideational structures. Constructivists do not focus on how ideas materialize, are enacted, and are reproduced in practice or on the practical processes through which ideas become influential on day-to-day activities. Their exploration of how identity influences interests often remain ideational, emphasizing for instance that when decision makers want to acquire nuclear weapons, they are driven by a sense of fairness or a notion that great powers possess nuclear weapons. In aspiring to attain or in already viewing themselves as great (regional) powers, they are trying to acquire these weapons mostly for the symbolic status they afford (Sagan 1996, 73–85; Hymans 2006).

Constructivists also tend to have a structuralist/holist/macro take on human activities. Several constructivists have emphasized agency or the coconstitution between agent and structure (e.g., Wendt 1999; Jackson and Nexon 1999; Checkel 1998; 2001; Finnemore and Sikkink 2001; Johnston 2001; Lebow 2009; on this debate see Adler 2013, 128–30). Yet constructivists often explain individual variations of behavior by looking at differences in the social norms to which individuals conform or their identity (Ross 2006). As Shannon explains, "in theory, constructivism claims to transcend either agent or structure to provide the 'middle ground' for each level's influence on the other. In practice, many constructivist studies have ended up structuralist in bent" (2012, 4; also see McCourt 2016). They seldom "recognize that actors have agency, can be strategic, are aware of the culture and social rules that presumably limit their practices, and as knowledgeable actors are capable of appropriating those cultural taproots for various ends" (Barnett 1999, 7). In a constructivist perspective, norms of behavior are characteristics of the collective: the risk is "the abandonment of free will, individualism, and personal sources of motivation" (Shannon 2012, 15; also see Kowert and Legro 1996).

Through a study of embodiments, relationality, and performances, PT brings more materiality and agency into the analysis of the social construction of reality. Practices are collectively shared, and this is where constructivism and practice theory meet. Practices are the common way of doing things; they are produced by the repetitive interaction between members of a group; they make sense in that group. They are "a social artefact" (Navari 2011, 614), "always linked to a collective" (Bueger and Gadinger 2014, 19) and "the products of social structures" (Hopf 2010, 548). They "are acquired through socialization, exposure, imitation, and symbolic power relationships . . . what may seem to be a set of individual dispositions is in fact profoundly social" (Pouliot 2008, 273–74). Because PT emphasizes shared structures of meaning within social fields, it also adopts a structural and ideational approach to IR.

Yet for PT, active agents perform practices. Practices not only constrain; they enable and empower social actors. As Adler and Pouliot put it, "when 'disaggregated,' practices are ultimately performed by individual social beings and thus they clearly are what human agency is about" (2011, 16). Practice can involve "strategic thinking as well as habit" (Brown 2012, 444), and PT makes "room for individual psychologies and improvisations" (Leander 2011, 300). This explains why there is a great deal of variation between practitioners performing a single role whose practices are quite well defined. For instance, in Hansen's analysis of the Muhammad cartoon crisis in 2005, there is a central place for differences of performances of practices. She looks at how "actors at key junctures mobilize specific practices in a manner that constitutes collective subjects with identities that embody or differ from the 'proper' values to be adopted" (Hansen 2011, 289–90). Similarly, Cornut shows that there were important differences regarding diplomats' ability to analyze social and political change during the Arab spring in Egypt in 2011. This was related to the extent to which their practices led them to be in regular contact with the public, NGOs, and grassroots organizations (2015a).

Norms, culture, and identity not only shape practice. Common ways of doing things in part stem from cultural and normative imperatives that have been internalized up to the point that they are taken for granted. On the other hand, as Pouliot (2008, 276) put it, "it is thanks to their practical sense that agents feel whether a given social context calls for . . . norm compliance [or not]."[2] In a study of the place in diplomatic circles of new members of the European Union, Merje Kuus (2014, 166) shows that some skillful diplomats from western Europe know how *not* to follow social rules, while newly arrived diplomats from eastern Europe tend to be identifiable because they follow them too carefully. She turns the constructivist logic of appropriateness on its head: "It s not enough to learn the [social] rules. To use these rules . . . one has to be able to break them. . . . Departures from [rules of the game] are also a part of the game. . . . It is these departures that signify a true insider." Others outline that practices change through a conscious process in which agents themselves realize that their practices are ill-adapted. Stein (2011) shows for instance how disruptions of the international environment after the end of the Cold War sparked discussions among humanitarian practitioners about what it means to "do good" and avoid "doing harm." Debates about competent and incompetent practices put background knowledge into the foreground and foster occasions for learning within the humanitarian community of practice.

A focus on practice thus provides an innovative solution to the agent-structure problem. The PT relational approach does not oppose structure and agency (on relationalism, see Jackson and Nexon 1999). Because practices—instead of agents or structure—are made "ontologically primitive," there "is no longer an agent who faces a structure, but instead practices that are responsible for the production of both" (Ringmar 2014, 17). Many practice turners take the same stance and feel that PT overcomes the agent-structure dichotomy (Hopf 2010, 547; Brown 2012, 444; Navari 2011, 618; Bueger and Gadinger 2014, 3; Bigo 2011, 236; in social theory, see Schatzki 2001). In a practice theory perspective, practices "enable structures to be stable or to evolve, and agents to reproduce or transform structures" (Adler and Pouliot 2011, 5). This uncovers the mundane processes through which ideas and background knowledge are (re)produced and changed in and through practice. For instance, the G20 emerges out of a combination of both transformation and reproduction of Western-dominated global order norms and practices (Cooper and Pouliot 2015). Similarly, the "ratchet effect" in the global governance of international security since 1814 explains how past practices tend to provide baselines for future negotiations (Pouliot and Thérien 2015).

PT further bridges the dichotomy between the ideational and the material. On the one side, practice "can change the physical environment as well as the ideas that individually and collectively people hold about the world" (Adler and Pouliot 2011, 7). On the other side, practices are "the bodily manifestations of what has already happened in the brain" (Hopf 2010, 546). For instance, Abrahamsen and Williams (2011) analyze how changes in security practices—in particular the emergence of a transnational commercial security sector—have been caused by a series of interlocking processes involving the relationship of private citizens to security, domestic, and global politics, in addition to technological and ideological changes. Neumann defines culture as a mutually conditioned play between discourse and practices. His analysis of regional cooperation between Norway and Russia at the end of the 1980s shows that the ending of the Cold War and the emergence of new actors allowed for possibilities of new relationships and thus new practices (2002).

For PT, what matters is the corporeal interaction of flesh-and-blood human beings in the course of everyday life. Take for instance the crisis between Russia and the West over Crimea in 2014. The clash of narratives that constitutes the conflict was embodied and performed by diplomats and other actors during the crisis. To understand the conflict, scholars thus need to look at various "narrative practices" associated with traditional diplomacy (secret meetings, top-level negotiations, and third-party interventions), public diplomacy (public speech making, media interviews, and diplomats' interaction with civil society), and nonstate actors influencing international politics (media reporting for instance). In this perspective, "narratives are more than texts and discourses" because they "are performed by flesh and blood people through their practice" (Faizullaev and Cornut 2016, 3). Similarly, writing a speech, gathering information, controlling a border, negotiating a treaty, are all performances of human bodies, though they are also informed by ideas in the mind of practitioners. Practitioners interact with one another, with their practices constantly reinforcing, emulating, imitating, and hybridizing one another. Ideas, norms, and identities emerge from and diffuse through these repeated physical interactions.

Emphasizing agency and materiality, PT thus broadens constructivism's ontology. The rest of PT's contribution to constructivism stems from this innovative ontology. It notably provides new ways to understand how power works in practice.

Conceptual Innovations to Think About Power

The rationalist approach to power outlines the external mechanisms of control that constrain individuals and states. On the contrary, the conceptualization of power in constructivism and PT both start with a focus on how unequal power relationships are constructed through social interaction. They emphasize the constraining power of shared hierarchical structures in the minds of actors (Adler 2013, 125). They "includ[e] that part of power which works by not being acknowledged, that part which makes agents conform . . . through some sort of internalised acceptance" (Guzzini 2013, 101). In Barnett and Duvall's typology, this conception of power understands it in terms of social relations of constitution (2005). Yet constructivists do not study how power relations work in practice. Constructivism says little about how the influence of some countries over others are produced and reproduced by individuals within social fields (Adler-Nissen and Pouliot 2014). In doing so, the processes through which power produces specific outcomes remain unexplored (Pouliot 2016). More generally, as Williams put it, "in the stress on norms, values, and identities that has marked [constructivism], the concepts of power and strategy have largely been left behind" (2007, 1).

PT gives a central place to power relationships between dominating social actors over dominated ones in the course of their performance (Guzzini 2013; Williams 2007; Pouliot 2010; Adler-Nissen 2011, 2012). Within social fields—defined as "a bundle of structured relations within which agents are variously positioned" (Pouliot 2010, 36)—power is the power to impose a specific conception of the social world, one whose rules are not contested because they are perceived as legitimate. Members of a field have opposing interests, and fields of practice are artifacts of past struggles that tend to be both reproduced and changed through day-to-day interactions. They are dynamic sites of contestation full of conflicts. They "are characterized by both struggles over the distribution of currently recognized forms of capital and by struggles to change the social relationship by changing the structures of valorization within the field" (Abrahamsen and Williams 2011, 313). For this reason, they are sometimes conceived as games (Williams 2007, 27–28).

Power relationships between dominating and the dominated structure and define fields. On the one hand, fields are hierarchical because practitioners do not hold equal positions in them. Depending on their positions, they have more or less capital of different forms, social, economic, cultural, or symbolic. It "is the control of a variety of historically constructed capitals, from economic through social to symbolic, that defines the structure of power relations in the field and the positions that result" (Pouliot 2008, 275). On the other hand, "all contestants agree on what it is they are seeking—political authority, artistic prestige, economic profit, academic reputation, and so on" (Pouliot 2008, 275). Practice turners—in the line of Pierre Bourdieu—call this "doxa," the knowledge, ideas, and values shared by members of a specific field. All in a field tacitly agree on the object of their struggle and the general contours of the game. To be part of a field is to share its doxa and, most of the time, not question these contours.

Practitioners in a given field defend their own interests. Dominant actors seek to use their mastery of the rules of the game and accumulated capital to maintain their domination and keep the field functioning to their advantage. The dominated can attempt to subvert the field through changing or challenging its rules. In rare occasions, the doxa itself can become an object of struggle and, as a consequence, is no longer doxa. For instance, Senn and Elhardt (2014) show how four influential decision makers and experts (William Perry, George Shultz, Henry Kissinger, and Sam Nunn) used their symbolic capital in a doxic battle over nuclear weapons to successfully promote the idea of nuclear disarmament. Adler-Nissen (2014) shows that the European External Action Service challenges European national diplomacies at a symbolic level.

Yet the dominated tend to abide by the rules of the game. This is what practice turners call "symbolic domination": "as a form of immediate adherence, a field's doxa is obeyed not only by dominant agents who benefit from it but also by the dominated ones who clearly do not" (Pouliot 2008, 275). For instance, informal practices, social norms, and interpersonal relations constantly inform diplomatic negotiations and decision-making processes. Those who have mastered the informal rules of the game often have a comparative advantage and are able to promote the interests of their country more efficiently. In his studies on informal rules, norms, and routines at the UN Security Council, Ambrosetti (2009, 2012) convincingly shows that these practices influence the organization, often to the advantage of its permanent members. In a similar vein, Schia (2013) demonstrates that representatives of the Security Council's smaller countries do not often perfectly master the informal rules of the game. As a consequence, they run the risk of "going native" by giving precedence to UN Security Council consensus to the detriment of their countries' interests.[3]

Uncovering Practices Through Interviews
and Participant Observation

With notable exceptions, constructivists tend to rely on discourse analysis and other text-based methods. For practice theorists, as Navari (2011, 622) explains, such "a focus on discourse or text alone threatens to leave practice behind." PT reinvigorates constructivist methodologies by inviting constructivists to leave their offices and look at how on-the-ground social realities are constructed. It stresses the need for scholars to conduct empirical research within the sites where practices are performed (Neumann 2002; Hopf 2010, 544).

Practice theorists generally look at practices inductively to infer practitioners' mental dispositions and strategies; practices are the observable traces of habits/habitus. This uncovering of practices often calls for a prolonged and deep involvement within practitioners' field of practice. Such engagement gives scholars an inside view of the field, critical to linking practices with the mental dispositions from which they emerge. As Bueger and Gadinger explain:

> Rather than trying to be "objective" and "distant" observers, [PT theorists] had to engage with their subject of investigation. This required not only to observe practices, but also learn and adapt and become active . . . doing practice theory is observing the practices of others, talking about practices, participating in practices, and reflecting on practices all at the same time. (2014, 4)

For this reason, several practice turners use participant observation and other ethnographic methods of inquiry. For instance, Neumann builds on his experience in the Norwegian foreign service to study diplomatic practices within ministries of foreign affairs (2012). Ambrosetti (2009, 2012) and Schia (2013) both started their studies from months of involvement within the UN Security Council.

When ethnographic methods of inquiry are not possible—whether requiring more time and resources than scholars can afford or involving sites with restricted access—scholars must resort to the other methods (Brown 2012, 442; Bueger 2014, 399–400; Pouliot 2014). Many PT scholars rely on interviews. Interviewees provide an insider's point of view that scholars do not have. Scholars can use various techniques to reconstruct through interviews practitioners' points of view, their mental dispositions, the doxa, and the rules of the game in the specific field of practice under study. Pouliot identifies four such techniques: "ask interviewees to recount their everyday practices," "ask interviewees to describe the practice of their colleagues and other interlocutors," "recreate part of the practical context by doing group interviews," and "treat interviews themselves as performances" (2012: 49). Adler-Nissen and Pouliot (2014) used dozens of interviews with diplomats, political experts, and international civil servants to reconstruct the concrete workings of power at the UN Security Council and NATO in negotiations over the Libyan war in 2011. Hardt (2014) uses interviews to show how informal practices influence diplomatic negotiations over peace operations within international organizations.

Whether through participant observation or interviews, practice theory invites IR scholars into the field to get access to the practices that constitute world politics, instead of relying on texts or discourses. Nonetheless, some practice theorists use texts, objects, and discourses to reconstruct practices: "praxiography analyzes documents—including manuals and handbooks—, ego-documents—such as letters and auto-biographies—, or artifacts which record practice—such as videos, paintings, or architecture" (Bueger 2014, 389). Texts and objects are here considered artifacts of the tacit knowledge and background assumptions of practitioners. Sometimes—as in a study of historical practices—there is just no other solution. Such is the case with Andersen and Neumann's study of "wampum diplomacy" (2012). It is moreover "perfectly possible to study practices . . . by using regression analyses or any other supposedly 'non-constructivist' procedure for generating knowledge" (2012, 465), even if practice theorists rarely do so.

Doing practice theory implies a deep grounding in empirical research. This empirical research program builds on a specific epistemology inspired by reflexive pragmatism.

Reflexive Pragmatism as an Epistemology

The epistemology of constructivism has been the subject of much debate (Adler 2013, 130–33). As Jackson put it, "no other identifiable subset of the contemporary IR scholarly literature has worried as long and as loudly about its epistemic standing over the past few years, probably in large part due to the repeated efforts to de-legitimate constructivism as either not scientific or as not yet scientific enough" (2011, 201). As a result of these debates, it can be difficult to see what the four categories of constructivists—modernist, linguistic, radical, and critical—identified by Adler (1997) or the two categories—critical and conventional—identified by Hopf (1998) have in common in terms of epistemology. There are entrenched epistemological oppositions between Wendt's scientific realism (1999), Weldes' critical constructivism (1999), and Guzzini's reflexive constructivism (2000, 2013). This leaves the question of constructivism's epistemology open and allows critics of constructivism to question its foundations. Building on pragmatism, PT rests on an interpretive, empirical, and reflexive epistemology that contributes to reinforce a meta-theoretical foundation to constructivism, while opening a space for critical involvement of scholars in the world.

Analyzing the traces left by habits and the disclosure of mental dispositions always depends on an analyst's point of view. PT therefore builds on a specific epistemology that locates it among interpretivist approaches. The position of the researcher is here characterized by a subtle equilibrium between distance and involvement, an understanding of practices from both "inside" and "outside" the field under study (Pouliot 2007). As Turner (1994, 24) put it, "practices are objects of a peculiar kind, dependent on a cultural perspective." For Bueger (2014, 389), "the praxiographic research process is one of turning implicit knowledge into explicit. This implies a high degree of interpretation." PT therefore stands against neopositivism and its "hubristic claims" that the world can be explained (Brown 2012, 456; McCourt 2012; Navari 2011; Pouliot 2014).

What Turner labeled the "Mauss problem" explains more precisely why practices cannot be studied objectively (Pouliot 2012). At the beginning of the twentieth century, French sociologist Marcel Mauss observed that French women were changing the way they walk to walk more like American women. Mauss's problem was that he needed to be situated within French society to identify and understand this change. Only through his position within that culture could he attribute causality. How can he be sure that this was not a "natural" phenomenon? Turner (1994, 21) explains: "Mauss could distinguish the walk as habit *because* he could say that the difference in walks he had noticed was not a natural difference, and he could say that it was not a natural difference because he could give a historical account of it. He started, so to speak, within a culture with its expectations." Turner imagines a Martian making the same observation. Martians would be unable to see the different ways women walk as a difference of habits and practices, because they are outside French (or US) culture. The attribution of causality to practice requires knowledge of that culture. Practices are always (implicitly) compared to other practices.

This locates PT in line with the pragmatic and postfoundationalist epistemological tradition of pragmatists William James, John Dewey, and

Charles Sanders Peirce and neopragmatists Hillary Putnam and Richard Rorty. In this tradition, the validity of scientific attribution is decided
through adjudication,by consensual agreement among scholars about the
validity of the knowledge claims. Pragmatism "implies turning away from
abstractions and ideal conceptions, from a prioris, axioms, and the ideal of
compelling demonstrations, to arguments and justifications" (Kratochwil
2011, 46). In this tradition, "'truth' is not simply given, revealed, or intuited
by theoretical reason; rather, it results from practical activity, from learning
and contestation" (Ibid.). In this context, IR scholars themselves become
legitimate objects of study. Sociology of knowledge production becomes
necessary, as it is impossible to understand what is held true in IR without
studying those who study IR.

As all practices are analyzed through the lenses of researchers' own practices, it is not possible to study practices without being reflexive (Bueger
and Gadinger 2015). Scholars should be aware that their potential biases
are a two-way street, going as much from the scholar to the object of observation as from the object of observation to the scholar. That is why practice
turners always need to reflect on their own practices as members of specific
social groups and cultures, even if few of them are doing it explicitly:

> If left unchecked, the habitus of the scientist will distort scien-
> tific claims both because s/he will look selectively at the observed
> but also because the observed text, person, image will speak back
> selectively. . . . By turning the sociological tools onto the socio-
> logical observer—analyzing his/her position, habitus and hence the
> strategy—the inherent biases and blindness are made visible and
> (hence) potentially controllable. This is not a "narcissist" navel gaz-
> ing exercise. It is a "scientific exercise." (Leander 2011: 307)

It is ontological coherence that makes necessary such an epistemological stance. If the social world is indeed constituted by fields of practice,
the world of scientists should also be considered as such. Put differently, if
each field has particular doxa, hierarchies, and rules of the game, the scientific field is defined by its own (scientific) doxa, hierarchy, and rules of the
game. Thus the tools used to analyze social realities could and should also
be used to analyze the field of research itself. As Turner (1994, 9) explains,
"if practices are diverse and therefore 'local,' then truth and validity are
themselves local, and only local, because they are always relative to practices that are themselves local." He continues: "the truths we can construct
within our practices are thus 'socially constructed'—constructed by relying

on practices that are themselves shared within a particular social group or network."

PT thus opens up the possibility of a critical involvement in the world. PT's analytical tools unravel the multiple ways in which domination is produced and reproduced in practice. They can generate critical reflections and create the condition for changes in the hierarchical distribution of social positions. For Leander, PT works to "open up scope for politics and revisions. It is only by unveiling and clarifying the positions/dispositions that underpin the constant reproduction in practices . . . that one can ever hope to alter it, that is to introduce politics into the process" (2011, 306). This being said, very few practice turners are themselves activists. Their critical contribution often remains exclusively theoretical.

Conclusion

What it means to be a constructivist is not always clear. Introduced in the discipline in various ways, constructivism at thirty gathers a wide range of different scholarship (see McCourt in this book). Like constructivism, PT is a diverse and sometimes contradictory research program. Nonetheless, its theoretical and meta-theoretical innovations point in a specific direction, expounded in this chapter. My contention is not that PT is entirely new; neither is it simply a new label for scholars revisiting constructivist ideas. PT both builds on and supplements constructivism. Taken together, PT's ontological, conceptual, methodological, and epistemological innovations push constructivism (and IR) in new directions. It answers some concerns raised against constructivism, thus clarifying and reinforcing constructivist thinking on crucial aspects.

NOTES

I thank Ben Foldy, Vincent Pouliot, Maïka Sondarjée, and Srdjan Vucetic for their comments and suggestions on an earlier version of this chapter. All errors are mine. This chapter builds on my contribution to the *International Studies Encyclopedia* "The Practice Turn in International Relations Theory" (Cornut 2015b).

1. While there are some conceptual affinities, both concepts are not synonymous. For Pouliot (2008, 274), "habitus is not habit, for the former is fundamentally generative while the latter is strictly iterative." Reciprocally, for Hopf, the logic of practice is "more reflective and agential than the logic of habit and, consequently, expects far more change in the world" (Hopf 2010, 544). The concept of habitus is linked to Bourdieu's vocabulary as one of his key concepts, whereas the concept of

habits is more broadly used in other practice approaches, for example in Giddens' social theory or in Dewey's pragmatism.

2. On this question, see Hopf 2010; Barnes 2001; Knorr Cetina 2001.

3. For analysis of symbolic power in the World Trade Organization, see Eagleton-Pierce 2013; on symbolic power and security, see Williams 2007; on symbolic power in the EU, see Kuus 2015.

REFERENCES

Abrahamsen, Rita, and Michael Williams. 2011. "Privatization in Practice: Power and Capital in the Field of Global Security." In *International Practices*, edited by Emanuel Adler and Vincent Pouliot, 310–31. Cambridge: Cambridge University Press.

Adler, Emanuel. 1997. "Seizing the Middle Ground: Constructivism in World Politics." *European Journal of International Relations* 3, no. 3: 319–63.

Adler, Emanuel. 2008. "The Spread of Security Communities: Communities of Practice, Self-Restraint, and NATO's Post-Cold War Evolution." *European Journal of International Relations* 14, no. 2: 195–230.

Adler, Emanuel. 2013. "Constructivism in International Relations: Sources, Contributions, and Debates." In *Handbook of International Relations*, edited by Walter Carlsnaes, Thomas Risse, and Beth A. Simmons. London: Sage.

Adler, Emanuel, and Vincent Pouliot. 2011. "International Practices." *International Theory* 3, no. 1: 1–36.

Adler-Nissen, Rebecca. 2011. "On a Field Trip with Bourdieu." *International Political Sociology* 5, no. 3: 327–30.

Adler-Nissen, Rebecca, ed. 2012. *Bourdieu in International Relations: Rethinking Key Concepts*. London: Routledge.

Adler-Nissen, Rebecca. 2014. "Symbolic Power in European Diplomacy: The Struggle Between National Foreign Services and the EU's External Action Service." *Review of International Studies* 40, no. 4: 657–81.

Adler-Nissen, Rebecca, and Vincent Pouliot. 2014. "Power in Practice: Negotiating the International Intervention in Libya." *European Journal of International Relations* 20, no. 4: 889–911.

Ambrosetti, David. 2009. *Normes et Rivalités Diplomatiques à l'ONU. Le Conseil de Sécurité en Audience*. Bruxelles: P. I. E. Peter Lang.

Ambrosetti, David. 2012. "The Diplomatic Lead in the United Nations Security Council and Local Actors' Violence: The Changing Terms of a Social Position." *African Security* 5, no. 2: 63–87.

Andersen, Morten Skumsrud, and Iver B. Neumann. 2012. "Practices as Models: A Methodology with an Illustration Concerning Wampum Diplomacy." *Millennium: Journal of International Studies* 40, no. 3: 457–81.

Barnes, Barry. 2001. "Practice as Collective Action." In *The Practice Turn in Contemporary Theory*, edited by Theodore Schatzki, Karin Knorr Cetina, and Eike von Savigny, 17–28. London: Routledge.

Barnett, Michael. 1999. "Culture, Strategy, and Foreign Policy Change: Israel's Road to Oslo." *European Journal of International Relations* 5, no. 1: 5–36.

Barnett, Michael, and Raymond Duvall. 2005. "Power in International Politics." *International Organization* 59, no. 1: 39–75.

Bigo, Didier. 2011. "Pierre Bourdieu and International Relations: Power of Practices, Practices of Power." *International Political Sociology* 5, no. 3: 225–58.

Brown, Chris. 2012. "The 'Practice Turn,' Phronesis and Classical Realism: Towards a Phronetic International Political Theory?" *Millennium: Journal of International Studies* 40, no. 3: 439–56.

Bueger, Christian. 2014. "Pathways to Practice. Praxiography and International Politics." *European Political Science Review* 6, no. 3: 383–406.

Bueger, Christian, and Frank Gadinger. 2014. *International Practice Theory: New Perspectives*. Basingstoke: Palgrave Macmillan.

Bueger, Christian, and Frank Gadinger. 2015. "The Play of International Practice: Minimalism, Pragmatism and Critical Theory." *International Studies Quarterly* 59, no. 3: 449–60.

Checkel, Jeffrey T. 1998. "The Constructivist Turn in International Relations Theory." *World Politics* 50, no. 2: 324–48.

Checkel, Jeffrey T. 2001. "Why Comply? Social Learning and European Identity Change." *International Organization* 55, no. 3: 553–88.

Cook, Scott, and John Seely Brown. 1999. "Bridging Epistemologies: The Generative Dance Between Organizational Knowledge and Organizational Knowing." *Organization Science* 10, no. 4: 381–400.

Cooper, Andrew F., and Vincent Pouliot. 2015. "How Much Is Global Governance Changing? The G20 as International Practice." *Cooperation and Conflict* 3, no. 50: 334–50.

Cornut, Jérémie. 2015a. "To Be a Diplomat Abroad: Diplomatic Practice at Embassies." *Cooperation and Conflict* 50, no. 3: 385–401.

Cornut, Jérémie. 2015b. "The Practice Turn in International Relations Theory." In *The International Studies Encyclopedia*, edited by Robert Denemark and Renée Marlin-Bennett, 24p. Oxford Reference Online: Oxford University Press.

Eagleton-Pierce, Matthew. 2013. *Symbolic Power in the World Trade Organization*. Oxford: Oxford University Press.

Faizullaev, Alisher, and Jérémie Cornut. 2017. "Narrative Practice in International Politics and Diplomacy. The Case of the Crisis in Crimea." *Journal of International Relations and Development* 20, no. 3: 578–604

Finnemore, Martha, and Kathryn Sikkink. 2001. "Taking Stock: The Constructivist Research Program in International Relations and Comparative Politics." *Annual Review of Political Science* 4, no. 1: 391–416.

Guzzini, Stefano. 2000. "A Reconstruction of Constructivism in International Relations." *European Journal of International Relations* 6, no. 2: 147–82.

Guzzini, Stefano. 2013. *Power, Realism and Constructivism*. Oxon: Routledge.

Hansen, Lene. 2011. "Performing Practices: A Poststructuralist Analysis of the Muhammad Cartoon Crisis." In *International Practices*, edited by Emanuel Adler and Vincent Pouliot, 280–309. Cambridge: Cambridge University Press.

Hardt, Heidi. 2014. *Time to React: The Efficiency of International Organizations in Crisis Response*. Oxford: Oxford University Press.

Hopf, Ted. 1998. "The Promise of Constructivism in International Relations Theory." *International Security* 23, no. 1: 171–200.

Hopf, Ted. 2010. "The Logic of Habit in International Relations." *European Journal of International Relations* 16, no. 4: 539–61.

Hymans, Jacques. 2006. "Theories of Nuclear Proliferation." *The Nonproliferation Review* 13, no. 3: 455–65.

Jackson, Patrick Thaddeus. 2011. *The Conduct of Inquiry in International Relations.* London: Routledge.

Jackson, Patrick Thaddeus, and Daniel H. Nexon. 1999. "Relations Before States: Substance, Process and the Study of World Politics." *European Journal of International Relations* 5, no. 3: 291–332.

Johnston, Alastair Iain. 2001. "Treating International Institutions as Social Environments." *International Studies Quarterly* 45, no. 4: 487–515.

Knorr Cetina, Karin. 2001. "Objectual Practice." In *The Practice Turn in Contemporary Theory*, edited by Theodore Schatzki, Karin Knorr Cetina, and Eike von Savigny, 175–88. London: Routledge.

Kowert, Paul, and Jeffrey Legro. 1996. "Norms, Identity and Their Limits: A Theoretical Reprise." In *The Culture of National Security*, edited by Peter Katzenstein, 451–97. New York: Columbia.

Kratochwil, Friedrich. 2011. "Making Sense of 'International Practices.'" In *International Practices*, edited by Emanuel Adler and Vincent Pouliot, 36–60. Cambridge: Cambridge University Press.

Kuus, Merje. 2014. *Geopolitics and Expertise: Knowledge and Authority in European Diplomacy.* London: Wiley Blackwell.

Kuus, Merje. 2015. "Symbolic Power in Diplomatic Practice: Matters of Style in Brussels." *Cooperation and Conflict* 50, no. 3: 368–84.

Leander, Anna. 2011. "The Promises, Problems, and Potentials of a Bourdieu-Inspired Staging of International Relations." *International Political Sociology* 5, no. 3: 294–313.

Lebow, Richard Ned. 2009. *A Cultural Theory of International Relations.* Cambridge: Cambridge University Press.

McCourt, David. 2012. "What's at Stake in the Historical Turn? Theory, Practice, and Phronēsis in International Relations." *Millennium: Journal of International Studies* 41, no. 1: 23–42.

McCourt, David. 2016. "Practice Theory and Relationalism as the New Constructivism." *International Studies Quarterly* 60, no. 3: 475–85.

Navari, Cornelia. 2011. "The Concept of Practice in the English School." *European Journal of International Relations* 17, no. 4: 611–30.

Neumann, Iver B. 2002. "Returning Practice to the Linguistic Turn: The Case of Diplomacy." *Millennium: Journal of International Studies* 31, no. 3: 627–51.

Neumann, Iver B. 2012. *At Home with the Diplomats: Ethnography of a European Foreign Ministry.* Ithaca, NY: Cornell University Press.

Pouliot, Vincent. 2007. "'Subjectivism': Toward a Constructivist Methodology." *International Studies Quarterly* 51, no. 2: 359–84.

Pouliot, Vincent. 2008. "The Logic of Practicality: A Theory of Practice of Security Communities." *International Organization* 62, no. 2: 257–88.

Pouliot, Vincent. 2010. *International Security in Practice: The Politics of NATO-Russia Diplomacy.* Cambridge: Cambridge University Press.

Pouliot, Vincent. 2012. "Methodology: Putting Practice Theory Into Practice." In *Bourdieu in International Relations: Rethinking the Key Concepts in IR*, edited by Rebecca Adler-Nissen, 46–58. London: Routledge.

Pouliot, Vincent. 2014. "Practice Tracing." In *Process Tracing: From Analytic Metaphor to Best Practices*, edited by Andrew Bennett and Jeffrey Checkel, 237–59. Cambridge: Cambridge University Press.

Pouliot, Vincent. 2016. *International Pecking Orders: The Politics and Practice of Multilateral Diplomacy*. Cambridge: Cambridge University Press.

Pouliot, Vincent, and Jérémie Cornut. 2015. "Practice Theory and the Study of Diplomacy: A Research Agenda." *Cooperation and Conflict* 50, no. 3: 297–315.

Pouliot, Vincent, and Jean-Philippe Thérien. 2015. "The Politics of Inclusion: Changing Patterns in the Governance of International Security." *Review of International Studies* 2, no. 41: 211–37.

Ringmar, Eric. 2014. "The Search for Dialogue as a Hindrance to Understanding: Practices as Inter-Paradigmatic Research program." *International Theory* 6, no. 1: 1–27.

Ross, Andrew. 2006. "Coming In from the Cold: Constructivism and Emotions." *European Journal of International Relations* 12, no. 2: 197–222.

Sagan, Scott. 1996. "Why Do States Build Nuclear Weapons?: Three Models in Search of a Bomb." *International Security* 21, no. 3: 54–86.

Schatzki, Theodore. 2001. "Introduction: Practice Theory." In *The Practice Turn in Contemporary Theory*, edited by Theodore Schatzki, Karin Knorr Cetina, and Eike von Savigny, 1–14. London: Routledge.

Schia, Niels Nagelhus. 2013. "Being Part of the Parade—'Going Native' in the United Nations Security Council." *PoLAR: Political and Legal Anthropology Review* 36, no. 1: 138–56.

Senn, Martin, and Christoph Elhardt. 2014. "Bourdieu and the Bomb: Power, Language and the Doxic Battle Over the Value of Nuclear Weapons." *European Journal of International Relations* 20, no. 2: 316–40.

Shannon, Vaughn P. 2012. "Ideational Allies—Psychology, Constructivism, and International Reations." In *Psychology and Constructivism in International Relations. An Ideational Alliance*, edited by Vaughn P. Shannon and Paul A Kowert, 1–29. Ann Arbor: University of Michigan Press.

Stein, Janice. 2011. "Background Knowledge In the Foreground: Conversations about Competent Practice in 'Sacred Space.'" In *International Practices*, edited by E. Adler and V. Pouliot, 87–107. Cambridge: Cambridge University Press.

Turner, Stephen. 1994. *The Social Theory of Practices. Tradition, Tacit Knowledge, and Presuppositions*. Chicago: University of Chicago Press.

Weldes, Jutta. 1999. *Constructing National Interests: The United States and the Cuban Missile Crisis*. Minneapolis: University of Minnesota Press.

Wendt, Alexander. 1999. *Social Theory of International Politics*. Cambridge: Cambridge University Press.

Williams, Michael C. 2007. *Culture and Security: Symbolic Power and the Politics of International Security*. London: Routledge.

TEN

Securitization Theory

Toward a Replicable Framework for Analysis

Thomas Jamieson

This chapter provides an examination of one midlevel theory within the constructivist approach to international politics—securitization theory—and proposes an analytical framework that could provide the platform for renewed academic interest in securitization and constructivist approaches more broadly. Although securitization is just one theoretical approach within constructivism, the unfulfilled promise of this research agenda over the past two decades is symptomatic of ontological limitations that have prevented constructivist approaches from achieving more of a foothold in North American international relations (IR). In particular, the rigid resistance to positivist research within some strands of constructivism is frustrating when there are some objective indicators that can be used to explore how international relations are constructed between and within states.

I do not self-identify as a constructivist, primarily because although I am sympathetic to constructivist approaches in IR, I make a different ontological wager about the creation of knowledge (Jackson 2011). I agree with Kessler and Steele (this volume) that moderate constructivists using positivist methods are not truly constructivist, so I do not consider myself a constructivist even though I am interested in intersubjective contestation over security threats. I see constructivism as a theoretical approach where states act on the basis of "their shared knowledge, the collective meaning they attach to their situation, their authority and legitimacy, the rules, institutions and material resources they use to find their way, and their practices, or even, sometimes, their joint creativity" (Adler 1997, 321). Ideas and norms are important areas of inquiry, and the constructivist research agenda is informed by the fact that the relationship between states and among states is socially constructed.

This approach has provided an important contribution to IR, but I argue that this has been stifled by many practitioners' refusal to employ positivist research methods. Kessler and Steele contend that damage has been done to constructivism where positivist methods have been adopted. But there is scope within constructivism for the adoption of tools such as content analysis, discourse analysis, or process tracing in a fashion that can be replicated by other researchers without sacrificing the epistemological foundations of constructivism. I find this rigidity frustrating and ultimately self-defeating because it prevents constructivist approaches from gaining more popularity among scholars trained to demand methodological rigor in IR.

Two canonical texts within constructivism stand out as my favorites. First, Wendt's *Social Theory of International Politics* (1999) is a critical contribution to constructivist approaches to IR. It particularly appeals to me because of his systematic approach to the examination of international politics as socially constructed. The second is Buzan, Wæver, and de Wilde's *Security: A New Framework for Analysis* (1998), a book that outlines how security threats are constructed through speech acts, leading to extraordinary political action after an intersubjective agreement is formed about the nature of the threat. Although they are considerably different texts, they both set the research agenda for the integration of constructivism within IR, each making persuasive arguments about how the approach broadens the understanding of international politics.

In this chapter, I advocate a return to the notion of securitization introduced by Buzan, Wæver, and de Wilde (1998). The publication of *Security: A New Framework for Analysis* prompted a flurry of scholarship into the securitization of political events with their introduction of securitization theory, which has added much to the understanding of how potential threats become security issues. They presented securitization as "a more extreme version of politicization" where actors construct security threats in order to justify extraordinary political powers (Buzan, Wæver, and de Wilde 1998, 23–24). This argument that security should be interpreted as the social construction of a threat has become an important alternative approach that has helped invigorate the study of security, even if there was some resistance from some vocal opponents of such moves (Walt 1991). Securitization theory has thus been an invaluable analytical concept for constructivist approaches to IR, but there appear to be two critical limitations that have prevented securitization from fulfilling its initial promise.

First, much scholarship has erroneously assumed that the articulation of the threat in a speech act constitutes securitization. The criteria proposed by Buzan, Wæver, and de Wilde, however, are much more stringent, requiring significant political effects and an intersubjective agreement about the nature of the threat between the public and the elites voicing the speech acts. Second, a lack of methodological guidance has led to a multiplicity of definitions and methods, preventing the establishment of a coherent research program in securitization. In an attempt to bridge this gap, this chapter operationalizes securitization into a four-stage process that involves the fulfillment of several necessary conditions. The chapter introduces this standardized framework to enable replicable research into the process of securitization. The goal is to take a first step toward reinvigoration of securitization studies in IR.

This chapter consists of five parts. First, the chapter outlines the introduction and the evolution of securitization theory in the study of international politics. I argue, however, that the research tradition overlooks how successful securitization is difficult to achieve; following the theoretical framework of Buzan, Wæver, and de Wilde, it is difficult for elite actors to securitize a security threat and fulfill all the necessary conditions for securitization. Second, the chapter reviews methodological limitations of the securitization literature. Third, in an attempt to address the preceding issues, the chapter introduces a framework for the evaluation of securitization in practice. This involves the fulfilment of four necessary conditions: (1) identification of the security threat, (2) articulation of the security threat, (3) an intersubjective agreement about the security threat, and (4) demonstrated political effects that cannot be easily reversed. Fourth, the chapter applies the analytical framework to two cases where the United States attempted to securitize threats. Through the application of the framework, it is evident that the US securitization of the Islamic State was successful, while the securitization of Venezuela as a security threat was unsuccessful because Washington failed to fulfil all the necessary conditions for successful securitization. Finally, the chapter concludes with a summary of the critical reasons behind the need for the framework and an acknowledgment that the explanation here does not prescribe methods for the study of securitization in the future.

Securitization Theory

While earlier discussions of securitization exist, the exploration of the concept by Buzan, Wæver, and de Wilde (1998) is the first fully formed articulation of the concept to international relations. The authors define securitization as "constituted by the intersubjective establishment of an existential threat with a saliency sufficient to have substantial political effects" (1998, 25). Later, Hayes (2012, 66) elaborated on this concept, discussing securitization as "the sociopolitical construction of security" where (a) a securitizing actor voices the claim about the threat and (b) the audience must both agree about the nature of the threat and that the threatened object is of value. Thus the bar for the successful securitization of a threat is high.

According to Buzan, Wæver, and de Wilde (1998, 25), securitization is not realized without subsequent political action; it can only be fulfilled through "cases of existential threats that legitimize the breaking of rules." Securitization of a threat occurs through a speech act, which works "to shift the issue from the arena of normal politics into the realm of security politics—characterized by urgency and exceptional measures, including power centralization and marginalized debate" (Hayes 2012, 66). A speech act by itself, however, does not constitute securitization.

Conflation of speech acts with securitization has led to assumptions that "calling something 'security' makes it into a security problem" (Huysmans 1998, 492). In fact, securitization actually involves fulfilling a more rigorous set of necessary conditions to qualify under the definition offered by Buzan, Wæver, and de Wilde. This is corroborated by Balzacq (2005, 172), who argued that "securitization is better understood as a strategic [pragmatic] practice that occurs within, and as part of, a configuration of circumstances, including the context, the psycho-cultural disposition of the audience, and the power that both speaker and listener bring to the interaction." Similarly, McDonald (2008, 566) noted that Buzan, Wæver, and de Wilde "began to place increased emphasis on the role of constituencies or audiences in 'backing up' speech acts." Accordingly, "speech acts were defined as 'securitizing moves' that became securitizations through audience consent" (McDonald 2008, 566). Securitizing moves hold risks for leaders if they are rejected by the domestic public, as leaders might avoid the political risk of securitizing perceived threats and ultimately "underbalance" if they anticipate problems persuading voters to accept their interpretation of the security environment (Schweller 2004). Essentially the message delivered in a speech act is not enough by itself. The reception of the audience is critical for successful securitization.

Additionally, securitizing actors must be operating from a position of power, with actors such as "political leaders, bureaucracies, governments, lobbyists, and pressure groups" being sufficiently influential to be considered as elites (Buzan, Wæver, and de Wilde 1998, 40–41). There must also be significant political effects, making a speech act insufficient by itself to securitize a particular threat; there must be some political action to accompany it. The political effects are contingent on the intersubjective agreement about the nature of the threat between the public and the elites: political action can only take place if the public believes the rhetoric they hear from the elites. In this fashion successful securitization must involve the fulfillment of several necessary conditions.

Some alternative definitions of securitization have included issue areas where the military is summoned to take over the control or response to a particular threat, such as in the response to natural disasters or the outbreak of contagious diseases (Dörrie 2014). The use of the term "securitization" in these cases, however, is void of meaning, and the term erroneously labels militarized responses to emergency situations as securitization. Instead, securitization refers to the constitutive process whereby a security threat becomes accepted as such, in a process akin to legitimation as discussed by Goddard and Krebs. This chapter introduces a framework for the replicable analysis of this process.

Methodological Challenges

In order to take into account various elements necessary for successful securitization, there are several important methodological challenges to overcome. Even a casual glance at the literature indicates the problems inherent with securitization: there has been much navel gazing about definitions and theoretical assumptions, but comparatively little empirical work on specific *instances* of securitization. Where empirical work has been conducted, it has all too often confirmed securitization through evidence of speech acts articulating the threat, paying little attention to the necessity of political effects or to the possibility of unsuccessful securitization. Too little work has also dealt with contingency as discussed by Kessler and Steele.

Fortunately, much recent work has wrestled with the difficulty in putting forward a framework for the analysis of securitization in empirical studies (Guzzini 2011; Balzacq 2011; Vultee 2010; Stritzel 2007; Holbraad and Pedersen 2012). Until this point, empirical research has tended to employ either discursive, critical, or anthropological methodologies, perhaps due to the fragmented nature of the concept. It is possible, however, to develop a workable set of qualitative and quantitative indicators to insert securitization in a framework that can be repeated by other scholars.

Vultee's (2010) content analysis of the newspaper coverage of the "war on terror" constituted a rare attempt at studying securitization through content analysis, but his constructs did not capture the entire process of securitization. Vultee focused on the securitizing voice, the status of the nouns describing the conflict, and the location of the enemy (2010). This chapter operationalizes the notion further into a set of necessary conditions for securitization, providing the platform for a more complete analysis of securitization in the news media coverage of foreign policy debates.

Before going further, it is important to note that there may be some resistance to the positivist analysis of a concept like securitization. As mentioned earlier, constructivist works in IR have tended to gravitate toward interpretivist methods, which help explain the social construction of interstate relations; this has meant that cross-case comparisons and nomothetic explanations of state behavior have been difficult using constructivist approaches. Accordingly, much like other midlevel theories within constructivism, securitization has not been the subject of much empirical study through replicable methods.

When positivist methods have been used to explore the securitization of security threats, the concept has been interpreted in different ways to create a "problematic range of contradictory empirical applications of securitization theory" (Stritzel 2007, 359). This situation has been exacerbated by the fact that "the theory does not point to one particular type of study as the right one," even if the theory does have a firm "postmodern/poststructural root" (Wæver 2003, 16–17; Stritzel 2007, 362).

Although the theory has a wide range of applications, that "the Copenhagen School offers little methodological guidance" has also helped cause the work on securitization to be methodologically and theoretically disjointed (Hayes 2012, 72). Additionally, the reflexive nature of the theory might also have contributed to the absence of replicable studies of securitization, even though Buzan, Wæver, and de Wilde popularized the concept almost two decades ago.

But this need not be the case. Jackson notes that "the default position in IR—whether one is talking about constructivist, rationalist, systemic, individualist, or any other variety of substantive claims—is and remains neopositivism" (2011, 204). He therefore could find "no compelling philosophical or methodological reason why norms, ideas, culture, and other intersubjective factors cannot be studied by using a neopositivist methodology," a sentiment that is pertinent to the study of securitization (Jackson 2011, 206). Jackson, of course, argues for methodological pluralism, and the alternative methods have many advantages over positivism in understanding the nature of securitization. But there is nothing in the theory of securitization that precludes its positivist testing, and if this research agenda is pursued in the future, it would be useful to have a framework in place to compare analyses across different issues, periods, and scholars. In fact, through such work, Sil and Katzenstein's (2010) call for more analytic eclecticism in the study of international politics might come to fruition. In this spirit, this chapter attempts to mark a first step in proposing an analytical framework for the replicable study of securitization.

By definition speech acts have to be observable. Indeed, one of the most trenchant critiques of the Copenhagen School is that securitization pays no heed to those incapable of voicing threat (Hansen 2000). It is in this spirit that this chapter proceeds, with a view to furthering social-scientific knowledge by operationalizing securitization to assess how and when an issue is securitized. Not only has securitization not been taken up for definitive empirical testing, but it has also developed parallel to theorizing about news media, an obvious primary forum for the articulation of the threat in order to form an intersubjective agreement about the nature of the threat. In particular, framing theory offers insights into "the process by which people develop a particular conceptualization of an issue or reorient their thinking about an issue" (Chong and Druckman 2007, 104). The absence of work in this area is perplexing given that speech acts must be made in a public forum, and be persuasive, for securitization to be successful.

The securitization literature has also shown signs of confirmation bias, where researchers are liable to find supporting evidence to confirm preexisting beliefs or expectations (Nickerson 1998). One of the interesting and underexplored areas of securitization, though, is that the speech acts of elite actors do not always work. These cases—where securitization does not succeed—are just as significant as those that do and are worthy of further exploration. The literature, however, has tended to confirm cases of securitization, a state of affairs that has stifled understanding of the concept, because to truly comprehend the process of securitization there should be variation in the dependent variable. This also detracts from the possibility of comparing securitization across cases, which would allow researchers to determine the conditions under which securitization fails as well as when it succeeds.

Toward a Framework for Analysis

A critical operational problem with definitions of securitization is that the concept is a messy one with many moving parts. As a result, while it has proved to be a useful analytical concept, it has been much more difficult to turn into a set of testable conditions for empirical hypothesis testing. In order to best encapsulate the process of securitization as outlined by Buzan, Wæver, and de Wilde, this chapter operationalizes securitization into a four-stage process. Although the process of securitization is undoubtedly complex, and the temporal order might not be set in stone, the framework is presented in this way for analytical clarity. This process involves the fulfillment of a set of necessary conditions that must be present for the successful securitization of a threat. First, a threat has to be identified by a political actor as something that has the potential to present an existential threat to their community. Second, the threat must be articulated through speech acts made by elite actors. The third stage involves the reaching of an intersubjective agreement about the nature of the threat. Finally, the fourth stage involves the achievement of significant political effects where the actions cannot be easily reversed. All four necessary conditions must be present for securitization of a particular threat to be successfully completed. In other words, the conditions are individually necessary and collectively sufficient.

It is most useful to conceive of the process as continuing along from the identification and articulation of the threat, before finally an intersubjective agreement about the nature of the security threat is formed. It should be noted, however, that the stages of the process might not follow in this temporal order. One can imagine a situation where the public is much more informed about the threat through everyday experiences than are the elites in a distant capital. This chapter, however, proceeds on the basis that securitization involves the dissemination of information about a security threat from the elites to the citizenry in order to justify extraordinary political actions. If the process followed from public opinion towards the elites, this would be a separate path to securitization as the government and policy elites respond to public opinion. On that basis, figure 10.1 demonstrates an analytical framework for the process of securitization as theorized in this chapter.

Identification of the Security Threat

First, a threat has to be identified by a political actor as something that might present an existential threat to their community. This chapter pro-

Figure 10.1. The four-stage process of securitization

ceeds on the assumption that the community referred to by the political actor is people within a state, although it is important to note that the community serving as the referent for the actor might instead be a group, an ethnicity, a race, a village, town, city, region, or state. In order for securitization to occur, the threat must be communicated by elites, so this identification of a threat must be done by people with the ability to get issues onto the policy agenda of elites. This expression could come out of a genuine concern about the potential security threat, but it could also be seized as an opportunity for political or economic gain for these actors to pursue in their rational self-interest.

Ultimately, the identification of the threat is an elite process where experts in security and foreign policy acknowledge the existence of the threat and communicate that to political elites. It is thus normally made up of elite-elite communication. Likely sources of information for the elites include political institutions, bureaucracies, the military, or academic research, with official papers and policy recommendations highlighting particular threats that get expressed by the elites.

Another intriguing possibility for examining the identification of the threat between elite actors would be to review private communication, much like Hayes' (2012) review of President Nixon's securitization of India. If access could be gained through Official Information Acts and similar legislation, unofficial documents such as e-mails, internal memos, private conversations, and meetings between elite actors could be even more useful than official documents in demonstrating how threats are identified by elites as potential security issues. Similarly, WikiLeaks might also provide data for scholars to review the identification of threats (de Zamaroczy 2015). When elites are engaged in unguarded private communication, they are more likely to be candid with one another, so the process through which a threat becomes identified could be observed by the researcher without the spin put on public speeches.

The key idea with the identification of the threat as a necessary condition for securitization is that speech acts do not come out of nowhere; the elite actors voicing that threat would have received information beforehand about the nature of the threat. The security threat does not necessarily have to be compelling or even "real"; its nature could be greatly exaggerated at this stage. Above all else, the security threat at this stage of securitization must be expressed as a threat that might be believed by the public in the future. Elite actors might therefore see the potential for securitizing the issue publicly by expressing the threat in the news media.

Articulation of the Security Threat

The next step in the securitization of the threat involves the articulation of the threat, which must be articulated by the elite actor in a speech act. Contrary to Huysmans, however, speaking about a threat does not necessarily make it so. In order for the speech act to result in an intersubjective agreement about the existence and the nature of the threat, it must fulfill a set of five necessary conditions. Without all these conditions being fulfilled, as pictured in figure 10.2, the security threat will not be successfully securitized.

First, for the fulfillment of the definition offered by Buzan, Wæver, and de Wilde, speech acts have to be consistently frequent. For securitization, the articulation of an existential threat should be made more than once, and it should not become less frequent with time. It is implausible for an existential security threat to disappear without any action after it has been articulated, so the articulation of the threat should either increase in frequency or remain consistently frequent for the speech act to be persuasive in securitizing the threat. Raw counts of elite speech acts, however, are insufficient by themselves to satisfy the requirements of successful securitization.

Second, successful securitization must involve negative sentiment in the articulation of the security threat. Articulation of the threat must invoke negative consequences that override any potential positive implications that might result from the security threat. If the overall tone of the coverage is consistently more negative than positive, and if the count of negative allusions does not increase over time, the articulation of the threat will meet this necessary condition for successful securitization of the threat.

Third, the threat should be framed as being relevant to a particular policy agenda across the coverage of the particular threat. The threat must be specifically and frequently identified as being relevant to the same portfolio for it to be successfully securitized. The threat should consistently be considered relevant to the region's defense or security policy agenda to be securitized successfully; if there is much variance in

Figure 10.2. The necessary conditions for successful articulation of the security threat

the policy agenda it would be difficult to argue that the threat has been sufficiently securitized to construct an intersubjective agreement about the nature of the security threat.

The fourth necessary condition for the successful articulation of the security threat is the consistent identification of the source of the threat. Vultee (2010) demonstrated how the threat can be constructed as more meaningful if it is formally and specifically identified by the newspaper. For an actor to argue persuasively that an issue is an existential security threat, one would need to be able to specifically identify where that threat is coming from. If a threat is conceived of in a general manner, as an abstract possibility, it is difficult to argue that it is actually an issue of concern to the general public.

For instance, if an actor articulates a threat such as global warming without specific details about where the threat is going to come from, it would not constitute successful articulation of the security threat as defined by Buzan, Wæver, and de Wilde. Similarly, American fears about communism during the Cold War would not qualify as a specific source of threat, whereas specific identification of the Soviet Union or China would meet these criteria. If a threat is identified by name, it is much more conducive for an eventual intersubjective agreement about the voiced threat. The threat must be specifically identified for it to be a genuine security threat.

Fifth, the successful articulation of a security threat requires it to be expressed by elites. Buzan, Wæver, and de Wilde classify elites as essentially those who have the ability to shape and inform the policy agenda, leading to eventual political effects. It is perhaps useful to invoke Mosca (1939, 50), who classified elites as a class who are "always the less numerous, performs all political functions, monopolizes power and enjoys the advantages that power brings." Likewise, Putnam (1976, 3–5) considered elites to be those in control of political power as part of a homogeneous group drawn from a small part of the population that is largely autonomous. This is a useful starting point for the consideration of who must articulate a threat to successfully securitize it as a security threat.

In this definition of political elite, journalists and academics are excluded from consideration as elites. Some critics, who correctly note that these figures have the opportunity to indirectly influence policy and public opinion through their work, might dispute this exclusion. For analytical clarity and to ensure consistency across different coders, however, it is most useful to consider elites to be those who are capable of influencing policy more directly.

In contrast to the identification of the threat, the articulation of the threat through speech acts must be in the public sphere. This is because the articulation of the threat is a process where elite actors pursue an intersubjective agreement about the nature of the threat. Although many state leaders and political actors increasingly communicate directly to their constituents through social media (Zeitzoff and Barberá 2014), the news media remain an influential source of information for the public, especially those without a continuing interest in politics. The best data to measure this process is therefore the news media, especially if one wishes to trace developments in securitization over time.

The news media provide the best lens to examine the articulation of a security threat as elites securitize a threat and communicate it to the public in the search for an intersubjective agreement. Because it is imperative for news organizations to achieve and sustain an audience, irrespective of their type of ownership or political sympathies, they are compelled to produce content that is relevant and significant for that audience (Galtung and Ruge 1965).

Construction of the news is also the result of an external set of conditions and conventions. One of these conditions is the interdependent relationship between journalists and the political elite, as "journalists, in attempting to fulfil public interest aims and present authoritative accounts, purposively seek out those who already appear knowledgeable, authoritative or representative" (Davis 2007, 40). At the same time, political elites require the media to communicate policies with the voting public. The result of these "symbiotic relationships" is that the news "reflects the strange mutual dependencies (punctuated by occasional bursts of antagonism) between reporters and officials" (Bennett, Lawrence, and Livingston 2007, 3). Because "reporters overwhelmingly turn to officials as sources for stories and for framing the content of stories," these political actors hold some influence over how the story is constructed (Bennett 1994, 177). Consequently, elite sources arguably come to "dominate the reporting of political as well as most other news sources" (Davis 2010, 69).

The process of securitization is best explained by the mutually beneficial relationship between the media and political actors. The news media's interests are served through access to the elite, and the securitization of threats is likely to attract interest from readers. Simultaneously, elites are able to voice the threat through speech acts in the news media, using them as a means of communication to local citizens and to foreign political actors. Although there might be contestation between elites about the nature of a security threat and whether it should be securitized, the assumption is that the ruling elite would have the ability to present their dominant frame to the public through their greater access to news media and other forms of information dissemination.

If the news media have the ability to "set the agenda," discussing the perceived threat might make the issue salient to the public (McCombs and Show 1972; Iyengar and Kinder 1987). As Cohen wrote, the news media "may not be successful much of the time in telling people what to think, but it is stunningly successful in telling its readers what to think about" (1963, 13). The news media are able to "force attention to certain issues" by "constantly presenting objects suggesting what individuals in the mass should think about, know about, have feelings about" (Lang and Lang 1966, 468). This suggests that securitizing actors can be successful in getting the issue into the public agenda, providing a platform for elites to pursue actions in the name of security that would otherwise be unavailable to them. For this reason, the news is an appropriate means to assess the elite articulation of security threats.

Intersubjective Agreement about the Security Threat

For the intersubjective agreement about the nature of the security threat to be met, there needs to be a widespread acceptance that the security threat has the potential to challenge the security of citizens within a state. Accordingly, a particular threat "is securitized only if and when the audience accepts it as such" (Buzan, Wæver, and de Wilde 1998, 25). Therefore, a speech act by itself is not enough; the public must find the threat credible.

This is a high standard to reach, and it presents a challenge to the researcher to find cases where this condition has been fulfilled. Vultee (2010) posits that the "war on terror" securitized the threat of terrorism after the events of 9/11, but it might be much more difficult to establish an intersubjective agreement about the nature of the threat without such a large unexpected shock as a focusing event that brings attention to the threat. This is a critical problem that has not been dealt with enough by securitization scholars; it is hard to achieve an intersubjective agreement through rhetoric alone. Instead, events might help to establish the security threat as being existential and requiring action from the state, fulfilling the condition of political effects as outlined by Buzan, Wæver, and de Wilde.

Intersubjective agreement about the threat requires relative consensus between the masses and the elites about the nature of the threat. More than anything, the intersubjective agreement is fulfilled when the public signals to the elites that they agree with the elite assessment about the nature of the threat. They can communicate their agreement through several different means. Before discussing that, though, it is important to acknowledge that the acceptance of a threat is subjective, which leads to problems with determining when this condition is fulfilled. It is also important to acknowledge that even though some people might correspond with political elites through social media or through consultations and public meetings with their elected official, there is not an equivalent to the news media that informs elites about the public acceptance of their speech act.

Some measurement is possible, however, to ascertain whether public opinion matches that of the elites who articulated the existential threat. For instance, public opinion polls with representative samples of the population could provide a measurement of the public acceptance of the threat as articulated by elites. If the majority of the population agrees about the nature of the security threat, one could interpret this as confirmation of an intersubjective agreement between the public and elites. Interviews with members of the public could also determine the nature of an intersubjective agreement.

Ultimately, election results in democratic regimes might also demonstrate the public's willingness to accept the elite framing of the threat, although drawing causal inferences about a single foreign policy issue and election results might be difficult. Popular protests also communicate directly with leaders, as the elites are able to assess the public's acceptance of elite rhetoric through its involvement in protests. Protests, however, also might be symptomatic of wider issues with the regime, so it is possibly not the best measure of the intersubjective agreement. Instead, public opinion polls provide the most appropriate way of measuring public acceptance of elite speech acts.

Demonstrated Political Effects

The fourth and final stage of the securitization process is that successful securitization must have demonstrated political effects. The voicing of the threat is not enough by itself; it must have some lasting political implications. As a result of the intersubjective agreement between elites and the general public, political action is possible. Furthermore, the articulation of the threat and a subsequent intersubjective agreement legitimates long-lasting political effects because elites can consequently enact legislation and spend money to confront the security threat without fear of punishment from the public. Accordingly, this final necessary stage fulfills the requirements for successful securitization as the process enables the creation of permanent political effects.

Demonstrated political effects could include legislation that enables the state to take action to confront the security threat. This could include binding legislation such as the creation of the US Transportation Security Administration [TSA] in the Aviation and Transportation Security Act after the events of September 11, 2011 (Pub. L. No. 107-71, 107th Cong., Nov. 19, 2001). This type of action is unlikely to be reversed and legislated out of existence because after the argument was made for it, the public or political elites are unlikely to accept that the need for such an institution will ever pass (Pierson 2000). Accordingly, political effects would include legislation that sets a state on a particular path that is difficult to deviate from (Thelen 1999). But political effects could also include less path-dependent actions.

Another example of demonstrated political effects could include spending money on countering security threats through specific programs or initiatives initiated after the securitization of the threat. For instance, if the Arctic was securitized within an Arctic state such as Norway, and the government subsequently increased its spending on militarized icebreaker ships, this could qualify as demonstrated political effects because the spending is irreversible; once the money has been spent, it cannot be returned. In such a way, government spending on initiatives aimed at targeting specific securitized threats can be interpreted as demonstrated political effects.

Limitations of the Framework

It is important to acknowledge that this analytical framework has a critical limitation. Like many other IR theories, the analytical framework described is the product of its environment, a Euro-US context where democracy is the norm and the press has the freedom to agree or disagree with the rhetoric of leaders. Implicit throughout the framework is the assumption that the state is a democracy, with leaders eager to legitimate their actions and the citizenry forming a crucial part of the securitization process, as their acceptance of elite speech acts is a necessary condition for securitization to be successful.[1] At the very least, there must be some avenue for leaders to be held accountable in this framework, otherwise the extraordinary steps taken to securitize a threat are completely unnecessary for autocratic leaders with no need to consult the public and convince them of the worthiness of their foreign policies. This is an important limitation of the framework, and it might be of limited value in analyzing securitization, or its absence, in states with authoritarian regimes.

A second limitation is that the framework implies that speech acts are transmitted primarily through verbal or written communication. Indeed, an exciting emergent field of research in IR is the analysis of visual moves (Sylvester 2009; Burke 2007; Bleiker 2009; Steele 2010). Although it is not covered in this chapter, it is certainly possible to develop a complementary framework that can encompass visual securitization, of which examples could be found in the Islamic State's beheading videos published on YouTube, and the television and film responses to them. While this is beyond the scope of this chapter, it would be a worthwhile exercise to better explore securitization in a nondiscursive setting and develop an appropriate coding scheme to explore visual securitization.

Application of the Analytical Framework

In order to illustrate how the analytical framework can be applied to empirical cases, two illustrative case studies are explored briefly to conclude this chapter: one where securitization was successful and one where it was not. The purpose of these case studies is to introduce examples of how the framework can be systematically applied, allowing for comparisons between cases across regions, states, or particular security threats. Although the cases could be explored in further depth, they are used here simply to illustrate how the framework might be applied in practice. The two cases of securitization are both from the US perspective. The first involves the securitization of the threat posed by the Islamic State of Iraq and the Levant (also known as the Islamic State of Iraq and Syria, Islamic State of Iraq and al-Sham, ISIS, or ISIL) to the United States, and the second involves the securitization of Venezuela.

Due to limitations of time and space, analysis of the securitization of these two cases is limited to selected secondary sources and the news coverage of the cases in the *New York Times* from January 1, 2013, to March 13, 2015.[2] As a prominent broadsheet newspaper of record in the United States, the *New York Times* was a suitable outlet for the exploratory analysis of the two cases. Table 10.1 presents a summary of the securitization in the two cases.

Successful Securitization: The Case of the Islamic State

The United States armed forces and intelligence agencies monitored the development of the Islamic State organization from its foundation groups in the late 1990s to the present time. After the invasion of Iraq in 2003 and the subsequent troop surge in 2007, the United States had scaled back its involvement in the country with a view to ensuring the Iraqi forces would be able to maintain territorial sovereignty by themselves. But the United States began to fly drones over Iraq from 2013 to gather information about the organization after ISIS had made significant territorial strides in northern Iraq (Entous 2014). That Iraq had lost territory to ISIS in northern Iraq and the reinvolvement of the United States suggests that the United States had identified the threat presented by the Islamic State to their interests, their allies, and their remaining troops in Iraq. As such, the United States had demonstrably identified the potential threat of the organization, as is evident in these surveillance activities.

Speech acts related to the threat presented by the Islamic State have frequently appeared in the *New York Times* from June 2014 to the time of writing, with 189 articles featuring the group in the context of security threats in 2014 and 61 in the first two and a half months of 2015. The sample featured a predominantly negative tone in the coverage of ISIS. This was particularly evident in headlines such as "Kerry Says ISIS Threat Could Hasten Military Action" (Gordon 2014), "The World Is Appalled by the Killing, Obama Says" (Shear and Davis 2014), and "Attacks in West Raise New Fears over ISIS' Influence" (Kirkpatrick 2014). The threat to national security and the security of US nationals was a feature of the coverage of the *New York Times*, which suggests that the group had been successfully

TABLE 10.1. Application of the Analytical Framework.

The Fulfillment of the Necessary Conditions for Successful Securitization	Islamic State	Venezuela
Identification of the Security Threat	Yes	No
Articulation of the Security Threat	Yes	No
Frequency of Speech Acts	Yes	No
Negative Tone	Yes	No
Relevant to the Security Policy Agenda	Yes	No
Specific Source of Threat	Yes	No
Speech Acts by Elite Actors	Yes	Yes
Intersubjective Agreement about the Security Threat	Yes	No available data
Demonstrated Political Effects	Yes	No
Successful Securitization?	**Yes**	**No**

securitized to the security policy agenda. Despite its various aliases, the group was consistently specifically identified as a threat to national security.

Perhaps most significantly, elite actors consistently identified ISIS as a security threat in the *New York Times*. President Obama was prominent in the newspaper coverage of the Islamic State. For instance, one article (Landler 2014: A1) quoted Obama's speech to the United Nations General Assembly in September 2014: "If there was ever a challenge in our interconnected world that cannot be met by one nation alone, it is this . . . terrorists crossing borders and threatening to unleash unspeakable violence." Obama was not the only elite actor voicing the threat; Senator Lindsey Graham was another high-profile voice who highlighted the threat posed by ISIL: "To those who say I'm trying to fight other peoples' wars, you don't understand what ISIL has in store for you and our nation. . . . The sooner we get on with it, the better" (quoted in Gabriel 2015). This was consistent across the coverage, with numerous political elites articulating the threat presented by ISIS. Collectively, this coverage fulfilled the necessary conditions identified in the analytical framework for the successful articulation of the threat.

Public opinion polls suggest that the securitization of ISIS has been successful in forming an intersubjective agreement about the nature of the threat of the organization. A recent Gallup public opinion poll found that "Islamic militants, commonly known as ISIS, operating in Iraq and Syria," were the most commonly cited critical threat, with 84 percent of respondents seeing the group as a "threat to the vital interests of the United States in the next 10 years" (Swift and Dugan 2015). This is corroborated by an earlier CNN/ORC poll in November 2014 that found "most Americans now believe ISIS poses at least a somewhat serious threat to the United States" (Diamond 2014). These polls suggest that the securitization of ISIS has been successful within the United States, with a majority of respondents agreeing that the Islamic State presents a real threat to the United States.

The American-led response to the Islamic State has been considerable. In September 2014, President Obama announced he had ordered air strikes on ISIS in Iraq and Syria because "if you threaten America, you will find no safe haven" (quoted in Cohen 2014). Since then, US officials claim that military operations in the region have killed more than six thousand ISIS militants, including several leaders of the group (Bergen and Schneider 2015). This military response has been possible due to the intersubjective agreement about the nature of the threat. At the time of writing, the United States is considering whether the deployment of ground troops would further assist the fight against the Islamic State. The considerable expense involved in the use of force against ISIS demonstrates that the securitization of the organization was successful in enabling extraordinary political action to be undertaken against the threat. In sum, the securitization of the threat presented by the Islamic State has been successful.

Unsuccessful Securitization: The Case of Venezuela

In contrast to the case of the Islamic State, the securitization of Venezuela in March 2015 almost came out of nowhere. Throughout the tenure of Hugo Chávez as president, Venezuela and the United States had experienced a tumultuous relationship. Chávez "led a nationalist movement that lashed out at the United States government," and he frequently accused the United States of supporting opposition to his leadership (Romero 2013; Kelman 2011). Since his death, however, even if they never quite reconciled, relations between the two states had appeared to calm down as they traded ambassadorial postings in each other's capitals (Neuman 2015a). Significant reductions in global oil prices in particular appeared to lessen Venezuela's capacity to be a menace for the United States. But, apparently in response to the prosecution of opposition politicians in Venezuela, President Obama attempted to securitize the regime.

Obama articulated the threat, claiming Venezuela presented "an extraordinary threat to the national security of the United States" (quoted in Neuman 2015a). But there is reason to doubt the president's assessment. One official, who spoke to the *New York Times* on condition of anonymity, claimed that:

> In order to carry out sanctions of this type, the law required the president to declare the nation whose officials are sanctioned to be a national security threat. The official cautioned that the declaration was meant to meet the legal requirement and did not represent "a recategorization of the actual circumstances in Venezuela" (Neuman 2015a).

Accordingly, it is possible that the United States does not genuinely perceive Venezuela as a security threat.

The securitization of the Venezuelan government fails to meet the necessary condition for a steady or increasing frequency of speech acts. Instead, that the *New York Times* coverage only includes eleven articles from 2013 and only two articles in 2015 indicates that, at the time of writing, the speech acts have been too infrequent to securitize the state. Similarly, the tone in the coverage is insufficiently negative to constitute fulfillment of the second necessary condition for the articulation of the threat. The securitization attempt is also not sufficiently relevant to the security agenda; it is unclear how the Venezuelan government relates to US national security.

Furthermore, the securitization move does not refer to a specific source of threat. President Obama mentioned that they are "committed to advancing respect for human rights, safeguarding democratic institutions, and protecting the U.S. financial system from the illicit financial flows from public corruption in Venezuela" (The White House 2015). Seven people are targeted for imposition of sanctions within the United States (The White House 2015), but it is unclear in the statement how they present a threat to the United States. The only necessary condition for the successful articulation of the threat that is met by the speech act is that President Obama was an elite actor who made the securitizing move, enforcing the Venezuela Defense of Human Rights and Civil Society Act that was passed in Congress in November 2014 (The White House 2015), thus fulfilling the necessary condition of elite actors voicing the threat.

At the time of writing, there have not been any public opinion polls published about US public support. But, given the incredulous reaction among commentators, it would be surprising if there was an intersubjective agreement about the security threat presented by Venezuela between the American public and political elites.

The final stage of the securitization process necessary for successful securitization is demonstrated political effects. At first glance, Obama's executive order might appear to fulfill the criteria for this because the order "authorized the American government to freeze any assets in the United States held by seven Venezuelan law enforcement and military officials whom Washington identified as being responsible for human rights abuses or violations of democratic due process" (Neuman 2015b). It is not readily apparent, though, whether this order has any real consequences. Neuman (2015a) elaborated on this fact:

> It was not clear, however, whether the officials being sanctioned actually owned property in the United States. An administration official said that designating those to be sanctioned was a first step and that a search to see whether they had assets that could be frozen would now begin.

There might thus not be any consequences as a result of the order. It is not clear either whether the sanctions can be reneged upon if relations improve between the two states, but they do not appear to be consequential or permanent at the moment. Given these doubts about the actions taken so far, it is most likely that the would-be securitization of Venezuela will not have irreversible political effects, despite the imposition of sanctions.

In sum, the two illustrations show how the analytical framework can be applied to different cases. A range of different methodological tools can be utilized to evaluate the success of the securitizing move. At the very least, the application of the framework demonstrates how the speech act is insufficient by itself to successfully securitize a security threat.

Conclusion

This chapter is a first step toward a replicable framework for the analysis of securitization. It makes the case that securitization can be interpreted as a four-stage process with a set of necessary conditions that must all be fulfilled for it to be successfully completed. The operationalization of securitization is aimed to allow for the systematic replication of empirical securitization analysis using the same framework.

The chapter has not contributed methodological prescriptions about how to conduct tests of securitization once the data has been collected. This is deliberate, because there are a variety of methods that can be successfully employed (Balzacq 2011), and I do not wish to suggest the use of any particular method. Ideally, the framework might be used as a guide to future research, but each scholar might wish to pursue different means to test for the fulfillment of the necessary conditions in her or his work. Rather than a methodological prescription, the chapter should be interpreted as a framework that still allows the researcher the freedom to establish his or her own interpretation of each stage and necessary condition. Accordingly, the chapter does not suggest any particular threshold for each condition that could become a baseline for use across different studies. This was a conscious decision in order to avoid drawing an arbitrary line in the sand, but future research would benefit from such impositions, especially if these thresholds emerge as norms from existing scholarship.

Future research stands to benefit from the replicable framework for the evaluation of securitization. This scholarship could further trace the process from the identification of a threat, the articulation of the threat, the intersubjective agreement about the threat, and the eventuality of demonstrated political effects to test the process of securitization across cases. This chapter marks a first step toward that end, providing the basis for the analysis of securitization through an analytical framework.

NOTES

1. My sincere thanks to Nicholas Onuf for pointing out this implicit assumption in the framework.

2. Searches were conducted on the LexisNexis database for articles from January 1, 2013, to March 13, 2015, using the search terms "islamic state" or "venezuela" w/p "threat."

REFERENCES

Adler, Emanuel. 1997. "Seizing the Middle Ground: Constructivism in World Politics." *European Journal of International Relations* 3, no. 3: 319–63.

Balzacq, Thierry. 2005. "The Three Faces of Securitization: Political Agency, Audience and Context." *European Journal of International Relations* 11, no. 2: 171–201.

Balzacq, Thierry. 2011. "A Theory of Securitization: Origins, Core Assumptions, and Variants." In *Securitization Theory: How Security Problems Emerge and Dissolve*, edited by Thierry Balzacq, 1–30. Abingdon: Routledge.

Bennett, W. Lance. 1994. "The Media and the Foreign Policy Process." In *The New Politics of American Foreign Policy*, edited by David A. Deese, 168–89. New York: St. Martin's Press.

Bennett, W. Lance, Regina G. Lawrence, and Steven Livingston. 2007. *When the Press Fails: Political Power and the News Media from Iraq to Katrina*. Chicago: University of Chicago Press.

Bergen, Peter, and Emily Schneider. 2015. "Is U.S. Coalition Winning War vs. ISIS?" *CNN.com*. www.cnn.com/2015/02/01/opinion/bergen-state-of-isis/. Last modified February 3.

Bleiker, Roland. 2009. *Aesthetics and World Politics*. London: Palgrave Macmillan.

Burke, Anthony. 2007. *Beyond Security: Ethics and Violence: War against the Other*. London: Routledge.

Buzan, Barry, Ole Wæver, and Jaap de Wilde. 1998. *Security: A New Framework for Analysis*. Boulder, CO: Lynne Rienner.

Chong, Dennis, and James N. Druckman. 2007. "Framing Theory." *Annual Review of Political Science* 10: 103–26.

Cohen, Bernard C. 1963. *The Press and Foreign Policy*. Princeton, NJ: Princeton University Press.

Cohen, Tom. 2014. "Obama Outlines ISIS Strategy: Airstrikes in Syria, More U.S. Forces." *CNN.com*. www.cnn.com/2014/09/10/politics/isis-obama-speech/. Last modified September 10.

Davis, Aeron. 2007. *The Mediation of Power: A Critical Introduction*. London: Routledge.

Davis, Aeron. 2010. *Political Communication and Social Theory*. Abingdon: Routledge.

de Zamaroczy, Nicolas. 2015. "Can Cables Speak? Reading Between the Lines of the Wikileaks Cables." Unpublished manuscript.

Diamond, Jeremy. 2014. "Poll: Most Americans Believe ISIS Serious Threat." *CNN.com.* http://www.cnn.com/2014/11/24/politics/isis-november-poll/. Last modified November 24.

Dörrie, Peter. 2014. "The Military Is the Worst Organization to Combat Ebola: But Now It's the Only Option." https://medium.com/war-is-boring/the-military-is-the-worst-organization-to-combat-ebola-75383fee54ab. Last modified September 28.

Entous, Adam. 2014. "U.S. Secretly Flying Drones Over Iraq; White House Could Expand Drone Flights Following Takeover of Two Iraqi Cities." *Wall Street Journal,* June 12.

Gabriel, Lindsey. 2015. "In Iowa, Lindsey Graham Talks Up Threat from Islamic State." *New York Times,* February 20.

Galtung, Johan, and Mari H. Ruge. 1965. "The Structure of Foreign News: The Presentation of the Congo, Cuba and Cyprus Crises in Four Norwegian Newspapers." *Journal of Peace Research* 2, no. 1: 64–90.

Gordon, Michael R. 2014. "Kerry Says ISIS Threat Could Hasten Military Action." *New York Times,* June 24.

Guzzini, Stefano. 2011. "Securitization as a Causal Mechanism." *Security Dialogue* 42, no. 4–5: 329–41.

Hansen, Lene. 2000. "The Little Mermaids Silent Security Dilemma and the Absence of Gender in the Copenhagen School." *Millennium: Journal of International Studies* 29: 285–306.

Hayes, Jarrod. 2012. "Securitization, Social Identity, and Democratic Security: Nixon, India, and the Ties That Bind." *International Organization* 66: 63–93.

Holbraad, Martin, and Morten Axel Pedersen. 2012. "Revolutionary Securitization: An Anthropological Extension of Securitization Theory." *International Theory* 4, no. 2: 165–97.

Huysmans, Jef. 1998. "Revisiting Copenhagen: Or, the Creative Development of a Security Studies Agenda in Europe." *European Journal of International Relations* 4, no. 4: 479–505.

Iyengar, Shanto, and Donald R. Kinder. 1987. *News That Matters: Television and American Opinion.* Chicago: University of Chicago Press.

Jackson, Patrick Thaddeus. 2011. *The Conduct of Inquiry in International Relations: Philosophy of Science and its Implications for the Study of World Politics.* Abingdon: Routledge.

Kelman, Ilan. 2011. *Disaster Diplomacy: How Disasters Affect Peace and Conflict.* Abingdon: Routledge.

Kirkpatrick, David D. 2014. "Attacks in West Raise New Fears Over ISIS' Influence." *New York Times,* October 25.

Landler, Mark. 2014. "President, at U.N., Vows to Counter Extremist Threat." *New York Times,* September 24, A1.

Lang, Kurt, and Gladys Engel Lang. 1966. "The Mass Media and Voting." In *Reader in Public Opinion and Communication,* edited by Bernard Berelson and Morris Janowitz, 2nd ed., 455–72. New York: Free Press.

McCombs, Maxwell E., and Donald L. Shaw. 1972. "The Agenda-Setting Function of Mass Media." *Public Opinion Quarterly* 36, no. 2: 176–87.

McDonald, Matt. 2008. "Securitization and the Construction of Security." *European Journal of International Relations* 14, no. 4: 563–87.

Mosca, Gaetano. 1939. *The Ruling Class*. Edited and revised by Arthur Livingston. Translated by Hannah D. Kahn. New York: McGraw-Hill.

Neuman, William. 2015a. "Obama Order Freezes Assets of 7 Officials in Venezuela." *New York Times*, March 10, A8.

Neuman, William. 2015b. "Obama Hands Venezuelan Leader a Cause to Stir Support." *New York Times*, March 12, A8.

Nickerson, Raymond S. 1998. "Confirmation Bias: A Ubiquitous Phenomenon in Many Guises." *Review of General Psychology* 2, no. 2: 175–220.

Pierson, Paul. 2000. "Increasing Returns, Path Dependence and the Study of Politics." *American Political Science Review* 94, no. 2: 251–67.

Putnam, Robert D. 1976. *The Comparative Study of Political Elites*. Englewood Cliffs, NJ: Prentice-Hall.

Romero, Simon. 2013. "Hugo Chávez, Leader Who Transformed Venezuela, Dies at 58." *New York Times*, March 6, A11.

Schweller, Randall L. 2004. "Unanswered Threats: A Neoclassical Realist Theory of Underbalancing." *International Security* 29, no. 2: 159–201.

Shear, Michael D., and Julie Hirschfeld Davis. 2014. "The World Is Appalled by the Killing, Obama Says." *New York Times*, August 21, A9.

Sil, Rudra, and Peter J. Katzenstein. 2010. "Analytic Eclecticism in the Study of World Politics: Reconfiguring Problems and Mechanisms across Research Traditions." *Perspectives on Politics* 8, no. 2: 411–31.

Steele, Brent. 2010. *Defacing Power: The Aesthetics of Insecurity in Global Politics*. Ann Arbor: University of Michigan Press.

Stritzel, Holger. 2007. "Towards a Theory of Securitization: Copenhagen and Beyond." *European Journal of International Relations* 13, no. 3: 357–83.

Swift, Art, and Andrew Dugan. 2015. "ISIS, Terrorism Seen as Graver Threats Than Russia, Ukraine." Gallup.com. http://www.gallup.com/poll/181553/isis-terrorism-seen-graver-threats-russia-ukraine.aspx?utm_source=ISIS&utm_medium=search&utm_campaign=tiles. Last modified February 13.

Sylvester, Christine. 2009. *Art/Museums: International Relations Where We Least Expect It*. Boulder, CO: Paradigm.

Thelen, Kathleen. 1999. "Historical Institutionalism in Comparative Politics." *Annual Review of Political Science* 2: 369–404.

U.S. Congress. Aviation and Transportation Security Act. Pub. L. No. 107-71, 107th Cong., November 19, 2001.

Vultee, Fred. 2010. "Securitization: A New Approach to the Framing of the "War on Terror." *Journalism Practice* 4, no. 1: 33–47.

Wæver, Ole. 2003. "Securitization: Taking Stock of a Research Programme in Security Studies." Unpublished manuscript.

Walt, Stephen M. 1991. "The Renaissance of Security Studies." *International Studies Quarterly* 35, no. 2: 211–39.

Wendt, Alexander. 1999. *Social Theory of International Politics*. Cambridge: Cambridge University Press.

White House, The. 2015. "Fact Sheet: Venezuela Executive Order." https://www.whitehouse.gov/the-press-office/2015/03/09/fact-sheet-venezuela-executive-order. Last modified March 9.

Williams, Michael C. 2003. "Words, Images, Enemies: Securitization and International Politics." *International Studies Quarterly* 47: 511–31.

Zeitzoff, Thomas, and Pablo Barberá. 2014. "The Empirical Determinants of Social Media Adoption by World Leaders and its Political Consequences." Paper presented at the American Political Science Association Annual Meeting, Washington, DC.

ELEVEN

A Realist Perspective on the Constructivist Project

Charles Glaser

This chapter addresses the relationship between constructivist theories and realist theories of international relations, with a focus on rationalist variants of realism. Although the two literatures are often characterized as competing "isms," I argue that key strands of these theoretical families *are better understood as complementary research projects that have much to offer each other.* The rational realist theory takes much as given, including states' preferences and norms that influence their identities; constructivist theories, especially those that focus on states—exploring the formation of their interests and of their beliefs about the international system—can contribute to explaining these inputs to the realist theory.[1] In combination, these theories have the potential to provide a much fuller explanation of international politics than either of them can alone.

At the same time, however, the rational realist theory and those constructivist theories that focus on the impact of the international system—which I term structural constructivism and associate most prominently with Wendt—are in direct competition on some of the key issues they address. The substance of this competition reflects their efforts to explain many of the same phenomena from different theoretical perspectives. *My assessment finds that the rational realist theory offers significant advantages for explaining states' strategic interaction and the possibilities for international cooperation under anarchy*. The rational theory relies on more analytically demanding assumptions about states' preferences and provides arguments that are more parsimonious and direct than the key structural-constructivist alternative.

Complementarity

Sketch of Structural Realism

To appreciate the potential complementarity between realist and constructivist theories, it is useful to begin with a summary of the foundations of realism. Realism is itself a complicated family of theories.[2] To focus the discussion, I use a rationalist version of realism: A state chooses a strategy that is designed to achieve its goals, given the constraints and opportunities created by international structure; the state acts strategically, that is, the state understands that other states will respond to its policies and may also make choices in anticipation of its policies.[3] The theory characterizes a state in terms of its motives, which reflects the state's fundamental interests and goals. It characterizes the international structure in terms of both material variables and information variables: the material variables determine the state's potential military capability, taking into account other states' abilities to respond to its decisions; the information variables capture the state's understanding of opposing states' motives and its beliefs about the opposing states' understanding of its own motives.

The key point for our discussion here is that the rational realist theory takes all these independent variables as *given*, that is, as inputs to the theory that are not explained by it. They are exogenous to the theory; they are untheorized. This is a pragmatic choice that leaves much unanswered, but is necessary to create a manageable theory capable of effectively exploring certain key questions:[4] How will changes in a state's international environment influence its choice between cooperative and competitive strategies? Similarly, should states that have different motives choose different strategies? And under what conditions can a state use its military policy to signal its motives? These questions, and many related others, are critically important to understanding how different strategic choices influence a state's prospects for achieving its goals and for understanding the factors that drive states' interactions. The analytic leverage that realism provides in answering these questions helps explain why realist theories hold such an influential place in both international relations theory and security studies.

Complementary Approaches

Because the rational realist theory takes its key independent variables as given, it is a partial theory. Theories that explain these independent variables could be combined with the realist theory to provide a more complete theory. Various constructivist theories focus on variables that in this context can contribute to building a fuller account of international politics. For example, a key distinction in the rationalist theory is between different types of states: states that are motived by security and states that are motivated to expand for more than security, which are commonly termed "greedy" states. A state's desire for security may require little explanation. The sources of greed are less obvious and more varied. Constructivist approaches have shed light on a number of important possibilities. For example, once source of greed could be status. A state motivated by the desire to achieve greater status could prefer to expand even when highly secure. Status is an ideational concept; how states define it and why they want it fits naturally into constructivist efforts.[5] Nationalism is a second potential source of greedy motives that is deeply ideational, and our understanding of it benefits from a constructivist lens. We do not need to develop an exhaustive list of examples to see that constructivist theories have a central role to play in a theory of state types, which themselves play a central role in the rationalist theory.[6]

Constructivist arguments can also play a role in theorizing other of the rational theory's independent variables. For example, the theory takes a state's initial information about its adversary's type—that is, the information it has before or at the beginning of their strategic interaction—as given, leaving open the question of the sources of states' *initial* information. One important answer provided by constructivists is that opposing states' identities and states' collective identities play a significant role in a state's assessment of threats.[7]

Furthermore, constructivist and ideational arguments have a role to play in explaining other givens in the rationalist realist theory. As a state evaluates the choice between the available options for achieving its goals, norms and identities may in effect take certain options off the table; the norm may be so strongly held or deeply embedded that the state does not even imagine the option being on the table. For example, a state that accepts the nuclear taboo would not use nuclear weapons in certain situations even when nuclear use might be most effective in achieving the state's goals with acceptable risk.[8] A full understanding of state behavior would require comprehending which norms restrict state behavior and how they develop and spread. Similarly, as a state evaluates the impact of a specific option, it needs to anticipate how other states will respond to its actions. The causal arguments that underpin the state's analysis are taken as given by the rationalist theory. A full understanding of a state's strategic choice would therefore require not only the rational realist theory, but also an understanding of how the state came to rely on specific causal arguments and how these arguments developed over time.[9]

In short, the key point here is that constructivist theories that help explain the inputs to the rational theory do not for the most part compete with the rational theory, but instead complement it. Each does its job separately and when combined can produce a more complete explanation of state behavior. The rational theory does not need to know *why* the opposing state is greedy, just that it is; it does not need to know how a norm or causal belief evolved and came to be accepted, just that it was. And neither type of theory can provide a full explanation on its own. Knowing that a state is greedy may tell us little about whether it will adopt a competitive policy and attempt to expand. For example, the greedy state might lack the power or military capabilities to achieve its objectives and may therefore understand that attempting to expand would be futile. Or it might face an adversary that possesses the military capabilities needed to deter the greedy state from trying to expand. Along our path toward the development of a full explanation of state behavior, we require both types of theories.

To put the preceding in a still larger perspective, we should note that combining theories of the inputs and the rational theory would not create a complete explanatory theory. At least one additional layer would be required. The rational realist theory assumes, not surprisingly, that states act rationally, that is, they make optimal choices given the constraints they face. If, however, a state instead chooses a suboptimal policy, the rational theory will not explain its behavior. The rational realist theory can, however, provide the foundation for explaining the state's behavior if it can be combined with a theory of suboptimal behavior that explains elements of the state's failure to act rationally. These theories of suboptimal behavior can address a state's failure to accurately assess the material and information variables that define its international situation, or a state's failure to make a rational choice given its assessment of these variables. Theories of suboptimal behavior could be constructivist, but they also have been built on a variety of other approaches, including cognitive theories, theories of domestic politics, organization theory, or theories of state capacity. An example of a constructivist theory in this category is a cultural explanation of states' military doctrines and, more specifically, of their choice between offensive and defensive doctrines.[10] Parallel efforts to explain these choices have focused on military organizational interests and the ability of these organizations to influence states' choices.[11] These alternative explanations of military doctrine are in much greater competition with each other than they are with the rational realist theories they complement.

The rational realist theory can therefore be envisioned as occupying the middle layer of a three-layer theory.[12] Constructivist theories could contribute to all three layers: by explaining the origins and values of certain of the realist theory's independent variables, by explaining the choice of causal theories that underpin the state's strategic choices in the rational theory and the norms that place limits on the strategies available to the state, and by explaining various types of suboptimality that plague the state's assessment of the inputs to the rational theory or its actual choices. Of course, constructivism is not the only theory that can contribute to the input and suboptimality layers. For example, theories of domestic politics, of organization theory, of state strength and preference aggregation, and of cognitive psychology also have made important contributions.[13]

Realism: Partial, Yet Powerful

In light of the partial nature of the rational realist theory, one might wonder whether the rational theory is fully useful on its own and why realist theories continue to have so much influence within IR. In fact, the rational realist theory stands well on its own for a variety of reasons.

First, and most important in this context, the inputs to the rational theory are often known sufficiently well that effective analysis is possible without a more complete theory. Values of the independent variables are often knowable, and known, without a theory that fully explains them. For example, we can measure a state's power without a full theory of the state that explains its productive potential and its ability to extract resources for national purposes. At the very least, basic material traits can be used to estimate power, with a well-established literature on that subject in place. Similarly, we can often be confident of the causal logics a state will employ to evaluate the impact of available strategies without having theories that explain the origins of the ideas and why one set of arguments was adopted instead of others. In other words, a theory of the inputs to the rational theory is not required to for the rational theory to support productive analysis.

Second, the rationalist theory is well matched to analyzing many of the key questions that the field of IR is most interested in. These include such questions as: What factors influence the probability of war and, closely related, when is war more or less likely? Are cooperative or competitive strategies best matched to achieving a state's security, economic, and other goals? When and why do states form alliances, engage in arms races, make territorial concessions, and join international institutions? Are states able to communicate information about their motives and intentions, and under what conditions is this possible? My point here is not that rational realist theories are the only theories capable of shedding light on these questions, as this would clearly undervalue other approaches. But the extensive realist literature that has productively tackled these questions, and many other related questions, should leave little doubt about the analytic value of the theories. This should not be a surprise, because the rationalist approach captures much of what is central to understanding the issues that drive these questions. And, of course, this is not an accident. Quite the opposite; this is why many analysts have chosen this approach to explore these questions.

Third, and closely related to the preceding discussion, the importance of these questions to real-world debates and states' most important security and foreign policy choices virtually guarantees that realist analyses will continue to have a prominent role within IR. More specifically, theories of foreign and security policy that are built on rational realist foundations focus on the strategies that states can choose from—including investing in economic growth, allying, arming, bargaining, fighting, etc.—and therefore have great potential to contribute to policy debates.

Competition

Origins of the Competition

Given the extensive complementarity between the constructivist and realist theories, why have these approaches been cast as competitors in IR theory? Many factors have contributed. Part of the answer undoubtedly lies in the professional inclination within IR theory to generate new arguments that can replace those that preceded them. Some of the answer may lie in the dominance of realist theory during the Cold War and arguably since then, which has made it a target for all other types of explanations. Part of the answer may lie in an underappreciation of realism, especially structural realism, as a partial theory, which meant that complementarity was not possible.

In addition to these more generic reasons, some of the competition likely reflects the order in which certain key arguments have been established, which in turn left them vulnerable to critiques from alternative approaches. Specifically, Waltz's seminal statement of structural realism made two arguments that were flawed or overstated, which left structural realism overly vulnerable: first, the theory was formulated and characterized as a purely material theory; and second, Waltz's central conclusion was that the anarchic nature of the international system generated a strong tendency toward competition, rendering cooperation both rare and limited.[14] As my sketch of structural realism explains, neither of these claims was sustainable, and strands of realism have been developed that correct these shortcomings.

Waltz's formulation therefore left the door open for constructivists (as well as realists and others) to offer as competitors the ideational arguments and the cooperation-under-anarchy arguments that were missing. Wendt's structural constructivism, which takes Waltz's structural realism as its central point of departure, develops many of these opposing arguments from a constructivist perspective.[15] If the rational realist theory had been more fully developed and appreciated before Wendt tackled these arguments, the debate might have proceeded rather differently. Instead of arguing that structural constructivism could explain and predict interaction and cooperation that were beyond the reach of Waltz's realism, Wendt would have had to argue that his approach produced similar results from an alternative perspective. Instead, the approaches ended up at least partly talking past each other and appearing to clash even more than they actually do. There is, however, some real competition between the rational realist theory and Wendt's structural constructivist theory.

Substance of the Competition

To appreciate how both competition and complementarity between realism and constructivism are possible, it is useful to distinguish different types of constructivism. Some constructivist work has focused on states and individuals, exploring the sources of beliefs, identifies, and norms. Other constructivist research has focused on the international system, exploring how structure influences states' choices; Wendt's is the defining work in the structural constructivist field.[16] The complementary nature of constructivist arguments that focus on states and individuals is clear; as explained above, these theories explain inputs to the rational theory. In contrast, structural constructivism emphasizes the role of the international system on states' actions and, therefore, runs largely parallel to structural realism, even though it defines the international system differently. This similarity and, closely related, the similarity in the questions the two approaches set out to answer makes them competitors.

Wendt argues that the key to understanding the possibility of multiple "logics" of anarchy is "conceptualizing structure in social rather than material terms." The sole variable in Waltz's international structure is the distribution of capabilities. Consequently, Waltz's theory is characterized as purely material.[17] Waltz concludes that international anarchy requires states to pursue competitive policies; in Wendt's terminology, this means that Waltz finds that anarchy has a single logic. Wendt argues instead that anarchy can take three principal forms, which vary in their tendencies to generate competition and cooperation. He defines the different anarchies in terms of the states' roles, specifically their orientation toward each other—enemy, rival, and friend—which reflect the rules that states expect others to observe. Working with these structural roles, Wendt explains how cooperation and even deep peace are possible within international anarchy. Enemies generate a Hobbesian anarchy that is highly competitive; although similar in some ways to the anarchy explained by Waltz's neorealism, the Hobbesian anarchy is more competitive and states are more insecure. Rivals generate a Lockean anarchy that is less competitive and that, Wendt argues, is in certain respects closer to Waltz's anarchy. Friends are concerned not only about their own security, but also other states' security, and their interaction generates a Kantian anarchy in which states do not fear that others will use force against them and in which confidence in a long-lasting peace is possible.[18]

Wendt's effort to explore the possibility that international anarchy can produce a much wider range of outcomes than is suggested by Waltz is a productive move. Whether extensive security cooperation is possible under anarchy is the central question posed by structural IR theories. Moreover, a variety of historical examples that run counter to Waltz's claim about the persistent presence of competition—including restraint and cooperation between powerful states, and substantial military capabilities that do not generate substantial insecurity—indicate the need for a more encompassing theory. Wendt's focus on social variables, however, masks the potential of structural realist and rational theories to explain variation in states' policies under anarchy and thereby incorrectly suggests that realist theories are incapable of explaining broad and basic variation in states' strategies in the face of anarchy. In fact, Wendt is explicit on this critical issue:

The real question is whether the fact of anarchy creates a tendency for all such interactions to realize a single logic at the macro-level. In the Neorealist view they do: anarchies are inherently self-help systems that tend to produce military competition, balances of power, and war. Against this I argue that anarchy can have at least three kinds of structure at the macro-level, based on what kind of roles—enemy, rival, and friend—dominate the system.[19]

To appreciate why structural realism can explain and predict cooperation but that this possibility is overlooked by Waltz, we need to return to his core argument. It turns out that the logic of Waltz's arguments requires the introduction of another variable: a state's information about the opposing state's motives. Waltz holds that although states may have motives beyond security, their international behavior can be understood largely by assuming that they are seeking only security. If, however, all states knew that all the other states were security seekers (and if all states knew that this is what the others knew), then the international system should not generate competition. This *uncertainty* about the opposing state's type lies at the core of the security dilemma, and, closely related, the security dilemma lies at the center of structural realism's ability to explain competition.[20] If states did not face a security dilemma, security seekers could always achieve their core objective while adopting policies that avoided generating competition. Once the importance of uncertainty about motives is made explicit, including it as a variable is the natural next step for the rational theory.

A key point for our discussion here is that structural realism, or at the least the more general rational theory that logically flows from it, is no longer a purely material theory. This matters because it means that distinguishing realist and constructivist theories in terms of material versus ideational arguments—a broad category that is typically understood to include information, norms, and causal ideas—no longer creates a sharp divide.

The implications reach beyond mere characterizations and definitions, however. Including information about motives as a key variable in a rational realist theory opens the door to arguments that address much of the terrain also covered by Wendt's structural constructivism. More specifically, the rational realist theory (1) explores the nature of interactions that can enable states to revise their assessments of the opposing state's type and thereby generate more cooperative or more competitive policies, providing a more straightforward explanation than Wendt's changes in interests, (2) explains international cooperation under anarchy as a result of information in combination with material factors instead of Wendt's focus on identities, and (3) shows that Wendt has both exaggerated and underestimated the potential for international cooperation, the former by underplaying the role of material factors in constraining states' choices and the latter by relying on states' collective interests instead of pure security seeking, which is more neutral regarding cooperation. The remainder of this section sketches these points.[21]

First, the realist theory provides an alternative explanation of how states' interactions can influence their relationship and, in turn, their behavior. Wendt argues that interaction between states is the key to their understandings of self and other, and that interactions play a central role in determining whether the international system is competitive or cooperative. He holds that interaction cannot play this important role in realist theories, because "realists would probably argue that each should act on the basis of worst-case assumptions about the other's intentions, justifying such an attitude as prudent in view of the possibility of death from making a mistake."[22] This is a reasonable reading of Waltz; since he barely touches on a possible role for information about the opposing side, assuming the worst can be seen as implicitly running through his formulation. Offensive realism makes fully explicit the requirement for states to assume the worst about opposing states.[23] Contrary to this position, however, rational states should not assume the worst when facing uncertainty about their adversary's motives and intentions. Instead, at least from a standard expected utility perspective, a state should consider the probability that the opposing state is a revisionist/greedy type as opposed to status quo/security type. The state should also consider the danger if the opposing state is a greedy type; many types of cooperation would not put the state at great risk, that is, death is not always, or even usually, the cost of misjudging the adversary's motives. These arguments lie at the core of the rationalist realist theory that includes information as a key variable defining a state's international environment, which in turn enables the theory to fully integrate the security dilemma into its arguments.

Given this realist formulation, states' interactions can influence their understanding (their information) of the opposing state's motives. When a state takes an action that would be more likely to be taken by a security-seeking state than by a greedy state, the opposing state should positively update its prior estimate of the probability that the state has security motives. Because states have an incentive to mislead adversaries, the opposing state should only find useful information when the state's action is costly, that is, when the state's action is a "costly signal." This occurs when a specific cooperative action would be more costly for a greedy state than for a security-seeking state. Wendt describes a similar process of interaction but emphasizes different changes and relies on different types of arguments—symbolic interactionism—not rational updating made possible by costly signals. His arguments describe how states' interactions can change their interests and identities, which in turn support cooperation in anarchy. The rationalist explanation has the advantage of greater simplicity—it holds interests constant, does not involve the creation of social structures, and does not require changes in interests—while appearing to explain essentially the same international phenomenon.

Second, the rational realist theory explains that anarchy can generate a variety of outcomes—including various degrees of competition, cooperation, and mixtures of the two—that have much in common with Wendt's three anarchies. According to the rational theory, whether a security-seeking state should choose cooperation over competition depends on both material variables, which include the state's power and offense-defense variables, and information variables, which capture what a state knows about its adversary's motives.[24] Material variables largely determine the military capabilities a state can acquire, given the opposing state's ability to build military forces of its own. They determine the types of military missions that states will be able to perform and their relative prospects for performing them successfully.

Information variables influence a state's expectations about its adversary's behavior, including reactions to the state's own policies. The theory explains that when defense has the advantage—that is, when holding territory or maintaining the capabilities required for deterrence are relatively easy—states can achieve high levels of security without engaging in intense competition. When offense and defense are distinguishable—that is, when the forces that support offensive missions would contribute less (or more) to defensive missions—states may be able to choose forces and strategies that signal benign motives and to use arms control to increase the feasibility of defensive force postures. Information variables also influence the prospects for cooperation. A state that believes the opposing state is likely to be a security seeker should be more willing to run the risks of restraint and cooperation. These strategies have the potential to generate positive political spirals, which can in turn make states willing to choose military strategies that pose smaller risks to others' security.

In short, the rationalist theory describes the conditions under which anarchy can produce cooperative international security policies and relatively peaceful international politics. It both corrects Waltz's conclusion about the general tendency for anarchy to generate competition and shows that Wendt's social structure is unnecessary to produce this result. Again, the rationalist theory has the advantage of being more straightforward, less complex, and more parsimonious than Wendt's constructivist alternative.

Third, and related, the rationalist theory shows that Wendt is both too pessimistic and too optimistic, in different ways, about the prospects for cooperation under anarchy. On the pessimistic side, the rationalist theory shows that cooperation is possible without introducing "friends," that is, states that have collective identities in which they value each other's security as well as their own. According to the rational realist argument, the states' international situation is doing most of the work; nonfriends—security seekers that do not value others' security—have fundamental preferences that are relatively neutral between cooperation and competition. In contrast, collective identities and altruistic preferences play a central role in the constructivist argument, and it views them as necessary for deep cooperation. My point here is not that considering the impact of collective identities is analytically flawed, but that relying on collective identities to make extensive cooperation possible is a significantly weaker finding regarding the potential of anarchy to allow and support cooperation. If, as seems likely, pure security seekers are much more common than friends, then Wendt is pessimistic about cooperation under anarchy, in that he finds the possibility of cooperation existing under narrower, less common conditions.

At the same time, however, Wendt is overly optimistic about the prospects for cooperation because he fails to adequately incorporate the constraints that information and material factors can impose on states' policies. A strength of the rational realist theory is that it explicitly explains how both material variables and information variables influence the prospects for cooperation, and how they interact. In contrast, Wendt's social theory does not bring in material factors and thereby implicitly ignores the constraints they could impose. Wendt is partially correct in arguing that "*History matters*. Security dilemmas are not acts of God; they are effects of practice."[25] States, however, do not get to choose their history at the time they are making forward-looking decisions. Of course, in the past they did have partial control over it via the policy choices they made, although these were constrained by information and material factors. At the time of a new choice, however, the past and its related history are fixed and thereby impose severe constraints on states' practice/choices. Their interactions may start under information conditions that prevent them from overcoming material conditions that make cooperative policies too risky. Moreover, these information conditions could reflect previous material conditions that required the security-seeking state to compete, thereby signaling greedy motives, which contributed to the initial information from which the states begin this round of interaction. Consequently, although certainty or near certainty that the opposing state is a security seeker could be sufficient to eliminate the security dilemma under even very dangerous material conditions, states will not always have this information. Moreover, a state can face material conditions—for example, offense dominance—that make cooperation too risky, even when the state believes that adversary is probably a security-seeking state. In short, states can face constraints that require them to choose competitive policies, which can make the security dilemma still more severe and cooperation a still worse option.

In Closing

What does this assessment of the dual nature—competitive and complementary—of the realist and constructivist research programs suggest for future progress? The most straightforward step would be broader appreciation that the most direct competition between them is limited and exaggerated. The literature no longer supports a characterization of these approaches in which realism and constructivism are depicted as offering fully divergent predictions for the feasibility of cooperation under international anarchy. Unlike Waltz's realism, rational realist theories now show that cooperation is a state's best strategy under certain material and information conditions. Structural constructivism also finds that cooperation under anarchy is possible. Thus the theories are no longer divided on this central question. They do, of course, provide different explanations. I have argued that the rational realist theory has significant advantages. Others may want to make the case for the constructivist logic or for combining the two approaches to provide a richer explanation.

The bigger challenge concerns the complementary nature of the two research programs. A complete theory of international relations will eventually integrate key features of both theories. This could result from an effort dedicated to this integration or from more isolated efforts in which one theory provides guidance for the development of the other. Either way, these efforts promise to advance the field.

NOTES

1. For discussion of rationalist and constructivist approaches, see James Fearon and Alexander Wendt, "Rationalism v. Constructivism: A Skeptical View," in *Hand-*

book of International Relations, ed. Walter Carlsnaes, Thomas Risse, and Beth A. Simmons (London: Sage, 2002).

2. On this family, see Charles L. Glaser, "Realism" in *Contemporary Security Studies*, 4th ed., ed. Alan Collins (Oxford: Oxford University Press, 2016); and William C. Wohlforth, "Realism," in *The Oxford Handbook of International Relations*, ed. Christian Reus-Smit and Duncan Snidal (New York: Oxford University Press, 2008).

3. This rationalist theory is fully developed in Charles L. Glaser, *Rational Theory of International Politics: The Logic of Competition and Cooperation* (Princeton, NJ: Princeton University Press, 2010); my discussion here draws heavily on chap. 2.

4. On pragmatic simplification in theory development, see David A. Lake and Robert Powell, "International Relations: A Strategic-Choice Approach" in *Strategic Choice and International Relations*, ed. David A. Lake and Robert Powell (Princeton, NJ: Princeton University Press, 1999).

5. For recent work on status in IR that draws on a variety of theoretical approaches, including constructivist approaches, see T. V. Paul, Deborah Welch Larson, and William C. Wohlforth, eds., *Status in World Politics* (Cambridge: Cambridge University Press, 2014).

6. Other important constructivist work on the sources of states' interests includes Martha Finnemore, *National Interests in International Society* (Ithaca, NY: Cornell University Press, 1996).

7. See for example, Thomas Risse-Kappen, "Collective Identity in a Democratic Community" and Michael N. Barnett, "Identity and Alliances in the Middle East," both in *The Culture of National Security: Norms and Identities in World Politics*, ed. Peter J. Katzenstein (New York: Columbia University Press, 1996); and "Security Communities in Theoretical Perspective," in *Security Communities*, ed. Emanuel Adler and Michael Barnett (Cambridge: Cambridge University Press, 1998).

8. On the nuclear taboo see Nina Tannenwald, "The Nuclear Taboo: The United States and the Normative Basis of Nuclear Non-Use," *International Organization* 53, no. 3 (Summer 1999): 433–68.

9. On this type of argument see Judith Goldstein and Robert O. Keohane, eds., *Ideas and Foreign Policy: Beliefs, Institutions, and Political Change* (Ithaca, NY: Cornell University Press, 1993).

10. Elizabeth Kier, *Imagining War: French and British Military Doctrine Between the Wars* (Princeton, NJ: Princeton University Press, 1997).

11. Barry R. Posen, *The Sources of Military Doctrine: France, Britain and Germany Between the World Wars* (Ithaca, NY: Cornell University Press, 1984); and Jack Snyder, *The Ideology of the Offensive: Military Decision Making and the Disasters of 1914* (Ithaca, NY: Cornell University Press, 1984).

12. These three layers do not capture the full spectrum of theories. For example, strategic choice theories assume that states and their international environment are separable and that interaction does not change the type of state. In contrast, second-image reversed theories add how interactions can lead to a change in a state's preferences; see for example, Peter A. Gourevich, "The Second Image Reversed: International Sources of Domestic Politics," *International Organization* 32, no. 4 (Autumn 1978): 881–912; Jack Snyder, "International Leverage on Soviet

Domestic Change," *World Politics* 42, no. 1 (October 1989): 1–30; and Charles L. Glaser, "Political Consequences of Military Strategy: Expanding and Refining the Spiral and Deterrence Models," *World Politics* 44, no. 4 (July 1997): 497–538.

13. See for example, Jack Snyder, *Myths of Empire: Domestic Politics and International Ambition* (Ithaca, NY: Cornell University Press, 1993); Barry R. Posen, *The Sources of Military Doctrine: France, Britain, and Germany Between the World Wars* (Ithaca, NY: Cornell University Press, 1986); Randall L. Schweller, *Unanswered Threats: Political Constraints on the Balance of Power* (Princeton, NJ: Princeton University Press, 2008); and Robert Jervis, *Perception and Misperception in International Politics* (Princeton, NJ: Princeton University Press, 1976)

14. Kenneth N. Waltz, *Theory of International Politics* (Reading, MA: Addison-Wesley, 1979).

15. Alexander Wendt, *Social Theory of International Politics* (Cambridge: Cambridge University Press, 1999).

16. This characterization simplifies these types of research, among other reasons because constructivists have stressed the infeasibility of separating state and structure; see for example David Dessler, "What's at Stake in the Agent-Structure Debate," *International Organization* 43, no. 3 (Summer 1989): 441–73; and Alexander E. Wendt, "The Agent-Structure Problem in International Relations Theory," *International Organization* 41, no. 3 (Summer 1987): 335–70. In significant ways, this degree of complexity parallels the second-image reverse arguments that apply to traditional levels-of-analysis categorizations; see note 12

17. This is itself a bit of a simplification because, among other reasons, Waltz's own list of the factors that influence a state's power includes "political stability" and "competence," which are not purely or even primarily material; Waltz, *Theory of International Politics*, 131.

18. Wendt, *Social Theory of International Politics*, chap. 6, quote at 249.

19. Wendt, *Social Theory of International Politics*, 247.

20. Andrew Kydd, "Game Theory and the Spiral Model," *World Politics* 49, no. 2 (April 1997): 371–400; and Charles L. Glaser, "The Security Dilemma Revisited," *World Politics* 50, no. 1 (October 1997): 171–201. A different, albeit not entirely unrelated, effort to explain cooperation under anarchy from a rationalist perspective is Kenneth A. Oye, ed., *Cooperation under Anarchy* (Princeton, NJ: Princeton University Press, 1986).

21. This following discussion draws heavily on Glaser, *Rational Theory of International Politics*, 167–71.

22. Alexander Wendt, "Anarchy Is What States Make of It: The Social Construction of Power Politics," *International Organization* 46, no. 2 (Spring 1992): 391–425, quote at 404.

23. John J. Mearsheimer, *The Tragedy of Great Power Politics* (New York: Norton, 2001); and the updated edition (Norton, 2014).

24. Related theories—defensive realism and offense-defense theory—provide similar arguments, but the role of the information variable is less fully developed. On offense-defense theory see George H. Quester, *Offense and Defense in the International System* (New York: Wiley, 1977); Robert Jervis, "Cooperation Under the Security Dilemma," *World Politics* 30, no. 1 (January 1978): 167–214; Charles L.

Glaser and Chaim Kaufmann, "What Is the Offense-Defense Balance and Can We Measure It," *International Security* 22, no. 4 (Spring 1998); and Stephen Van Evera, *Causes of War: Power and the Roots of Conflict* (Ithaca, NY: Cornell University Press, 1999); on defensive realism see Charles L. Glaser, "Realists as Optimists: Cooperation as Self-Help," *International Security* 19, no. 3 (Winter 1994/95): 50–90.

25. Alexander Wendt, "Constructing International Politics," *International Security* 20, no. 1 (Summer 1995): 77.

TWELVE

Realism, Uncertainty, and the Security Dilemma

*Identity and the Tantalizing Promise of
Transformed International Relations*

David Blagden

That ideational, social, and cultural variables "matter" in international politics is now widely accepted. Culture may condition threat perceptions and military doctrine. Domestic-political ideational factors can contribute to a particularly belligerent or pacifistic foreign policy. The pursuit of status or performance of role can be a motivating interest of state behavior. Nationalism, a symptom of a particularly pervasive form of political-social identity, is the very underpinning of the nation-state system. Indeed, while even post–Cold War international relations (IR) theory textbooks used to begin frequently with the refrain "realism is the most influential theory of international politics," such a claim would today surely be historical: if anything, since the start of the twenty-first century, constructivist and liberal approaches have risen to enjoy the theoretical primacy that was once realism's assumed prerogative.[1]

Yet just how far can social forces offer to transform international politics away from the intractable competition for security—and thus military power—that realists see as endemic to the anarchy of the international system? This chapter will answer, "not reliably," by suggesting that states' need to survive in the face of potential threats from similarly capable political units (that is, other states) whose intentions can never be known with certainty—a caveated claim, explored subsequently—forces them to hedge against others' potential to do harm. Such harm can be thought of as movement along a spectrum from cooperation to conflict, whether that be alliance abandonment, coercion—militarized or otherwise—or total warfare. Other states' ability to do such harm—and one's own state's ability to guard against it—rests on underlying material resources, which means that states must always pay attention to their position in the balance of power.[2] This comes despite the social pressures undoubtedly influencing their foreign policies in other directions.

Throughout, the chapter understands "constructivism" as an approach to theorization in IR defined by a focus on the causal power of social forces, including norms of "legitimate" behavior, intersubjective recognition of status/role and regime type, domestic culture and its impact on foreign and defense policy choices, and the interstate friendship/hostility-inducing consequences of "self" versus "other" distinctions. Of course, constructivists themselves disagree vigorously over the paradigm's analytical core.[3] This chapter takes no view of that exchange and limits itself instead to critical appraisal of one key constructivist ambition.

Its particular target is the argument that whether or not the balance of military power compels states toward security competition can be transcended by states coming to see each other as "friends," and the implicit promise of transformed international politics that such an argument offers. This transformational promise—while not a necessary component of the original constructivist turn or indeed a characteristic of much of the most seminal constructivist scholarship[4]—has added to constructivism's progressive appeal and thus its theoretical ascendance. Yet, as the chapter argues, it is also one of the more contestable elements of the constructivist contribution. Note that this argument does not deny or challenge the valuable contribution of constructivist explanations of other international-political phenomena, many of which are wholly compatible with a "realist" (meaning pessimistic and power-centric) worldview,[5] as the chapter will recognize.

The chapter proceeds in five parts. First, it outlines several key areas in which social, cultural, and ideational variables are accepted as impacting international politics and foreign policy by IR scholars of all theoretical persuasions. Second, it discusses how these variables could—if they fulfilled an expansive vision of their seeming transformational promise—be thought to carry hope for a changed, amicable international relations that finally leaves persistent interstate security competition behind. Third, it explains why these variables are not in fact capable of fulfilling such transformational promise. In particular, while playing a social role may be *an* interest of states, it is necessarily subordinate to state survival, and since survival has a material base, so too must protecting materially underpinned interests remain a pressing concern for states. Fourth, it develops these claims by suggesting why—short of the unlikely emergence of a single world-state—enduring uncertainty over other states' intentions, particularly their future intentions, will ensure that security concerns remain a pervasive feature of international politics. Moreover, while nationalism is an ideational variable on one level, it is iteratively forged through security competition between mutually threatening political groups, so recognizing that a form of identity underpins the international system does not mean that such identities can be readily shifted to enable the world to escape competition over materially underpinned interests. Structurally based variants of realism thus remain informative approaches to explaining international relations at the systemic level, particularly between major powers, alongside the undoubted contributions of the constructivist research program. Fifth, it concludes by suggesting grounds for future research, focusing on exploring the space in which states pursue socially constituted interests *within* the overall material-structural constraints of the need to survive in an anarchic international system.

This topic is of pressing relevance in contemporary international politics. The rise of China as an industrial superpower and the partial resurgence of Russia from its 1990s nadir—although they are both now faced by precipitous economic challenges if growth is to continue—have seen the potential for conflict between major powers reintroduced to the international system. In each key theater, uncertainty over possible behavior coupled with a shifting balance of capabilities has seen an escalation of security competition with the potential for war, the structural realists' bread and butter. Yet other key contemporary flashpoints, such as the West's confrontations with Iran and North Korea, seem to lend themselves most obviously to ideational explanations. And in some ways even more troubling, political relations even within the Euro-Atlantic "security community"— the greatest apparent success story for the progressive social transformation of international politics—have recently displayed a dramatic backsliding, via both Trump and Brexit, raising the specter of alliance breakdown and coercive confrontation. These developments themselves represent ideationally motivated reorientations in foreign policy outlook (albeit partly motivated by underlying economic shifts), in line with constructivist arguments. Yet the relative power of all sides is critical to their ability to resist/

dispense such coercion and safeguard future security and prosperity even in the possible absence of alliance support, which is why it has continued to be recognized as such, as realists would expect. In short, contemporary world politics demands that "analytic eclecticism" be not just tokenistically professed by IR theorists, but practiced too.[6]

Social Variables in International Politics

The days when committed realist IR scholars would deny any causal role in international politics for social, cultural, and ideational factors—if there ever were such days—have now come to an end. On the contrary, there are many areas where there is a compelling case to suggest that such constructivist variables are important drivers of state behavior and thus international outcomes. What follows in this section is not an attempt at an exhaustive list, but rather an illustrative grouping of some important examples: examples that even structural realists, constructivists' principal theoretical antagonists, appear to embrace.

First, the pursuit of international standing, status, and role fulfillment—all social variables—can condition states' foreign policy choices.[7] In particular, the quest for "great power" status, and its associated social trappings and perceived influence, can drive states toward activist and even belligerent strategic postures.[8] Contemporary major-but-not-super-powers, such as Russia, France, and the United Kingdom, seem particularly prone to such status and role obsession.[9] The acquisition of certain symbolic military capabilities—most obviously, nuclear weapons, but also various implements of naval power projection or other assets symbolic of greatness/modernity—can also be driven by status anxiety.[10] Tellingly, moreover, the leading role of an eminent realist scholar, Wohlforth, in driving recent work on states' status concerns shows the extent to which even materially inclined IR scholars are today relaxed about the incorporation of such social explanations of foreign policy behavior.[11]

Second, cultural factors can condition both threat perception and military doctrine. States' perceptions of cultural "otherness" can elevate their assessments of the dangerousness or otherwise of their potential foes.[12] For example, the differing attitudes of US policymakers towards the Israeli, British, and Indian nuclear programs on the one hand, and those of Iran, Russia, and China on the other, are particularly instructive.[13] Again, moreover, variations of such arguments can be discerned in places that a strictly pigeonholed, stove-piped approach to paradigmatic "schools" of theory would not anticipate: Snyder's *Myths of Empire*, for instance—an iconic work of the realist canon—attributes an important causal role to domestic social structure and the self/other images of opponents created by imperial domestic culture.[14] Similarly, the formation of military doctrine—an essential component of military capability and thus a necessary step in generating defense against external threats—has historically been influenced by both the domestic culture of the state in general and the specific institutional culture of particular militaries.[15] The fixation of interwar French military culture on static defensive doctrine proved to have dire consequences in 1940, for example.[16] Cultural perceptions of others' military culture can also make this relationship one of iterative reinforcement, such as Western militaries' views of Asian forces' inherent "martial virtues.".[17] And again, social variables creep into this debate in unexpected quarters. Posen's thoroughly "realist" take on *The Sources of Military Doctrine*, for example, touches on the military's desire for prestige—a form of social status—among its other, materially grounded variables.[18] Likewise, Walt's ascertainment that states balance against assessments of threat, rather than mere concentrations of power, codes threats as constituted by total power, geographic proximity, offensive capability, *and* offensive intentions.[19] This introduces scope for identity to play an important part in both the offensiveness or otherwise of others' intentions *and* in states' (subjective) evaluations of the threats they face. Indeed, insofar as all threat assessment and the foreign policy behavior that follows from it is a product of cognitive processes,[20] anything that conditions leaders' cognition and interpretation—including cultural, social, and ideational context—must be playing a part here.

More broadly, aspects of domestic identity can be seen skewing foreign policy behavior in not necessarily sensible—even reckless—ways. Leading torch bearers for the realist flame have recently found themselves making arguments about the detrimental influence of particularly influential domestic identity groups on US policy choices, for instance, and seeking to explore the connections between structural IR theory and such an analysis of domestic policy capture as a consequence.[21] Looking beyond the US superpower to the UK context, moreover, there is a striking disconnect between a foreign policy elite consensus over both the desirability and utility of British military interventionism on the one hand—based, again, on ideational arguments about the "sort" of country that the UK should seek to be—and a combination of the balance-of-power imperative to eschew unnecessary entanglements (plus deep public skepticism over the merits of military interventionism) on the other.[22] Scrutinizing the filtration of balance-of-power pressures through such domestic ideational lenses to explain foreign policy outcomes has even given rise to a new theoretical school, neoclassical realism.[23]

To make a final point in this vein, it is worth noting that to the extent that the contemporary international system is composed of sovereign nation-states, even the most structural of realists accepts that the system itself is partly underpinned by an idea: the political units competing under anarchy may have varying degrees of material capability, but the formation and reinforcement of those units rests on variations of an ideology, nationalism.[24] Thus, at the most fundamental level—in understanding the existence of the very units whose interactions constitute "inter*national* politics"—IR scholars are united in an acceptance that social variables "matter."

Of course, some of the causal role here attributed to ideational, cultural, and social variables could just as readily be attributed to the material interests of domestic interest groups, which might suggest a "neoliberal" rather than a "constructivist" theoretical pathway.[25] In pointing to the initial capture of imperial foreign policy by elites seeking to advance their private financial interests, for example—as well as to the self/other images projected and the subsequent balancing coalitions that form against imperial overextension—Snyder's *Myths of Empire* can be read as including liberal, constructivist, *and* realist arguments.[26] The point of this section, however, is not to establish which theoretical paradigm is "best." The point, rather, is to observe—as a contribution to a volume on the merits and limitations of constructivism—that all IR theoretical perspectives can admit at least some causal role for ideas. Moreover, as the discussion above suggests, states clearly *do* harm their strategic position via identity-driven foreign policy choices.[27] Just how far they do so is an important question, however, because there is a significant causal difference between a state that actually jeopardizes its survival through "crazy" ideational foreign policy choices, on the one hand, and a state that merely uses its "spare capacity" to pursue such choices while still being careful to guard its fundamental security interests and preserve its position in the balance of power, on the other. This is therefore a question that will be returned to later in the chapter.

Transformational Promise?

The previous section documented several examples of ideational, social, and cultural variables that IR scholars of all stripes are likely to see as conditioning international outcomes. This section now turns to consider how a selection of these variables might, if they fulfilled an expansive vision of their potential, promise to transform international politics away from the realist prediction of pervasive interstate security competition and balance-of-power concerns. The point is not to *endorse* such transformational claims, but rather to elucidate the expansive transformational claims that *could* be (and are) made. As noted from the outset, the argument here is also not that such transformational implications are common to all constructivists, nor that they are a necessary component of the overall school of thought, but simply that they are present in one element of constructivist thought and have come to be perceived as part of the progressive political appeal of the wider research agenda.

First, ambitious constructivists go so far as to argue that social role *constitutes* state interests, rather than merely ranking among them.[28] This is a necessary claim if one is to advance the argument that great powers are defined by the social roles they play rather than by their standing in the balance of power. It is also an argument that, if true, suggests that states can escape balance-of-power concerns and security competition, provided that they retain the ability to discharge their chosen international-social role, which may be based more around diplomatic mediation, neutrality, humanitarian intervention, cultural attractiveness, or any number of other role-values that are not linked to the ability to balance against other (materially-capable) major powers.[29] Indeed, if being "friends" with one or more other states comes to be seen domestically as part of the state's international-social role, then that would point toward a profound transformation of the international system toward an international "society" and, perhaps ultimately, an amicable "culture of anarchy."[30]

Second, if culture routinely impacts threat perception or military performance to the point of fatal misalignment with other interests, then this might also suggest that international politics is not the arena of cautious, competitive, survival-inclined security seeking that realists assume—although in quite a different way to that posited in the previous paragraph. If cultural factors commonly cause states to *under*perceive emerging threats, leaving them ill-prepared for subsequent conflict, and subsequently imperil their survival to the point of regular "state death," this would undermine the notion of an international system composed of broadly rational security seekers.[31] The same would hold in the opposite case, that is, if states' culture leads them to routinely *over*perceive dangers and thus destroy themselves by initiating unnecessary wars against adversaries that did not pose a threat until attacked. Likewise, if cultural factors render states so incapable of adapting sufficiently to meet military necessity that state "death" is again frequent—that is, if culture so severely inhibits Waltzian "socialization" toward prevailing strategic best practice that state survival is imperiled—then that again points toward a fundamentally different sort of international system to that envisaged by structural realism.[32]

Of course, none of this necessarily provides grounds for optimism about the prospects for cooperative, amicable international relations. But if states' culture and identity can cause them to set aside balance-of-power "imperatives," and show that such imperatives are in fact choices that can be forgone through an ideational decision to accept higher strategic risk in order to accommodate domestic preferences, that does offer at least the possibility of moving beyond pervasive interstate security competition.

Third, following from the previous two points about the possibility of ideationally driven domestic preferences offering the possibility of "nonrealist" foreign policy behavior and a subsequent transformation of international politics, it is worth noting that particular states' versions of nationalism itself—often assumed to be a constantly divisive force—could itself adapt and evolve to include valuing the other as the self. To the extent that visions of national role and status—like visions of potential threats and preferred ways of fighting—may flow from national identity, all of these variables are to a degree underpinned by a given state's particular variant of nationalism. While nationalism may certainly be an inherently nostalgic, self-referential, usually slow-to-change force, moreover, this does not mean that change is impossible. So in a group of countries with a sufficiently amorphous and malleable set of national identities, there could even be potential for the very underpinning of the nation-state system itself to change in a way that would bring about a transformation of international politics toward permanent amicability—although note that plenty of constructivists, let alone realists, are not optimistic about the prospects for such change given the logic of international habit.[33]

Taken together, then, if the social variables that most IR scholars accept as having at least some causal role were to fulfill expansive understandings of their transformative potential, then they would indeed carry the promise of an international system that could move beyond pervasive balance-of-power positioning and security competition. In such a world, states could aspire through effective policy to transform the culture of international anarchy—to make of it what they will, paraphrasing Wendt—and come to relate to each other as friends.[34] The point of this section has not been to argue that such a transformation is readily achievable, or even possible; rather, it has sought to briefly elucidate how a selection of widely endorsed constructivist variables *could* offer such transformational promise *if* they played the profound causal role which is often credited to them. This progressive promise has—along with the seeming inadequacies of realism in accounting for the peaceful end of the Cold War in particular[35]— undoubtedly played a significant role in the booming popularity of constructivism since the 1990s. Assessing whether ideational, social, and cultural factors do in fact carry such transformational promise—whether they do indeed have the potential to change the consequences of international systemic anarchy and enable states to escape a reliance on security through military power and the mutual threat and subsequent competition that it brings—is the purpose of the next section.

The Hierarchy of Interests

The previous section documented how social variables might be taken as having the potential to transform international politics. This section now turns to an explanation of why it is so hard to fulfill such seeming transformational promise. Running throughout is the argument that while playing a particular social role or expressing a particular cultural identity are certainly state interests, they are necessarily subordinate to political survival (as a sovereign entity with control over its own foreign policy), "physiological" security (the safety from death and harm of the state's population), and economic prosperity (a baseline level of which is necessary to ensure physiological security). Put simply, if a state and its population do not exist, it cannot achieve anything else—such as fulfilling a social role or expressing a cultural identity—either.[36] And since survival, security, and prosperity all have a material base—as Wendt recognizes via his "rump materialism" (he simply does not think the material base yields determinate outcomes)—so too must states necessarily put the defense of such interests ahead of social role fulfillment if they want to be in a position to play any sort of role in future.[37] That is not to suggest that states do not sometimes—or, indeed, often—make ideationally driven foreign policy choices that are detrimental to their other interests. It is simply a description of states' incentive structure, which much of the time they end up following.

It is necessary at this point to defend the notion that there is, in fact, a material base independent of the social world and that characteristics of that material base can yield causal outcomes. After all, military technology does not descend as manna from heaven, but rather is created via human agency in response to perceived threats, and thus it necessarily contains a dose of military culture and broader social identity from the outset. The same goes for the overall share of national economic resources allocated to defense, and indeed, money itself is a socially constructed store of value, albeit one premised upon underlying materially underpinned wealth.[38] Any assessment of strategic priorities is necessarily filtered through the strategic-cultural lens of the institution(s) doing the assessing; asking one's navy for an analysis of the relative merits of sea denial versus power projection, for example, necessarily delivers an answer infused with that navy's historical trajectory, its sense of its role in the nation and the world, its internal politics, and so forth. The broader question of whether the sea—like other geographical features—constitutes a strategic barrier or a highway similarly requires cultural interpretation.

Even technologies with such seemingly self-evident destructive power as nuclear weapons are not self-evidently "good" or "bad," either morally or strategically, absent social interpretation. One might see them as "bad" because of the potential humanitarian consequences of their use (or because of the constraints they impose on conventional military options), or "good" because of the casualties in conventional war they prevent (and deterrence that they enable at low relative cost). Their political *meaning* is thus socially constructed, even if the physiological effects on human bodies of their detonation have only one possible outcome. If military technology and resources require a social component to be both developed and meaningfully deployed, then Wendt's contention that there is indeed a "rump" material base but that it is simply indeterminate—in the absence of a friend/enemy distinction—as a cause of international outcomes becomes alluring.[39]

Crucially, however, each of these social choices involves a decisive material effect that is not open to interpretation. It may be debatable whether nuclear weapons are "good" or "bad," but the effect that one will have on the city and its population of frail, carbon-based human animals over which it detonates represents a single, determinate outcome—and a state facing another state armed with them must therefore make certain necessary calculations based around that capability.[40] In the same vein, while the strategic threat/opportunity constituted by geographical features, such as the oceanic moats enjoyed by the United States and United Kingdom, may be a matter of interpretation, the underlying material factor—humans' inability to cross water without spending resources on capital (ships) that could otherwise have been spent on further ground forces—yields certain necessary outcomes. Indeed, the very foundation of relations between major powers after 1945—secure second-strike nuclear deterrence and its disincentivization of conventional aggression[41]—rests on a physical "fact":

the relative impenetrability of water to the electro-magnetic spectrum and the associated survivability that it provides to ballistic missile submarines.

The same goes for the decision over what share of national economic resources to allocate to defense. Choosing a proportion may indeed be a socially and ideationally informed political choice, but the underlying size of the resource pools—and the military potentiality that they underpin—rests on the total size of the state's capital stock (both human and physical), which is not a matter of social interpretation. And while military technology is indeed developed in response to human agency, it is done so from within the technical bounds of the feasible. Such rebuttals apply more widely: while the balance of power, including resources and technology, is indeed necessarily interpreted through states' social lenses, it nonetheless conditions the bounds of the possible even in the absence of social content. And when those possibilities include hostile use, certain behaviors are necessitated by prudent states seeking survival for their populations.

Realists should indeed be castigated if they infer predictions solely from the balance of currently existing military hardware—a thin and intellectually impoverished understanding of relative power—and critics are correct to point out that a large stock of materiel is not the same as being able to compel another to do that which they would not otherwise have done, in line with the behavioral output understanding of power commonly associated with Dahl (as distinct from the input understanding).[42] But viewing total state power in terms of overall assets, defined as the state's total stock of physical,[43] financial,[44] and human capital,[45] does a better job of first encompassing *all* the relevant resources—equipment, stores of value, human bodies and brains—and, second, providing an effective measurable proxy for the underlying causes of behavioral power (given that the latter can only be observed *ex post*, and is therefore not an effective predictor of outcomes). None of this is to deny that there is a social element to the construction of all these power resources, or indeed that the "material" itself involves a large dose of social input, and this chapter is therefore not attempting to "settle" the debate over the precise nature of the relationship. It is simply to point out, rather, that states' power resources and their effects are not *wholly* socially constructed and that the nonsocial element produces certain effects.

Turning to specific arguments over states' pursuit of status, the notion that achieving a particular elevated status and thus fulfilling a certain international-social role might be *a* goal of states is relatively uncontentious.[46] For instance, one insightful recent constructivist work on Britain's pursuit of international status suggests at the outset that states' social roles are not the same as their interests, ambitions, values, or capabilities.[47] Yet the same work later asserts that social role actually *produces* national interests, thus implying that states *cannot* in fact have interests besides those constituted by identity.[48] Such conceptual tensions are symptomatic of a theoretical dilemma: the more minimal former assertion is the harder to refute, yet the more ambitious latter claim is necessary if constructivists are to escape the realist retort that fulfilling a social role is merely *an* interest of states—and a subordinate one to materially underpinned survival at that—rather than *the* interest. Escaping this retort is in turn necessary if constructivists are to be able to claim that anarchy is indeed what states make of it socially, since transforming the prevailing culture of anarchy would require states to lower their guard against each other—and thus accept higher risk to their survival, at least while the hoped-for transformation was taking place—in pursuit of an international-social value.

The less contentious point—that playing a particular social role is one of multiple interests—opens the way to conceding that the *most* fundamental state interests remain "political" survival (of state territory and institutions), "biological" security (of the citizenry's bodies), and preserving some baseline level of economic prosperity, since a state that cannot survive cannot achieve anything else. But if that is the case, then from these materially underpinned vital interests follows a need to be capable of defending them against potential foes—and that, if it comes to it, means accomplishing certain military missions.[49] Such military capability is necessarily underpinned by material resources, even as it also has a socially constructed dimension. Such capability can be provided independently (internal balancing), via allies (external balancing), or through some combination of the two—prudent strategy, including eschewing avoidable confrontation and aligning with the preferences of powerful allies, is a key aspect of state success[50]—but either way, it rests on some friendly actor's underlying resources. And reliance on external balancing brings its own dangers, as recently experienced by European NATO, when one's allies turn coercive.[51]

In short, such an analysis—while conceding that social role and status are important to states, all else held equal, and that such concerns sometimes drive them to act in imprudent ways—nonetheless suggests that hedging against abandonment, coercion, or outright destruction via balance-of-power positioning is likely to remain pervasive. This is not to say that there will not be variation in the extent and severity of such competition. All manner of ideational variables might exacerbate or reduce tensions, as discussed above, and even in the absence of such social forces, overt, intensive competition may yield self-destructive outcomes if it increases another side's insecurity and causes them to adopt a more offensively capable strategic posture in response.[52] The point, rather, is simply that conflict will never be a wholly absent possibility and that that reality must condition states' calculations—often to the point of some level of defensive hedging, if the state has the resources and technology to make that feasible—even in times of broadly cooperative relations.

A similar retort can be made against the claims that threat perception and military doctrine are both so fundamentally skewed by culture that they may be commonly and wholly disconnected from balance-of-power concerns, and which subsequently allow for an end to military balancing, mutual threat, and security competition. While this short chapter is clearly not the place for an extensive review, the success of many states—particularly resource-rich ones—in aping military technological and professional best practice would seem to suggest that much of the time states are able to achieve what Gray, borrowing from marketing theory, dubs "good enough" force postures in the face of strategic uncertainty.[53] Similarly, when states do "die" in the face of foreign aggression—a rare occurrence in post-1945 international politics—it is more often as a consequence of their relative military weakness and geographical vulnerability than as a consequence of a failure to perceive a looming threat.[54] Indeed, a key contribution of the neoclassical realist research program has been to demonstrate that while domestic-political variables may filter strategic behavior in multifarious and often nefarious ways, there are still underlying balance-of-power structural pressures at the international-systemic level that states usually respond to, even if they do so belatedly or imperfectly.[55]

In short, while Waltzian "socialization" toward accurately perceiving threats and formulating effective military doctrine may frequently be hindered—and sometimes terminally compromised—by cultural factors, as a description of the workings of the international system as a whole (as he intended his theory to be), realist predictions of enduring concern and possible competition over the distribution of material power are not undermined by this recognition.[56] Tellingly, despite their strong ideational commitments toward democracy promotion and human rights enforcement under the banner of upholding international order, Western states have recently had the reprioritization of balancing against increasingly capable rivals forced upon them by developments in the balance of power, whether that be China's rise in Asia for the United States or Russia's (partial) resurgence in Europe for the rest of NATO.[57]

Finally, even national identity and the nationalism it engenders—the ideational "master variable" underpinning the nation-state system—is itself forged by the interaction of political group identity and the survival imperative under structural anarchy. To paraphrase Tilly, war makes the state, and the state makes war.[58] Modern nation-states may have origi-nated as political groups of individually weak human beings with some shared identity connection, but their choice to form states as protective war machines capable of generating the military power necessary to defend against similar political units, and the subsequent mutual reinforcement of national identity and state strength, is very much consistent with real-ism's predictions of the consequences of international structural anarchy. Indeed, as noted earlier, Mearsheimer uses these grounds to argue that nationalism and realism are mutually supportive theories.[59] In the post–Cold War world, moreover, mutually threatening political groups' need to generate the military power necessary for security under anarchy—the security dilemma, in short—helps to explain the explosion of ferocious ethnonationalist and sectarian conflict within and between the new states emerging from the collapse of previously multiethnic communist federa-tions, secular Middle Eastern autocracies, and so forth.[60] Such conflict has in turn forged the identity of the states and state-like entities emerging from it. In short, while it is certainly not impossible for national identities to shift, as noted above, the process of their generation nonetheless sug-gests that they are endogenous to—rather than readily capable of exog-enously shifting to transform—international systemic security competition and balance-of-power positioning, that they are as much a dependent vari-able as an independent variable.

Uncertainty and the Menacing Shadow of the Future

The previous section outlined why some of the otherwise most convinc-ing constructivist variables at work in international politics nevertheless cannot promise to transform international politics away from a world of "realist," security-motivated balance-of-power positioning. This section turns to discuss why this is something that social variables will continue to struggle with as long as there is an inter*national* system.

The principal barrier to states ever setting aside their inclination to guard against each other and instead embrace each other as "friends"—no matter how strong their leaders' or citizens' desire to transform the cul-ture of international anarchy—is uncertainty over others' intentions, par-ticularly their future intentions.[61] Following the logic of the prisoners' dilemma, a state[62] that trusts that another means it no harm while the other state concludes that it now has an opportunity to pursue advantage may be punished severely for its complacency, rendering such trust perilous, particularly in security affairs, where defection from cooperation could result in the end of the "game" for one party.[63]

The meaning and implications of this "uncertainty" assumption merit consideration, however. Human beings are constantly trying to impose certainty on a contingent world via cognitive heuristics and neural shortcuts, for the sake of their own mental well-being.[64] Indeed, since humans derive meaning and value from the self-imposed certainty of ideational reinforcement, so too they can derive benefit from the entrenchment of both amity with and enmity against "others," even when this creates other complications and dangers.[65] As a result, much of international politics is influenced by habit, both the habit of friendship *and* the habit of animosity.[66] "Uncertainty" also means different things to different people: for realists, it is a condition from which to infer fear about others' possible behavior; for constructivists, by contrast, it may simply refer to the inherent indeterminacy of information until it is imbued with social content.[67] It may be possible to build trust in others' benign intent over time and thereby escape security competition, meanwhile, through their costly signaling: forgoing capabilities and policy options that a potential aggressor would not want to do without.[68] States can also have the certain "friendship" of those with whom they are balancing against a third-party threat, and if that threat is long-lived, then so too may be the certainty of alliance.[69]

Illustrating this "uncertainty about uncertainty,"[70] consider one of the highest profile oft-invoked security dilemmas: the Cold War escalation of U.S.-Soviet hostility, during which the most seminal security dilemma theorization took place.[71] Robert Jervis—one of the concept's foremost progenitors—subsequently questioned whether the Cold War can be understood as a security dilemma after all, understood as a tragic cycle of mutual threat between nonrevisionist security seekers driven by uncertainty over the other's intentions. Neither side was "uncertain" over whether the other was an adversary. And as subsequent archival revelations document, each side *did* want to destroy the other, and correctly inferred as much of its opponent.[72]

Jervis's "recantation" of the Cold War-as-security-dilemma is itself bounded, however, and this bounding sheds light on the ways in which varieties of uncertainty can still operate even between states with "certain" mutual intent. "Greedy" states versus "security-seeking" states are themselves binary ideal types that mask an underlying spectrum. Practically all states are greedy, in terms of wanting to improve their lot, if the costs are low enough.[73] Conversely, few states are greedy to the point of total unconcern for security; not even Nazi Germany desired limitless global war. While there may not have been uncertainty over each side's Cold War *intent*, therefore—enmity-driven desire to defeat and ultimately destroy the other—there was still uncertainty over underlying *motivations*.[74] A desire to exterminate an enemy population may entail quite different behavior than a desire for ideological supremacy, for example, and the two may therefore merit different policy responses, even though both fall within the domain of "hostile" intent. Such doubt over motivations—even within the cognitively "certain" domain of U.S.-Soviet enmity—still added up to a variety of security dilemma: the most salient question for Americans was not "is the Soviet Union an enemy?" but rather "what might Moscow do about situation X, in Y circumstances, at time Z?" The same is evident in major power politics today. Washington is not "uncertain" over whether or not China and Russia are its "adversaries," defined in broad and obvious terms, but there *is* a high degree of uncertainty over what *types* of rivals they represent and their associated future strategic choices. Recognition of uncertainty's nonbinary nature, in short, does not undermine the argument that states' inability to know others' future behavior with perfect reliability incentivizes them to worry about possible future dangers. Realists disagree over prospects for avoiding security competition through signaling motivations, of course,[75] but all variants are united by recognizing the enduring significance of the balance of material power.[76]

On top of these qualifications to the uncertainty-over-intentions assumption come disagreements over the most appropriate response to such uncertainty. Conceding that we can never know another state's future intentions with mathematical certainty, and therefore that the worst-case outcome—surprise attack by a concealed aggressor—will always remain a hypothetical possibility does not necessarily imply that security is maximized by treating such a scenario as likely. Provoking war for fear of possible future war is like committing suicide for fear of death, and given the balancing often generated by hostile behavior, provoking others into uniting against oneself through attempted power maximization can ultimately reduce one's security.[77] While worst-case contingencies always merit consideration, policy planning—particularly decisions over how much of the national resource base to devote to defense ("guns") versus consumption and productive investment ("butter")[78]—necessitates probabilistic calculations of the relative dangers of overarmament (provoking balancing alongside domestic economic immiseration) versus underarmament (attack by a better-armed adversary).[79] Intense security competition can therefore be an irrational and self-defeating response to mere uncertainty over future intentions, in the absence of other threat data.[80] Both "realist" and "constructivist" variables can feature among this threat data and therefore play a crucial part in determining the optimal strategic response to such intentions uncertainty, and that in turn conditions whether the potential threat posed by each side's capabilities, be they latent or realized, manifests itself as a security dilemma. For many realists, the offense-defense balance of technology and geography determines whether uncertainty over others' intentions merits military confrontation and determines the (in)stability of states' strategic relations.[81] For constructivists, the solidarity/enmity borne of sociocultural similarity/difference may be equally decisive.

But neither of these observations—that uncertainty neither carries a single meaning nor prescribes a single strategy—undermines the core claim that survival has a material base that necessitates continual security-motivated concern for one's position in the balance of power. Survival may indeed be "multiply realizable," with social/ideational variables informing the path taken, alongside various "realist" variables. But given all states' need to safeguard a materially based hierarchy of interests without wholesale reliance on others' politically contingent (and therefore capricious) benevolence—whether that be potential abandonment by erstwhile allies, potential attack by erstwhile neutrals, or potential coercion by either—their position in the balance of power will always remain relevant to their future security. And given that situation, the conditions for mutual threat and an associated security dilemma to re-emerge are unlikely to be permanently expunged, despite such a deterioration going unrealized indefinitely in many cases due to other overlying factors.[82] Fear of future conflict—at least against *some* state, if not against any *specific* state—thus remains an endemic feature of international politics. And much of that is still down to the enduring concerns of structurally based realism: international-systemic anarchy, its absence of a reliable sovereign enforcer of global peace, and the associated dangers of offensively capable peers of unreliably benevolent intent.

Tellingly, while many contemporary states have achieved mutual "friendship," they have rarely sustained it once the strategic factors holding them together—such as alliance against a mutual threat, shared membership of a great(er) power's dependency network, or some other mutually beneficial exchange—have disappeared. This suggests that such "friendship" is as much a dependent variable (an outcome of realist balancing behavior) as an independent variable (a transformational force in international politics).[83] Even within the zone of friendship that had come to characterize the European "community" by the late 1980s, for example—

probably the deepest case of intersubjective recognition, cooperation, and sovereignty pooling to date—Britain and France still worried intensely about the potential power imbalances created by German reunification, and they were not content until reunified German power was subordinated via a restated US commitment to NATO.[84] As noted previously, moreover, via both Trump and Brexit—ideationally motivated shifts in foreign policy orientation[85]—Euro-Atlantic security relations have recently displayed a dramatic backsliding, raising the specter of alliance breakdown and coercive confrontation. The relative power of all sides is critical to their ability to resist/dispense such coercion and safeguard future security even in the possible absence of alliance support. Even within the EU, the ability of members to resist or dispense coercion comes down to relative power: witness Greece's experience at German hands in the context of the Eurozone crisis, and contrast it with the lack of sanction for Franco-German breaches of EU rules.[86] And between NATO and Russia, a 1990s moment of optimism over developing friendship has retrenched to coercive confrontation as an outcome of each other's choices.[87] All these developments—which can be interpreted as negative movement along the spectrum between cooperation and conflict—illustrate the continuing centrality of relative power to safeguarding a hierarchy of national interests without dependence on the changeable commitments of others.

As a consequence, the base conditions for the security dilemma will always exist between sovereign states under anarchy, even if it lies wholly dormant for most states most of the time, thanks to overlying factors. Interstate friendship does not render deterioration to a security dilemma impossible, and neither does interstate animosity preclude stable and durable cooperation.[88] So while identity—which in any case is "sticky" and slow to change—certainly matters to security relations, it is unlikely to trump some combination of power and informational variables.[89] Of course, if international relations were transformed by the emergence of a single world-state, the system would no longer be anarchic and the units-formerly-known-as-states would not need to rely on relative power for their security, and thus such competition would end.[90] That requirement, however, does not look likely to be fulfilled anytime soon.

Conclusion

Conflict and cooperation is not some binary "either/or" condition, but rather a spectrum. So too the security concerns borne of uncertainty over motivations are not some irreversible "on/off" switch, be that permanently severe *or* permanently solved. There is certainly far more peace in the world than the most pessimistic readings of realism would seem to imply,[91] and ideational similarity and solidarity—as well as the power and informational variables beloved of realists—clearly have something to do with this. Interests within the parameters of continuing to survive are socially constituted, and even the route to survival itself represents an ideationally informed choice. But the need to safeguard a materially underpinned hierarchy of interests if states are to continue to exist—a necessary prerequisite to performing any kind of social role—still incentivizes them to value their position in the balance of power as a safeguard against future dangers. Of course, states can and do disregard certain incentive structures in favor of others.[92] But until *all* states are *known* to have done so—a high bar indeed—the potential for security competition to re-emerge in the international system will continue to exist. And knowing *that*, states will continue to prize the capabilities to provide for their own security . . . and so on, creating enduring conditions for security dilemmas to one day reappear, even though they go overlain by other factors in most international relationships most of the time.

Both realists and constructivists therefore have work to do, in terms of both refining their paradigmatic cores *and* recognizing the necessity of analytically eclectic cross-pollination to explain many of the most pressing questions of real-world international politics. Realists must do more to incorporate identity as a variable that produces systemically significant variation in behavior rather than as some adjunct bolt-on, whether that be via the post-1990s boom of neoclassical theorization or attempts at microfoundationally elaborated structural realism.[93] Porter's work on the interaction of power and habit in determining US grand strategy is a good recent example, while—as noted earlier—Snyder's *Myths of Empire* remains a key benchmark.[94] Constructivists, for their part, must continue to investigate the relationship between states' potentially infinite array of socially constituted interests, their materially underpinned hierarchy of core survival requirements, and the enduring concern for relative power that the latter generates. Along the way, both sides must be circumspect in their appeals to allegedly "smoking-gun" examples. For realists to claim that structure alone explains World War II or the Cold War, for example— missing the universalist ideologies of German Nazism, Soviet communism, or US liberalism—would be a stretch indeed. Equally, constructivists' most beloved examples—amicable US-Canadian relations along an easily passable land border, the relative underarmament of Germany and Japan, greater American fear of a few North Korean atomic bombs than hundreds of British thermonuclear warheads, the rise of European Union, and so forth—can all be readily explained with reference to balances of capability and information. "Analytic eclecticism" is easy to profess, but the most pressing contemporary questions of world politics require that theorists practice it too.

For those not interested in resolving paradigm wars or "isms" debates, meanwhile, the intersection of material-structural pressures on state behavior with socially constituted foreign policy preferences provides ample scope for investigating crucial real-world questions of our time. Viewed in rationalist terms, this might involve investigating the role of social variables in informing leaders' utility functions, and thus their preference orderings under the overall structural constraint of needing to ensure continued survival. Just how far could the United States meddle in the Middle East at the behest of domestic interests, for example, before it critically harmed its power position vis-à-vis China? Extending the previous point, has US unipolarity created unique space for a "crazy" foreign policy that disregards the balance of power—both by the United States itself and by close US allies—and will this change if or when unipolarity wanes?[95] Relatedly, just how far can the likes of Germany and Japan sustain their pacifistic foreign policy orientations in the face of US relative decline or disengagement and the likely associated need for them to provide more for their own security? Changing tack, how does a small power like Sweden—say—make its trade-off between providing mobile forces for an EU Battlegroup (a cause it values), on the one hand, and maintaining large amounts of conscripts and armor on its eastern border to hedge against Russia (a threat that it cannot be rid of), on the other? Are UK efforts to rebrand as an "aid superpower" facilitated by a nuclear deterrent and the US alliance, say, providing leeway to follow an ideational foreign policy under the cover of a "good enough" military umbrella? In short, there is scope for any number of midlevel theories of foreign policy under the constraint of still recognizing that interstate balance-of-power considerations continue to structure the international system.

NOTES

1. For a turn-of-the-millennium instance of this refrain, see Burchill 2001, 70.

2. Defined as some function of presently extant military forces and the underlying economic wherewithal necessary to generate further military forces if required. The notion that there is a material world independent of—and with certain determinate consequences in the absence of—social forces will be defended subsequently.

3. McCourt 2016; Nexon et al. 2017. See also other contributions to this volume.

4. Leveling the charge that constructivism's allure lies in its transformational promise is Mearsheimer (1994–95). Retorting that constructivism is in fact agnostic at best—and deeply pessimistic often—over the prospects for such transformational change are Hopf (1998, 180) and Barkin (2003, 326), with the latter reaching a "realist worldview" characterized by an expectation of persistent power competition via "constructivist," ideational logic. See also the Sjoberg chapter in this volume, which contends that while constructivism was indeed initially agnostic or even pessimistic over prospects for progressive change, Mearsheimer's argument has in fact been partially borne out, since it has come since then to be seen by many as holding the (in his view unjustified) transformational allure that he accused it of, even while that was—certainly in Hopf's (1998) view—not a fair characterization of the research agenda at the time of his original interjection. Both Hopf and Sjoberg caution that such transformational allure may promise something that it is not within constructivism's gift to deliver, and that may undermine the insightful—but often deeply pessimistic—contributions of nontransformational constructivist explanations.

5. Barkin 2003.

6. Sil and Katzenstein 2010.

7. The notion of great powers as states that not only possess certain capabilities but that also discharge certain international-social roles was first formulated by Bull (1977).

8. Paul, Larson, and Wohlforth 2014; Volgy et al. 2011; Lebow 2010.

9. McCourt 2014; Neumann 2008.

10. Sagan 1996–97; Ross 2009.

11. Paul, Larson, and Wohlforth 2014. See also Schweller 2008. "Materially inclined" here refers to Wohlforth's past work (1999) on the international-political consequences of US unipolarity, which is fundamentally an argument about the international-political consequences of the contemporary United States' unrivaled and unprecedented preponderance of material capabilities.

12. Hayes 2014; Stein 2013; Rousseau and Garcia-Retamero 2007; Goodwin, Wilson, and Gaines 2005; Hopf 2002.

13. Hayes 2014.

14. Snyder 1993, 3–6.

15. Johnston 1995; Katzenstein 1996; Kier 1997; Farrell 1998, Gray 1999.

16. Kier 1996.

17. Porter 2009.

18. Posen 1984.

19. Walt 1990.

20. Jervis 1976.

21. Mearsheimer and Walt 2008; Mearsheimer 2009.

22. Blagden 2015.

23. Lobell, Ripsman, and Taliaferro 2009; Kitchen 2010.

24. For seminal perspectives on the role of nationalist ideas in state formation, see Gellner 2009 (1983); Anderson 2006 (1983). For a contemporary realist take on the role of nationalism in underpinning the competitive nation-state system, see

Mearsheimer 2011. Note, of course, that nationalism and national identity are not identical terms, but varieties of nationalism are instrumental in forming a national identity, and however liberal/civic the latter, it invariably contains a desire for the biological survival of some group.

25. Moravcsik 1997.

26. Snyder 1993. Indeed, Snyder's work can be seen as an admirable example of "analytic eclecticism" before the term was popularized (Sil and Katzenstein 2010).

27. Mitzen 2006.

28. McCourt 2014, 174.

29. Thies and Breuning 2012.

30. Bull 1977; Wendt 1999, 297–308.

31. That is, if terminal "underbalancing" is common. Schweller 2008.

32. Waltz 1979, 74. The interwar French case may be one such example (Kier 1996); the question, then, is how common is such behavior, if this is indeed what explains France's experience in 1940?

33. Hopf 2010.

34. Wendt 1992, 1999, 297–308.

35. Lebow 1994. This charge against realism was never wholly fair, given that few realists ever professed to have a theory of domestic economic change/growth/collapse and given that the USSR's collapse as a "pole" owed more to domestic economic crisis than international pressure.

36. Mearsheimer 2001, 31. Of course, a key contribution of constructivist IR scholarship has been the identification that states have multiple interests, which are both partially constituted *and* hierarchically rank-ordered by state identity (Klotz 1995 and Hopf 1998, 174–77). A key contribution of realist thought, however, has been the recognition that this rank-ordering must always be topped by the survival of the state and its population, whatever the prevailing form and identity of the underlying state, and that survival has a material base, meaning that interests are not *wholly* socially constituted. Indeed, this can be understood via Maslow's (1943) "hierarchy of needs," applied at the state level. Likewise, sovereignty is itself a social construction, but one with a "survivalist" base; that is, the formation of state-like political entities owes to human communities' biologically underpinned imperative to survive and, crucially, reliant upon material power for its defense (Krasner 1999). This latter claim does not preclude recognition that security for self- and state identity is something that people value in its own right, alongside "physical" security, even to the point of incurring other risks to reinforce such identity (Mitzen 2006). Of course, a state might *not* want to survive (consider cases of states voluntarily giving up sovereignty to enter political union with others), so in that sense, it is a generalization rather than a categorical rule. But it is assumed that those that do exist want to continue to do so (otherwise they would already no longer do so) (Barkin 2003, 328).

37. Wendt 1999, 109–13.

38. Hence the notion of money's long-run "neutrality" vis-à-vis the real economy. See, for example, Lucas 1972.

39. Wendt 1999, 109–13.

40. Moreover, while the first use of nuclear weapons saw a decade of consideration of their warfighting utility—so Hiroshima did not immediately "speak for

itself" in terms of social interpretation—the diffusion of their possession to multiple actors and associated retaliatory implications saw all sides rapidly migrate toward the deterrent strategies necessitated by their destructive potential (albeit with variation in deterrent posture, based on strategic position (Narang 2014).

41. Jervis 1989.

42. Barkin 2003, 329 and Dahl 1957.

43. Defined broadly to include military materiel, the means of economic production, natural resource endowments, and favorable geographic assets (such as oceanic moats).

44. Defined as the means of storing and trading the value of underlying physical and human assets.

45. Defined similarly broadly, to include military personnel, nonmilitary contributors to economic activity, and the overall quality of both of those two categories (education, training, and so forth), with the latter in turn yielding such assets as effective doctrine and strategy, as well as general military and nonmilitary operational effectiveness.

46. On international-social performance/practice as a determinant of state behavior, see—for example—Hopf 1998, 177–80.

47. McCourt 2014, 166.

48. McCourt 2014, 174.

49. On the relationship between the achievement of national objectives and the possession of sufficient capability to accomplish key associated military missions, see Glaser 2010, 40–41.

50. Geyer 1986.

51. Gray 2017.

52. Jervis 1978; Glaser 2010.

53. Horowitz 2010; Gray 2014.

54. Fazal 2007.

55. Lobell, Ripsman, and Taliaferro 2009.

56. Waltz 1979, 74.

57. Blagden 2015.

58. Tilly 1992.

59. Mearsheimer 2011. On this relationship between national identity and realist predictions of conflict and competition more broadly, see also Barkin 2003.

60. Posen 1993.

61. Mearsheimer 2001, 31–36; Copeland 2000, 2003, 2011; Lieber 2000; Rosato 2014–15.

62. Or nonstate group, in the context of civil conflict.

63. Lipson 1984. Of course, the game may itself be socially conditioned; if the "prisoners" have a communitarian rather than an individualist group identity, say, then they may value the other as the self (Schelling 2018). But given the game's survival-motivated incentives toward defection if there is any doubt over the strength of that communitarian spirit, it will remain challenging for states—at least those of similar power and capability to do each other harm—to reach this transformational level of ideationally motivated trust.

64. Kahneman 2012.

65. Mitzen 2006; see also Porter 2016.

66. Hopf 2010. Such mentally generated certainty can cut both ways, moreover: just as states may be fearful of the implications of conflict, this can give way at certain points to misplaced confidence over both the necessity of war and prospects for success (Johnson and Tierney 2011).
67. Rathbun 2007.
68. Kydd 2000; see also Booth and Wheeler 2007.
69. Walt 1990.
70. Rathbun 2007.
71. Herz 1950; Jervis 1978.
72. Jervis 2001.
73. Jervis 2001, 39.
74. Jervis 2001, 41.
75. Kydd 1997; Glaser 2010; Lieber 2011.
76. Edelstein 2002, 1.
77. Waltz 1979; Walt 1990; Glaser 1992, 2000, 2010; Kirshner 2012.
78. Powell 1993.
79. Brooks 1997, 447–450; Glaser et al. 2015–16, 197–202.
80. Copeland 2011, 442; Kydd 1997; Schweller 1996; Montgomery 2006; Tang 2008.
81. Jervis 1978; Glaser and Kaufmann 1998; Montgomery 2006; Goldstein 2013.
82. Taliaferro 2000–1.
83. Walt 1990.
84. Hayes and James 2015.
85. Blagden 2017, 8–9.
86. *The Economist* 2015; Little 2012.
87. Blagden 2015; Shifrinson 2016.
88. Edelstein 2002; Montgomery 2006.
89. Glaser 2010, 166–71.
90. Wendt 2003.
91. Blagden 2016, 200.
92. Mearsheimer 2009.
93. Rose 1998; Rathbun 2008; Freyberg-Inan, Harrison, and James 2009, 3–8.
94. Porter 2017; Snyder 1993. Many question-driven research projects on particular empirical puzzles combine both "realist" and "constructivist" variables, but without being positioned "within" a paradigm.
95. Monteiro 2014; Brooks and Wohlforth 2008; Blagden 2015.

REFERENCES

Anderson, Benedict. 2006. *Imagined Communities: Reflections on the Origin and Spread of Nationalism* (new ed.). London: Verso.
Barkin, J. Samuel. 2003. "Realist Constructivism." *International Studies Review* 5, no. 3: 325–42.
Blagden, David. 2015. "Global Multipolarity, European Security, and UK Grand Strategy: Back to the Future, Once Again." *International Affairs* 91 no. 2: 333–53.
Blagden, David. 2016. "Induction and Deduction in International Relations: Squar-

ing the Circle between Theory and Evidence." *International Studies Review* 18, no. 2: 195–213.

Blagden, David. 2017. "Britain and the World after Brexit." *International Politics* 54, no. 1: 1–25.

Booth, Ken, and Nicholas J. Wheeler. 2007. *The Security Dilemma: Fear, Cooperation and Trust in World Politics*. New York: Palgrave Macmillan.

Brooks, Stephen G. 1997. "Dueling Realisms." *International Organization* 51, no. 3: 445–77.

Brooks, Stephen G., and William C. Wohlforth. 2008. *World Out of Balance: International Relations and the Challenge of American Primacy*. Princeton, NJ: Princeton University Press.

Bull, Hedley. 1977. *The Anarchical Society: A Study of Order in World Politics*. New York: Columbia University Press.

Burchill, Scott. 2001. "Realism and Neo-Realism." In *Theories of International Relations* (2nd ed.), edited by S. Burchill et al., 70–102 Basingstoke: Palgrave Macmillan.

Copeland, Dale C. 2000. "The Constructivist Challenge to Structural Realism: A Review Essay." *International Security* 25, no. 2: 187–212.

Copeland, Dale C. 2003. "A Realist Critique of the English School." *Review of International Studies* 29, no. 3: 427–41.

Copeland, Dale C. 2011. "Rationalist Theories of International Politics and the Problem of the Future." *Security Studies* 20, no. 3: 441–50.

Dahl, Robert A. 1957. "The Concept of Power." *Behavioral Science* 2, no. 3: 201–15.

The Economist. 2015. "Why Germany and Greece Are at Odds" February 19. Available at: http://www.economist.com/blogs/economist-explains/2015/02/economist-explains-11. Accessed June 17, 2017.

Edelstein, David M. 2002. "Managing Uncertainty: Beliefs About Intentions and the Rise of Great Powers." *Security Studies* 12, no. 1: 1–40.

Farrell, Theo. 1998. "Culture and Military Doctrine." *Review of International Studies* 24, no. 3: 407–16.

Fazal, Tanisha M. 2007. *State Death: The Politics and Geography of Conquest, Occupation, and Annexation*. Princeton, NJ: Princeton University Press.

Freyberg-Inan, Annette, Ewan Harrison, and Patrick James. 2009. "What Way Forward for Contemporary Realism?" In *Rethinking Realism in International Relations: Between Tradition and Innovation*, edited by Annette Freyberg-Inan, Ewan Harrison, and Patrick James, 1–18. Baltimore: Johns Hopkins University Press.

Gellner, Ernest. 2009. *Nations and Nationalism* (2nd ed.). Ithaca, NY: Cornell University Press.

Geyer, Michael. 1986. "German Strategy in the Age of Machine Warfare." In *Makers of Modern Strategy from Machiavelli to the Nuclear Age*, edited by Peter Paret, 527–97. Princeton, NJ: Princeton University Press.

Glaser, Charles L. 1992. "Political Consequences of Military Strategy: Expanding and Refining the Spiral and Deterrence Models." *World Politics* 44, no. 4: 497–538.

Glaser, Charles L. 2000. "The Causes and Consequences of Arms Races." *Annual Review of Political Science* 3: 251–76.

Glaser, Charles L. 2010. *Rational Theory of International Politics: The Logic of Competition and Cooperation*. Princeton, NJ: Princeton University Press.

Glaser, Charles L., and Chaim Kaufmann. 1998. "What Is the Offense-Defense Balance and Can We Measure It?" *International Security* 22, no. 4: 44–82.

Glaser, Charles L., Andrew H. Kydd, Mark L. Haas, John M. Owen IV, and Sebastian Rosato. 2015–16. "Can Great Powers Discern Intentions?" *International Security* 40, no. 3: 197–215.

Goldstein, Avery (2013). "First Things First: The Pressing Danger of Crisis Instability in U.S.-China relations." *International Security* 37, no. 4: 49–89.

Goodwin, Robin, Michelle Willson, and Stanley Gaines. 2005. "Terror Threat Perception and Its Consequences in Contemporary Britain." *British Journal of Politics and International Relations* 96, no. 4: 389–406.

Gray, Colin S. 1999. "Strategic Culture as Context: The First Generation of Theory Strikes Back." *Review of International Studies* 25, no. 1: 49–69.

Gray, Colin S. 2014. *Strategy and Defence Planning: Meeting the Challenge of Uncertainty.* Oxford: Oxford University Press.

Gray, Rosie. 2017. "Trump Declines to Affirm NATO's Article 5." *The Atlantic,* 25 May. Available at: https://www.theatlantic.com/international/archive/2017/05/trump-declines-to-affirm-natos-article-5/528129/. Accessed June 16, 2017.

Hayes, Jarrod. 2014. *Constructing National Security: U.S. Relations with India and China.* Cambridge: Cambridge University Press.

Hayes, Jarrod, and Patrick James. 2015. "Theory as Thought: Britain and German Unification." *Security Studies* 23, no. 2: 399–429.

Herz, John H. 1950. "Idealist Internationalism and the Security Dilemma." *World Politics* 2, no. 2: 157–80.

Hopf, Ted. 1998. "The Promise of Constructivism in International Relations Theory." *International Security* 23, no. 1: 171–200.

Hopf, Ted. 2002. *Social Construction of International Politics: Identities and Foreign Policies, Moscow, 1955 and 1999.* Ithaca, NY: Cornell University Press.

Hopf, Ted, 2010. "The Logic of Habit in International Relations." *European Journal of International Relations* 16, no. 4: 539–61.

Horowitz, Michael C. 2010. *The Diffusion of Military Power: Causes and Consequences for International Politics.* Princeton, NJ: Princeton University Press.

Jervis, Robert. 1976. *Perception and Misperception in International Politics.* Princeton, NJ: Princeton University Press.

Jervis, Robert. 1978. "Cooperation Under the Security Dilemma." *World Politics* 30, no. 2: 167–214.

Jervis, Robert. 1989. *The Meaning of the Nuclear Revolution: Statecraft and the Prospect of Armageddon.* Ithaca, NJ: Cornell University Press.

Jervis, Robert. 2001. "Was the Cold War a Security Dilemma?" *Journal of Cold War Studies* 3, no. 1: 36–60.

Johnson, Dominic D. P., and Dominic Tierney. 2011. "The Rubicon Theory of War: How the Path to Conflict Reaches the Point of No Return." *International Security* 36, no. 1: 7–40.

Johnston, Alastair Iain. 1995. *Cultural Realism: Strategic Culture and Grand Strategy in Chinese History.* Princeton, NJ: Princeton University Press.

Kahneman, Daniel. 2012. *Thinking, Fast and Slow.* London: Penguin.

Katzenstein, Peter J. 1996. *Cultural Norms and National Security: Police and Military in Postwar Japan.* Ithaca, NJ: Cornell University Press.

Kier, Elizabeth. 1996. "Culture and French Military Doctrine Before World War II." In *The Culture of National Security: Norms and Identity in World Politics*, edited by Peter J. Katzenstein, 186–215. New York: Columbia University Press.

Kier, Elizabeth. 1997. *Imagining War: French and British Military Doctrine between the Wars*. Princeton, NJ: Princeton University Press.

Kirshner, Jonathan. 2012. "The Tragedy of Offensive Realism: Classical Realism and the Rise of China." *European Journal of International Relations* 18, no. 1: 53–75.

Kitchen, Nicholas. 2010. "Systemic Pressures and Domestic Ideas: A Neoclassical Realist Model of Grand Strategy Formation." *Review of International Studies* 36, no. 1: 117–43.

Klotz, Audie. 1995. "Norms Reconstituting Interests: Global Racial Equality and U.S. Sanctions Against South Africa." *International Organization* 49, no. 3: 451–78.

Krasner, Stephen D. 1999. *Sovereignty: Organized Hypocrisy*. Princeton, NJ: Princeton University Press.

Kydd, Andrew H. 1997. "Sheep in Sheep's Clothing: Why Security Seekers Do Not Fight Each Other." *Security Studies* 7, no. 1: 114–54.

Kydd, Andrew H. 2000. "Trust, Reassurance, and Cooperation." *International Organization* 54, no. 2: 325–57.

Lebow, Richard Ned. 1994. "The Long Peace, the End of the Cold War, and the Failure of Realism." *International Organization* 48, no. 2: 249–77.

Lebow, Richard Ned. 2010. *Why Nations Fight: Past and Future Motives for War*. Cambridge: Cambridge University Press.

Lieber, Keir A. 2000. "Grasping the Technological Peace: The Offense-Defense Balance and International Security." *International Security* 25, no. 1: 71–104.

Lieber, Keir A. 2011. "Mission Impossible: Measuring the Offense-Defense Balance with Military Net Assessment." *Security Studies* 20, no. 3: 451–59.

Little, Allan. 2012. "Did Germany Sow the Seeds of Eurozone Debt Crisis." *BBC News*, January 19. Available at: http://www.bbc.co.uk/news/world-europe-16761087. Accessed July 17, 2107.

Lipson, Charles. 1984. "International Cooperation in Economic and Security Affairs." *World Politics* 37, no. 1: 1–23.

Lobell, Steven E., Norrin M. Ripsman, and Jeffrey W. Taliaferro, eds. 2009. *Neoclassical Realism, the State, and Foreign Policy* Cambridge: Cambridge University Press.

Lucas, Robert E. 1972. "Expectations and the Neutrality of Money." *Journal of Economic Theory* 4, no. 2: 103–24.

Maslow, Abraham H. 1943. "A Theory of Human Motivation." *Psychological Review* 50, no. 4: 370–96.

McCourt, David M. 2014. "Has Britain Found Its Role?" *Survival* 56, no. 2: 157–78.

McCourt, David M. 2016. "Practice Theory and Relationalism as the New Constructivism." *International Studies Quarterly* 60, no. 3: 475–85.

Mearsheimer, John J. 1994–95. "The False Promise of International Institutions." *International Security* 19, no. 3: 5–49.

Mearsheimer, John J. 2001. *The Tragedy of Great Power Politics*, New York: Norton.

Mearsheimer, John J. 2009. "Reckless States and Realism." *International Relations* 23, no. 2: 241–56.

Mearsheimer, John J. 2011. "Kissing Cousins: Realism and Nationalism." Paper presented at the Yale Workshop on International Relations, New Haven, May 5 Accessed online 18/12/2014 at http://mearsheimer.uchicago.edu/pdfs/kissing-cousins.pdf.

Mearsheimer, John J., and Stephen M. Walt. 2008. *The Israel Lobby and U.S. Foreign Policy*. New York: Farrar, Straus and Giroux.

Mitzen, Jennifer. 2006. "Ontological Security in World Politics: State Identity and the Security Dilemma." *European Journal of International Relations* 12, no. 3: 341–70.

Monteiro, Nuno P. 2014. *Theory of Unipolar Politics*. Cambridge: Cambridge University Press.

Montgomery, Evan Braden. 2006. "Breaking Out of the Security Dilemma: Realism, Reassurance, and the Problem of Uncertainty." *International Security* 31, no. 2: 151–85.

Moravcsik, Andrew. 1997. "Taking Preferences Seriously: A Liberal Theory of International Politics." *International Organization* 51, no. 4: 513–53.

Narang, Vipin. 2014. *Nuclear Strategy in the Modern Era: Regional Powers and International Conflict*. Princeton, NJ: Princeton University Press.

Neumann, Iver B. 2008. "Russia As a Great Power, 1815–2007." *Journal of International Relations and Development* 11, no. 2: 128–51.

Nexon, Daniel H. et al. 2017. "Seizing Constructivist Ground? Practice and Relational theories." ISQ Symposium, April 3. Available at http://www.isanet.org/Publications/ISQ/Posts/ID/5473/categoryId/102/Seizing-Constructivist-Ground-Practice-and-Relational-Theories. Accessed June 16, 2017.

Paul, T. V., Deborah Welch Larson, and William C. Wohlforth, eds. 2014. *Status in World Politics*. Cambridge: Cambridge University Press.

Porter, Patrick. 2009. *Military Orientalism: Eastern War through Western Eyes*. London: Hurst.

Porter, Patrick. 2016. "Taking Uncertainty Seriously: Classical Realism and National Security." *European Journal of International Security* 1, no. 2: 239–60.

Porter, Patrick. 2018. "Why America's Grand Strategy Has Not Changed: Power, Habit, and the U.S. Foreign Policy Establishment." *International Security* 42, no. 4: forthcoming.

Posen, Barry R. 1984. *The Sources of Military Doctrine: France, Britain, and Germany between the World Wars*. Ithaca, NY: Cornell University Press.

Posen, Barry R. 1993. "The Security Dilemma and Ethnic Conflict." *Survival* 35, no. 1: 27–47.

Powell, Robert. 1993. "Guns, Butter, and Anarchy." *American Political Science Review* 87, no. 1: 115–32.

Rathbun, Brian C. 2007. "Uncertain About Uncertainty: Understanding the Multiple Meanings of a Crucial Concept in International Relations Theory." *International Studies Quarterly* 51, no. 3: 533–57.

Rathbun, Brian C. 2008. "A Rose By Any Other Name: Neoclassical Realism as the Logical and Necessary Extension of Structural Realism." *Security Studies* 17, no. 2: 294–321.

Rosato, Sebastian. 2014–15. "The Inscrutable Intentions of Great Powers." *International Security* 39, no. 3: 48–88.

Rose, Gideon. 1998. "Neoclassical Realism and Theories of Foreign Policy." *World Politics* 51, no. 1: 144–72.

Ross, Robert. 2009. "China's Naval Nationalism: Sources, Prospects, and the U.S. Response." *International Security* 34, no. 2: 46–81.

Rousseau, David L., and Rocio Garcia-Retamero. 2007. "Identity, Power, and Threat Perception: A Cross-National Experimental Study." *Journal of Conflict Resolution* 51, no. 5: 744–71.

Sagan, Scott D. (1996–97). "Why Do States Build Nuclear Weapons? Three Models in Search of a Bomb." *International Security* 21, no.3: 54–86.

Schelling, Thomas C. 2018. "The Game Theory of Conflict: The Prisoners' Dilemma – An Unsympathetic Critique." In *Games: Conflict, Competition, and Cooperation*, edited by David Blagden and Mark de Rond. Cambridge: Cambridge University Press.

Schweller, Randall L. 1996. "Neorealism's *Status Quo* Bias: What Security Dilemma?" *Security Studies* 5, no. 3: 90–121.

Schweller, Randall L. 2008. *Unanswered Threats: Political Constraints on the Balance of Power*. Princeton, NJ: Princeton University Press.

Shifrinson, Joshua R. Itzkowitz. 2016. "Deal or No Deal? The End of the Cold War and the U.S. Offer to Limit NATO Expansion." *International Security* 40, no. 4: 7–44.

Sil, Rudra, and Peter J. Katzenstein. 2010. *Beyond Paradigms: Analytic Eclecticism in World Politics*. New York: Palgrave Macmillan.

Snyder, Jack. 1993. *Myths of Empire: Domestic Politics and International Ambition*. Ithaca, NY: Cornell University Press.

Stein, Janice Gross. 2013. "Threat Perception in International Relations." In *The Oxford Handbook of Political Psychology* (2nd ed.), edited by L. Huddy, D. O. Sears, and J. S. Levy, 364–94. Oxford: Oxford University Press.

Taliaferro, Jeffrey W. 2000–1. "Security Seeking Under Anarchy: Defensive Realism Revisited." *International Security* 25, no. 3: 128–61.

Tang, Shiping. 2008. "Fear in International Politics: Two Positions." *International Studies Review* 10, no. 3: 451–71.

Thies, Cameron G., and Marijke Breuning. 2012. "Integrating Foreign Policy Analysis and International Relations Through Role Theory." *Foreign Policy Analysis* 8, no. 1: 1–4.

Tilly, Charles. 1992. *Coercion, Capital, and European States, AD 990–1992*. Oxford: Blackwell.

Volgy, Thomas J., et al., eds. 2011. *Major Powers and the Quest for Status in International Politics: Global and Regional Perspectives*. New York: Palgrave Macmillan.

Walt, Stephen M. 1990. *The Origins of Alliances*. Ithaca, NY: Cornell University Press.

Waltz, Kenneth N. 1979. *Theory of International Politics*. New York: Random House.

Wendt, Alexander. 1992. "Anarchy Is What States Make of It: The Social Construction of Power Politics." *International Organization* 46, no. 2: 391–425.

Wendt, Alexander. 1999. *Social Theory of International Politics*. Cambridge: Cambridge University Press.

Wendt, Alexander. 2003. "Why a World State Is Inevitable." *European Journal of International Relations* 9, no. 4: 491–542.

Wohlforth, William C. 1999. "The Stability of a Unipolar World." *International Security* 24, no. 1: 5–41.

THIRTEEN

If It Is Everything, It Is Nothing

An Argument for Specificity in Constructivisms

Laura Sjoberg

J. Samuel Barkin

Where we place ourselves in relation to constructivism depends on which performance of constructivism we are being asked to engage. There are many tenets of and performances of constructivism with which we are sympathetic and to which we are deeply emotionally, politically, and intellectually attached.

The constructivism that intervenes in materialist realism and utilitarian liberalism to suggest that people exist in and are constitutive of global politics, that those people have social relations, and that therefore social relations matter in global politics: that constructivism is near and dear to our hearts (e.g., Newman 2001; Conteh-Morgan 2005; Prugl 1999). The constructivism that challenges and expands the boundaries of acceptable research in international relations (IR) (e.g., Onuf 1989; Wendt 1992) is a condition of possibility of the existence of the sort of work that we generally do (e.g., Sjoberg 2013; Barkin 2010) in the field. This constructivism creates space for research on many of the things that can broadly be thought of as social forces, including gender (e.g., Locher and Prugl 2001), nationality (e.g., Christiansen, Jorgensen, and Wiener 1999), race (e.g., Klotz 1995; this volume), culture (e.g., Finnemore 1996), and religion (Philpott 2000).

The constructivism that dispenses with the agent/structure dichotomy (e.g., Wendt 1987) is also a constructivism that speaks to us. This constructivism that gives us permission to think about relational autonomy (e.g., Hirschmann 1989) and communicative action (Risse 2000) in/as global politics. The constructivism that recognizes the existence of norms (Finnemore and Sikkink 1998), and the deeper constructivism that recognizes the existence of rules that create states of rule (Onuf 1989, 1991), supply us with a language palatable to disciplinary IR with which to discuss the complicated web of restraints, constraints, and resultant interactions in global politics.

The constructivism that widens the political spectrum in the study of global politics—that positions itself outside of the neo-neo synthesis (see discussion in Guzzini 2000)—is particularly important to us. It is, however close to the neo-neo synthesis it falls, simultaneously a transgression of the traditional narrowness of IR theorizing and a creation of space for creativity (e.g., Barkin 2003, 2010; Adler 2005). We identify with the widening effect of this sort of constructivism.

Even with all the constructivisms with which we identify, however, we sometimes have trouble thinking of ourselves as constructivists. That is because, in addition to (and sometimes within) the constructivisms we find intellectually and normatively useful, there are many that seem less useful and even problematic. For example, the constructivism that sees itself as the "middle ground" between realism and liberalism because it provides a causal mechanism that explains both (e.g., Wendt 1999; Checkel 1997) feels underspecified and unattractive. Constructivisms that valorize norms but fail to theorize the constitutive dimensions of the normative (see discussion in Hurrell 2002) seem like exercises in self-reassurance and self-engagement rather than outward-looking theorizing.

The constructivisms that constitute the social as an empty signifier—as a word that means everything that is not materially power as traditionally conceived (e.g., Wendt 1999; Wendt 1987; Ruggie 1998)—possess the potential to be infinitely regressive. That assumption is almost by definition at once completely right—tautological—and completely meaningless—without direct lessons, depth, or theoretical implications. The constructivisms that pretend to be apolitical (Pollack 2001; Moravcsik 1999) feel incomplete at best and disingenuous at worst. The constructivisms that claim an internally-driven progressive politics (e.g., Price and Reus-Smit 1998; Barder and Levine 2012) feel weak. The constructivisms that focus on discourse feel like they miss the complexity of political performativity (e.g., Milliken 1999). The constructivisms that are structurationist (e.g.,

Wendt 1999; Diez 1999) feel like they lack a theoretical foundation with which to evaluate the richness of human, cultural, national, state, and global interaction.

It is our problems with these constructivisms that cause us to worry about the label "constructivist" and of research programs that self-identify as a part of "constructivist IR." This chapter will discuss in more detail three of our key misgivings: the tendency to associate constructivisms with progressive politics, the tendency to apply overbroad notions of the social and of norms to global politics, and problematic (mis)understandings of the notion of "social construction." In engaging all three of these problems, we make the argument that the politics of *having a constructivism in IR* is a positive one, but that IR constructivisms often destroy their potential contributions by overreaching their theoretical and political potential.

The Politics of Constructivisms?

Much of the constructivist literature in IR has implied that constructivism has an easy or natural association with progressive politics, both in the discipline and in global politics.[1] Some constructivists (e.g., Price and Reus-Smit 1998; Price 2008; Hoffman 2009; Barder and Levine 2012) have explicitly argued that constructivism *as a paradigm* has a claim on normative theorizing. We see this as the constructivist equivalent of imperial overstretch, trying to make constructivism more than what it is at the expense of its internal coherence. As we argue, "when scholars attempt to associate constructivism with a particular politics, or long for the simpler days when it appears constructivists had a shared politics, . . . they make an intellectual mistake with political consequences" (Barkin and Sjoberg 2019).

Constructivists who claim an association with progressive politics do so in different ways. Barder and Levine (2012) write a history of constructivism in IR that sees it as *originally* political and clearly associated with the 1980s critical theorists in the field. Price (2008), on the other hand, argues that constructivist IR should *adopt* or *be paired with* a progressive politics. Duvall and Varadarajan (2003) argue that constructivism can serve as a practical tool for or complement to critical IR's politics.

We argue that all these pairings of constructivism and *a politics* are problematic. This is not an argument that constructivisms are without political significance. All IR scholarship has political implications that stem from interpretations of what knowledge is and how it is accumulated. It is also not an argument that constructivisms cannot be paired with political theories that have a political agenda. Instead, it is an argument that constructivism is compatible with *multiple* political theories and approaches rather than being stuck to one of them.

That is because, conceived of appropriately, constructivism is a social theory. As a social theory, its use is political, as is all knowledge, but that is different than it having *a politics*. A social theory with political implications, however, is different than either a political theory or a politics. To look for *a* constructivist politics, or *a* constructivist morality, is, in our view, an intellectual mistake, though one a number of constructivists make. What constructivisms have in common is that they *study* normative structures, not that they have a *particular* normative approach to those normative structures. As we argue elsewhere (Barkin and Sjoberg 2019), the only coherent accounts of constructivism are as social theory that sees political structures (including the politics of theory) as socially constructed and contextually specific. It therefore, *by definition*, cannot have a *stable* politics.

Instead, constructivist research can be used in service of a number of different (and diverse) political approaches to the theory and practice of international relations. Take, for example, constructivist research on the civilian immunity principle, which has been a feature both of just war theory (e.g., Walzer 1977) and international law (Valentino, Huth, and Croco 2006). Constructivism can be paired with a liberal research agenda to show how the civilian immunity principle has been used to promote international rules to constrain weapons that have a disproportionate, negative effect on civilians (e.g., Gardam 1993). Constructivism can be paired with a critical research agenda to show how it has been used to privilege technologies of war used by the powerful over those used by the weak (e.g., Orford 2006). Constructivism can be paired with a liberal feminist research agenda to demonstrate that the norm of protecting women from wars is salient in advocacy organizations' efforts to provide noncombatants protection (e.g., Carpenter 2005). Constructivism can be paired with a critical feminist research agenda to show that the same normative forces that cause advocacy organizations to promote the protection of women reinforce women's subordination to men and encourage belligerents to attack women in wars (e.g., Sjoberg 2006; Sjoberg and Peet 2011). Constructivist analysis can be paired with postcolonial or poststructuralist research agendas to show that norms of labeling peoples as barbarians lead to brutality against civilians (e.g., Kinsella 2011) and that civilian protection is (therefore?) more effective in places of cultural similarity (e.g., Salter 2002).

All these examples have in common a focus on social construction, the use of social constructivist epistemology, and the employment of what can be thought of as constructivist methods. In this way, it is possible to do liberal, feminist, critical, postcolonial, and poststructuralist analysis of civilian immunity using the tools of constructivism. Not only is it possible to use constructivism's epistemology and tools in service of all those ends, doing so provides a greater contribution to knowledge about the civilian immunity principle than does limiting constructivism to deployment in service of one of those political-theoretic ends. As theoretical analyses, each of these approaches is distinct. As empirical analyses, the approaches are compatible and complementary.

When we say that, as theoretical analyses, each of these approaches is distinct, we mean that they differ in their politics. Liberal, critical, feminist, postcolonial, and poststructuralist analyses of the noncombatant immunity principle draw on different political moralities and suggest different avenues for political engagement. To limit "constructivism" to an a priori association with one morality as opposed to others does two things. First, it artificially narrows the range of political moralities that constructivist analysis can be deployed to further, and by extension it narrows the potential empirical contribution of constructivism to the field of IR. Second, it makes a false claim to the coherence of (existing and future) constructivist contributions to normative theorizing.

Back to the example of civilian immunity; we are not arguing that constructivism cannot by itself provide knowledge about the subject. Constructivist analysis can be useful as an approach to deal with the tough questions about what happens to civilians in wars: to know the social norms surrounding civilians, the social interactions of actors in wars as they relate to civilians, the ways those norms and interactions manifest in and produce the daily lives of civilians, and how different policy options are likely to affect civilians differently. Constructivist analysis could even be used to understand the constitution of the category of "civilian." What we are arguing is that this analysis is not inherently tied to *a politics*. Instead, this work can be done with, and informed by, a number of different (positive and negative, policy and theoretical, progressive and conservative) political interests, with different results.

As a result, constructivism alone *cannot* provide answers to questions like what *should* happen to civilians in wars, what we should wish for civilians in wars, whether the category of "civilian" is itself a normative good, or if war is sufficiently or insufficiently humane to civilians. While constructivist research can be used to determine whether the standard set by a particular approach is (or even is likely to be or could be) met, the standard-setting always comes from outside of constructivism. It is, for example, liberalism that inspires an interest in human rights, feminism that inspires a gender-based concern for civilian well-being, postcolonialism that inspires a concern for race- and ethnicity-based targeting in war and conflict, and critical theory that inspires an interest in human emancipation and the deconstruction of oppression. In other words, it is liberalism, feminism, postcolonalism, and critical theory (alone or in combination) that provide the progressivist teleology to constructivist theorizing interested in civilian immunity, or any other phenomenon in global politics. It is constructivism that supplies the *how* to the analysis, but other *political theories* that supply both the objects to be analyzed and the politics that should be endorsed in that analysis. Therefore, as we argue (Barkin and Sjoberg 2019), one needs *more than* constructivism to deal with *political* questions: What are the moral benefits of a civilian immunity principle? Do those moral benefits outweigh the strategic calculations that encourage violation of such a principle? Who counts as a civilian and when and why is it wrong to target them in war? These are questions that constructivism can provide empirical evidence about, but that evidence needs a pre-existing moral framework to be a part of any actual answer.

In other words, epistemologically and methodologically, there are constructivists in IR. Politically, there are not constructivists. The claim to *a politics* of constructivism is itself a political act. That is, those who implicitly or explicitly tie constructivism to a particular political morality assign a morality to a research community that does not share that morality. Such a claim has the effect of privileging one moral claim over others, and cutting off the others *by definition*. It constrains "insiders" *within* constructivism and creates a false impression to "outsiders" that there is a political morality that the research community shares, when in fact it does not.

Assigning *a politics* or *a morality*, then, claims that constructivism is more than it can be (because it assigns it political content it cannot provide), and constrains the contributions that constructivism can make to the discipline. The constraining effect is twofold. As we discussed above, one constraint is the exclusion of work inspired by political theories and political moralities other than that with which constructivism is being (incorrectly) matched. The second constraint is the resultant limitation of uses of constructivist empirical methodology to explore discussions of the ethics of political action in global politics. This is why claims to *a politics* for constructivism are unnecessarily limiting. Seeing constructivism as not tied to any particular politics actually expands rather than constricts constructivism's potential influence in IR and leverage for providing explanation and understanding of global politics.

Norms Everywhere (and Nowhere)

In addition to being often inappropriately associated with a particular politics, the word constructivism also feels both underspecified and overused in IR. This is largely the result of tendencies to call everything in IR that is not realist or liberal "constructivist" as a shorthand. But it is also because there are many constructivisms in IR and many disagreement *among constructivists* about what constitute constructivisms' core assumptions, including but not limited to assertions about the politics of constructivism. Reading the claims to and labels of constructivism in disciplinary IR, it is not clear that those constructivisms have a lot in common except either self-identification or categorization by others (Srivastava 2012).

Legro and Moravcsik (1999) asked if anyone is still a realist, and correspondents (Feaver et al. 2000) asked if anyone was *ever* a realist; we wonder if *everyone* is a constructivist. There are realist constructivists (Barkin 2003, 2010; Sterling-Folker 2002; Jackson and Nexon 2004), liberal constructivists (Risse-Kappan 1996; Keck and Sikkink 1998), feminist constructivists (Prugl 1999; Locher and Prugl 2001; Confortini 2012), critical constructivists (Weldes 1998; Steele 2007), and postmodern constructivists (see discussion in Smith 2000). Whether the field is mapped as paradigms, research programs, or Weberian ideal-types (e.g., Jackson and Nexon 2009), constructivisms are everywhere. To some, constructivism is a method; to others an epistemology; to others social theory; and to still others ontology and politics. If constructivisms reach across paradigms, research programs, and tools, then the everywhereness of constructivisms expand even further. If constructivisms are everywhere in IR, are they nowhere? Does the concept of constructivism become meaningless?

If constructivisms have a commonality, perhaps it is understanding social construction as a *mechanism* of the constitution of global politics and norms/rules/discourses as the *vessels* for that social construction. In that sense, constructivisms would be seen to identify the norms inherent in the realist, liberal, feminist, and critical *functioning* of global politics. For constructivisms not to be devoid of meaning, though, that identification has to be more than providing a more complicated explanation for the same (Desch 1998). In other words, if constructivisms tell a more complicated story with the same basic account as the paradigmatic approaches they intend to supplant, there is a question about the ultimate utility of thinking about constructivism as paradigmatic.

In other words, what is the "value added" of thinking of constructivism as a paradigmatic approach to IR? If the "value added" of constructivism is that social constructions are the *mechanism* that fuels realist, liberal, feminist, and critical theory "results," then constructivism as a social theory of norms supersedes paradigmatic IR and can be used as a tool of all paradigms. At the same time, there is then a risk of constructivisms being theories of *everything* and therefore of nothing. By "everything and therefore nothing," we mean that if constructivism does not have *limits*, then it cannot be specified or defined, and it cannot be honed, grown, or critiqued.

We should note that we do not think that constructivism is the only research program that could potentially have this problem. For example, there is work in "hierarchy studies" (Zarakol and Bially Mattern 2016; Lake 1996) in the field that risks a similar tautology. The study of global politics is the study of hierarchy, therefore the study of hierarchy *within* global politics seems to leave nothing out (after all, what in global politics is not some sort of hierarchy?) One can study types of hierarchies, different operationalizations of hierarchies, the interactions of different hierarchies, and the like, but one cannot just study "hierarchy" or have a theory of hierarchy. We think constructivisms are at their best, then, when they study particular social constructions, different types of social constructions, different operationalizations of social constructions, the interactions of different social constructions, and different processes of interactions among social constructions. That, however, makes constructivisms *theories of social constructions* rather than constructivism *a paradigm of social construction.*

In other words, to the extent that contructivisms broadly construed share an interest in the ways that social constructions operate in global politics, then that is the unifying strand in what work counts as "constructivist." The unification of work as "constructivist," though, must in our view be done with some care, because it could very easily become infinitely regressive, where everyone sees social constructions in everything and recognizes but doesn't theorize them (Hacking 1999) or overly limited, where "constructivist theorizing" is used as a tool to delineate where norms, for example, are and where they (supposedly) are not. The specification of work as "constructivist," then, needs to include more than the operation of social constructions in a particular situation in global politics, but less than a particular politics of norm or discourse operation that would convert constructivism to social theory in political theory's clothes. To some, that is where social construction comes in; theory is constructivist where it recognizes and analyzes the ways norms, etc., are socially constructed, and falls outside of constructivism where it fails to analyze the existence, and function, of social construction in global politics. That is, that constructivism is a theory of the social construction of international politics. Even accepting that, however, the label of constructivism is still problematic, because of our third issue with constructivism: lingering questions about whether "social construction" has a strong enough definition and meaning to unify theorists as constructivists.

Socially Constructing Social Construction

When we say we are concerned about the ability of the term "social construction" to unify constructivisms, we do not mean that constructivists fail to specifically explain the idea that global politics is "socially constructed." Those explanations are contained in a significant amount of constructivist scholarship, and many of them are quite rigorous. For example, Wendt (1999) talks about the social constitution of power and interest based on a structurationist account of power, agency, and culture. Onuf (1989) sets up a system of rules that transform into a state of rule which then reifies and reconstitutes (and is reified and reconstituted by) rules. As Onuf notes, "neither has causal or temporal primacy." Wendt relies on structurationist sociology, and Onuf on Wittgensteinian philosophy of language. Both explain what they think is happening when something is "socially constructed," as do a number of other constructivists.

Because these explanations exist in some detail, it is hard to argue that constructivists do not know what they think is happening when they say that global politics is socially constructed. In the remainder of this short chapter, though, we will sketch out such an argument, because we think it is key to the underspecification and overreach of constructivisms that makes it difficult to identify as a constructivist in IR.

Almost universally, the statements about *what's happening* when something is *being* socially constructed are *not* actually statements about *what's happening* when something is *being* socially constructed. They are statements about the *elements* of the thing that is socially constructed, or the thing that is socially constructed as an *element* of other things that are socially constructed. Onuf (1989, 78, 82, 98, 157) comes perhaps the closest to thinking about what is happening: rules are a matter of language, language is both representative and performative, performative language is a human universal, performative speech is also figurative speech, and [therefore] "the ongoing (re)construction of reality is rarely distinguishable from the known, felt, lived-in world that we inhabit." In Onuf's (1989, 229, 257) view, people can game the performative-speech system, and what people do is almost entirely a product of what they say to each other.

That detailed account of what happens to make social construction is built out of *is* statements: how things *are*, rather than how they work. These *is* statements provide hints and make implications about how things work, but they do not explicitly theorize what is happening when something is being socially constructed. Onuf (1989, 96) frequently uses the word "process," engaging cognition to map categories of performative language to match modes of reasoning. In Onuf's account, social construction, then, is performative language mapped to modes of reasoning to create sorts of rules that create and are created by states of rule.

We are focusing on Onuf's account because we think it comes closest to giving a sense of substance to the idea of social construction. Still, after reading *World of Our Making* (Onuf 1989) a number of times and asking Onuf and a number of other constructivists, we still have not heard a compelling account of *what happens* when something goes through the *process* of "social construction." While we might be expecting more out of constructivisms than they are able to give, it seems like *how* something comes to be socially constructed, and *how* you would know *what happened* would be important elements to understanding *what* social construction is, and giving it independent meaning.

Even if Onuf's (1989) account of social construction of rules and rule *did* meet that expectation (which we think it does not, because a mechanism remains missing), the depth in that notion of social construction has, in large part, left constructivist research in IR. Even more now than then, "social constructivism" seems to be currently a signifier (of membership in a constructivist community) without a referent (substance in itself).

In Baudrillard's (1981a) terms, the moment it was introduced to IR, social construction became "an object of consumption" to the IR scholars discontented with the combined dominance of neorealism and neoliberalism in the discipline (what Ole Waever [1992] called the "neo-neo synthesis"). The transformation of social construction into an object of consumption separated "social construction" *per se* from "social construction" *as consumed*. In this differentiation, the phrase "social construction" in IR became "external to a relation which it now only signifies, a-signed *arbitrarily* and non-coherently to this concrete relation, yet obtaining its coherence, and consequently its meaning, from an abstract and systematic relation to all other object-signs" (Baudrillard 1981a). This self-externality *mandates* the reproduction of the concept to fulfill the absence of reality/substance (Baudrillard 1981a). That makes the sign of "social construction" an "operative abstraction" that IR scholars use, assume to be fixed, and ascribe universally understandable meaning to even though it is not fixed, universal, or even usable (Baudrillard 1975). Instead, the utterance "absorbs meaning and empties itself of meaning in order to better fascinate others" (Baudrillard 1991). In terms of Baudrillard's (1981b) description of the evolution of images in *Simulation and Simulacra*, it is possible see social construction discourses in IR going from reflections of basic observation (that there are social forces in global politics was empirically important), to the masking of that observation (where social construction becomes a shorthand for *something* happening, though no one really knows what but everyone pretends they know what), to masking the *absence* of basic observation (where analysis of "social construction" masks the absence of analyses of social processes of relating), to bearing no relation to observation whatsoever (where "social construction" is stand-in language rather than representative of "what is happening" out there in the world being studied).

Though abbreviated for space, this account has a *how*, that (especially broad and multipurpose) consumption and regurgitation of the concept of social construction reproduces it multiply and incoherently, making the phrase (much like "just cause" or "e pluribus unum") one that signifies a basic agreement on the principles that underlie it, whether or not such principles exist or could be agreed upon. Its repetition (and reconsumption) functions as confirmatory and seductive; there's something there, and you want it, which reproduces the consumptive process of distancing sign and referent.

In this view, the automatic language of social construction (especially insomuch as it describes the "is" rather than the "how"), then, rather than revealing the "how" of the social in global politics, obscures the failure to reveal the how, all the while presenting an indication of revelation. *Knowing* that something is "socially constructed" then could be more problematic than *knowing* nothing about it, because the *knowledge* that the thing is "socially constructed" is a signifier without a referent, a misleading approximation of reality rather than a recognition of emptiness.

This *is not* a call to collapse analysis of social construction into causal analysis. The "how" questions asked here are not positivist, result-focused questions that take for granted the possibility of disaggregating what leads to or causes what else. Instead, it is a suggestion that *what constitutes* many of IR's accounts *of constitution* is "social construction" as an empty signifier that marks differentiation from the "other" in the field but no other necessary commonality. If this is the case, then Baudrillard's (1981b) analysis suggests that the idea of "social construction" needs to be rejected in whole to determine if it ever had, or could have, content, rather than functioning as a stand-in for absence.

Thinking about Constructivisms and IR Theories

To us, then, though the *idea* of constructivisms in IR is a nice one, the *practice* of constructivisms in IR is often vague, violent, overstretched, and underspecified. The deployment of the term "constructivism" and the notion of "social construction" without a clear referent is intellectually counterproductive and politically problematic. At the same time, however, we opened this chapter talking about the many constructivisms in IR to which we are drawn, along with the many constructivisms in IR with which we are frustrated.

We are drawn to constructivisms in IR because they function to create space (even if the space they create is made artificially narrative by the means of its creation), and because they provide interesting epistemological and methodological tools (even if those tools are often inappropriately framed as paradigmatic). Because we are drawn to some constructivisms and think the idea of the presence of constructivisms in the field is a net positive, we do not want to conclude that constructivisms should be rejected in the field of IR. At the same time, we argue above that the idea of "social construction" needs to be rejected to be saved. This sort of *retraction* is, in our view, the best path forward for constructivist analysis in IR.

Particularly, a large-scale *retraction* and *introspection* of constructivist IR might just "save" it, intellectually speaking. Retracting constructivism from a normative theory of the social construction of norms (or many normative theories of the social construction of norms) would leave constructivist scholars of IR with a clear target of analysis and a clearer set of questions to answer, individually and collectively. Retracting constructivism from a theory of all social constructions everywhere and therefore a theory of everything to a targeted theory or group of theories about specific functions of particular social constructions or specific processes by which specific sorts of social constructions diffuse, happen, or engage might provide constructivisms with an opportunity to develop better senses of *processes* of social construction and constitution.

As it is now, constructivist description of social constructions remains often in the realm of what something is constituted as, and the substantive relationships among constitutions, taking "social construction" as given. Introspection *within* constructivism about the meaning and place in global politics of "social construction" might decrease the violence associated with the seductiveness of the concept as an empty signifier, and enrich knowledge of both concepts absent the alienation of operative abstraction. Until then, constructivism, like its key concepts, is an attractive but often dangerous mirage in the study of global politics.

NOTES

1. We expand on this subject significantly in Barkin and Sjoberg (2019).

REFERENCES

Adler, Emmanuel. 2005. *Communitarian International Relations: The Epistemic Foundations of International Relations*. New York: Psychology Press.

Barder, Alexander, and Daniel Levine. 2012. "'The World Is Too Much with Us': Reification and the Depoliticising of *Via Media* Constructivist IR." *Millennium: Journal of International Studies* 40, no. 3: 585–604.

Barkin, J. Samuel. 2003. "Realist Constructivism." *International Studies Review* 5, no. 3: 325–42.

Barkin, J. Samuel. 2010. *Realist Constructivism: Rethinking International Relations*. Cambridge: Cambridge University Press.

Barkin, J. Samuel, and Laura Sjoberg. 2019. *International Relations' Last Synthesis*. New York: Oxford University Press.

Baudrillard, Jean. 1975. *The Mirror of Production*. St. Louis, MO: Telos Press.

Baudrillard, Jean. 1981a. *For a Critique of the Political Economy of the Sign*. St. Louis, MO: Telos Press.

Baudrillard, Jean. 1981b. *Simulacra and Simulation*. Paris: Editions Galilee.

Baudrillard, Jean. 1991. *Seduction*. London: Palgrave MacMillan.

Carpenter, R. Charli. 2005. "'Women, children, and other vulnerable groups': Gender, Strategic Frames, and the Protection of Civilians as a Transnational Issue." *International Studies Quarterly* 49, no. 2: 295–335.

Checkel, Jeffrey T. 1997. "International Norms and Domestic Politics: Bridging the Rationalist-Constructivist Divide." *European Journal of International Relations* 3, no. 4: 473–95.

Christiansen, Thomas, Knud Erik Jorgensen, and Antje Wiener. 1999. "The Social Construction of Europe." *Journal of European Public Policy* 6, no. 4: 528–44.

Confortini, Catia. 2012. *Intelligent Compassion: Feminist Critical Methodology in the Women's International League for Peace and Freedom*. New York: Oxford University Press.

Conteh-Morgan, Earl. 2005. "Peacebuilding and Human Security: A Constructivist Perspective." *International Journal of Peace Studies* 10, no. 1: 69–86.

Desch, Michael. 1998. "Culture Clash: Assessing the Importance of Ideas in Security Studies." *International Security* 23, no. 1: 141–70.

Diez, Thomas. 1999. "Speaking 'Europe': The Politics of Integration Discourse." *Journal of European Public Policy* 6, no. 4: 598–613.

Duvall, Raymond, and Latha Varadajan. 2003. "On the Practical Significance of Critical International Relations Theory." *Asian Journal of Political Science* 11, no. 2: 75–88.

Feaver, Peter, Gunther Hellman, Randall L. Schweller, Jeffrey W. Taliaferro, William C. Wohlforth, Jeffrey W. Legro, and Andrew Moravcsik. 2000. "Brother, Can You Spare a Paradigm? (Or Was Anybody Ever a Realist?)" *International Security* 25, no. 1: 165–93.

Finnemore, Martha. 1996. "Norms, Culture, and World Politics: Insights from Sociology's Institutionalism." *International Organization* 50, no. 2: 325–47.

Finnemore, Martha, and Kathryn Sikkink. 1998. "Constructivist Approaches: International Norm Dynamics and Political Change." *International Organization* 52, no. 4: 887–917.

Gardam, Judith. 1993. *Non-Combatant Immunity as a Norm of International Humanitarian Law*. London: Martius-Nijhoff.

Guzzini, Stefano. 2000. "A Reconstruction of Constructivism in International Relations." *European Journal of International Relations* 6, no. 2: 147–82.

Hacking, Ian. 1999. *The Social Construction of What?* Cambridge, MA: Harvard University Press.

Hirschmann, Nancy. 1989. "Freedom, Recognition, and Obligation: A Feminist Approach to Political Theory." *American Political Science Review* 83, no. 4: 1227–44.

Hoffmann, Matthew. 2009. "Is Constructivist Ethics an Oxymoron?" *International Studies Review* 11, no. 2: 232–33.

Hurrell, Andrew. 2002. "Norms and Ethics in International Relations." In *Handbook of International Relations*, edited by Walter Carlsnaes, Thomas Risse-Kappen, and Beth A. Simmons, 137–54. London: SAGE.

Jackson, Patrick Thaddeus, and Daniel H. Nexon. 2004. "Constructivist Realism or Realist-Constructivism." *International Studies Review* 6, no. 2: 337–41.

Jackson, Patrick Thaddeus, and Daniel H. Nexon. 2009. "Paradigmatic Faults in International-Relations Theory." *International Studies Quarterly* 53, no. 4: 907–30.

Keck, Margaret, and Kathryn Sikkink. 1998. *Activists Beyond Borders: Advocacy Networks in International Politics*. Ithaca, NY: Cornell University Press.

Kinsella, Helen. *The Image Before the Weapon: A Critical History of the Distinction between Combatant and Civilian*. Ithaca, NY: Cornell University Press.

Klotz, Audie. 1995. "Norms Reconstituting Interests: Global Racial Equality and U.S. Sanctions Against South Africa." *International Organization* 49, no. 3: 451–78.

Lake, David A. 1996. "Anarchy, Hierarchy, and the Variety of International Relations." *International Organization* 50, no. 1: 1–33.

Legro, Jeffrey W., and Andrew Moravcsik. 1999. "Is Anybody Still a Realist?" *International Security* 24, no. 2: 5–55.

Locher, Birgit, and Elisabeth Prugl. 2001. "Feminism and Constructivism: Worlds Apart or Sharing the Middle Ground?" *International Studies Quarterly* 45, no. 1: 111–29.

Milliken, Jennifer. 1999. "The Study of Discourse in International Relations: A Critique of Research and Methods." *European Journal of International Relations* 5, no. 2: 255–54.

Moravcsik, Andrew. 1999. "A New Statecraft? Supranational Entrepreneurs and International Cooperation." *International Organization* 53, no. 2: 267–306.

Newman, Edward. 2001. "Human Security and Constructivism." *International Studies Perspectives* 2, no. 3: 239–51.

Onuf, Nicholas Greenwood. 1989. *World of Our Making: Rules and Rule in Social Theory and International Relations*. Columbia: University of South Carolina Press.

Onuf, Nicholas Greenwood. 1991. "Sovereignty: Outline of a Conceptual History." *Alternatives: Global, Local, Political* 16, no. 4: 425–46.

Orford, Anne, ed. 2006. *International Law and its Others*. Cambridge: Cambridge University Press.

Philpott, Daniel. 2000. "The Religious Roots of Modern International Relations." *World Politics* 52, no. 2: 206–45.

Pollack, Mark A. 2001. "International Relations Theory and European Integration." *JCMS: Journal of Common Market Studies* 39, no. 2: 221–44.

Price, Richard, ed. 2008. *Moral Limit and Possibility in World Politics*. Cambridge: Cambridge University Press.

Price, Richard, and Christian Reus-Smit. 1998. "Dangerous Liaisons? Critical International Theory and Constructivism." *European Journal of International Relations* 4, no. 3: 259–94.

Prugl, Elisabeth. 1999. *The Global Construction of Gender: Home-Based Work in the Political Economy of the 20th Century*. New York: Columbia University Press.

Risse, Thomas. 2000. "'Let's Argue!': Communicative Action in World Politics." *International Organization* 54, no. 1: 1–39.

Risse-Kappen, Thomas. 1996. "Exploring the Nature of the Beast: International Relations and Comparative Policy Analysis Meet the European Union." *JCMS: Journal of Common Market Studies* 34, no. 1: 53–80.

Ruggie, John Gerard. 1998. "What Makes the World Hang Together? Neo-Utilitarianism and the Social Constructivist Challenge." *International Organization* 52, no. 2: 855–85.

Salter, Mark. 2002. *Barbarians and Civilization in International Relations*. London: Pluto.

Sjoberg, Laura. 2006. *Gender, Justice, and the Wars in Iraq*. New York: Lexington Books.

Sjoberg, Laura. 2013. *Gendering Global Conflict*. New York: Columbia University Press.

Sjoberg, Laura, and Jessica Peet. 2011. "A(nother) Dark Side of the Protection Racket: Targeting Women in Wars." *International Feminist Journal of Politics* 13, no. 2: 163–82.

Smith, Steve. 2000. "Historical Sociology and International Relations Theory." In *Historical Sociology of International Relations*, edited by Stephen Hobden and John M. Hobson, 223–44. Cambridge: Cambridge University Press.

Srivastava, Swati. 2012. "Varieties of Constructivism." Paper presented at the annual conference of the International Studies Association Northeast.

Steele, Brent J. 2007. "Liberal-Idealism: A Constructivist Critique." *International Studies Review* 9, no. 1: 23–52.

Sterling-Folker, Jennifer. 2002. "Realism and the Constructivist Challenge: Rejecting, Reconstructing, or Rereading." *International Studies Review* 4, no. 1: 73–97.

Valentino, Benjamin, Paul Huth, and Sarah Croco. 2006. "Covenants Without the Sword: International Law and the Protection of Civilians in Times of War." *World Politics* 58, no. 3: 339–77.

Waever, Ole. 1992. "International Society—Theoretical Promises Unfulfilled?" *Cooperation and Conflict* 27, no. 1: 97–128.

Walzer, Michael. 1977. *Just and Unjust Wars.* New York: Basic Books.

Weldes, Jutta. 1998. "Bureaucratic Politics: A Critical-Constructivist Assessment." *Mershon International Studies Review* 42: 2216–25.

Wendt, Alexander. 1987. "The Agent-Structure Problem in International Relations Theory." *International Organization* 41, no. 3: 335–70.

Wendt, Alexander. 1992. "Anarchy Is What States Make of It." *International Organization* 46, no. 2: 391–425.

Wendt, Alexander. 1999. *Social Theory of International Politics.* Cambridge: Cambridge University Press.

Zarakol, Ayse, and Janice Bially Mattern. 2016. "Hierarchy in International Relations." *International Organization* 70, no. 3: 623–54.

FOURTEEN

Moving Forward

Mariano E. Bertucci
Jarrod Hayes
Patrick James

Overview

After three decades of sustained activity, a review of constructivism is in order. While resembling *Neorealism and Its Critics* (Keohane 1986) in some ways, the present volume does not focus on a *magnus opus* such as *Theory of International Politics* (1979). As will become apparent, it instead makes sense to seek answers to two basic questions about the diverse and interesting set of studies identified with constructivism. First, what extent of (dis)agreement exists with regard to the meaning of constructivism? Second, to what degree is it regarded as a success? To answer these questions, evidence is assembled from the preceding chapters of this book.

This chapter will proceed in seven further sections that combine to answer the two basic questions about constructivism. The second section focuses on concept formation. Section three conveys the origins of constructivism. Content and programs of research from constructivism are covered in the fourth section. Section five explores the set of causal mechanisms identified via constructivist research. Critiques from a general standpoint, along with those associated with realism and critical approaches, appear in the sixth section. A discussion of how constructivism and analytic eclecticism relate to each other takes place in section seven. Constructivism is assessed in an overall sense in the eighth and final section, which explicitly answers the two basic questions.

Concept Formation

What is constructivism? The most common answer is quite encompassing, namely, a theoretical approach. This is the position adopted by most contributors to this volume and rejected by none, at least in reference to how constructivism looks today. For example, "constructivism is not a theory of politics, like realism or Marxism, but a broader approach or 'social theory'" that focuses on "social construction of knowledge and of social reality, respectively" (Branch). Constructivism, as introduced in more detail by McCourt, is an "interpretive and ideational approach that stresses the role of intersubjective meaning in world politics, manifested through norms, identity and culture." Glaser offers a nuance through use of the term "theoretical family," and Blagden adds that constructivism is "an approach to theorizing in IR defined by a focus on the causal power of social forces." Constructivism as a "big tent" probably reflects a general opinion that it refers to social theory and can work in tandem with ideas from various paradigms, as long as an ideational element is present.

More directive and specific concept formation, which entails concerns about the evolution of constructivism up to today, goes back to Onuf. This self-proclaimed dinosaur still speaks, with his words echoing among constructivists and beyond. Onuf sees constructivists as those who, collectively speaking, do not take for granted the "useful, moderate-sized social objects with material properties" that populate the social world, but rather seek to explore the "myriad of cognitive and linguistic operations" by which they are created. By contrast, all other scholars start with the above-noted goods in place. Furthermore, Onuf sees constructivism as a social process of constructing reality, which is not objective but instead comes through the mind and takes the form of language and rules. The greater specificity of these views makes the constructivist tent look smaller than when it is characterized as an approach that comes about because positivist research becomes problematic.

Some contributors to the volume connect with this more circumscribed and normatively oriented sense of what constructivism *should* be about. McCourt, Goddard and Krebs, Ramos, and Sjoberg and Barkin, to varying degrees, are more in line with Onuf than are other contributors to the volume. (Blagden, a critic of constructivism, identifies a more normative strain of constructivism that he views less favorably than its empirical variant.) McCourt emphasizes constitutive theory as opposed to strictly causal analysis, with the implication that the quest for knowledge should focus on understanding rather than explanation.[1] The axiomatic basis of constructivism, according to Goddard and Krebs, is that human beings are meaning-making and social animals. Thus the content of global events and material structures is not self-evident. "Constructivism's main set of assumptions," observes Ramos, "center on the socially constructed nature of global affairs, in which agents and structures are co-constructed." These observations tilt at least partially toward the exposition from Onuf (1989), which emphasized coconstitution and rejected positivist cause and effect.

Sjoberg and Barkin are quite detailed in their reflections about the meaning of constructivism. While they assert that constructivism is "compatible with *multiple* political theories and approaches rather than being stuck to one of them," the boundaries they draw are more in line with Onuf and exclude, in particular, positivism. For Sjoberg and Barkin, the significant common trait among constructivisms is that they study normative structures. The way this happens is in line with Onuf's emphasis on a social process that calls for understanding rather than explanation: "If constructivisms have a commonality," observe Sjoberg and Barkin, "perhaps it is understanding social construction as a *mechanism* of the constitution of global politics and norms/rules/discourses as the *vessels* for that social construction." This summary stands apart from constructivism as an approach with the door open to positivism and its emphasis on cause and effect.

Agreement is clear as far as the *idea* of constructivism in concerned. It is an approach. It is a social theory. It focuses on the social construction of international relations (IR). Consensus breaks down, however, with greater specificity and especially when discussion turns to epistemology. As will become apparent, constructivism's origins are outside of positivism, yet much of what is described today as constructivist engages in empirical research.

Origins

When and why did constructivism start in IR? The time frame is not in dispute. Initially labeled as such by Onuf, constructivism begins in the 1980s. Contributors to this volume identify works from Onuf, Wendt, and Kratochwil as the iconic texts of the initial phase of constructivism. Given this timing, Onuf correctly points out that constructivism did *not* arise in reaction to the end of the Cold War. Of course, the apparent failure of existing paradigms to account for such a huge event in world politics encouraged further interest in constructivism as an alternative approach.

Several precursors to constructivism, which operated in tandem with each other, are identified throughout the chapters of this book. Onuf points to overlapping intellectual developments, such as postmodernism and feminism, which had become pronounced by the 1980s. A key intellectual change took the form of an uprising among scholars in the humanities against the shifting of resources from the liberal arts to the sciences. The disenchanted focused particularly on what they saw as shortcomings in the philosophical assumptions underlying modern science, which seemed headed for hegemonic status throughout the intellectual world. With regard to the initial advocates of what become known as constructivist IR, Onuf recalls an interest in applying ideas from the philosophy of science that argued against the adoption of positivism. This movement dovetailed with what later became known as critical IR.

Constructivists took critical aim from the outset at theories with a strictly material basis. Without an ideational foundation, such theories inherently lacked meaning.[2] This curiosity about the role of ideas became even more intense when the Soviet Union collapsed without a fight and gave up its empire along the way. Neither neorealism nor neoliberalism, the dominant material explanations in IR, had a satisfying answer for the great events of that time (Sjoberg and Barkin). Thus Branch (see also Cornut) observes that constructivism attracted support because of its "emphasis on ideational factors in opposition to the then-dominant focus on material interests and drivers." In other words, if a superpower could disappear seemingly through the force of ideas, could other things be understood more effectively for such reasons as well? Intuition said "yes" and constructivists went to work.

Consensus emerged about the timing and reasons behind constructivism's origins. Those dissatisfied with the two main strands of positivist IR, neorealism and neorealism, searched for something better. As the 1980s progressed, scholars who became known as constructivists turned to social theory to derive ideational accounts for events that seemed increasingly beyond the grasp of existing materialist explanations of one stripe or another. The collapse of the USSR and its empire accelerated the growth of constructivism and expanded its boundaries via increasingly diverse new adherents.

Content and Programs of Research

Constructivism's content is introduced effectively in summary form, respectively, by an advocate and a critic from this volume. Its focus, according to the advocate, is on "the role of norms, identities, and other broadly social features of world politics" (McCourt). The critic provides further detail; constructivism includes "norms of 'legitimate' behavior, intersubjective recognition of status/role and regime type, domestic culture and its impact on foreign and defense policy choices, and the interstate friendship/hostility-inducing consequences of 'self' versus 'other' distinctions" (Blagden). Thus representative exponents and skeptics share a view of constructivism as focusing on norms and other cognate features of the social world.

What constructivism does, put simply, is provide a counterpoint to the ontology of rationalism (McCourt). Constructivism looks beyond the individual as an isolated monad with known and fixed preferences, from its perspective, the narrowly reductionist *homo economicus* of positivist IR. Instead of taking the individual as given, constructivism moves away from rationality-based explanation and toward socially constructed understanding.

Constructivism features a wide range of research programs in subject areas that include the role of norms, collective and state identity, and political culture. Contributors to this volume have built upon accomplishments in those areas and opened up new vistas. What follows is an attempt to summarize what respective chapters have discovered.[3]

Within a constructivist frame of reference, Goddard and Krebs explore a previously neglected social process, namely, legitimation. While legitimacy as a concept is not without serious attention, the workings of *legitimation* deserve more scrutiny. Security threats are not only revealed, but also constructed, in the course of legitimation (Goddard and Krebs). Moreover, legitimation becomes necessary "whenever publics, be they domestic or global, must be mobilized, and it lurks in the background wherever there is a reasonable chance that the glare of attention will turn" (Goddard and Krebs). Thus a focus on legitimation may uncover aspects of strategic interaction not previously considered.

Along two dimensions, Goddard and Krebs theorize conditions under which the need for legitimation will vary: Legitimation matters most "when officials need to mobilize resources—from either domestic or foreign audiences, whether mass or elite—and when relevant publics are attentive." The basic inference is that rhetoric to provide legitimation will be most in demand under that combination of conditions.

Additional propositions are identified by Goddard and Krebs for further research:

- The broader the scope of policy, the more important legitimation is for its success.
- The more private interests stand to gain or lose from the adoption of a particular policy, the more legitimation determines actors' success.
- The more divided the contending interests, the greater the need to mobilize the public.
- The greater a government's demand for resources, the greater its need to engage in legitimation.

Note that the program of research on legitimation and rhetoric emerges as a quite ambitious and interesting bridge between the emphasis on the "making of meaning" on the one hand and a "'pragmatic' model of rhetorical politics that centers on specific rhetorical deployments in particular political and social contexts" (Goddard and Krebs). These observations are relevant to the two-level or nested game framework that is prominent within rationalism (Putnam 1988; Tsebelis 1990). Rhetorical deployments have not been studied previously within that framework, but could turn out to be significant in identifying the set of policies that are viable in both domestic and international terms.

Constructivist research on the propositions from Goddard and Krebs would have additional value in connecting with a classic work from IR, namely, Organski and Kugler (1980) on the subject of differential tax effort. Their final proposition from the preceding list, which focuses on the need for resources, is the most relevant one here. In an effort to explain war outcomes, Organski and Kugler developed metrics that distinguished states from each other in terms of their relative capacity for devoting resources to overall national purposes. Anomalous results, such as the US defeat in Vietnam, become more understandable when the concept of relative effort, quantified through government extraction of resources, is taken into account. Goddard and Krebs draw attention to one explanation for why some states might succeed more than others in prosecuting a war: whether leadership rhetoric succeeds in legitimation. Thus legitimation might be the foundation of what initially appears as a strictly material difference among states, clearly the type of contribution that is available only through a constructivist approach.

Branch opens up a new program of research for constructivists vis-à-vis science and technology studies (STS). Technology is dual—material and ideational—and would seem to be a domain in which neither is properly treated as a foundation for the other.[4] Branch adopts an encompassing definition: technology is "understood broadly as the application of knowledge to specific practical purposes." Two illustrative examples from STS, military (nuclear weapons) and communication (mapping) technologies, are offered.

Possible contributions from STS into constructivism include social construction of technology (SCOT) and actor-network theory (ANT). With regard to nuclear weapons or other military technology systems, Branch observes that it is important to "look simultaneously at their ideational and material features." In that regard, ANT "shifts the focus to looking for the relevant actors (both human and nonhuman) and the networks they create" (Branch). An example of a research question where ANT and SCOT intersect is this one: "How are digital mapping tools used in territorial negotiations?" (Branch). This question also is interesting to ponder in the greater context of IR vis-à-vis the prominent debate over the territorial explanation for war (Senese and Vasquez 2008). More specifically, are advancements in mapping technology likely to facilitate negotiations and discourage the choice of war? Answers to queries such as this one are of obvious interest to IR as a whole.

Further priorities for STS in relation to constructivism are easy to identify. For example, Goddard and Krebs observe that "effects of legitimation are not constant through time and space" and that technologies of communications and information affect legitimation. A focus on social media and the (mislabeled and more nuanced) Arab Spring is just one direction that could be followed here.

Ramos asks the question of how norms change over time. Her approach is to bring an idea from social psychology, cognitive dissonance, into an account of sovereignty. With an emphasis on the "legitimizing narrative" from elites about intervention, a link with the research agenda of Goddard and Krebs is clear to see. A proposition connected to the presumed effects of cognitive dissonance—"the higher the costs and/or the murkier the prospects for success, the more strenuously the case justifying contingent sovereignty must be made" (Ramos 2013, 38)—is assessed through case studies of US wars in Afghanistan and Iraq. Both cases produce evidence of the need for cognitive consistency, with the different levels of success in each instance creating different effects on norms such as contingent sovereignty.

Jamieson puts securitization into a four-stage process: identification of security threat; articulation of security threat (frequency of speech acts, negative tone, relevant to security policy agenda, specific sources of threat, speech acts by elite actors); intersubjective agreement about security threat; and demonstrated political effects. Once again the concept of legitimation enters into state-of-the-art constructivist research. Leaders eager to legitimate their actions and the citizenry form a crucial part of the securitization process as their acceptance of elite speech acts is a necessary condition for securitization to be successful (Jamieson). The analytical framework is applied to two cases of conflict for the US, the Islamic State and Venezuela, to show how securitization succeeds when all stages of the process are present, but not otherwise. The contribution resembles that of Goddard and Krebs, who also focus on legitimation *and* elaborate their key concept. In sum, the contribution from Jamieson follows in the tradition of Harvey (1999), who took the concept of deterrence and elaborated it to show how success or failure occurs in stages as a function of the presence or absence of multiple conditions.

Realist critics acknowledge and demonstrate how constructivism can help to explain inputs into their theory. "One important answer provided by constructivists," observes Glaser, "is that opposing states' identities and states' collective identities play a significant role in a state's assessment of threats." Constructivist theories that explain inputs into rational theory do not compete with it, but instead complement it (Glaser). An example would be how cognitive dissonance impacts foreign policy interactions involving the elite and mass public (Ramos). Furthermore, "the pursuit of international standing, status, and role fulfillment—all social variables—can condition states' foreign policy choices" (Blagden). Thus constructivism as an approach and realist theories can complement, rather than compete, with each other in numerous ways.

Research programs within constructivism are expanding from a relatively macro-oriented sense of norms and how they might rival the distribution of capabilities for influence on systems processes. The sample of topics in this volume—which include legitimation, science and technology, and sovereignty—are sufficient to establish a significant widening of the constructivist research agenda.

Causal Mechanisms

Another way of looking at the subject matter of constructivism, beyond a review of its research programs, is to focus on completeness in terms of potential causal mechanisms. The principle of *systemism*, developed by Bunge (1996) and applied throughout the social sciences, is well-suited to application in that context.[5] Systemism rejects holism and reductionism because of their inherent incompleteness. In the language of IR, holism would correspond to theorizing like Waltz (1979), which focuses exclusively on macro-level cause and effect (i.e., M → M). In other words, Waltz's structural realism is holistic because it concentrates on the structure of the system as a cause of international (in)stability. Reductionist theory, in the eyes of systemism, also is incomplete because it examines the micro-level exclusively (i.e., m → m).[6]

Systemists argue that such theorizing is fundamentally incomplete because there are *four* types of connection in IR: the two noted above, but also two other hybrids: Macro to micro (M → m) and micro to Macro (m → M). Thus a basic criterion for theoretical completeness emerges: Does a program of research explore all four of the preceding connections? The unsatisfying alternative is to invoke ceteris paribus. Constructivism, moreover, arose from the critique of materialism and, at least indirectly, rejection of neorealist and neoliberal holism. Thus it would seem even more appropriate to pursue a full set of linkages across levels of analysis.

Before embarking on the review that follows, definitions are in order. The international system of states constitutes the macro level, with states and nonstate actors as the micro level. This corresponds loosely to structure and agency as these terms often are used in IR, although as critics of Waltz (1979) pointed out long ago, the distribution of capabilities is only one sense of international structure.[7]

From a systemist point of view, progress is evident within constructivism as evidenced throughout the pages of this book. Constructivist theorizing with a focus on causal mechanisms—as opposed to the variants beyond the boundaries of positivism—favored the macro level for some time. The idea of a social structure conditioning interactions at the interstate level reached a point of culmination with Wendt (1999; see also Glaser). His familiar argument about anarchy being what states make of it summarizes the macro-macro variants of constructivism that predominated for some time. Social structure is a macro-level entity that resembles, for instance, a market within the domain of economics in the sense that both condition the behavior of agents.

Macro-macro links are acknowledged but not developed much. The simplest explanation is that among the elements of constructivism, this type of cause and effect is so well-established already. Contributors to this volume acknowledge that M → M linkages operate and then move on to explore other connections. For example, structure is "composed of the ideas that are held by actors" (Ramos; see also Cornut). It is striking that at this stage of constructivism's development, macro-macro linkages seem to be in the background, acknowledged as a matter of course, but not activated and integrated all that much into purportedly original theorizing.

Micro-micro connections, by contrast, are quite evident throughout the chapters of this volume. Consider, in exploring science and technology through a constructivist approach, the emphasis Branch places on networks of individual scientists in laboratories and their actions. "I am assuming," observes Ramos about transmission of the sovereignty norm within the state, "an elite-driven process, one in which leaders shape the content of public information." More emphatic about the need for a micro-micro shift is Cornut in assessing the deeper value of the practice turn: "scaling down analyses of social construction to the micro level." Jamieson provides the most detailed treatment of a micro-micro process, in which securitization is elaborated into four conditions and outcomes accounted for in terms of their collective presence (likely success) or individual absence (likely failure).

Consider also the importance of m m connections among realists who see value in incorporating the constructivist approach. Blagden identifies multiple and quite specific instances about how ideational theorizing plays a role in foreign policy. Culture can "condition both threat perception and military doctrine" via states' perceptions of "otherness" and "elevate their assessments of the dangerousness or otherwise of their potential foes" (Blagden). The potentially harmful influence of domestic identity groups on US policy choices is cited by a realist critic as a well-established causal mechanism in which an ideational element is essential (Blagden).

Macro-micro links also are explored in this volume. Goddard and Krebs observe that "strategizing elites cannot escape the bonds of legitimacy." States must react to this macro-level force. As a result, they will "cultivate legitimacy" through public rhetorical practices," and that can include domestic as well as international audiences. Cornut adds that "constructivists often explain individual variations of behavior by looking at differences in the social norms to which individuals conform"; more specifically, "norms, culture, and identity also shape specific practice." And Ramos sees a cycle of cause and effect—"states both influence norms and are affected by them"—which for a systemist would be written m $\rightarrow$ M $\rightarrow$ m.

Striking is the relative level of interest that constructivists reveal in the micro-macro connection, which had been left alone during the initial era of structural (i.e., M $\rightarrow$ M) dominance. One m $\rightarrow$ M connection is singled out by Goddard and Krebs: "Audiences' insistence that officials explain themselves is a key driver of legitimation." Branch sees potential for constructivist IR theory in the issue area of science and technology in "scaling up from micro processes to macro-level outcomes based on the constraining and driving effects of ideas that emerge and are reproduced through networks." A micro-macro connection is the focal point of the case studies pursued by Ramos; how does the outcome of military intervention influence the evolution of one specific norm, state sovereignty? Results bear out the curiosity and affirm a macro-micro linkage: "Thus, at least in part, as a by-product of the intervention, counterterrorism norms within the international system became widely understood to be an important part of states' responsibilities." And Cornut asserts that the logic of practice precedes the logic of appropriateness. In other words, repetitive behavior generates a norm, clearly an m $\rightarrow$ M connection. For example, consider this point from a realist contributor to the volume; lack of certainty "about the opposing state's type lies at the core of the security dilemma," which in turn explain competition in the international system (Glaser). The practice of policy based on suspicion becomes a self-fulfilling prophecy at the level of the system.

When looking back at the respective linkages enumerated through systemism, several points become clear. One is that macro-macro connections have evolved into well-accepted background conditions. Another is that the remaining three types of connection, initially not explored much, now provide the focal points for active research programs. Finally, given their incorporation of all types of linkages, collectively speaking, the research programs of constructivism emerge as theoretically comprehensive and in line with the recommendations of systemism.

Critiques

This volume features a diverse set of contributors and associated viewpoints. Believers, agnostics, and nonbelievers coexist in its pages. As will become apparent, at times the critiques of insiders and outsiders converge.[8] The main points of criticism concern clarity and integration, possibly harmful associations with particular political beliefs, lack of economy of explanation, shortcomings in the research agenda and associated methods, and drifting away from normative thinking. It almost goes without saying that the critics do not all speak with one voice.

Most fundamental among the critiques is one that arises naturally from the initial definition of constructivism at the outset, quite broadly, as an approach rather than anything more specific like a theory or paradigm. Cornut observes that what it means to be a constructivist is "increasingly unclear," and McCourt adds that there is "strikingly little consensus on the essence of constructivism and its boundaries." Sjoberg and Barkin elaborate on that point and describe constructivism as "both underspecified and overused" as a result of the tendency to adopt the term as a label for everything that is not realist or liberal in IR. Constructivisms, as a result, "are everywhere": epistemology, ontology, methods, and social theory, depending upon the study (Sjoberg and Barkin). At this stage of its development, constructivism therefore looks like a graphic illustration of conceptual stretching (Sartori 1970) in practice.

Sjoberg and Barkin ask a revealing question: What happens when something goes through the process of "social construction"? It becomes obvious that the answer would depend on the context; is the question about theory, method, or something else? In the quest to move constructivism in the best possible directions, Sjoberg and Barkin effectively channel Vasquez (1999), minus the commitment to explanatory theory. A shift is recommended toward a "targeted theory or group of theories about specific functions of particular social constructions or specific processes by which specific sorts of social constructions diffuse, happen, or engage might provide constructivisms with an opportunity to develop better senses of *processes* of social construction and constitution." This recommendation is in line with the tradition of middle-range theory as articulated by Merton (1949), albeit without implications that favor positivism.

Putting Vasquez and Merton together, in effect, Sjoberg and Barkin see constructivisms, with an emphasis on the plural, as badly in need of reorganization into something that resembles a coherent whole. The idea is *not* to turn constructivism into an explanatory theory, but instead to restructure its contents in a Linnean sense to promote coherent dialogue.

Constructivism's association with a particular kind of politics is regarded as problematic by several critics. After the Cold War, as McCourt (see also Blagden) observes, "came to focus on the transformative and progressive potential of norms, human rights, taboos, culture, identity, and argument and persuasion in world politics." Constructivism thus became associated with idealist thinking, but events—9/11, wars in Iraq and elsewhere, and the rise of the Islamic State—cast doubt on the transforming effect of liberal norms (McCourt). The realist critique of the idealist element in constructivism is conveyed effectively by Blagden. He issues a challenge to the "most ambitious constructivists," who argue that "social role *constitutes* state interest, rather than merely ranking among them." Social variables cannot, however, transform the world because of the primacy of state interests: political survival, biological security, and economic prosperity.

Thus it is essential to recognize "a material base independent of the social world and that characteristics of that material base can yield determinate outcomes." The preceding observation emphasizes what Guzzini (2000) labeled "brute facts" as compared to "social facts," which are the prime movers for material and ideational theories, respectively. Blagden provides an example of how brute facts work within the material world of realism. "It may be debatable whether nuclear weapons are 'good' or 'bad,'" he observes, "but the effect that one will have on the city and its population of frail, carbon-based human animals represents a single, determinate outcome, and a state facing another state armed with them must therefore make certain necessary calculations based around that capability." In sum, realism teaches that neither the capabilities of states nor their effects are *wholly* socially constructed and that nonsocial elements produce certain effects, one of which is the ongoing possibility of conflict even in times of broadly cooperative relations (Blagden).

Another realist critique, put forward by Glaser, concerns relative economy of explanation. Glaser asserts that including information about motives as a key variable in a rational realist theory "opens the door to arguments that address much of the terrain also covered by Wendt's structural constructivism." A realist theory can provide, more elegantly, an alternative account of how states interact and influence their relationship and, in turn, future conduct. From a "standard expected utility perspective," Glaser argues that "a state should consider the probability that the opposing state is a revisionist/greedy type, as opposed to status quo/security type." This amounts to Bayesian updating. In comparison to what Wendt offers, the rational realist account possesses "the advantage of greater simplicity" (Glaser), and Blagden adds that while identity "certainly matters to security relations, it is less decisive than a combination of power and informational variables." Rationalism coupled with realism, according to Glaser, demonstrates that "anarchy can generate a variety of outcomes—including various degrees of competition, cooperation and mixtures of the two—that have much in common with Wendt's three anarchies." The overarching point about theory construction is that Wendt "fails to adequately incorporate the constraints that material factors can impose on states' policies" (Glaser).

Constructivists also express concerns about the research agenda and associated methods. Ramos observes that "a structural explanation alone does not take into account actors' behavior, and it therefore provides only a partial explanation of norm change." More specifically, constructivism suffers from "a lack of a micro-level foundation that enables understandings of social change and inattention to how actions (via elites) shape the normative environment" (Ramos). In response, she urges input from social psychology because of its attention to actors within a social context (Ramos). This recommendation can be taken more broadly as a critique of holistic, even disembodied, constructivism that starts and finishes with social structure and its presumed effects. Cornut throws down the gauntlet with the claim that practice theory "reinvigorates constructivist methodologies by inviting constructivists to leave their office and look at how on-the-ground social realities are constructed." More than purely abstract theorizing is needed to obtain a full understanding of IR.

This point is reinforced by McCourt and Jamieson, from inside and outside of constructivism, respectively. McCourt is quite graphic, asserting that the reputation of constructivism in the United States is weakened "as a result of its nonscientific associations." While not explicit, Goddard and Krebs may be talking about much the same thing in asserting that "like many constructivists, we have found the critical linguistic turn unsatisfying in its refusal to engage in causal dynamics and in its static presentation of dominant discursive structures that stripped agency and politics out of the analysis." This point about self-limitation is reinforced by Jamieson's assertion that constructivism suffers because "many practitioners refuse to employ positivist research methods"; for example, nothing in the theory of securitization precludes its empirical testing.

All of the preceding discussion points in the same direction, toward a fault line within constructivism over epistemology. While under the umbrella of a constructivist approach, critical and empirical strands of constructivist research differ strongly over positivism. While constructivism began among those dissatisfied with the materialism of liberal and realist IR, it gradually picked up more diverse adherents. While not enamored of liberalism or neorealism, these scholars—unlike those present at the creation—saw a place for empirical research in the study of ideas. Sjoberg and Barkin may be closest to the truth among critics in pointing out the need for reassessment of terminology to facilitate more effective dialogue in the future.

Kessler and Steele see constructivism as becoming too "moderate" in the sense of moving away from a normative orientation. From the standpoint of critical IR, Sjoberg and Barkin are dissatisfied with the current trajectory of constructivism. When constructivism constitutes "the social as an empty signifier," it creates the potential to be infinitely regressive. This is the basic problem with constructivism labeled loosely as an approach that ends up incorporating so many ultimately incompatible things. In a quest for greater coherence, Sjoberg and Barkin issue a reminder that the constructivism of Onuf began with a set of rules that transform into a state of rules, which in terms reifies and reconstitutes rules. Thus coconstitution, not cause and effect, is inherent in constructivism as the term originated. Sjoberg and Barkin urge movement away from triumphalism about constructivism as a middle ground between various positivist theories of IR—liberalism, realism, or whatever—and toward normative analysis.

Constructivism and Analytic Eclecticism

Striking is the presence of analytic eclecticism throughout the pages of this volume.[9] Its call for pragmatism in theorizing, as opposed to paradigmatic purity, is answered by constructivists and their critics. Sjoberg and Barkin assert that "constructivist research can be used in service of a number of different (and diverse) political approaches to the theory and practice of international relations." Examples of helpful transgressions of paradigmatic boundaries are easy to fined. According to Goddard and Krebs, actors are "both strategic and social" but "legitimation cannot be reduced to self-interest." Obviously concepts from rational choice and constructivism are intertwined in those assertions. Goddard and Krebs add that legitimation "*is* power politics," a symbiotic assertion regarding a social process in connection with the essence of traditional realism.

Self-interest and norms come together across the chapters in ways that reflect analytic eclecticism. While the multistage model from Jamieson assumes that efforts toward securitization follow from perceived self-interest, the case-based analysis is about speech acts that (un)successfully construct a desired mindset into the public. Similarly, Ramos asserts that "states are self-interested actors" and "ideas inform what these interests are" with regard to sovereignty.

For obvious reasons, the most graphic instances of analytic eclecticism come together during the more friendly engagements of realist critics with constructivism. Consider this list of assertions from Blagden:

- Military doctrine historically has been influenced by both the domestic culture of the state in general and the specific institutional culture of particular militaries.

- There is a military desire for prestige in terms of the sources of military doctrine.
- The system itself is party underpinned by an idea: formation of and reinforcement of states as units rests on variations of an ideology, nationalism.
- Snyder's *Myths of Empire* includes liberal, constructivist, and realist arguments.
- A key contribution of the neoclassical realist research program has been to demonstrate that while domestic-political variables may filter strategic behavior in nefarious ways, there are still underlying balance-of-power structural pressures at the international-systemic level that states usually respond to, even if they do so belatedly or imperfectly.
- Social and ideational variables play an important causal role in contemporary international politics.

Each of these assertions goes beyond paradigms in its subject matter. The level of detail is useful in driving home the point that engagements across paradigms are worthwhile and may even produce the most interesting prospects for advancement in the field of IR.

Final Thoughts

Over the past thirty years, there can be little doubt that constructivism has had an amazing run in the study of international relations. While the research program has not followed the trajectory its initiators imagined, constructivism has enriched international relations as a discipline and created a space for scholars to study the social relations that make humans distinct from the natural systems that physicists study. And yet, despite the many accomplishments of constructivism, there is also greater reason for concern for its future than at any time in the past thirty years. While the semiregular Teaching, Research, and International Policy survey shows constructivism as having the largest percentage of self-identified scholars, Subotic (2017) and Zarakol (2017) show in compelling fashion that constructivism is marginalized in American IR. These findings are thus in accord with McCourt's pessimistic assessment of constructivism's present and future in the practice of IR.

There are good reasons for constructivists and nonconstructivists alike to lament this state of affairs. As Rofer (2016) noted, events in the real world of international affairs are overdetermined: any given outcome has more motivators than are necessary for it to happen. This characteristic of the social world can produce a state of affairs in which scholars can legitimately find evidence in support of a given theory or approach and claim to have found *the* cause. In reality, the scholar has only found *a* cause, just as a person in a dark room with a single flashlight sees only a small piece of it.

The problem, of course, is that other causes (we use this word guardedly in recognition that causation is itself a complex thing in human society) go unrecognized, leading to at best a partial explanation. Thus, the complex, contingent nature of international relations outcomes *requires* multiple theoretical perspectives. Returning to the room metaphor, we can only really know the room by shining multiple flashlights from different angles at the same time. If the goal of IR scholars is to truly understand what international relations are and how they work (not to mention produce work that is relevant to policymakers), then rationalist materialists need constructivists as colleagues in their departments and across the discipline, and vice versa. The social psychology of academia makes this truth difficult to accept (Hayes 2017), but it is a truth nonetheless. The repeated re-emergence of theoretical perspectives concerned with the ideational foundations of social relations—regardless of the name—is testament to the fact that if IR did not already have constructivism, it would have to invent it. This volume, and the constructivist scholarship it outlines, demonstrates the ongoing vibrancy and vigor of constructivism as well as the ways in which it is addressing the problems of complexity and contingency in a world that looks increasingly characterized by both.

NOTES

1. Understanding and explanation are used throughout in line with Hollis and Smith (1991).

2. This reasoning goes back to Collingwood (1946) on historical processes.

3. Some chapters are covered here and not others. This is because some of the chapters in this volume are more purely abstract and include neither propositions nor testing of them.

4. Blagden puts this very directly in his critique of constructivism in its most purely ideational form within the domain of security studies: "military technology does not descend as manna from heaven, but rather is created via human agency in response to perceived threats, and thus it necessarily contains a dose of military culture and broader social identity from the outset."

5. Systemism is presented briefly here and without the diagrammatic exposition of cause and effect and other features that a full-fledged application of its principles normally would include. For an example of how systemism can be used to assess

theories in IR for comprehensiveness and logical consistency, see James (2002) on structural realism.

6. Upper and lower case characters are used to express macro and micro level connections, respectively.

7. A few illustrations should help to distinguish the use of terms here. Traits of the system as a whole constitute the macro level. For example, a macro-macro linkage would be from the type of international system—say, Kantian versus Hobbesian—to its overall frequency and intensity of warfare. (This is analogous to the Waltzian macro-macro linkage of polarity with war.) At the micro-micro level, an example would be two states signing a treaty or one of them quarreling with a transnational actor. A real-world example of a micro-macro linkage would be massive increases in energy usage that produce global climate change. A macro-micro linkage would be bandwagoning, where a state faces overwhelming power and its leaders decide to join in with, rather than balance against, a principal actor.

8. McCourt, Branch, and Cornut all urge a reflexivist approach toward constructivism; in other words, the field of research itself should be assessed with its own tools. Those identified with constructivism have done so, while others, not surprisingly, offer critiques that are more in line with either a positivist or critical IR point of view.

9. Sil and Katzenstein (2010) provide a full-length exposition of analytic exposition, with illustrations from research in IR. It is beyond the scope of the present study to introduce analytic eclecticism in such detail; its most important trait for present purposes concerns encouragement of theorizing that crosses paradigmatic boundaries. Applications in IR are building quickly (Cornut 2015).

REFERENCES

Bunge, Mario. 1996. *Finding Philosophy in Social Science*. New Haven, CT: Yale University Press.

Collingwood, R. G. 1946. *The Idea of History*. Edited by Jan van der Dussen. Oxford: Clarendon Press.

Cornut, Jérémie. 2015. "Analytic Eclecticism in Practice: A Method for Combining International Relations Theories." *International Studies Perspectives* 16: 50–66.

Guzzini, Stefano. 2000. "A Reconstruction of Constructivism in International Relations." *European Journal of International Relations* 6: 147–82.

Harvey, Frank. 1999. "Practicing Coercion: Revisiting Successes and Failures Using Boolean Logic and Comparative Methods." *Journal of Conflict Resolution* 43: 840–71.

Hayes, Jarrod. 2017. "Reclaiming Constructivism: Identity and the Practice of the Study of International Relations." *PS: Political Science & Politics* 50: 89–92.

Hollis, Martin, and Steve Smith. 1991. *Explaining and Understanding International Relations*. Oxford: Clarendon Press.

James, Patrick. 2002. *International Relations and Scientific Progress*. Columbus: Ohio State University Press.

Keohane, Robert O. 1986. *Neorealism and Its Critics*. New York: Columbia University Press.

Merton, Robert K. 1949. *Social Theory and Social Structure*. New York: The Free Press.

Onuf, Nicholas. 1989. *World of Our Making*. Columbia: University of South Carolina Press.

Organski, A. F. K., and Jacek Kugler. 1980. *The War Ledger*. Chicago: University of Chicago Press.

Putnam, Robert D. 1988. "Diplomacy and Domestic Politics: The Logic of Two-Level Games." *International Organization* 42: 427–60.

Ramos, Jennifer. 2013. *Changing Norms Through Actions: The Evolution of Sovereignty*. New York: Oxford University Press.

Rofer, Cheryl. 2016. "A Scientist's View of Realism." *Nuclear Diner* (blog). https://nucleardiner.wordpress.com/2016/02/16/a-scientists-view-of-realism/.

Sartori, Giovanni. 1970. "Concept Misformation in Comparative Politics." *American Political Science Review* 64: 1033–53.

Senese, Paul D., and John A. Vasquez. 2008. *The Steps to War: An Empirical Study*. Princeton, NJ: Princeton University Press.

Sil, Rudra, and Peter J. Katzenstein. 2010. *Beyond Paradigms: Analytic Eclecticism in the Study of World Politics*. New York: Palgrave Macmillan.

Subotic, Jelena. 2017. "Constructivism as Professional Practice in the US Academy." *PS: Political Science & Politics* 50: 84–88.

Tsebelis, George. 1990. *Nested Games: Rational Choice in Comparative Politics*. Berkeley: University of California Press.

Vasquez, John A. 1999. *The Power of Power Politics: From Classical Realism to Neotraditionalism*. Cambridge: Cambridge University Press.

Waltz, Kenneth N. 1979. *Theory of International Politics*. New York: McGraw-Hill.

Wendt, Alexander. 1999. *Social Theory of International Politics*. Cambridge: Cambridge University Press.

Zarakol, Ayşe. 2017. "TRIPping Constructivism." *PS: Political Science & Politics* 50: 75–78.

Epilogue

Constructivism and Global International Relations: False Promise to Vanguard

Amitav Acharya

I did not start out as a constructivist and still hesitate to call myself one, although I do not mind (and secretly enjoy) when others call me a constructivist. The reasons for my ambivalence about constructivism go back to its initial years, when I found myself asking: What, if any, relevance does the the supposedly new, optimistic, and progressive theory (in terms of its stress on moral transformation and community building in world politics) have for the study of international relations of the *non-Western* world? While IR theories generally tend to be Western-centric, would constructivism be any different by offering more space to the study of non-Western states and societies? The reasons for IR's Western-centrism—including the dominance and gatekeeping role of Western IR scholars, institutions, and publication outlets, and the resource and intellectual constraints in which scholars from the Global South find themselves and how to remedy them intellectually and institutionally—have already been identified and discussed (Acharya 2000; Acharya and Buzan 2007; Acharya 2014b). Frankly, I was not hopeful that constructivism would make a big difference in this state of affairs, at least based on my first reading of Wendt's *Social Theory of International Politics* and an exchange with him at a roundtable on his book at the annual convention of the International Studies Association in Chicago in 2001. There went some of my early enthusiasm for a theory that was rapidly gaining ground as the principal challenge to the hitherto dominance of realism and liberalism.

While constructivism seemed different, I did not (and still do not, despite major strides it has made in recent years) see it as a sufficiently universal framework of inquiry and analysis of international relations. Its founding literature, beginning with Wendt, fell short of my understanding of what a truly global IR should be, that is, a discipline that "draw(s) from a broad canvass of human interactions, with their multiple origins, patterns, and distinctions, to challenge IR's existing boundary markers set by dominant American and Western scholarship and encourage new understandings and approaches to the study of world politics" (Acharya 2014b). Onuf's chapter in this volume dealing with the origins of constructivism confirms my view that the key founders of the theory (Onuf being among them) did not see it necessary or important to engage with the ideas, worldviews, and agency claims of non-Western societies. Yet, constructivism is not without such potential, and while it cannot be identical to it, it can be, along with such critical theories as postcolonialism and feminism, a vanguard theory of Global IR.

Constructivism's (Initial) False Promise

Constructivism poses a particular challenge to anyone who saw it as a savior against the dominance of realism and liberalism as the mainstream theories of international relations. Despite its claim to novelty and its affinity with critical theories of international relations, constructivism has become fairly *mainstream* theory. It has made such rapid strides over the past two decades in shaping the research agendas of young scholars and winning converts from among older ones that it has become, in the eyes of its critics, *the new orthodoxy*. In the 2014 Teaching, Research, and International Policy (TRIP) Survey (2014), constructivism came out the top choice of an IR paradigm with 22.5 percent, followed by realism and liberalism. (It should be noted, however, that the numbers of those who opted for "I do not use a paradigm" exceeded constructivism, attesting to the aforementioned point about the declining interest in paradigm debates).[1] Wendt has displaced Keohane as "the scholar whose work has had the greatest influence on the field of IR in the past 20 years."[2]

Despite its growing popularity, my initial misgivings about constructivism's affinity with the two other mainstream theories—realism and liberalism—in neglecting non-Western voices and experiences are borne out by two of the contributions to this volume. They suggest that constructivism might be no better than realism and liberalism when it comes to IR theory's gross neglect or marginalization of the non-Western world. Different methods are pursued in chapters 2 and 6, but on this matter they end up in the same place.

Consider first one of the findings of chapter 2, the contribution by Bertucci, Hayes, and James. Analyzing an extensive journal-based dataset, they find that "despite constructivism's place as the leading theoretical alternative to rationalist approaches to the study of international relations, in terms of its substantive and empirical scope constructivism does not look much different than rationalist alternatives like realism and liberalism. In all cases, scholarship primarily focuses on security processes and outcomes taking place in the North Atlantic region and Europe." They note that about 45 percent of their sampled constructivist research relates to the North Atlantic region, followed by 13.1 percent on Asia, whereas "regions such as Latin America, Africa and, most notably, the Middle East, have received only scant attention." In the conclusion of the chapter, they further note that "constructivism is an approach to the study of international relations that . . . makes security issues in the North Atlantic region its salient substantive and empirical focus of analysis." Aside from the substance or issue areas of constructivist research, they also find that scholars from Europe, North America, and Oceania (Australia and New Zealand) account for 93.5 percent of all articles by constructivist scholars. Among other regions, Asia leads at a mere 4.1 percent.

The other contribution that shows constructivism's false promise in engaging the Global South is by Klotz (chapter 6), who examines and laments constructivism's "race gap," or its neglect of race. To be sure, race and racism are not exclusively "non-Western" issues. But Klotz is not entirely correct in my view in saying that "no one to my knowledge has undertaken a thorough critique regarding the race gap in IR theory." While much depends on what one means by "thorough" here, race is the salient issue for a large section of the IR academic community in the Global South, and its neglect in traditional IR has attracted much criticism from them (Persaud and Walker 2001; Henderson 2013; Hobson 2012; Bell 2013; Persaud 2014). What justifies Klotz's lament about constructivism's "race gap," however, is that none of these contributions is from a constructivist.

Constructivism itself may not have the racial baggage of its older cousins, realism and liberalism (Hobson 2012), but it still suffers from a heavy dose of Western ethnocentrism. I have outlined some of these areas before, especially the "moral cosmopolitanism" bias in the early literature on norm diffusion (Acharya 2004, 2009). Whether consciously or not, at least to a non-Western observer, these narratives were mostly built around how good global norms promoted by transnational norm entrepreneurs (who happen to be mostly Western), drove out bad local beliefs and practices (which happened to occur mostly in the non-Western world). Although not all norm literature was like this, most of it took little note of the legitimate normative priors of non-Western societies and the agency of non-Western actors in norm creation and propagation. A good deal of my own work on norms was inspired by acute frustration with constructivism's neglect of southern agency, which has led to the concepts of constitutive localization (Acharya 2004, 2009), norm subsidiarity (Acharya 2011b), and norm circulation (Acharya 2013b).

But such criticisms of constructivism should not blind us to the efforts made by constructivist scholars to engage with issues and concerns of the Global South. To some scholars, constructivism holds significant promise as a theory relevant and applicable to the non-Western world. This is particularly true in light of constructivism's greater capacity to account for local practice, identity, custom, and how these shape international behavior (see, for instance, Solomon and Steele (2016).) As a German scholar notes:

> Constructivism has always had a strong academic base outside of the US; European IR has even been characterized by its preference for constructivist ontologies. . . . Furthermore, constructivism is a paradigm often characterized as frequently "traveling" to non-core regions . . . and even as "bridge-builder" between core and periphery IR. . . . It can therefore be expected that constructivist approaches to IR can be found even outside of the transatlantic core. All in all, it is a most likely case of a branch of IR that is *not* US-dominated. (Wemheuer-Vogelaar 2013, 2)

Yet much of this potential remains unrealized to date. But it need not be. Among the three "mainstream" IR theories today, realism has some broad resonance with non-Western history and culture, as its occasional if superficial engagement with Chinese (legalism) and Indian (Kautilya) traditions attests. Liberalism is perhaps the most ethnocentric of IR theories (Hobson 2012). It derives its foundational narratives, core ideas, and policy practices almost exclusively from the West. Thus free trade is the result of British and American policy preferences and dominance, multilateralism is a unique product of *American* hegemony, and the current world order is the exclusive product of American power and purpose. Liberalism also insists on co-opting non-Western actors into its ambit without making a serious effort at recognizing the unquestionably multiple and global heritage of its core ideas such as free trade, human rights, rights of protest against authority, and ruled-based interstate cooperation. By comparison, there is nothing innate or inevitable about constructivism's disconnect with or neglect of the Global South. It is largely the result of how the theory originated and evolved and of the larger issue of the narrow training that IR scholars offer and receive in the dominant Western centers of knowledge production, which are under increasing scrutiny and challenge.

Where Constructivism Can Make a Difference

How does constructivism differ from realism and liberalism? At least in three ways. The first has to do with its emphasis on ideational forces in world politics. Here, I do not see constructivism as "ideas all the way down," but as an "ideas first" approach. Since a hallmark of non-Western (Third World) countries has been their relative lack of material power (which may be changing in the case of the emerging powers), a theory that stresses the power of ideas over ideas of power has a broader, more universal resonance in the study of world politics. Writing around the time constructivism began to obtain a substantial following, Puchala noted that for "Third World countries, ideas and ideologies are far more important" than power or wealth. This is because whereas "powerlessness" and "unequal distribution of the world's wealth" are "constants," ideas can be empowering (Puchala 1998, 151). In other words, by broadening the notion of agency to include both material and ideational elements, constructivism, to a much greater extent than materialist theories like realism and liberalism, gives more space to the consideration of the agency of weaker actors in the international system, which includes much of the Global South. Since a good deal of IR theory rests on considerations of agency, constructivism offers an important avenue for recognizing the role of non-Western actors in world politics.

Second, and this is really fortunate for the admirers of the theory, some of the best constructivist work since the founding literature by Onuf, Wendt, and Ruggie, etc., has been concerned with the study of regional dynamics in the Global South. While taking note of the important observation by Bertucci, Hayes, and James about constructivist scholarship's preoccupation with the North Atlantic region, I can point to scholarship that has already done much to render constructivism more global. Some of the best proponents of constructivism are also some of the best regional specialists and many focus outside Europe. Here I have in mind scholars such as Barnett (1995, 1998) on the Middle East, Kacowitz (2005) and Sikkink (2014) on Latin America, Johnston (1998) and Hemmer and Katzenstein (2002) on East Asia, and many others. The hallmark of the highly influential book *Security Communities* (Adler and Barnett 1998), was its focus on regions, both Europe and outside. This literature has been invaluable in stimulating my own work on the intersection of IR theory and Asian and comparative regionalism (Acharya 2001, 2004, 2009, 2011b).

A third reason why constructivism is better suited than either realism or liberalism for the study of non-Western societies has to do with its deep association with culture and identity. Cultural distinctiveness, or claims about it, are often the starting point of the study of international relations in many parts of the developing world. In the words of Iriye, international relations is primarily about the study of intercultural relations (Iriye 1979). And a Malaysian IR scholar (Karim 2007) writes, "Thinking in the constructivist vein has been about the best gift made available to scholars and leaders in the region."

What Is to Be Done?

Different people have different ideas as to what IR theory should do to shed its Western-centrism (Acharya 2000, 2014b; Agathangelou and Ling 2009; Tickner 2003; Tickner and Waever 2009; Behera 2010; Bilgin 2008, 2013; Chowdhry and Nair 2004; Ling 2002; Neuman 1998; Parasar 2013; Shilliam 2010; Smith 2006; Thomas and Wilkin 2004; Tadjbakhsh 2010). But common to all these attempts is to reject the claim of IR as a truly global discipline unless and until it accounts for the ideas, experiences, and voices of all civilizations, societies, and states. This leads me to return to the topic of a global IR (Acharya 2013a, 2014b).

By global IR, I mean the collective efforts by the IR community, both from the West and the Global South, to expand the horizons of IR theory beyond the histories, ideas, identities, and practices of Europe and the United States. The origins of the global IR idea reflected growing and widespread dissatisfaction with American and Western dominance in IR theory. Global IR supersedes Acharya and Buzan's (2007, 2010) "Non-

Western IRT" or the idea of a "post-Western" IR (Bilgin 2008, 2013). Indeed, it transcends the distinction between West and non-West. While these categories might persist as terms of convenience, they lose analytical significance in the world of global IR.

Global IR is not an attempt to build a new or distinctive theory. Nor is it a paradigm to be juxtaposed against realism, liberalism, constructivism, or postcolonialism. Its purpose is not to launch another grand debate, like the "interparadigm" debates between idealism and realism, behavioralism and postpositivism, or rationalism and constructivism, which often end up in synthesis. Global IR begins with a syncretism, or eclecticism, with its chief goal being to develop a truly inclusive and universal discipline. Global IR subsumes, rather than supplants, existing IR theories and methods. It embraces both mainstream (realism, liberalism, and constructivism) and critical approaches (especially postcolonialism and feminism) but is agnostic about the theoretical and methodological instincts and preferences of the scholars. For example, global IR has much common ground with postcolonialism. But unlike some postcolonial scholarship, global IR does not reject mainstream theories, but challenges their parochialism and urges that they be infused and broadened with ideas, experiences, and insights from the non-Western world.

Global IR is a framework of enquiry and analysis of international relations in all its diversity, especially with due recognition of the experiences, voices, and agency of those actors—both state and nonstate—that have been marginalized by the discipline of international relations. These include, but are not limited to, those that are outside of, and challenging to, the interstate system of Europe and its colonial expansion, which has been central to the construction of dominant IR theories, including constructivism. Hence global IR is grounded in world history (or global history), rather than just Greco-Roman, European, or US history. While eschewing cultural exceptionalism, global IR seeks to uncover endogenously driven patterns of interaction around the world, paying attention to local, regional, and interregional dynamics and through them the agency of non-Western actors. Global IR prizes and integrates the study of regions, regionalisms, and area studies. As mentioned above, some of the best constructivist work deeply is focused on regional dynamics and engages area studies. One cannot develop a global discipline of IR out of North America or western Europe alone; global IR is an impossibility without having its foundation in local IRs around the world. Some of this is already happening, at least conceptually, in some regions of the world outside of Europe, especially in Latin America (Deciancio 2016; Frasson-Quenoz 2016) and

Southeast Asia, with the development of ASEAN studies in Southeast Asia (Rother 2012).

Finally, Global IR recognizes and investigates the multiple and complex ways civilizations and states interact with each other, including through peaceful processes of mutual learning.

There is much that constructivism—with its focus on ideas, identity, and interactions—can do to inform and contribute to the development of global IR. But to do so, constructivism needs to reimagine and reorient itself and perform several tasks. This volume contains a number of essays that challenge constructivism to rethink, reform, and redefine itself. This effort can immensely benefit from a global IR approach that fully engages the ideas, histories, and approaches found in the non-Western world. Let me offer some pathways to this broadening and redefining of constructivism to play the role of vanguard to a global IR.

The first concerns the issue of agency. Kessler and Steele (chapter 4) call for a rethinking of agency in constructivist theory and in this context stress the importance of language. That the concept of agency on Western IR theory, including earlier version of constructivism, has been too narrow is not difficult to prove, especially when looking at the construction of global order and governance. Goddard and Krebs' (chapter 5) plea for more attention to legitimation, itself a form of agency, can also benefit from more attention to the different concepts and approaches found in the non-Western world, where normative legitimation and delegitimation have been far more empowering and consequential than dissent or resistance through material (economic and military) means. (See the discussion of the delegitimation of US Cold War alliances in Acharya 2009.)

Thus, constructivism should promote a broader definition of agency, backed by an elaborate research agenda. Global IR recognizes multiple forms of agency beyond material power, including resistance, normative action, and local constructions of global order. Global IR is founded upon a pluralistic universalism. Moreover, global IR questions the early constructivist literature's "power bias," or its emphasis on the role of powerful actors in norm diffusion in world politics. Indeed, the realist-liberal-constructivist divide breaks down when it comes to privileging the role of materially powerful actors in shaping world order. This is true of the hegemonic stability theory, which synthesizes the realist notion of structural power with the liberal notion of public good, as well as constructivism, which subjects the dynamics of socialization and norm diffusion (Florini 1996) to the logic of power.

A broader understanding of agency would see it not just as the prerogative of the strong, but also as the weapon of the weak. Agency can be exercised in global transnational space as well as at regional and local levels. Agency can describe acts of resistance to and localization of global norms and institutions. Agency also means constructing new rules and institutions at the local level to support and strengthen global order against great power hypocrisy and dominance. Agency means conceptualizing and implementing new pathways to development, security, and ecological justice. Recent work on global governance highlights many examples of agency by non-Western actors, such as the extension of universal sovereignty at the 1955 Bandung Conference (Acharya 2014a), the invention of the idea of international development by Sun yat-Sen (Helleneier 2014), the idea of universal participation (Finnemore and Jurkovitch 2014), and contributions to the development of the human rights idea by postcolonial states (Sikkink 2014). Add to this literature that traces the emergence of the ideas of human development and human security and even responsibility to protect from non-Western contexts and thinkers (Acharya 2013a, 2013b). The fact that many if not all of these contributors are constructivists suggests that the theory can be at the forefront of the pluralization of agency in IR theory, which is vital to making it less Western-centric and building a global IR. Other theories could follow the example set by these constructivists, since the purpose of global IR is not to displace them or constructivism itself, but challenge them to look beyond the West in rethinking their assumptions, developing new concepts, understandings, methodological tools, and appreciating the work of those non-Western scholars who have already done so.

Aside from agency, constructivism needs to make a conscious effort to bring in the ideas of the non-Western world as a source of concepts and theories of IR. While realism has done so to a limited degree from classical China and India to illustrate the workings of competition, war, balancing, hegemony, and power politics (i.e., to illustrate how their approach is unbounded by time or space), constructivism can similarly help with the sources of existing and new international norms. Here constructivism, with its emphasis on culture and identity, can be of much help. As an ideational theory, one would have expected constructivism to pay more attention to the study of non-Western civilizations. Yet such work remains scarce and needs to be further encouraged, with constructivism playing a vanguard role. The kind of constructivist contributions on constitutive norms and culture of IR drawing on Greco-Roman civilizations (Reus-Smit 2001; Lebow 2008) is conspicuously scarce when it comes to classical interactions in the Indian Ocean region and elsewhere.

But such work holds much promise. For example, in presenting his "relational theory of world politics," Qin (2016) argues that international relations scholars should look beyond rationality and embrace relationality, in explaining foreign policy and international behavior and outcomes in a more universal context. Relationality not only deeply resonates within Chinese culture, it can also be applied to other contexts, even the West. In his view, it is not that the Western actors do not behave relationally; it may well be that Western IR theories, because of their obsession with rationality, have overlooked or rendered invisible the relationality aspect. Qin does not regard rationality and relationality as mutually antithetical, but complementary to each other. At the same time, it should not be overlooked that Qin is also a constructivist, and there are obvious echoes of constructivism in Qin's idea of relationality. To that extent, Western and non-Western approaches to IR can converge or find common ground and be mutually reinforcing. Global IR after all does not seek to displace but to subsume existing IR theories and enrich them with the infusion of ideas and practices from the non-Western world. Qin's relational theory is also significant because unlike some other members of the "Chinese School of IR," it offers a concept and explanation that have relevance beyond China or East Asia, rather than simply capture China's international behavior or the East Asian international system.

A related task here involves a full-scale embracing of world history (or global history), featuring especially the study of pre-Westphalian interstate (or "international") systems. Both anarchic and hierarchic systems should be included and studied, and their definition should be based as much on ideational sociocultural interactions (here one can specify flow of ideas as a crucial type of interaction) as on political/strategic and economic ones (which is central to most traditional definitions of international systems). These broadenings open the space to considering a variety of classical interactions and relationships, such as the maritime orders of Asia and the Indian Ocean. Again, given that a good deal of such interactions is ideational and intercivilizational, constructivism can play a major role in the investigation into non- and pre-Westphalian systems. Furthermore, neither "global history" nor any of its variants are taught very often within doctoral programs in the United States.

A further task for constructivism concerns the philosophy of science. The project of turning IR scientific, even by those who take a broader view of science, has led to the insistence that only phenomena that is "this worldly" is worthy of investigation. Yet as noted above, a good deal of the potential and actual sources on non-Western or global IR come from philosophy of religion, where the distinction between "this worldliness" and "otherworldliness" is often thin. Many religious philosophies straddle both. The lines between rationality and instrumental thinking are frequently blurred in a good deal of classical thought and practice in non-European civilizations, with the Indian epic *Mahabharata* being a leading example (Acharya 2011a). If one is to broaden the scope of IRT, one cannot exclude such hybrid causal logics, which do explain war, peace, interdependence, foreign policy behavior, the creation and distribution of wealth, and the spread of ideas and norms. This approach resonates with the call, following others such as Fearon and Wendt and Checkel, by Glaser (chapter 11) to find common ground between rationalism and constructivism. IR theorists are asked to view them more as friends than rivals.

Fourth, constructivism must overcome the related problem of false universalism (Acharya 2013a) in mainstream IR theories. (The universalism comes from an effort to emulate physics/economics in the pursuit of covering laws. These are false only after one steps out of the neopositivist mindset.) For global IR, true universalism is one that recognizes the diversity of human interactions, rather than one that legitimizes the imposition of a temporally and temporarily dominant Western civilization. Liberalism is especially beholden to what Cox (2002, 53) would say is Enlightenment of universalism. In this sense, universalism meant "true for all time and space—the perspective of a homogenous reality." For Cox, an alternative understanding of universality would mean "comprehending and respecting diversity in an ever changing world." Constructivism, with its focus on identity, can point to an alternative direction, where universalism was less about "applying to all" and more about recognizing diversity and finding common elements and common ground among agents and structures.

The fifth task, which closely follows from the above, concerns the language and vocabulary of international relations, which are closely tied to the issue of identity that occupies a central place in constructivist theory. IR theory often purports to speak in a universal linguistic code, but many of the core concepts or vocabulary of IR theory—such as power, sovereignty, balancing, peace, empire, norms—derive directly or indirectly (e.g., via old French) from Greek and Latin. This partly explains the persisting Western-centrism in the field, given that the common tendency to view key political terms in terms of their etymological origins often leads us back to interactions during the Greek and Roman worlds, ignoring that they might have been the unique product of a specific time and context that the West has claimed as its cultural and intellectual heritage. Hence a key challenge where constructivism can be of particular value is the recognition of the cultural and historical context of existing concepts so that they do not become part of an artificial universal code that ignores or obscures other origins. This may be the most daunting challenge of all tasks that constructivism and global IR face today.

Because of the hegemony of Greek and Latin origins of the core concepts of IR, scholars think of these terms in a specific way. If you want to understand hegemony, you start with Greek *hēgemonía*, and you think of the Hellenistic world, which by the way was a world where legitimizing ideas spread with the backing of competition and force. When you think of empire, you think of *imperium* and *imperator*, and your mind travels to Rome as the archetype empire, with all its violent direct political control. Yet if you think of the spread of ideas in the Indian Ocean, the situation is different, where Indian ideas spread without the backing of force and where the Chinese imperium ruled more by symbolic authority that brute physical force.

TABLE E.1. Ten Key Concepts in IR: Greek and Latin Origins

Power	Vulgar Latin *potere*; Latin *potis*	Powerful
Sovereign	Latin *super*	Above
Balance	Medieval Latin *bilancia*; Latin *bilanx*	scale, having two pans
		twice + dish, plate, scale of a balance
	Latin *bis* + *lanx*	
Hegemony	Greek *hēgemonía*	leadership, supremacy
Liberalism	Latin *liber*	free
	Latin *līberālis*	of freedom, befitting the free, equivalent to free
Democracy	Greek *demokratia*	popular government
	Greek *demos* + *kratos*	common people (district) + rule, strength
	Medieval Latin *democratia*	
Peace	Latin *pacem* (*pax*)	compact, agreement, treaty of peace, tranquility, absence of war
Empire	Latin imperium	rule, command
	Latin imperare	to command
Colony	Latin *colonia*	settled land, farm, landed estate (ancient Roman settlement outside Italy)
	Latin *colonus*	
	Latin *colere*	husbandman, tenant farmer, settler in new land
	Roman translation of Greek *apoikia*	to inhabit, cultivate, frequent, practice, tend, guard, respect
		people from home
Norm	Greek *anomalos*	abnormal
	Latin *abnormis*	irregular
	Latin *ab-* + *norma*	from + norm ("away from the norm")

To compound matters, other languages may not have the equivalent meaning to these core concepts. The Chinese are often puzzled by the steady stream of words that the West comes up with to deal with them that have no equivalent in their own language, such as "engagement," "confidence-building," "human security." They do not even have an exact equivalent of "sovereignty" ("*zhu quan*" or master/patron rights). For them, "engagement," a favorite policy term of the United States, is "*jie chu*," meaning "touch and connect." The term "security" is translated as "*an quan*" in Chinese, but this exact Chinese term can also be used for "safety," which has less of a military connotation.

The Chinese have no sense of "international-ness" as it is understood in the West (Qin 2010); hence, how do they relate to the discipline of international relations? In response, the Chinese have come up with their own terms like "*Tianxia*" (space under heaven), "*datong*" (universal great harmony), and other such terms to describe their worldview. There are also more politically charged concepts like "peaceful rise," "peaceful development," "convergence of interests," and "community of interests." While their deployment is sometimes (but not always) self-serving, it is not entirely different from the purposes to which the West's "democratic peace" or "liberal hegemony" are employed. In the orthodox Islamic world, IR becomes meaningless because the idea of sovereign state is regarded as but a temporary aberration rather than a permanent condition (Tadjbakhsh 2010). Just think of the day when ten key and widely used concepts in IR theory are taken from Mandarin or Sanskrit or Arabic. Consider this possibility in comparison to the contents of table E.1. What a different world of IR it might be?

The above tasks and challenges are not just for constructivism to address. IR theory in general must confront them if it is to assert a credible claim to be universal and retain relevance in a post-Western world. But constructivism, with its stress on ideas, identity, and interactions, can play a vanguard role if it can rise above its narrow Western origins and concerns. Its willingness and ability to do so is critical not only to its own future, but to IR theory and the discipline as a whole.

NOTES

1. Teaching, Research and International Policy (TRIP) Survey (2014). Available at https://trip.wm.edu/charts/#/questions/38.

2. Teaching, Research and International Policy (TRIP) Survey (2014). Available at https://trip.wm.edu/charts/#/bargraph/38/5045.

REFERENCES

Acharya, Amitav. 2000. "Ethnocentrism and Emancipatory IR Theory." In *Displacing Security*, edited by Samantha Arnold and J. Marshall Bier, 1–18. Toronto: Centre for International and Security Studies, York University.

Acharya, Amitav. 2001. *Constructing a Security Community in Southeast Asia: ASEAN and the Problem of Regional Order*. London: Routledge.

Acharya, Amitav. 2004. "How Ideas Spread: Whose Norms Matter? Norm Localization and Institutional Change in Asian Regionalism." *International Organization* 58, no. 2: 239–75.

Acharya, Amitav. 2009. *Whose Ideas Matter? Agency and Power in Asian Regionalism*. Ithaca, NY: Cornell University Press.

Acharya, Amitav. 2011a. "Dialogue and Discovery: In Search of International Relations Theories Beyond the West." *Millennium* 39, no. 3: 619–37.

Acharya, Amitav. 2011b. "Norm Subsidiarity and Regional Orders: Sovereignty, Regionalism, and Rule-Making in the Third World." *International Studies Quarterly* 55, no. 1: 95–123.

Acharya, Amitav. 2013a. *Rethinking Power, Institutions and Ideas in World Politics: Whose IR*. Abingdon: Routledge.

Acharya, Amitav. 2013b. "R2P and Theory of Norm Diffusion: Towards a Framework of Norm Circulation." *Global Responsibility to Protect* 5, no. 4: 466–79.

Acharya, Amitav. 2014a. "Who Are the Norm Makers? The Asian-African Conference in Bandung and the Evolution of Norms." *Global Governance: A Review of Multilateralism and International Organizations* 20, no. 3: 405–17.

Acharya, Amitav. 2014b. "Global International Relations (IR) and Regional Worlds: A New Agenda for International Studies." *International Studies Quarterly* 58, no. 4: 1–13.

Acharya, Amitav, and Barry Buzan, eds. 2007. "Why Is There No Non-Western International Relations Theory? Reflections on and from Asia." Special Issue of *International Relations of Asia Pacific* 7, no. 3.

Acharya, Amitav, and Barry Buzan. (2010). "Why is there no Non-Western International Relations Theory: An Introduction. In *Non- Western International Relations Theory: Reflections on and Beyond Asia*, edited by Amitav Acharya and Barry Buzan, 1–25. Abingdon: Routledge.

Adler, Emmanuel, and Michael Barnett, eds. 1998. *Security Communities*. Cambridge: Cambridge University Press.

Agathangelou, Anna M., and L. H. M. Ling. 2009. *Transforming World Politics: From Empire to Multiple Worlds*. London: Routledge.

Barnett, Michael. 1995. "Nationalism, Sovereignty, and Regional Order in Arab Politics." *International Organization* 49, no. 3: 479–510.

Barnett, Michael. 1998. *Dialogues in Arab Politics*. New York: Columbia University Press.

Behera, Navnita Chaddha. 2010. "Reimagining IR in India." In *Non-Western International Relations Theory*, edited by Amitav Acharya and Barry Buzan, 92–116. Abingdon: Routledge.

Bell, Duncan. 2013. "Race and International Relations." *Cambridge Review of International Relations* 26, no. 1: 1–4.

Bilgin, Pinar. 2008. "Thinking Past 'Western IR.'" *Third World Quarterly* 29, no. 1: 5–23.

Bilgin, Pinar. 2013. "Pınar Bilgin on Non-Western IR, Hybridity, and the One-Toothed Monster called Civilization." *Theory Talks*, December 20. http://www.theory-talks.org/2013/12/theory-talk-61.html Accessed September 12, 2016.

Chowdhry, Geeta, and Sheila Nair, eds. 2004. *Power, Postcolonialism, and International Relations: Reading Race, Gender, and Class.* London: Routledge.

Cox, Robert W. 2002. "Universality in International Studies." In *Critical Perspectives in International Studies*, edited by Michael Brecher and Frank Harvey, 45–55. Ann Arbor: University of Michigan Press.

Deciancio, Melisa. 2016. "International Relations from the South: A Regional Research Agenda for Global IR." *International Studies Review* 18: 106–19.

Finnemore, Martha, and Michelle Jurkovich. 2014. "Getting a Seat at the Table: The Origins of Universal Participation and Modern Multilateral Conferences." *Global Governance: A Review of Multilateralism and International Organizations* 20, no. 3: 361–73.

Florini, Ann. 1996. "The Evolution of International Norms." *International Studies Quarterly* 40, no. 3: 363–89.

Frasson-Quenoz, Florent. 2016. "Latin American Thinking in International Relations Reloaded," Available at http://revistas.uexternado.edu.co/index.php/oasis/article/viewFile/4525/5200. Accessed October 22, 2016.

Hemmer, Christopher, and Peter J. Katzenstein. 2002. "Why Is There No NATO in Asia: Collective Identity, Regionalism, and the Origins of Multilateralism." *International Organization* 56, no. 3: 575–607.

Helleiner, Eric. 2014. "Southern Pioneers of International Development." *Global Governance: A Review of Multilateralism and International Organizations* 20, no. 3: 375–88.

Henderson, Errol. 2013. "Hidden in Plain Sight: Racism in International Relations Theory." *Cambridge Review of International Relations* 26, no. 1: 71–92.

Hobson, John A. 2012. *The Eurocentric Conception of World Politics.* Cambridge: Cambridge University Press.

Iriye, Akira. 1979. "Culture and Power: International Relations as Intercultural Relations." *Diplomatic History* 3, no. 2: 115–28.

Johnston, Alastair Iain. 1998. *Cultural Realism: Strategic Culture and Grand Strategy in Chinese History.* Princeton, NJ: Princeton University Press.

Kacowitz, Arie. 2005. *The Impact of Norms in International Society: The Latin American Experience, 1881–2001.* Notre Dame, IN: Notre Dame University Press.

Karim, Azhari. 2007. "ASEAN: Association to Community: Constructed in the Image of Malaysia's Global Diplomacy." In *Malaysia's Foreign Policy: Continuity and Change*, edited by Abdul Razak Baginda, 109–32. Singapore: Marshal Cavendish Editions.

Lebow, Richard Ned. 2008. *A Cultural Theory of International Relations.* Cambridge: Cambridge University Press.

Ling, L. H. M. 2002. *Postcolonial International Relations: Conquest and Desire between Asia and the West.* London: Palgrave Macmillan.

Neuman, Stephanie G. 1998. *International Relations Theory and the Third World.* New York: St. Martin's Press.

Persaud, Randolph B. 2014. Points on Race and Global IR. [Personal e-mail]. August 20.

Persaud, Randolph B., and R. B. J. Walker. 2001. "Race in International Relations." *Alternatives* 26, no. 4: 373–76.

Puchala, Donald J. 1998. "Third World Thinking and Contemporary International Relations." In *International Relations Theory and the Third World*, edited by Stephanie Neuman. New York: St. Martin's Press.

Qin, Yaqin. 2010. "Why Is There No Chinese International Relations Theory?" In *Non-Western International Relations Theory: Reflections on and Beyond Asia*, edited by Amitav Acharya and Barry Buzan, 26–50. Oxford: Routledge.

Qin, Yaqing. 2016. "A Relational Theory of World Politics." *International Studies Review* 18, no. 1: 33–47.

Reus-Smit, Christian. 2001. *The Moral Purpose of the State: Culture, Social Identity, and Institutional Rationality in International Relations*. Princeton, NJ: Princeton University Press.

Rother, Stefan. 2012. "Wendt Meets East: ASEAN Cultures of Conflict and Cooperation." *Co-operation and Conflict* 47, no. 1: 49–67.

Shilliam, Robbie, ed. 2010. *International Relations and Non-Western Thoughts: Imperialism, Colonialism and Investigations of Global Modernity*. London: Routledge.

Sikkink, Kathryn. 2014. "Latin American Countries as Norm Protagonists of the Idea of International Human Rights." *Global Governance: A Review of Multilateralism and International Organizations* 20, no. 3: 389–404.

Smith, Karen. 2006. "Can It Be Home-Grown: Challenges to Developing IR Theory in the Global South." Paper presented to the 47th Annual Convention of the International Studies Association, San Diego, March 22–25.

Solomon, Ty, and Brent J. Steele. 2017. "Micro-moves in International Relations Theory." *European Journal of International Relations*,. 23, no. 2: 267–91

Tadjbakhsh, Shahrbanou. 2010. "International Relations Theory and the Islamic Worldview." In *Non-Western International Relations Theory*, edited by Amitav Acharya and Barry Buzan, 174–96. Abingdon: Routledge.

Thomas, Caroline, and Peter Wilkin. 2004. "Still Waiting after All These Years: 'The Third World' on the Periphery of International Relations." *The British Journal of Politics & International Relations* 6, no. 2: 241–58.

Tickner, Arlene B. 2003. "Seeing IR Differently: Notes from the Third World." *Millennium: Journal of International Studies* 32, no. 2: 295–324.

Tickner, Arlene, and Ole Waever, eds. 2009. *International Relations Scholarship Around the World*. London: Routledge.

Wemheuer-Vogelaar, Wiebke. 2013. "Intellectual Rooting in IR: Converging Citation Patterns in Constructivist Publications Around the World." Paper prepared for the Theories of Hegemony and Hegemony of Theories panel, International Studies Association annual convention 2013, San Francisco.

About the Authors

Amitav Acharya: American University
J. Samuel Barkin: University of Massachusetts, Boston
Mariano E. Bertucci: Loyola Marymount University
David Blagden: University of Exeter
Jordan Branch: Brown University
Jérémie Cornut: Simon Fraser University
Charles Glaser: George Washington University
Stacie E. Goddard: Wellesley College
Jarrod Hayes: MIT and University of Massachusetts, Lowell
Patrick James: University of Southern California
Thomas Jamieson: University of Southern California
Oliver Kessler: University of Erfurt
Audie Klotz: Syracuse University
Ronald R. Krebs: University of Minnesota
David M. McCourt: University of California, Davis
Nicholas Onuf: Florida International University
Jennifer M. Ramos: Loyola Marymount University
Laura Sjoberg: University of Florida
Brent Steele: University of Utah

Index

Abbott, Andrew, 40–41
Abrahamsen, Rita, 142
Acheson, Dean, 77
actor-network theory (ANT), 110–11, 249
Adler, Emanuel, xv, 98n1, 138, 140, 146
Adler-Nissen, Rebecca, 144, 146
Africa: coverage in constructivist research, 22, 265; prevalence of peaceful dyads, 94. *See also* South Africa
agency: classical realism vs. early constructivism views, 6; constructivism's tendency to structuralism vs., 139–40; need for non-Western scholarship on, 270–71; practice theory understanding of, 140–42; social concept of, 51
agent-based modeling, 89
agent-structure problem, 51, 63n6, 110, 139–42
Allport, Gordon, 130n5
Ambrosetti, David, 144, 145
analytic eclecticism: growing enthusiasm for, 12, 200, 260n9; recommendations for future research, 215–16, 257–58
anarchy: logics of, 188–89; types of, 188; unlikeliness of ending, 214; varying outcomes of, 191–92. *See also* cooperation under anarchy
Andersen, Morten Skumsrud, 146
Anglosphere, defined, 96. *See also* Austra-

lia; Canada; United Kingdom; United States
antiapartheid sanctions research, race-based variables in, 88–89
Arab spring (2011), 140, 249
articulation of security threats: failed securitization of Venezuela, 171, 173–74; forums for, 161; in four-stage model, 157, 164–67, 250; securitization as, erroneous assumption of, 157; US views of ISIS, 171–72
Asia: coverage in constructivist research, 21, 22, 265; local IR development, 269
assessment of constructivist publications. *See* quantitative assessment of constructivist publications
audiences, role in legitimation, 80
Austin, J. L., xvi, 5, 84n38
Australia: Anglosphere membership, 96; legitimacy of constructivism, 34; women's suffrage, 93, 94

balance of power: defined, 216n2; domestic identity and, 201–2, 258; enduring significance in security competition, 212, 258; normative dimension of, 51; recent developments in, 209; as relational space, 53; states' attention to position in, 198, 208–9, 213; as three combined problems, 60; types of contingency in, 61–62. *See also* power